SAP PRESS e-books

Print or e-book, Kindle or iPad, workplace or airplane: Choose where and how to read your SAP PRESS books! You can now get all our titles as e-books, too:

- By download and online access
- For all popular devices
- And, of course, DRM-free

Convinced? Then go to www.sap-press.com and get your e-book today.

Open Client

Su 56   Page 118   Display User Authorization
Buffer

Svo3 - maintain your own Settings

PFud- User Master Data Reconciliation

Su10 - Maintain multiple users

Su01 -   "   one   user

SAP PRESS is a joint initiative of SAP and Rheinwerk Publishing. The know-how offered by SAP specialists combined with the expertise of Rheinwerk Publishing offers the reader expert books in the field. SAP PRESS features first-hand information and expert advice, and provides useful skills for professional decision-making.

SAP PRESS offers a variety of books on technical and business-related topics for the SAP user. For further information, please visit our website: *www.sap-press.com*.

Jonathan Haun
SAP HANA Security Guide
2017, 541 pages, hardcover and e-book
www.sap-press.com/4227

Lehnert, Luther, Christoph, Pluder, Fernandes
GDPR and SAP: Data Privacy with SAP Business Suite and SAP S/4HANA
2018, 430 pages, hardcover and e-book
www.sap-press.com/4652

Sebastian Schreckenbach
SAP Administration—Practical Guide (2nd Edition)
2015, 912 pages, hardcover and e-book
www.sap-press.com/3639

Thomas Schneider
SAP Performance Optimization Guide: Analyzing and Tuning SAP Systems (8th Edition)
2018, 892 pages, hardcover and e-book
www.sap-press.com/4370

Joe Markgraf, Alessandro Banzer

SAP® System Security Guide

Rheinwerk
Publishing

Editor Hareem Shafi
Copyeditor Melinda Rankin
Cover Design Graham Geary
Photo Credit Shutterstock.com/230426353/© Andrey_Popov
Layout Design Vera Brauner
Production Hannah Lane
Typesetting SatzPro, Krefeld (Germany)
Printed and bound in the United States of America, on paper from sustainable sources

ISBN 978-1-4932-1481-5
© 2018 by Rheinwerk Publishing, Inc., Boston (MA)
1st edition 2018

Library of Congress Cataloging-in-Publication Data
Names: Markgraf, Joe, author. | Banzer, Alessandro.
Title: SAP system security guide / Joe Markgraf and Alessandro Banzer.
Description: 1st edition. | Bonn ; Boston : Rheinwerk Publishing, 2018. |
  Includes index.
Identifiers: LCCN 2017025849 | ISBN 9781493214815 (alk. paper)
Subjects: LCSH: SAP NetWeaver. | Computer networks--Management. | Database
  security. | Computer security.
Classification: LCC TK5105.8885.S24 M364 2017 | DDC 005.8--dc23 LC record available at https://lccn.loc.gov/2017025849

All rights reserved. Neither this publication nor any part of it may be copied or reproduced in any form or by any means or translated into another language, without the prior consent of Rheinwerk Publishing, 2 Heritage Drive, Suite 305, Quincy, MA 02171.

Rheinwerk Publishing makes no warranties or representations with respect to the content hereof and specifically disclaims any implied warranties of merchantability or fitness for any particular purpose. Rheinwerk Publishing assumes no responsibility for any errors that may appear in this publication.

"Rheinwerk Publishing" and the Rheinwerk Publishing logo are registered trademarks of Rheinwerk Verlag GmbH, Bonn, Germany. SAP PRESS is an imprint of Rheinwerk Verlag GmbH and Rheinwerk Publishing, Inc.

All of the screenshots and graphics reproduced in this book are subject to copyright © SAP SE, Dietmar-Hopp-Allee 16, 69190 Walldorf, Germany.

SAP, the SAP logo, ABAP, Ariba, ASAP, Concur, Concur ExpenseIt, Concur TripIt, Duet, SAP Adaptive Server Enterprise, SAP Advantage Database Server, SAP Afaria, SAP ArchiveLink, SAP Ariba, SAP Business ByDesign, SAP Business Explorer, SAP BusinessObjects, SAP BusinessObjects Explorer, SAP BusinessObjects Lumira, SAP BusinessObjects Roambi, SAP BusinessObjects Web Intelligence, SAP Business One, SAP Business Workflow, SAP Crystal Reports, SAP EarlyWatch, SAP Exchange Media (SAP XM), SAP Fieldglass, SAP Fiori, SAP Global Trade Services (SAP GTS), SAP GoingLive, SAP HANA, SAP HANA Vora, SAP Hybris, SAP Jam, SAP MaxAttention, SAP MaxDB, SAP NetWeaver, SAP PartnerEdge, SAPPHIRE NOW, SAP PowerBuilder, SAP PowerDesigner, SAP R/2, SAP R/3, SAP Replication Server, SAP S/4HANA, SAP SQL Anywhere, SAP Strategic Enterprise Management (SAP SEM), SAP SuccessFactors, The Best-Run Businesses Run SAP, TwoGo are registered or unregistered trademarks of SAP SE, Walldorf, Germany.

All other products mentioned in this book are registered or unregistered trademarks of their respective companies.

Contents at a Glance

Dear Reader,

As an administrator, you understand the stakes like few others: the risks associated with an unsecured system are immense. But it can be daunting to acquire the breadth of knowledge necessary to implement a strong security policy—where do you begin?

The answer is, here.

This book is a result of the effort of two excellent authors: Joe Markgraf and Alessandro Banzer. Over countless days and nights they've worked to compile their knowledge of system security into one easy-to-reference book. Between these covers you'll find the information you need to confidently build a long-lasting security policy and protect your SAP NetWeaver system.

What did you think about *SAP System Security Guide*? Your comments and suggestions are the most useful tools to help us make our books the best they can be. Please feel free to contact me and share any praise or criticism you may have.

Thank you for purchasing a book from SAP PRESS!

Hareem Shafi
Editor, SAP PRESS

hareems@rheinwerk-publishing.com
www.sap-press.com
Rheinwerk Publishing · Boston, MA

Contents

2 Configuring Profiles and Parameters 45

3 Restricting Transactional Access 69

7 Configuring Authorizations

9   Patching

13   Configuring Encryption   433

14   Database Security 489

15   Infrastructure Security 513

Preface

This book introduces to you the tools, challenges, and mindset needed to fill the role of an SAP security administrator. The role of security administrator is most commonly held by a technically-minded person who understands how the SAP NetWeaver platform works on a technical level. Often, a security administrator is also a Basis administrator or comes from a system administration background.

Security administrators are responsible for the overall security of an SAP system. This includes technical and some functional security. Because SAP security is such a broad topic, you may find several subpositions within this topic. Regardless of how the roles may be split up, it's crucial for any administrator to have a sound understanding of the fundamentals of system security.

Target Audience

This book is aimed at the following groups of readers:

- SAP system administrators, traditionally called Basis administrators, in small- to medium-sized enterprises (SMEs) and large enterprises
- Newcomers to SAP security
- Administrators who are tasked with the total security of an SAP system
- Junior consultants

Some sections or procedures may not be applicable to senior security administrators or senior consultants. However, the concepts of security design and security fundamentals can be useful at all experience levels as a reference.

This book is not intended to be an introduction to SAP NetWeaver. Although it does cover many of the basics, these topics have been carefully selected because they are often skipped in traditional introductions due to their technical or security-focused nature. A solid understanding of SAP NetWeaver will help you understand the background of each security issue we'll be discussing. We also advise you to have a basic understanding of Basis administration to fully understand the material covered in this book.

System Administration: A Vast Field of Options

There are many possible roles for a system administrator. Notable subroles for a Basis administrator include the following:

- **System administrator**
  Responsible for the configuration and maintenance of the SAP NetWeaver Application Server.

- **User administrator**
  Responsible for creating, modifying, and deleting user accounts on an SAP NetWeaver system.

- **Authorization administrator**
  Responsible for configuring authorizations for end users. This role is semifunctional and requires a working knowledge of the application in use.

- **Security administrator**
  Responsible for the total technical security of SAP NetWeaver systems. This role could be considered a subrole of every role listed, but it's commonly referred to as its own role.

- **Transport administrator**
  Responsible for moving code in an SAP NetWeaver landscape using the Transport Management System.

- **Backup administrator**
  Responsible for creating, maintaining, and restoring backups of an SAP system and its underlying infrastructure (operating system [OS], database).

- **Database administrator**
  Responsible for maintaining the underlying database.

- **Operating system administrator**
  Responsible for administration of the OS that SAP NetWeaver runs on.

- **Network administrator**
  Responsible for the networking internal to the SAP NetWeaver system and between the corporate network and any other networks or subnets that business systems reside in.

- **Virtualization administrator**
  Responsible for maintaining the hypervisor and virtual machines that an SAP NetWeaver system may run on.

Depending on the size of your organization, several positions may be the responsibility of a single administrator. In some organizations, the roles of user, authorization, and security administrators are combined. In others, strict segregation of duties may prevent an administrator from being able to perform user administration and system administration. Every organization is different.

This book's goal is to dig deeply into the subrole of the security administrator.

Small and Medium Organizations

An administrator for a small or medium organization may be tasked with performing all the roles listed above. You may think that a scope of responsibility this large would be nearly impossible to manage. However, with careful planning and documentation, such a position is easily manageable by an administrator with a broad skillset and an eye for detail. A solid understanding of the concepts put forth in this book will give such an administrator a great foundation for the skill set needed to manage such an expansive area.

What Is Basis?

This book uses the term *Basis administrator* quite frequently. One of the most frequently asked questions from newcomers to SAP is: What is a Basis administrator? To answer that question, we need to dig back into the history of the SAP NetWeaver Application Server product.

The term *Basis* came about during the early days of the original SAP ERP product, at that time called R/3 (R for real-time data processing, 3 for the third release of the product). R/3 introduced the concept of a standard core system that consisted of a technical "basis" layer, which served as the foundation of the system. On top of this basis layer, applications for financial accounting, logistics, and human resource management could be run. A *Basis administrator* was the administrator responsible for system maintenance on this layer.

Today's successor to the Basis foundation layer, SAP NetWeaver Application Server (AS) ABAP, is a common system that SAP's products run on top of. These products include SAP S/4HANA, SAP Business Warehouse (SAP BW), SAP ERP, and many more ABAP-based solutions from SAP. The term *Basis* isn't used actively in marketing by SAP, but most people that have been around SAP still use the Basis title because it's a good descriptor for what a Basis administrator does in his or her day-to-day work.

SAP also produces the SAP NetWeaver Application Server (AS) Java, which is the foundation for products such as SAP Enterprise Portal and half of the technical foundation of SAP Solution Manger. SAP NetWeaver AS Java is a technical subtopic of its own; complex enough to warrant its own book. Too often, technical texts attempt to cover more material than is practical on multiple topics and lose the level of detail needed to fully understand each product. For this reason, this book has been written for administrators focusing on SAP NetWeaver AS ABAP 7.5. Although there are many SAP NetWeaver AS Java systems, this book won't cover the specific steps for securing those systems. However, many of the security concepts are similar for both ABAP- and Java-based systems.

Depending on the size of your organization, you may be the sole Basis administrator who is also responsible for security. You also could be singularly focused on SAP security. You might even be responsible only for user creation and role assignment. Every company is different, and every role will have its own responsibilities. The goal of this book is to cover the entirety of a Basis administrator's role when tasked with system security. In your role, you may or may not be hands on with the technical Basis tasks. One thing is clear: as a security administrator, you must have a solid understanding of the Basis layer. Even if you aren't performing day-to-day Basis work, you'll need to know how things technically work so that you can protect the system from all threats on the technical level.

The terms *Basis administrator, system administrator*, and *SAP administrator* can be used interchangeably. Most often, a Basis administrator with a specialty in security administration will be referred to simply as an *SAP security administrator*. To make things simple, we'll refer to this position as *security administrator* in this book. To refer to the role of Basis administrator, we'll use the term *system administrator*.

You'll also find a wealth of information that's applicable to database administrators, network administrators, virtualization administrators, and so on; though it would be worthwhile for each of these infrastructure roles to understand SAP security concepts on the whole, it's impractical because these infrastructure administrators typically only spend a portion of their day on SAP. For this reason, an SAP system administrator often is tasked with working with these groups to support an SAP NetWeaver system. SAP system administrators often will be consulted by other infrastructure administrators to provide guidance in these infrastructure areas. Therefore, we've devoted Chapter 15 to this subject so that the security administrator will be able to provide recommendations to infrastructure administrators for how best to secure all components of an SAP NetWeaver system.

Structure of This Book

The content of this book is structured as follows.

Chapter 1 explains the basic security concepts relevant to SAP systems and introduces the system administrator's role in security.

Chapter 2 dives into a technical understanding of profiles and parameters, two key tools for configuration of the SAP NetWeaver system.

Limiting access to transactions using transaction locking is covered in **Chapter 3.** This ensures that only authorized users can use certain transactions. Chapter 3 also explores why it's essential to lock certain transactions through the use of authorizations.

A single SAP NetWeaver system is often used by several companies (e.g., subsidiaries). In such cases, a client is assigned to each company to keep the companies' data separate. **Chapter 4** describes the strategies and procedures used to secure different clients on an SAP NetWeaver system.

Securing the kernel, the core technical executables that run an SAP NetWeaver system, is covered in **Chapter 5**.

In **Chapter 6**, we cover the topic of managing users. Administration, password security, and segregation of duties are all topics of interest within this chapter.

Authorizations and their use in controlling access to functionality are covered in **Chapter 7**. This is an important overall skill to have as a security administrator.

Chapter 8 covers enabling and using authentication technologies such as single sign-on (SSO)—including the SAP-specific solution, SAP Single Sign-On—and LDAP authentication.

In **Chapter 9**, you'll learn about SAP's approach to patching and the system administrator's role in staying up to date with critical security patches. This chapter includes how to find information about critical vulnerabilities released by SAP and how to apply patches to address these vulnerabilities.

The transport system is used to import changes to all applications in an SAP NetWeaver system. **Chapter 10** explains how to secure the mechanics of the transport system, including the transport process and technical transport configuration. It assumes some technical knowledge of how transports work.

To keep a system secure, it's essential to have eyes on all parts of the system and the changes being made therein. Security audit logging records all security events for later analysis, whereas table logging records changes made to tables, including when the changes were made and who made them. **Chapter 11** explains how to configure and enable security audit logging, table logging, and auditing, and how the administrator is typically involved in the process.

Chapter 12 discusses how SAP handles network communications and what a system administrator must do to secure communications on the local network and the Internet. It also explains how to secure system-to-system communications (via Remote Function Calls [RFCs]) and system-to-user communications.

Chapter 13 is dedicated to securing an SAP system using encryption. It explains the concepts of and technical reasoning behind encryption and how it's implemented on an SAP platform. You'll learn to choose the level of encryption that best suits your organization's needs and how to enable encryption.

Chapter 14 explains step-by-step how to configure SAP NetWeaver to ensure security at the database level. Some of these settings are controlled from within SAP and do not differ based on the database in question; however, for those that do differ, instructions are provided based on the most common databases in use.

In **Chapter 15**, you'll learn about a system administrator's role in policy creation, planning, and maintaining infrastructure components to ensure that the SAP NetWeaver system is as secure as possible. This includes the OS, hypervisor, networking, and physical layers. All of these make up the stack which must be secure in order to protect your SAP NetWeaver AS ABAP system.

Chapter 1
Introduction

Before reading this chapter, you should have an understanding of the Basis or system administration role and its responsibilities within an organization.

In this chapter, we will explain the basic security concepts relevant to SAP systems, and introduce the system administrator's role in security. A thorough understanding of the ideas in this chapter is integral to grasping the concepts laid out throughout this rest of this book, so be sure to refer back here as needed as you make your way through each chapter.

The technical focus of this book is the SAP NetWeaver AS ABAP platform and the business applications that run on this platform. You will find that the majority of the practical material in this book is specific to the SAP NetWeaver platform, and while most of the security concepts will apply to nearly any system or platform within an organization, from a technical standpoint, you should expect slight differences between SAP's approach to platform security and other software vendors' approach. With that in mind, this chapter will focus more on the conceptual side of business system security. To start, we will explore the business system's role in an organization and learn how the security administrator works to protect such a critical system.

Modern day businesses rely on software to support their business processes and manage their resources. Enterprise resource planning (ERP) software and other business applications are often essential to an organization's operations; organizations likely could not function without them. This creates a dependency on these systems, which makes their operation and security critical to the organization's ongoing success.

To ensure continuing operation of these business systems, organizations require administrators. These administrators take care of the system, making sure it is stable and available for business. Given their critical nature, the security of these systems is a significant concern. For this reason, a security administrator is entrusted to protect the system from harm, which brings us to our formal definition of a security administrator's role:

The fundamental job of a security administrator is to protect an organization's business computer systems from threats, both internally and externally.

Let's discuss what "threat" means in this context.

1.1 Potential Threats

A threat is anything that could possibly cause harm to a computer system. Given that many SAP NetWeaver AS ABAP systems are mission critical to organizations, an attack on these systems will also cause direct harm to the organization itself. Therefore, it is in an organization's best interests to protect their computer systems from threats.

Threats can come from anywhere, internal or external to the organization. Specifically, Internet exposure is the biggest source of threats, or *attack vector*, on a technical level. Whenever an SAP system is connected directly to the Internet your *attack surface*, or the sum of a system's vulnerabilities, is larger. We'll dig further into attack vectors and attack surfaces later on in this chapter, but for now if you're in a scenario in which your SAP systems are reachable via the Internet, you're at a greater risk for attack.

Complacency, or ignorance to the potential threats that face an organization's systems, can be costly. Ignoring a risk because it hasn't been considered a risk in the past is a dangerous practice that can completely compromise security. And yet, this mindset is so typical that security administrators often consider addressing this ignorance a top priority. It comes as no surprise that when attackers are able to compromise a system entirely, there is no end to the cost of the attack. Depending on the attack, destruction of the system, or even destruction of the organization are both very possible. However, developing and executing a plan to address security risks—both known and unknown—can help avoid these scenarios.

The following sections will explore the types and sources of some of the most common attacks. When working as a security administrator, it is often useful to frame your efforts with the following known approaches in mind. For each section, you may want to evaluate your current security practices against the attack. Are you vulnerable? Could an attacker compromise your organization?

1.1.1   Data Breach

A *data breach* is the release of any secure, private, or confidential data. In many scenarios, a breach is the result of attackers having access to an organization's database and everything in it. Data breaches are always costly and when an SAP system experiences a data breach, the damage can be catastrophic for an organization.

Data breaches can occur when an outside party gains access to the database or an inside party gains enough authorizations through normal channels to read or copy private or sensitive data and export it into their own systems. Both scenarios are remedied using proper system hardening and account authorization management.

1.1.2   Privacy Violations

Privacy violations often go hand in hand with a data breach. A data breach that includes personal information about users or customers is considered a *privacy violation* and can incur significant legal repercussions in the event of a violation. Privacy laws vary from country to country; if you have users or customers that reside in a country with strict privacy laws, you may be legally obligated to follow the laws in the location in which your user or customer resides. Therefore, an approach to maintain the privacy of your users in line with these regulations is a good practice.

1.1.3   Phishing

A *phishing attack* is an attack in which customers or business users are tricked into providing confidential or valuable data to a third party. It is important for security administrators to be aware of their end users' practices and make sure that users are well educated about phishing attacks and understand how to identify them. A common method for a phishing attack is over email or a phone call. Clear policies need to be put in place to ensure that users never divulge login credentials or system information to an unverified third party.

When specific users, for example C-level executives or system administrators, are targeted, the attack is known as *spear phishing*. This means that an attacker creates a specific communication for the target in an attempt to get them to give up confidential information. The most common example of this attack is by impersonating trusted support, through either a malicious email or phone call. The goal of the attacker is to gain credentials or critical information to gain access to the organizations data or systems. While it may seem like spear phishing attacks are easy to detect, they aren't. Attackers may go to great lengths to impersonate trusted individuals, which, when successful, provides them with a significant advantage over an organization's existing security practices.

1.1.4   Theft

In terms of security, *theft* refers to the taking of anything of monetary value, intellectual property, and proprietary information about your organization. Attackers with access to your financial system can manipulate financial data to steal and cover up their tracks, or they may access restricted financial reports to gain an advantage when trading stocks. The number of potential theft risks is only limited by the attacker's imagination.

For example, many companies have dedicated printers that are able to print checks. They also have a process that is initiated to send a check to someone they owe money to. A malicious party may be able to manipulate both human process and the SAP system to have a check printed and mailed to them. Without careful security, they would be able to steal from the company.

Theft often goes hand in hand with our next type of attack: fraud.

1.1.5   Fraud

Fraud is the act of covering up illicit or illegal activity. Fraud can occur when external adversaries compromise the system or internal users have malicious intentions and access in which they can manipulate the system to cover their tracks. This can lead to a variety of exploits in which theft occurs and the attackers attempt to use their system access to cover up the evidence that any illicit activity has occurred.

An example of fraud would be forging financial records to attempt to cover up missing funds that were taken from cash operations. This is also known as *skimming*. This is difficult to detect because there is no record that would show an issue—the malicious party would need to be caught in the act.

Any opportunity for fraud poses a threat and organizations should take steps to install appropriate controls to mitigate these threats. A common area for fraud to occur is with accounts that have access to both financial and audit portions of systems. This includes many system administrator-type roles, so scrutiny of these assignments is critical to safeguarding your systems. This is mitigated by monitoring and documenting of what is called *segregation of duties* (SoD). This means that each business role or access privilege must be separate from other roles that may give the user access which could be abused. SoD auditing is a topic that the security administrator can send a great deal of time performing, because it can become very vast when an organization has many users.

1.1.6   Brute Force Attacks

Using a trial-and-error method to guess passwords and gain access to accounts or systems is called a *brute force attack*. Brute force attacks have been a factor in security since the early days of computing. Due to advances in technology and attacking methods, this age-old practice is still an active threat in today's world. Attackers use computer programs to attack systems or even to crack secured password storage files in order to gain login credentials to a system. These programs are able to generate millions or billions of login attempts per second and can quickly guess simple passwords. By using more advanced methods, attackers can even guess complex passwords in a short amount of time.

As technology and attacks mature, the time needed to brute force attack passwords decreases. Password policy, single-sign on, and password controls can be implemented to make brute force attacks much more difficult.

1.1.7   Disruption

Attackers sometimes have considerable *botnets*, or a network of compromised computers, that are able to execute commands in unison, remotely. The use of these botnets to perform an attack is known as a *distributed denial of service* (DDoS) attack (see Figure 1.1). These attacks attempt to disrupt their target by overwhelming servers with traffic in order to either damage the systen or otherwise make the system unavailable. They are difficult to block because they are distributed, coming from many different compromised computers all over the world, making it difficult to distinguish from legitimate traffic.

> **Internet Connections**
>
> Only open your systems to the Internet if it is required. Chapter 12 contains information on how to mitigate the threat of network and Internet-based attacks.

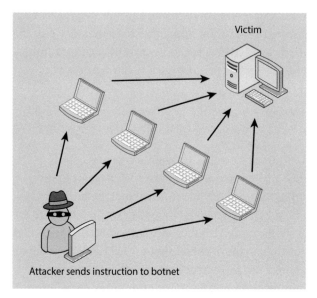

Figure 1.1 A DDoS Attack

A DDoS attack can overwhelm business systems, making it impossible to conduct ecommerce, send email, or even communicate. Disruption of critical services can cause lost revenue or damage an organization's public image.

1.1.8   Who Represents a Threat?

Terms like adversaries, attackers, malicious parties, bad actors, hackers, crackers, and cybercriminals all describe a hostile person or persons who intend on compromising the security of your business systems. They can be foreign governments, competitors, and even angry users. These parties act as a threat to your business systems and their security and stability.

> **Know Your Adversary**
>
> We will use the above standard terms when describing parties that intend on harming your system. Be aware that the industry uses many terms for these parties, so be sure to understand them in the context of the documentation you may be reading.

In the past, malicious parties were required to possess extensive knowledge and a significant skillset in order to attack complex business systems. However, due to advances in processing power, social exploitation techniques, and even lessons learned from past security breaches, the amount of knowledge required to damage an organization's business systems has decreased considerably.

It's important to mention that attackers can also be internal users who are untrustworthy. It may seem impossible to guard against these types of users, but proper security measures and authorizations can prevent even internal users from causing significant harm to your organization. Additionally, auditing your users' authorizations and permissions regularly can help make sure that users who are attempting to gain critical combinations of access rights can be stopped. You should set up ongoing review processes to keep access rights in check. Understand that every user with a critical combination of access rights may not be an attacker. However, if this user's account were to be compromised by spear phishing activity, the attacker would have all the access rights required for fraud or theft. Be mindful that users do not typically consider this when requesting access rights, so your intentions in denying access may not be apparent to them.

1.1.9 Understanding Modern-Day Vulnerabilities

Security administrators should keep up with current tactics employed by attackers. As new vulnerabilities are discovered, the paradigm in which attackers attempt to exploit systems can change. For example, in the early days of computing, attacks centered around authentication. Today, attacks tend to focus on encryption and memory vulnerabilities within servers. Consider using projects like Metasploit, which make available a framework for exploiting preassembled attacks with ease from a point-and-click interface. Figure 1.2 shows an SAP-specific attack in Metasploit. This tool is important to understand because it forces software vendors to actively develop fixes for software vulnerabilities and deploy them as quickly as possible. It also forces organizations to keep up with the latest security practices since otherwise they run an increased likelihood of being exploited.

Metasploit

Metasploit is outside the scope of this book, but it would serve any security professional well to be aware of the project and it's uses in exploitation and penetration testing. Given that the project has SAP-specific vulnerabilities, you can assume that it's being used by attackers in the wild.

Figure 1.2 The Metasploit Framework

Other things to consider are that, over time, many password creation tendencies have been discovered or leaked, enabling intelligent password-cracking algorithms to decode passwords or deploy brute force attacks much more quickly than in the past.

Finally, like anyone, attackers learn from the past. Lessons from successful attacks are applied to future attempts to gain an advantage.

Attacks are continuously evolving alongside the advancement of security measures. The most notable example of this is the many attacks that attempt to gain credentials from users. These attacks mask themselves as "authorized" password resets that are required for "strong security," and convince users that they are legitimate requests from a service provider they trust. Attacks like these are known as *man-in-the middle* attacks, convincing the user to enter their old password in order to change it to a new one (see Figure 1.3). In the past, the only goal would be to obtain the user's current login credentials by showing a login page. However, modern attempts will capture the user's current credentials, what the user enters as new credentials, and then change the user's password in the targeted system to the new credentials so that the user is completely unaware of the attack.

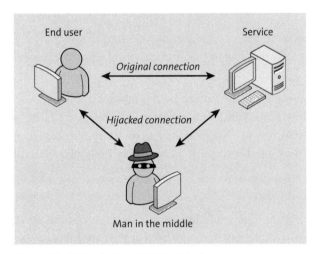

Figure 1.3 A Man-in-the-Middle Attack

In the era of two-factor authentication (2FA), attackers will even request the user verify their identity with an app that generates a login code. The code that the attacker sends or requests is actually a legitimate code that is being requested or displayed by the target system when the malicious party attempts a login. When the user receives the request and replies, the malicious party is able to login, defeating the security measure.

Threats Are Ever-Evolving!
Every day new vulnerabilities are discovered and one can find attackers that are trying every latest trick possible to reach your data.

As you perform your duties as a security administrator, keep in mind that attackers may use a combination of different methods to accomplish their goals. Regardless of what their end goal may be, you should strive to keep yourself well-versed in whatever methods they may use. Often you will find attackers using a combination of old and new techniques. Be sure to understand what exploits are being used by attackers and the strategies being used by vendors and other security professionals to defend against these attacks.

1.2   The Onion Concept

As we study common methods of attacking organizations, we find that many security risks exist in both electronic format and in the physical world. Consider the following scenario:

A clever attacker could compromise an SAP system by calling a business user and claiming to be a system administrator. This attacker may talk a user into sharing a password that the attacker could then use to create fake invoices and process payments. This would trigger a check printer to print a check that the attacker could physically obtain.

How would one defend against this attack?

As we have learned from Section 1.1, this scenario is a combination of both spear phishing and theft. There is no single activity that one could perform to mitigate this attack. The solution to this scenario is multiple approaches. A good approach may be the following security activities:

- Educating users about phishing and not disclosing passwords
- Putting in proper SoD policies that enforce appropriate role assignments
- Enacting an approval process on payments like checks

Each of these activities on its own will not prevent the attacker from accomplishing his or her objective. However, together, these policies can make it difficult, even impossible, for the attacker to execute their attack. Therefore, a good security plan is a lot like an onion. Layer upon layer of preventative measures that protect the stability of your SAP system.

The following sections will explore each layer that can be used to help mitigate the threat posed by complex attacks on your organization.

1.2.1   Perimeter

The *perimeter* consists of firewalls, application-level gateways, and load balancers. This layer is most commonly your network; your corporate network, and any subnetworks you define for your business systems, including SAP NetWeaver AS ABAP systems. It can also be ancillary systems, like your corporate phone system, or even the physical doors to your building or data center. The perimeter must be protected by authentication. Users must be required to log in, present ID, or use a key in order to access your systems. Guarding the perimeter helps prevent unauthorized access to your systems, both online and in person.

Perimeters are often breached. While disturbing to think about, this is the first wall an attacker must scale and they are often quite talented at doing so. Your goal needs to be to make it as difficult as possible to obtain and keep access.

1.2.2   Operations

The next layer in our onion is operational security tasks. These tasks are the routine work of a security administrator, and primarily involve reviewing access logs, role assignments, SoD reports, and other reporting and observation mechanisms. Secondarily they involve planning and executing security policy and practices.

Once an attacker breaks into a network, the next layer would be discovering the attacker's presence. The longer an attacker is able to remain undetected, the more information he or she might gather, and the more time he or she has to further dig into the organization's systems. Many attackers go undiscovered for months. It is important for the security administrator to design processes and operations that are able to identify signs that an attacker is present in the system.

1.2.3   Patching

Patching all devices, systems, and software on your network is your best line of defense against the majority of attacks that exist. As software (and hardware) is exploited, vendors release patches to fix the issues that allowed the exploit. However, it's up to the user to make sure that the fixes are implemented in their software. So it's common for the security administrator to catalog all devices, software, and hardware and dictate a patching schedule to make sure that the latest security patches are installed. This goes for SAP software, as well as all the software that is used in the SAP stack: the database, operating systems, hypervisors, networking equipment, even the end users' workstations. Patched systems are much more secure than non-patched systems.

> **SAP Specific Vulnerabilities**
> The majority of SAP-specific vulnerabilities exist for software versions that are old, often out of SAP support. Be sure to stay current with your patch levels.

1.2.4   Human Factor

Protecting against phishing or spear phishing is a difficult challenge for many security administrators because it has no technical connection to the system. It is purely a person problem. Nonetheless, it is very important that proper measures are taken to educate users so that they are able to resist attackers and report incidents to the security administrator. Preventing a phishing attack is much easier when you know that someone is actively attempting to find a vulnerable employee to exploit. Proper training and friendly reminders are a prudent practice and should be included in any operations and policy planning executed by a security administrator.

1.2.5   Physical Security

As with perimeter security, security measures that affect an SAP system also need to exist in the real world. It is important to safeguard critical portions of an organizations physical infrastructure, such as invoice printers, ID badge printers, and check printers. The ability to print a check, company ID, or invoice can be a major advantage to an attacker. Also, protecting your physical servers, hard disks, and backup media is also critical. If an attacker has physical access to a disk or backup media, they could easily obtain your critical data.

1.2.6   Security Awareness

Finally, and most importantly, a security administrator must be aware. Checking authorization logs and current vulnerabilities is important for a security administrator, but knowing what threats are new and which are being actively used against organizations is of an even greater importance.

Security is a continual practice, meaning that it's never complete. Each day new threats and vulnerabilities are discovered and it's a security administrator's job to mitigate those threats and vulnerabilities.

In closing, each layer you implement may not stop a threat or attack on it's own. But layer after layer, security becomes stronger and stronger, until it's such a burden to compromise that attackers will look for easier targets.

Now that we've explored the threats possible and how to work to prevent these threats, let's discuss two topics that are major players in the development of a security policy: risk and cost.

1.3   Risk and True Cost of Security

There is no predictive mechanism that an organization can use to determine the risk that they are taking on by neglecting their business system's security—the consequences can range from no impact to the complete shuttering of a business, from lawsuits to the loss of shareholder or brand equity. Often, this risk isn't even taken into account by an organization. It only exists due to neglect and, therefore, it's ignored.

It's important to remember that organizations and, more importantly, people depend on SAP systems. Critical business activities, paycheck processing, flight scheduling and logistics, may all depend on SAP systems being available for use. Downtime can translate into lost revenue and impact lives and livelihoods. While the SAP system you're charged with safeguarding may not be this critical it's important to take into account what could happen if security is ignored or underestimated and take the necessary precautions before the risk becomes a reality.

Alongside discussions of risks comes the topic of cost. Cost is significant to system security in two ways:

- The cost of setting up and operating a security policy and securing an organization's systems.
- The cost of a security lapse that results in a system breach.

It's difficult to give these costs a dollar value, and yet this is often the first step a security administrator must take when developing a security policy.

Organizations tend to focus explicitly on the latter cost; that is, how much they stand to lose if their systems are breached. As we discussed earlier, risk is often the yardstick by which security efforts are measured. Therefore, a security administrator may be asked to estimate the cost of the risk itself and the cost to mitigate that risk.

It can be useful to discuss the following topics with your organization's management when broaching the topic of security risks and costs:

- What can a business interruption cost?
- What does downtime mean for the company, both in terms of monetary loss and damage to reputation?
- What occurs if a business is unable to function as a whole?
- How much will be lost if business systems are not functional?
- What would data theft cost the business?

Since the cost of a potential breach is often more than an organization can easily imagine, these questions ensure that management is thinking about security in clearer terms than they may have been before.

For example, in the case of a data breach, the cost to the organization may be monetary damages caused by the exposure of private information. However, it could also result in the loss of brand equity. As of the writing of this book, one of the largest consumer credit information agencies has suffered a significant security breach, which has tarnished the name of this company immeasurably and has also affected its stock price.

So far we've discussed the costs an organization might incur as a result of a poorly-secured system. However, there are also costs associated with maintaining security. Take the example of role and access provisioning and SoD. Violating SoD may have no immediate affect—however, if an attacker obtains the proper roles, breaches the system, and runs unchecked, there is limitless potential for theft and fraud. Therefore, SoD reviews may need to be conducted quarterly, or even monthly, adding to the cost of maintaining security. Determining these types of direct costs is an essential step in bringing your organization's security to an acceptable level.

Fort Knox

As a security administrator, it's important that you do your due diligence when estimating the costs associated with security. Just don't lose sight of the importance of determining what your organization actually needs. In the SAP security industry there is a general tendency to assume that a "Fort Knox" must be built around an organization's small stack of coins. However, it may suit the organization more to put the stack of coins in a sturdy jar—both in terms of cost and in the level of security needed. The "Fort Knox" approach tends to be better suited to governments and banks—if you work at a bank, by all means, opt for maximum security and accept the high cost. But if you work for an organization that doesn't require all the stops, remember to build the most sturdy and secure jar that is appropriate for them.

Cost-Benefit Analysis of Security Projects

When evaluating the type of "jar" your organization needs, it's a good idea to weigh the potential costs of security implementation against the received benefit. Security projects may slow administrators and users down, forcing them to adjust their current processes for security-oriented processes. This can be an inconvenience. The level of inconvenience should be measured against the tangible benefit of these security processes. For example, how much will a specific process slow down an attacker? How much more difficult does it become for an attacker to breach a system? Is the time it takes to perform 2FA reasonable when compared to the increase in difficulty for attackers?

A failure to consider this can cause users to abandon security processes, defeating the purpose of their implementation. Keep in mind that your security processes should result in a return that is supported by both management and your user base.

These discussions with management should result in a decision. If the risk is deemed high enough to warrant action—and more costly to the organization than establishing a security policy—an administrator will be given the go-ahead to "fix" the problem.

The "fix" begins with addressing the lack of a good security policy (see Chapter 15 for more information). However, a general security policy is not enough. Many organizations choose to enact specific SAP security policies due to the unique nature of SAP systems. Local workstations and SAP systems tend to have little in common, so a single policy isn't a good idea. Security protocols must be specific to the system they are trying to protect.

Once a policy is established, you can begin planning and developing goals around the risk areas that were identified based on discussions with your organization's management.

The Advantages of a Secure SAP System

We've discussed the direct costs associated with maintain security, but it is also important to recognize that a secure system can save money. During a compliance or financial audit, organizations that can demonstrate consistent security and auditing practices often need to do less post-audit work. Additionally, good security practices like implementing SSO and SoD reviews can save a large amount of time during user-maintained activities. The cost of the time required to maintain insecure processes that have not been optimized can, therefore, be substantial.

1.4 The Administrator's Role in Security

The position of security administrator may have various meanings within different organizations. The aim of this book is to prepare you for the many responsibilities that you may have. For example, in some organizations, a security administrator may never perform a kernel upgrade. In others, the activity is driven by the security administrator in charge of Basis or system administration. Regardless of the responsibility, it's important for a security administrator to know and understand the kernel and how it is upgraded. For that reason, this book in broad in its scope.

In the following sections, we will discuss the variety of responsibilities a security administrator may be required to undertake and, based on these responsibilities, what you can expect to learn from this book.

1.4.1 Planning

Security administrators do a significant amount of system planning, and participate in almost every planning activity. From a new implementation to an upgrade of an existing system, the security administrator has a role to play in evaluating each activity and how it pertains to or effects security. Administrators should always seek to play an active role in these activities, since security can be much more difficult if it's an afterthought. A good example of this is a system upgrade. Testing the roles delivered with an upgrade is much easier during the upgrade as the organization will be doing testing to verify the upgrade itself. Testing roles is a small extension of the testing procedures that are already occurring. However, finding out that roles must be tested *after* the upgrade may cause a significant amount of rework, or worse, result in the choice to skip testing altogether.

Planning the policy and making improvements to overall security is also a continual task for the system administrator. New threats and vulnerabilities are constantly being discovered. It is within a security administrator's best interests to develop a monthly or quarterly security-planning meeting in which upcoming activities can be discussed.

1.4.2   Execution

In general, a security administrator is responsible two types of execution tasks: operations, or the ongoing day-to-day task that are usually governed by policy, and implementation of planning activities. Usually these tasks are project activities centered on improving security. They often involve an activity called *hardening*. Hardening is the practice of incrementally improving the security of any device, process, or system. Hardening usually includes two areas denoted by specific terminology that is important to understand. Many times, this terminology will be used in SAP Notes and security briefings or notices from other vendors. The two most critical concepts regarding security are attack vectors and attack surfaces. They will be used throughout this book and are important to understand.

- **Attack Vector**
  An attack vector is a path or method in which a malicious party is able gain access to a server or the network in order to exploit a vulnerability. This typically is a virus, web page, connection to the Internet, or path through a firewall to a business system.

- **Attack Surface**
  An attack surface is the sum of all parts or portions of a computer system or network in which it is possible to perform an attack on. An example of this would be the total attackable group of unpatched software vulnerabilities, open ports, and unsecured servers themselves.

  An attack vector leads to an attack surface. Successful exploitation of a portion of the attack surface will lead to a breach or compilation of security.

Attack Vectors and Attack Surfaces

As a rule, a security administrator should minimize both attack vectors and attack surfaces. Unfortunately, because users need to interact with your business systems, elimination of all attack vectors and attack surfaces is not possible.

Distilling down the role, a great deal of a security administrator's responsibility comes to execution tasks focused on minimizing possible attack vectors and surfaces. One might argue that it's the security administrator's only role. This role is complex and requires much planning and analysis, beyond just elimination of known attack points.

1.4.3   Segregation of Duties

Every organization is going to have a different approach to corporate security, especially for administrators, due for the potential for fraud. The role of enforcing SoD may fall to the security administrator. SoD may also apply to Basis administrators or system administrators. This restriction of abilities or roles can be intensely frustrating for administrators. However, always keep in mind that SoD increases the overall level of security, even for administrators. SoD policies of this type would include practices such as separating an administration team into administrators that can manage users, and administrators that have system configuration abilities. The security administrator may be caught in the middle of this, only being able to perform a subset of the required functions for his or her job. If this is the case, then working with other administrators to perform tasks is a critical skill that will be required to keep up the SoD rules. To be clear, SoD rules that affect administrators are still beneficial. They must be respected.

Forming a clear policy in which SoD achieves it's purpose without hampering administrative work is critical if this situation occurs. There are many tools, such as SAP GRC's firefighter functionality, that can help maintain SoD while still allowing administrators or developers to perform mission critical tasks. If you find your organization paralyzing it's administrators with SoD burdens, a good solution would be to implement this type of functionality.

1.4.4   Audit Support

Along with SoD, security administrators are routinely involved in supporting financial or regulatory audits. One of the most common areas of difficulty for a security administrator comes during an audit. There are many different types of audits, many of which we will cover later on in this book. A security administrator will be expected to help auditors run reports and gather the information needed to prove compliance. Once the audit is complete, a security administrator may be asked to remedy deficiencies found during the audit. This activity usually involves roles and SoD.

1.4.5 Basis versus Security

In your organization, you may share the roles of both Basis administrator and security administrator. Alternatively, you may not have a dual role. Regardless, good SAP security requires a good understanding of the Basis level of the SAP NetWeaver AS ABAP system. It is ideal to have a strong Basis background, or be in a role in which you are responsible for both Basis and security administration. The reason for this is that the ultimate responsibility for the SAP system falls upon the system administrator. Nobody knows or understands the system better. This also gives credence to the idea that a good security administrator has an understanding of the theoretical vectors of attack. Learning the details of how to secure an SAP NetWeaver system is an ongoing process. New vulnerabilities are discovered every day, forcing security administrators to be nimble, learning new techniques to defend as they go. Therefore, dual roles and a multifaceted experience in Basis administration is helpful when taking on the role of a security administrator.

1.5 Summary

In this chapter we explored the potential threats to an SAP NetWeaver system, including each type of threat and how it might affect an organization. We then learned about modern-day system vulnerabilities, including multi-approach attacks, and how these vulnerabilities can be remedied using a layered approach to security. Finally, we discussed the administrator's role in security planning, execution, and support.

In the next chapter we'll begin our practical discussion of SAP system security with profiles and parameters, which help establish many of the security-relevant settings for your system.

Chapter 2
Configuring Profiles and Parameters

Security administrators must have a sound understanding of profile parameters and how they're used to define the running state of an SAP NetWeaver system. This chapter presents the fundamentals along with some tips for security-minded administrators.

One of the most fundamental tasks of configuring any SAP NetWeaver system is setting *profile parameters*. Profile parameters control many aspects of the system's behavior and operation. For example, a profile parameter is responsible for limiting the number of times you can attempt to login to the system or what you can or can't use as a password. Many settings that are crucial to the security of the SAP NetWeaver system are set using profile parameters.

Profile parameters, often referred to as system parameters, are individual system settings that an administrator is able to set. A collection of these settings is kept in what is called a *profile*. There are several profiles that an instance will have which will determine what that instances active system parameters are when running.

As discussed in Chapter 1, security administrators often share many of the same tasks as system administrators. In smaller shops, the Basis administrator and security administrator is often the same person. Larger companies may elect to keep the responsibilities separate to segregate duties. However, a good security administrator will also be familiar with systems administration, even if it's not within their day-to-day job responsibilities.

Maintaining profile parameters is one of a system administrator's main duties. If you're both a system administrator and a security administrator, then profile know-how is doubly important for you. If you're a security administrator, then a sound understanding of profile parameters will help you secure your system, even if you're not setting the actual parameters yourself. After all, profile parameters control how a system behaves, and we want to make our systems behave in the most secure way. A security administrator is typically responsible for checking parameter values, evaluating risks, and suggesting or setting the proper values. Therefore, understanding how parameters are used is a core skill for the both system and security administrators.

To get the most out of from this chapter, you'll need to know the administration basics of what a system, instance, and host are. You'll also need to be able to navigate to transactions using transaction codes. You may already know how to adjust system parameters as a system administrator, but the information in this chapter is geared toward a full understanding to safeguard your administration practices and prevent inadvertent or malicious parameter changes to your SAP NetWeaver System. It's important to note that a security administrator protects the SAP NetWeaver system from both internal and external threats.

2.1   Understanding System Parameters

System parameters can be thought of as basic operating instructions for your SAP NetWeaver system. These instructions tell the system things like how much memory to allocate to a work process, how to negotiate secure connections, even how many times a user can try a password before that user's account is locked. These instructions can be read at startup, or some can even be evaluated as the system is running. Most system-wide settings are set with parameters, as are many client-specific settings.

System parameters live both in the database and on the OS. The reason for this is that when the administrator can't login to the system due to it being down, incorrectly configured, or in an error state, he can still login to the OS and manually change parameters before startup is attempted. Although this is fine in an emergency cases, in regular situations an administrator should always use the SAP system to change parameters for proper change tracking and control.

The advantage to keeping profile parameters in the database is twofold: First, multiple versions can be easily kept. The active version is used, and inactive versions can be kept for historical reference or even reactivated if the need arises. Second, changes can be tracked more easily by SAP user ID rather than the OS administrative use ID, SIDADM. Therefore, many auditors require that profile changes only be allowed using the proper transactions in the system.

For this reason, it's prudent to only allow administrators to set system parameters within the SAP system itself. Sometimes it will be necessary to edit parameters directly on the OS level, but SAP recommends doing this only in an emergency situation.

2.2   System Profiles

System profiles, like those in Figure 2.1, can be defined as a collection of parameters intended for a defined scope. This scope could be a single instance, an application server, all servers, the message server, the dispatcher, and so on. The reason for this distinction is that we don't want to be setting the exact same values in every single profile if we know that they'll be the same for each system. Furthermore, if we only want a value set in a single instance or application server, using the correct profile will allow us to do that.

There are two major types of profiles that we're most interested in. The instance profile applies to a single instance, commonly an application server. The default profile, on the other hand, applies to all instances within the system. We'll touch on all major profiles in this section, as well as others you might run into.

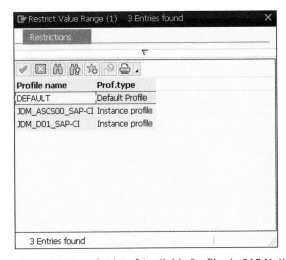

Figure 2.1 Sample List of Available Profiles in SAP NetWeaver 7.5

2.2.1   Instance Profile

The instance profile contains parameters that only apply to the instance that the profile belongs to. Each instance of your SAP NetWeaver system should have its own instance profile. Although this isn't a requirement, it usually holds true.

The instance profile is typically named as follows:

<SID>_<InstanceName>_<Hostname>

Where *SID* is the system ID of the system, *InstanceName* is the technical instance name, and *Hostname* is the host that runs the instance. For example, an application server for system ID JDM, instance D01, and hostname sap-ci would be named *JDM_D01_sap-ci*.

What goes into the instance profile? Anything that is set on a per-instance basis, such as hostnames or parameters that are intended only to be set to that value on that instance. For example, if you have a grouping of instances that you'd like to use only for batch processing, the instance profiles of those servers would have an increased value of batch processes set by parameter rdisp/wp_no_btc to a value higher than its default value of 0. Thus, the value set in the instance profile is the value that the system will use for that particular instance.

Profile Changes in SAP NetWeaver 7.5

You will also find in SAP NetWeaver 7.5 that the contents of the start profile can now be found in the instance profile. This change was for simplicity because two independent profiles weren't really needed. We'll cover more about the start profile in Section 2.2.3.

Security parameters are often set in the instance profile when they're instance-specific and require a specific variable, such as the hostname or instance name.

2.2.2   Default Profile

The default profile provides parameter values to all instances that don't have entries for a given parameter. That is, if the parameter is set in the default profile, each instance will inherit that value as if it were set in its instance profile. When a parameter is entered into the default profile, you can think of this as setting the default value for your system.

Default Profile

Instance profile parameters will override default profile parameters. Be sure that parameters set in your default profile aren't also set in an instance profile if you intend them to be set to the value in your default profile.

Therefore, the default profile sets the system default for that particular parameter. The system itself also has a predefined default value for some parameters. This is called the *system default value*. If you set a parameter to a specific value in the default profile, the system default value will be overridden.

The default profile is always named DEFAULT.

Because there aren't any instance-specific qualities of the default profile, it's always simply called the default profile.

The default profile is a valuable tool to a security administrator because security parameters often are set system-wide. It's worth noting that this can be done once in the default profile and will then affect all systems.

2.2.3   Other Profiles

Some systems may have the legacy start profile. The *start profile* is the first profile read when starting an instance. It provides the instance information, such as where to find its executables and what its own name is. Normally, there aren't many parameters in the start profile that a security administrator would concern herself with. In SAP NetWeaver 7.5, the start profile and the instance profile have been combined within the instance profile.

Other profiles you may see in use are the ASCS profile and the ERS profile. These profiles apply to the message server and enqueue replication server, respectively. These profiles are also instance profiles, but the instances they refer to are not your typical ABAP application servers. The message server is responsible for coordinating instance-to-instance communication, and the enqueue replication server is responsible for replicating the lock table to another host in a high-availability scenario. Both instances are potential security attack vectors, so understanding what parameters are set in each is prudent for a security administrator. Also recall that parameters set in the default profile will apply to the ASCS and ERS profiles.

2.3   Profile and Parameter Structure

As with profile names, profiles themselves have an exact structure in an SAP system. Typos, mistakes, and bad formatting can cause a system not to come up or a security hole to be left open. The effects of either of these scenarios could be devastating and must be avoided. Thus, a sound understanding of profile and parameter structure is needed.

Notice in Figure 2.2 that the profile has a header and several comment lines. In a profile, any line that begins with a pound sign (#) is ignored by the system. Comments can also be entered in the **Comment** field and will be added with the proper formatting in the parameter file.

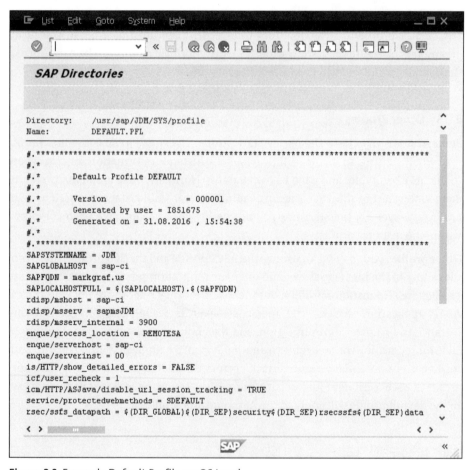

Figure 2.2 Example Default Profile on OS Level

Each parameter has three parts. The first is the application area. This tells you the group that the parameter belongs to. For example, a parameter with a "login" application area will have something to do with user authentication and logon. The application area is always followed by a forward slash (/). The second portion is the name of the parameter. This is a descriptive name used to briefly describe what the parameter does. However, a few words sometimes aren't enough to understand what the parameter does, so the documentation will better explain the parameter. Finally, the third part is the value. The value is separated from the rest of the parameter by an equals sign (=). Again, the documentation for that particular parameter will specify the acceptable values. Putting this all together, a parameter looks like this:

```
login/min_password_digits = 6
```

2.3.1   Profiles on the Operating System Level

As previously discussed, profiles are stored in the database and on the OS level. The file system path for profiles is */usr/sap/<SID>/SYS/profile* (see Figure 2.3). Because system profiles must be shared between systems that may be on different application servers or physical hosts running their own instances, the profile directory uses the global mount, sapmnt. On an SAP NetWeaver application server, the profile directory can be reached at a command prompt by simply typing the standard SAP-delivered alias, "cdpro".

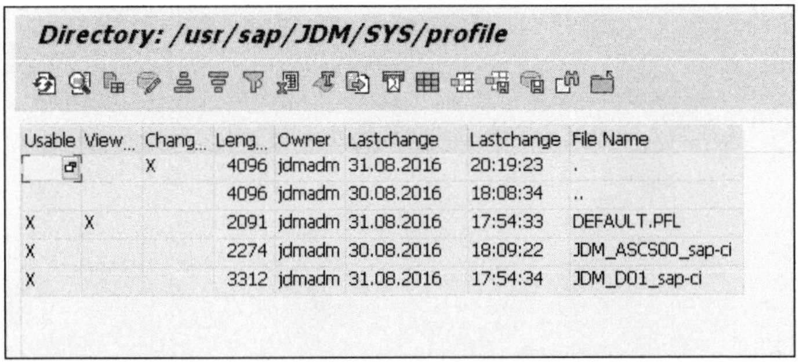

Directory: /usr/sap/JDM/SYS/profile

Usable	View...	Chang...	Leng...	Owner	Lastchange		Lastchange	File Name
		X	4096	jdmadm	31.08.2016	20:19:23	.
			4096	jdmadm	30.08.2016	18:08:34	..
X	X		2091	jdmadm	31.08.2016	17:54:33	DEFAULT.PFL
X			2274	jdmadm	30.08.2016	18:09:22	JDM_ASCS00_sap-ci
X			3312	jdmadm	31.08.2016	17:54:34	JDM_D01_sap-ci

Figure 2.3 Operating System-Level View of System Profiles

It's useful to be able to read profile parameter values on the OS level. If a security administrator is in a situation in which he or she has multiple application servers to audit, then a simple text search command (e.g., grep on Linux or the find function of Notepad in Windows) may come in handy to locate specific values quickly from multiple instances or systems. It's also advantageous for a system administrator to back up profiles during an upgrade or before major system changes. The same can be done for a security audit for a security administrator.

> **Warning: Editing Parameters on the OS Level**
>
> SAP advises that you should not edit profile parameters directly on the OS. Editing profile parameters on the OS is only permissible for cases in which the system won't start up otherwise.

2.3.2   Profiles on the Database Level

To maintain history, traceability, and backups, the profiles are also stored in the database, where profile parameters reside in table TPFET. An example view is shown in Figure 2.4. Table logging can be enabled on this table to track changes. We'll explore table logging in Chapter 11.

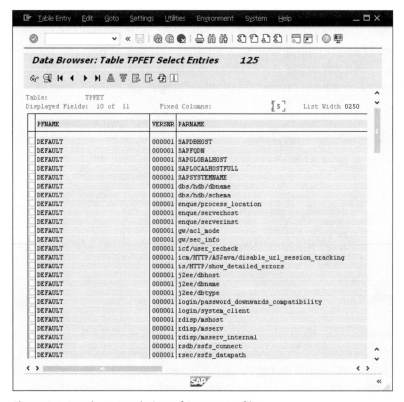

Figure 2.4 Database-Level View of System Profiles

> **Warning: Changing Parameters in the Database**
>
> *Never* change profile parameters directly in the database. Furthermore, don't directly edit any table in your database using database tools. Doing so could damage your system and void your SAP support contract.

Notice the **VERSNR** column in Figure 2.4. This indicates the version number of the profile. In the database, many old versions of the profile can be stored, and reviewed or activated in case of an issue with the current active profile.

2.4   Static and Dynamic Parameters

There are two types of profile parameters in an SAP NetWeaver system. The first are *static parameters* that are evaluated once at system startup. Changing these parameters during running operation will have no effect on the system. The system must be restarted for these profile parameters to come into effect.

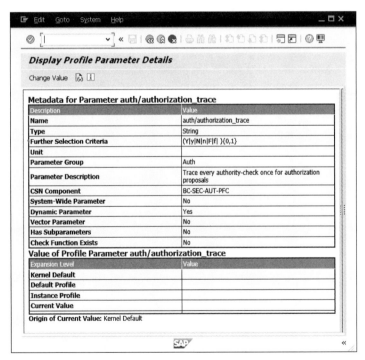

Figure 2.5 Transaction RZ11: The Display Profile Parameter Screen

Dynamic parameters, on the other hand, can be switched while the system is running and take effect immediately. These parameters are evaluated at runtime, so setting them can be done on the fly and the effect will be instant. No system restart is required.

A simple way to check if a profile parameter is dynamically switchable is to use Transaction RZ11. Simply specify the parameter you would like to look up and the **Dynamic Parameter** field will indicate if this parameter can be activated without restarting the system (see Figure 2.5). This is found in the **Metadata for Parameter** table under the **Dynamic Parameter** row.

Viewing Profile Information with Transaction RZ10

Transaction RZ10 is used by the security administrator to view profile information. Follow these steps to view profile information:

1. Navigate to Transaction RZ10.
2. Select the profile you'd like to access in the **Profile** field. You can use the input help to view a list of available profiles or type in the profile name.
3. To view profile information, select the **Administrative Data** radio button and click **Display** (Figure 2.6).

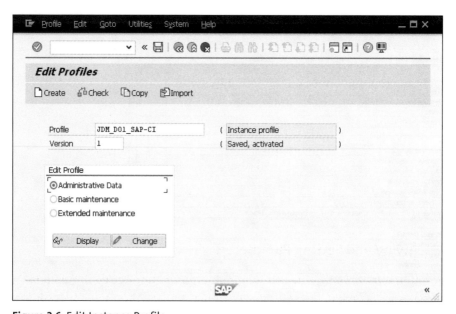

Figure 2.6 Edit Instance Profile

Several important items can be found in the profile data displayed in Figure 2.7. The path to the OS file that corresponds to your profile can be found in the **Activation in operating system file** field. The **Modification/activation data** dates and user information can help indicate the last change to a profile. The **Profile type** indicates the type of the profile, and the **Reference server for profile parameter check** shows which server the profile belongs to in the case of an instance profile.

Figure 2.7 Viewing Administrative Profile Data in Transaction RZ10

2.5   Viewing and Setting Parameters

There are several ways to view and manipulate parameters. There are three main tools that are used most often by security administrators. They may differ slightly from tools used by system administrators, but they accomplish the same goals. These tools are ABAP report RSPARAM for viewing parameters, Transaction RZ11 for viewing parameter documentation, and Transaction RZ10 for viewing and changing profile parameters.

2.5.1   Viewing Parameters with ABAP Report RSPARAM

ABAP report RSPARAM is an excellent resource for security administrators to get a holistic or focused view of system parameters of interest. This report is delivered standard with all recent SAP NetWeaver versions.

To view a list of system parameters, follow these steps:

1. Navigate to Transaction SA38.
2. Enter the **Program** name: "rsparam" (see Figure 2.8).

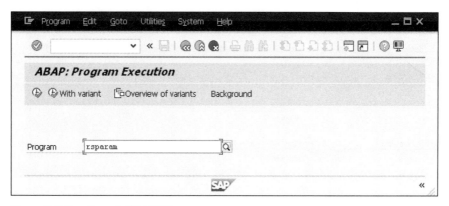

Figure 2.8 Run Report RSPARAM

3. Click the **Execute** button to launch the program. You'll be prompted again by the program to execute. Click the **Execute** button once more.

The program will now display output for all parameters that are active in the system (Figure 2.9). The following fields will be displayed:

- **Parameter Name**
  This is the technical name of the parameter. It's what you use when setting the parameter.
- **User-Defined Value**
  This is the value that has been set by the active profile.

- **System Default Value**
  This is the value that the system would assume if it were not set by a profile value in either the default or instance profiles.

- **SystemDefaultUnsubst (system value, unsubstituted form)**
  This is the same as **System Default Value**, but it shows the variables that are evaluated by the system to come up with the above value.

- **Comment**
  Short text about what the parameter does. Often, this field is brief and you'll need to look at the documentation for the parameter for more information.

Figure 2.9 Output of Report RSPARAM

Useful Tips for ABAP Report RSPARAM

You can use normal ABAP report tools like search and filter to narrow down what's displayed and find whatever you're looking for. You can also export the entire list to a spreadsheet for manipulation and display purposes. For these reasons, ABAP report RSPARAM is a very useful tool for the security administrator looking to audit and evaluate system parameters.

2.5.2   Viewing the Documentation with Transaction RZ11

Transaction RZ11 is used by security administrators to view the built-in documentation for SAP parameters. There are several ways to view documentation, but Transaction RZ11 is a quick and easy way to get directly to what you need.

To view documentation for a parameter, follow these steps:

1. Navigate to Transaction RZ11.
2. Specify the parameter you want to view (see Figure 2.10) and select the **Display docu** button. The documentation for the parameter login/fails_to_user_lock are shown in Figure 2.11. The parameter's values can be viewed with the **Display** button.

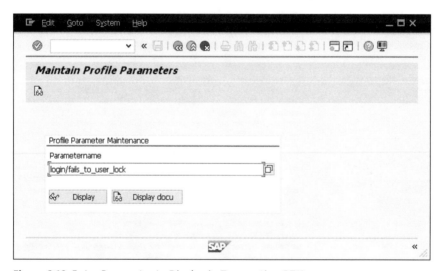

Figure 2.10 Enter Parameter to Display in Transaction RZ11

Figure 2.11 Documentation for Parameter login/fails_to_user_lock

2.5.3   Changing Parameters with Transaction RZ10

Transaction RZ10 is used by the security administrator to edit profiles and change parameter values. It can also be used to view data about profiles and to upload profiles from the OS to the database.

Follow these steps to maintain profile parameters:

1. Navigate to Transaction RZ10.

2. Select the profile you'd like to access in the **Profile** field (Figure 2.12). You can use the input help to view a list of available profiles or type in the profile name.

3. To change parameter values, select the **Extended maintenance** radio button and click **Change** (Figure 2.13).

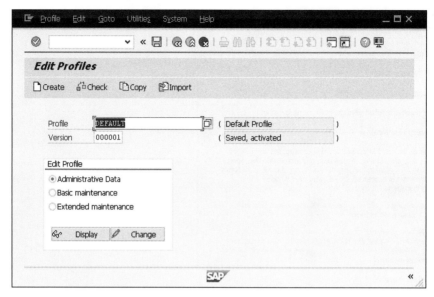

Figure 2.12 Select Profile to Access in Transaction RZ10

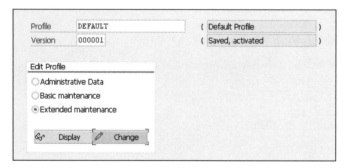

Figure 2.13 Changing Parameters in Transaction RZ10

4. Click the parameter that you'd like to change in the **Parameter Name** list, then click the **Edit Parameter** button in the toolbar (Figure 2.14).

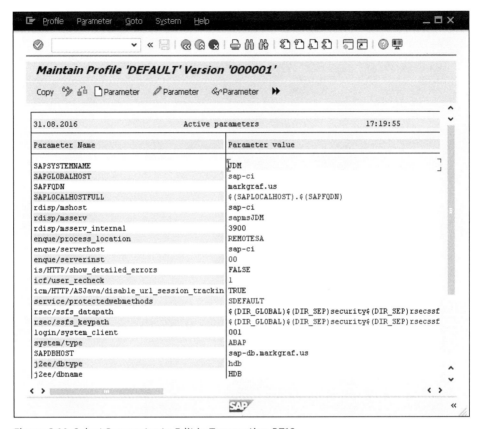

Figure 2.14 Select Parameter to Edit in Transaction RZ10

5. At this point, the profile maintenance screen will appear for the selected parameter (Figure 2.15). Enter the value you want to change in the **Parameter val.** field. You can also enter comments in the **Comment** field.

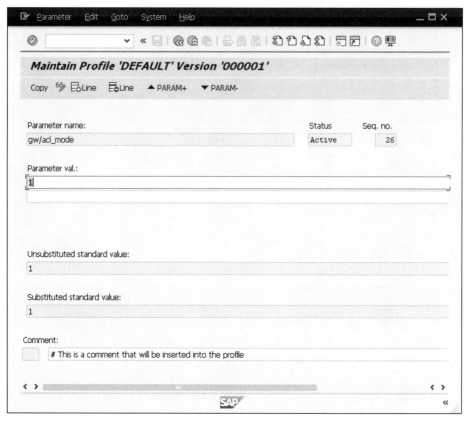

Figure 2.15 Profile Maintenance Screen in Transaction RZ10

6. When you're finished, click the **Copy** button. The system will indicate that the changes were saved in the lower-left corner of the window (Figure 2.16).

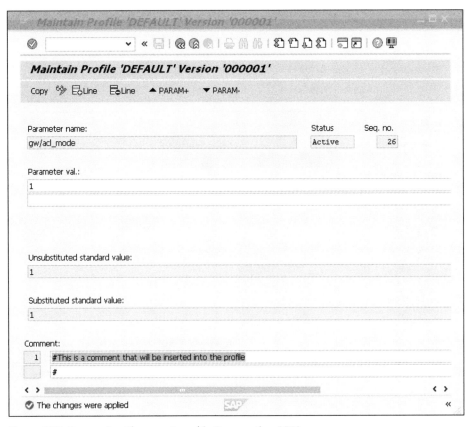

Figure 2.16 Parameter Changes Saved in Transaction RZ10

7. Once you're done editing the profile, click the **Exit** button. The system will prompt you to save your changes to the profile (Figure 2.17). You may also save your changes at any time by clicking the **Copy** button.

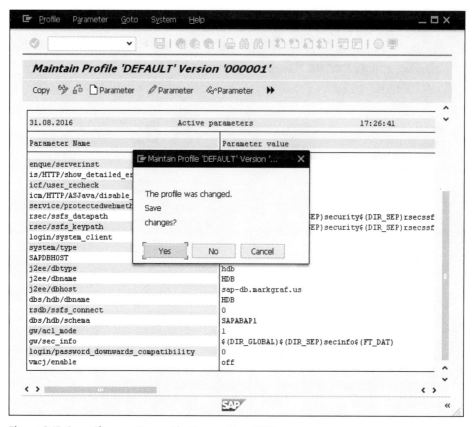

Figure 2.17 Save Changes Prompt in Transaction RZ10

2.6   Key Security-Related Parameters

This section describes some of the many profile parameters you'll want to evaluate during your day-to-day security analysis. As you continue through this book, you'll find many parameters relevant to the subject areas covered. The list in Table 2.1 is a starting point for investigation of basic levels of security.

Most of the parameters in Table 2.1 are directed toward the end user. Specifically, the login application area- and SAP GUI-related parameters. That's because user login and credentials are two of the most overlooked parts of an SAP NetWeaver system. Having solid password policies and SAP GUI safeguards will go a long way toward securing your system. The second, and equally important, area of focus is network communication. We'll cover this in depth during Chapter 12. For now, Table 2.1 is a good starting point to evaluate your security.

Parameter Name	Description
gw/acl_mode	Enables a whitelist of servers your SAP system can communicate with.
snc/enable	Enables Secure Network Communications (SNC) module.
login/no_automatic_user_sap*	Controls the automatic login user SAP*.
login/min_password_lng	Sets the minimum password length.
login/fails_to_session_end	Sets the number of invalid login attempts until a session will be terminated by the system.
login/fails_to_user_lock	Sets the maximum number of failed attempts before a user is locked.
login/failed_user_auto_unlock	Disables automatic unlocking of locked user at midnight.
login/password_expiration_time	Sets the validity period of passwords (in days).
sapgui/user_scripting	Enables or disables user scripting on SAP GUI.
rdisp/gui_auto_logout	Sets the maximum idle time for an SAP GUI connection until it's automatically logged out.

Table 2.1 Security-Related Parameters

The next logical question a security administrator should ask is, "What should I set parameter X to?" The answer depends on many factors. The first thing to check is your company's audit policies. Most often, setting your security parameters' values can be done easily by simply mapping each to an audit policy or corporate security policy. Second, you need to take into account the system performance impacts of setting a parameter. For example, parameters like table or audit logging can produce significant overhead on high-volume transactional systems. Only enable these parameters with adequate research and planning because they can impact performance significantly in certain scenarios.

Although we're specifically security administrators, it's always important to recognize that we're also *administrators* and our parameter settings may have unanticipated effects or, more commonly, unfavorable usability implications. Your security approach must be planned carefully because setting parameters incorrectly can lead to downtime or even data loss in extreme cases.

As we cover additional material, we'll introduce more parameters that will help you control the behavior and strength of security of your SAP NetWeaver system. Each area of the system (user authentication, authorizations, and network security, to name a few) has many important parameters you'll use. Having the tools to view, evaluate, and understand these parameters is a crucial starting skill.

2.7   Controlling Access to Change Parameters

It's very important for a security administrator to understand all methods of changing system parameters. The reason for this is simple: unauthorized or accidental changes to system parameters can compromise the security of your SAP system, causing downtime or even a data breach.

For example, internal or external bad actors could change key parameters via the OS level on a single-instance profile, opening a single application server to attack.

Safeguarding an Application Server
More information about safeguarding against these types of attacks can be found in Chapter 15.

In this scenario, you can see a practical example of why it's important for a security administrator to know and understand the personnel with access to the OS level, the profile tool (Transaction RZ10), and the database. Profile changes are possible on each of these levels and access must be controlled. Periodic auditing and change control are both effective techniques to combat this potential threat.

Auditing Security Parameters

One of the main tasks of a security administrator is to perform audits of system parameters periodically on systems. These audits, though not always specifically requested by external auditors, can help ensure that all SAP systems are secure and continue to stay secure as time passes. Using tools like ABAP report RSPARAM, the security administrator can check each system in his or her landscape against a reference configuration to ensure that the proper parameters are set. Often during periodic activities like system copies, the system administrators responsible for maintenance must relax some security parameters for technical reasons (e.g., to be able to login to a newly created client using account SAP*). These things are part of everyday business, but unfortunately sometimes are forgotten—and it's then up to a security parameter audit to catch these mistakes before a malicious user or external force can exploit them.

We'll cover an auditing program more in depth in Chapter 11. For now, understanding the importance of making sure your systems are in an expected safe state is the key takeaway.

2.8   Summary

This chapter described the use and operation of system parameters in a security administrator's day-to-day work. Many of the settings that are crucial to the security of the SAP NetWeaver system are set using profile parameters as described in this chapter. You learned that a security administrator is responsible for checking parameter values, evaluating risks, and suggesting or setting the proper values. This chapter also introduced you to transactions and reports you can use to research, view, and set parameters.

In addition, this chapter taught you the mechanics of profiles and parameters and what methods are used to set and store profiles on the OS and database levels.

In the next chapter, we will discuss transaction locking. Transaction locking gives the security administrator the ability to prevent specific transactions from being executed by all users, temporarily or permanently, in a single client or in multiple clients.

Chapter 3
Restricting Transactional Access

Before reading this chapter, you need to understand what a transaction is, what a client is, and how to navigate within SAP GUI.

The first tool in our repertoire when it comes to restricting users from accessing transactions within an SAP system is transaction locking. *Transaction locking* is the ability to lock *all* users from executing a specific transaction code. Keep in mind that when locking a transaction, administrators will also be prevented from executing the locked transaction code.

When a user attempts to execute a locked transaction, the system will display a notification in the notification area in the lower-left corner of the screen that the transaction is locked. The system won't execute the transaction. Upon clicking the message in the notification area, system help will show a window that explains that the transaction was locked, as shown in in Figure 3.1.

If the transaction in question is needed for daily use, then locking it isn't the correct approach. If preventing all users from executing a transaction code isn't flexible enough for your needs, the alternative is to control access to a transaction code using authorizations. We'll cover controlling transaction access with authorizations in depth in Chapter 7.

For now, we'll explore the situations and process of locking transactions. Often, transactions are locked to protect an accidental change by a user who may be otherwise authorized to perform a task. Sometimes the request to lock a transaction is due to a situation that requires users not to execute certain functionalities within in the SAP system during a specific timeframe. For example, a development freeze could be called for in a test system. Therefore, it would make sense to lock Transaction STMS so that users can't move transports using the Transport Management System (TMS) without an administrator first unlocking the transaction, signaling that it's acceptable for use.

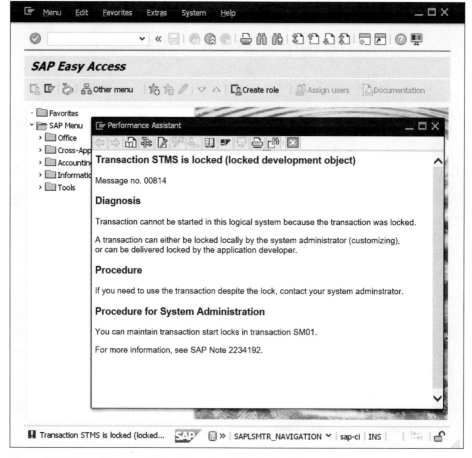

Figure 3.1 System Response When User Executes Locked Transaction

Locking transactions can be part of a process designed to make sure that users are authorized to perform work in high-security or productive-system scenarios. For example, a developer that needs to make an emergency fix in a production system may have to request that Transaction SE38 (ABAP Program Editor) is unlocked by a security administrator. The benefit of performing this extra step is that it allows the security administrator to be included in the loop so that she can verify that the developer has a proper ticket, documentation, and approval to perform the change before granting access to the transaction.

3.1   Clients

Transaction locking can be *client-dependent* or *client-independent*. A client-dependent lock is made only in one specific client, while a client-independent lock is made in all clients. For example, if you lock a transaction in your productive client—say, client 100—the locked transaction can be locked in all other clients, including client 000, 066, and so on. The decision of which clients are locked and which remain unlocked is made during the locking process.

Since transaction locking can be cross-client, client-independent locking is a secure way of ensuring that users cannot use a different client to adjust client-independent settings.

3.2   Who Should Be Able to Lock and Unlock Transactions?

Transaction locking is a very powerful feature of SAP NetWeaver and typically, only security administrators or developers should be allowed to lock or unlock transactions. Be very careful about which users are given these authorizations because they'll be able to unlock any transaction that has been previously locked. End users or business users should not be given access to lock or unlock transactions.

For a more granular approach to who can and cannot use this mechanism, authorizations can control transaction locking permissions. We'll discuss authorizations more in Chapter 7.

As for unlocking, usually, a business process is put in to place such that a user submits a ticket to a security administrator for the unlocking of a transaction for a specific time period. The request and action of the system administrator are both logged and should be kept for auditing purposes. Typically, it is only the security administrator that is tasked with unlocking transactions.

3.3   Which Transactions to Lock

As with many judgment calls when it comes to SAP security, the decision about which transactions to lock depends on various business and technical factors. A security administrator may be provided a list of transactions to lock by his auditor or corporate security department. You might also be asked by power users or department heads to lock certain functional transactions.

There are scenarios in which administrative transactions should be locked, but also keep in mind that many business situations may benefit from having a transaction locked. For example, at quarter- or year-end, the financial team may request that the security administrator lock financial transactions to prevent users from accidently entering data that could impact financial reporting. The key is to understand what the risks are and use transaction locking as a tool to mitigate those risks.

Any transaction that requires a second safety mechanism before being executed is a great candidate for locking. Table 3.1 lists some examples.

Transaction Code	Name
SCC1	Client Copy
SCC5	Client Delete
SE11	Data Dictionary Maintenance
SW37	Function Builder
SE38	ABAP Editor
SU10	User Mass Maintenance
SE01/STMS	Transport Management
SM30	Table Maintenance
SM49	Execute OS Command
SU21	Authorization Objects
SU24	Maintain Assignment of Authorization Objects
SA38	ABAP Reporting

Table 3.1 Technical Transactions to Consider Locking

By no means is Table 3.1 an exhaustive list; it's more of a starting point for consideration. In addition to these technical transactions, you may want to consult with your power users to come up with some functional transactions that you may need to lock as well. These transactions would be powerful HR or finance transactions, for example, that could cause issues if used in an inappropriate manner. Table 3.2 provides a list of some functional transactions to consider locking. Consult your business users to discuss the approach to be used with these commonly locked transactions.

Transaction Code	Name
PA20	Display HR Master Data
PA30	Maintain HR Master Data
MMPV	Close Periods
MMRV	Allow Posting to Previous Period
CAT6	Transfer External -> Time Management
CATS	CATS: Cross-Application Timesheet
OKP1	Maintain Period Lock
F110	Parameters for Automatic Payment
MIRO	Enter Incoming Invoice

Table 3.2 Functional Transactions to Consider Locking

Remember, some transactions are more sensitive in production environments than sandboxes. For example, the transaction used to open a client (Transaction SCC4) is much more likely to be locked in a production system than in a sandbox system. However, if your organization requires high security, there's nothing wrong with locking transactions in any system.

Developing a security plan that takes into account the roles of each of your systems within your landscape (dev/QA/production), as well as important business events (quarter end/year end/payroll/audit), will go far in securing your systems against both user error and malicious intent. Working with your power users and auditors can help you develop practices and procedures that can not only secure your system, but also make audits and critical business processing events easier and shorter, and accomplish your business goals with less overall risk.

3.4   Locking Transactions

Traditionally, transaction locking was done in Transaction SM01. As of SAP Net-Weaver AS ABAP 7.5, however, SAP has declared Transaction SM01 obsolete and has replaced it with Transaction SM01_DEV and Transaction SM01_CUS. The reason for this change is to introduce increased functionality around transaction locking and logging of locks.

> **Note**
>
> The steps for locking a transaction in Transaction SM01_DEV and Transaction SM01_CUS are almost identical. The steps in this section can be applied to both transactions.

Let's briefly compare these two transactions:

- **Transaction SM01_DEV**
  - Used by system administrators and developers
  - Locks created with this transaction can be transported as development requests
- **Transaction SM01_CUS**
  - Used by system administrators and business users
  - Locks created with this transaction can be transported as customizing requests
  - If this transaction is called in client 000, an administrator can lock a transaction for all clients or just for a specific client. If called in other clients, the administrator can only set the lock for that client. It may make more sense in your organization to lock transactions using the Transaction SM01_CUS from client 000 and lock all transactions.

> **Transaction SM01_DEV and Transaction SM01_CUS**
>
> As of the writing of this book, Transaction SM01_DEV is the only way to lock transactions in SAP NetWeaver 7.5. Enhancements to Transaction SM01_CUS will be delivered in future support packages and kernel updates. Updates to the status of this functionality will be published in SAP Note 2234192.

Use the following steps to lock a transaction:

1. Navigate to the client you wish to lock a transaction in, and then navigate to Transaction SM01_DEV (Figure 3.2).
2. Enter the code for the transaction you wish to lock into the **Transaction** field (Figure 3.3). Check the **Locked** and **Not Locked** check boxes. Then press the **Execute** button .

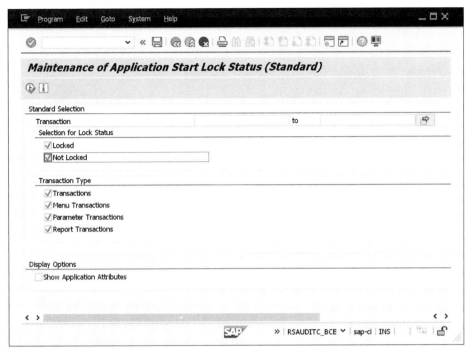

Figure 3.2 Transaction SM01_DEV: Initial Screen

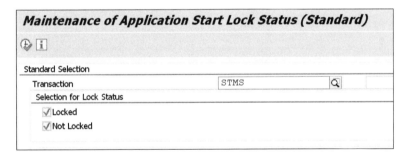

Figure 3.3 Transaction Search

3. Select the line which contains the transaction you'd like to lock and click the lock button 🔒 in the toolbar (Figure 3.4). Then click the save button 💾.

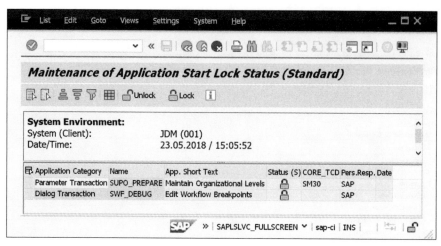

Figure 3.4 The Lock Selection Screen

4. You may be prompted for a transport request if your system is set up for transports. Only import this transport in downstream systems if you do want this transaction locked.

The process of unlocking is the reverse of locking: simply click the unlock icon, and the selected transaction will be unlocked. The system activates locks and unlocks system-wide as soon as the **Save** button is selected, so you won't need to sync a buffer or restart the system for a lock to be changed.

> **Don't Lock Yourself Out!**
>
> Don't make the mistake of locking Transaction SM01_DEV because you'll lock it for all users, including SAP* and even super users with the profile SAP_ALL. In the event of the accidental locking of Transaction SM01_DEV, you'll need to contact SAP support; direct database updates are the only way to correct the issue.

3.5   Viewing Locked Transactions

From time to time, it may be prudent to review which transactions are locked in your system. A list of locked transactions can be viewed by executing the following steps:

1. Go to Transaction SM01_DEV (Figure 3.5).

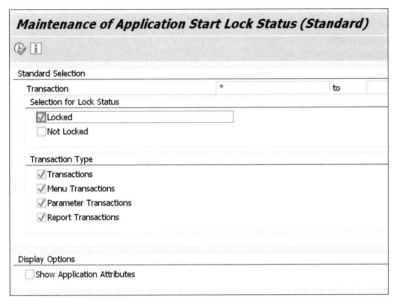

Figure 3.5 Selection for Locks

2. Enter an asterisk (*) in the transaction field. Check the **Locked** check box. Then press the **Execute** button. A window with a list of all locked transactions will appear (Figure 3.6).

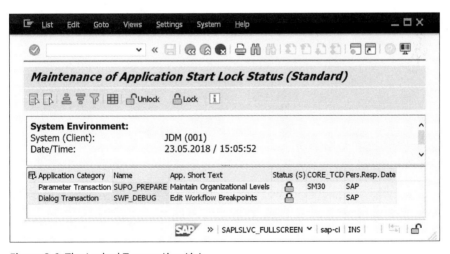

Figure 3.6 The Locked Transaction List

Exporting or Printing a List of Locked Transactions

You can export or print this list of locked transactions by using the **System • Output** menu in the menu bar.

3.6   Summary

In this chapter, you learned how to use the transaction locking tool (Transaction SM01_DEV) to both lock and unlock transactions. You also learned about why to lock a transaction and the different reasons you might be asked to do so. It's important to remember that locking is one tool in the security administrator's toolbelt to control transaction access. The other tool, authorizations, will be discussed in Chapter 7.

In the next chapter, we'll discuss how to further secure the system by managing settings on the client level. While transaction locking only restricts transaction use, controlling client settings allows for more granular control over what users are able to change in a system.

Chapter 4
Securing Clients

Before reading this chapter, you must have a basic understanding of the client concept in an SAP system. You must also understand how to navigate within SAP GUI.

In an SAP NetWeaver system, all business data is isolated on the client level. This means that users that work in one client can't access the data of another client. This architecture is ideal for shared systems that multiple organizations might use. It also allows for the separation of different clients for different activities or use cases. For example, testing clients and development clients could be created on the same SAP installation to allow users to develop and test in the same system without getting in each other's way. Some organizations will choose to have multiple development clients, or multiple test clients. Others will use different clients to separate HR and finance activities. Some organizations will have each of their subsidiaries operate in a separate client in the same master system.

Here are the basic rules that define clients:

- Clients can never read or write to other clients.
- The business data of a client is separated from other clients.
- Clients share the same SID but have different client numbers.
- Multiple clients may exist in an SAP system.
- Clients may be copied or deleted and won't affect other clients.

How is a client different than just having another system? To start, multiple clients can exist in a single system. A client will typically represent a separate organization or company within an SAP system but share the same technical SAP NetWeaver instance. Therefore, the overhead to maintain the instance is shared. However, some organizations will adhere to a strict, productive single client per system. It all depends on the architecture your organization has chosen.

You can think of clients as floors of an office building. Multiple organizations can occupy offices on different floors in an office building. All the building tenants share the same infrastructure (power, water, Internet, heating), but they operate as separate entities isolated from each other by the floor and ceiling. What's said on one floor isn't overheard on another. A disruption on the top floor won't affect the bottom floor.

One key takeaway from this example is that in the office building some infrastructure is shared; in an SAP system, this shared infrastructure is called *client-independent*. Client-independent objects or tables are common for all clients. On the other hand, *client-dependent* objects are never shared with other clients.

Client-Dependent Database Tables: MANDT Field

The technical table field that denotes a client is the MANDT field. This field is present in all client-dependent tables. Client-independent tables don't have a MANDT field and represent any and all clients. Use care when changing client-independent tables as they affect all clients.

Most SAP NetWeaver systems have at least two clients, if not more. To identify what clients exist in your SAP system, simply look at table T000, the clients table (see Figure 4.1).

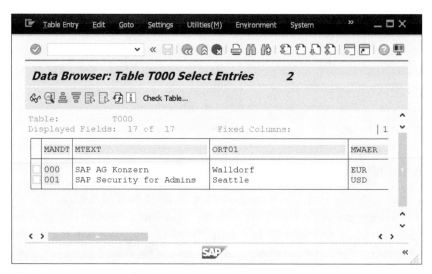

Figure 4.1 Table T000: Client List

Common clients you will see are client 000, client 001, and client 066. These clients are usually delivered/created by SAP. You may see more or fewer clients, depending on how your SAP system has been set up. You'll also see one or more productive clients, or clients that contain your business data. These are clients that your users will log in to and perform work on. Later in this chapter (Section 4.1.3), we'll cover more about securing clients, but for now let's explore the basics.

Now that you're familiar with the concept of multiple clients, let's explore the possible settings for each client. Some clients will be used to change code, others could be used for testing, and some will always be used by business end users in production. Client settings tell the SAP system what's allowable and what's restricted in each of these clients.

In a production or testing client, you wouldn't want a developer to be able to change objects. On the other hand, in a development client you would want this activity to be allowed. Settings like this are what we use to achieve a desired client scenario. In Section 4.1, we'll walk through how to check the current settings for a client.

As security administrators, we're interested in client settings because we'd like to prevent users from being able to change objects unless absolutely necessary. Even if the client settings are correct in one client, an errant setting in another client could lead to changes being made and passed to another client within the same system, *even if that client had the correct settings*. It's imperative that client settings are closely managed for all clients within both an SAP system and all SAP systems within a landscape.

From time to time an administrator may be asked to change the settings of a client. This activity should always be done temporarily because a client should have a steady state in which its settings are fixed. Often, clients are opened for simple changes and are then forgotten about and stay open until the next audit—or even worse, a malicious user—discovers the issue. Take care not to let this happen in your organization.

4.1 Client Settings

It's important for a security administrator to know and understand the different possible client settings and what they may be used for. Before we explore specific settings in depth, let's walk through how to check client settings in the system.

To check client settings, follow these steps:

1. Navigate to Transaction SCC4 (see Figure 4.2).
2. Double-click the client you'd like to view. For this example, client 001 has been selected (Figure 4.3).

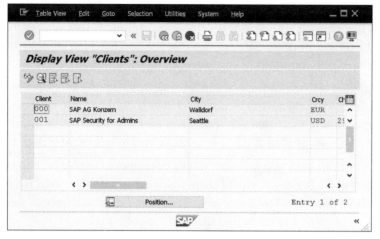

Figure 4.2 Transaction SCC4: Display Clients

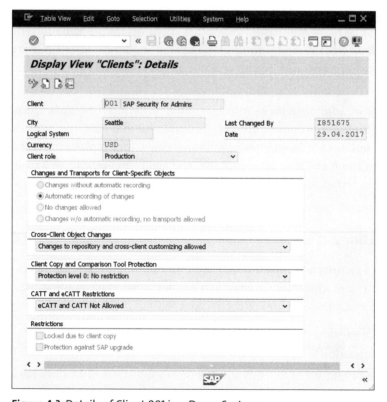

Figure 4.3 Details of Client 001 in a Demo System

Now that you know how to navigate to these settings, let's explore the information on this screen in more detail.

4.1.1   Client Setting Fields

When viewing a client's settings, you'll see the following fields:

- **Client number**
  This is a three-digit number that identifies the client within the system. This must be unique and is assigned when the client is created.

- **Client name or short text**
  Each client can have a short name assigned to it that helps identify it.

- **City**
  The city designation helps differentiate different clients when multiple organizations or divisions are used.

- **Logical System**
  The logical system is a technical identifier that comes into play when using system-to-system communication. It's very important to have a proper logical system name defined.

- **Currency**
  This field denotes what standard currency the client uses.

- **Last Changed By**
  This field denotes which user last changed the settings of the client. It is often checked for auditing purposes.

- **Date**
  This field denotes the date the client was last changed.

- **Client Role**
  Possible choices are as follows:
  - **Production**
    For the active use of business users. It's essential that no changes are made in this client.
  - **Test**
    Developers use this client setting to test their Customizing settings and workbench developments.
  - **Customizing**
    For the creation of Customizing settings and workbench developments.

- **Demo**
  For demonstration or prototyping purposes.
- **Training/Education**
  Typically used to train users on changes before import into production.
- **SAP Reference**
  Clients used by SAP.

- **Changes and Transports for Client-Specific Objects**
  Client-specific objects have values based on a client value. This means that a client-specific object can have a different value based on what client it's contained in. These options cover changes to these objects and how they're transported using the transport system. Possible choices are as follows:
  - **Changes without automatic recording**
    This means that changes in the customizing settings of the client are allowed. They aren't automatically captured in a transport for moving to other systems or clients. Changes can be manually transported to other clients or systems.
  - **Automatic recording of changes**
    This means that changes to the customizing settings of the client are allowed. They're automatically captured in a transport for moving to other systems or clients.
  - **No changes allowed**
    Changes to the customizing settings of the client aren't allowed with this setting.
  - **Changes w/o automatic recording, no transports allowed**
    Changes are allowed to the customizing settings of the client but may not be transported with this setting.

- **Cross-Client Object Changes**
  Cross-client objects have a single value for the entire system. This means that cross-client objects have the same value regardless of what client the user's logged into. These options cover changes to these objects and how they're transported using the transport system. Possible choices are as follows:
  - **Changes to repository and cross-client customizing allowed**
    There are no restrictions on the changes of cross-client objects for the client when this setting is used. Both cross-client Customizing objects and objects of the SAP repository can be changed.

- **No changes to cross-client customizing objects**
  Cross-client Customizing objects can't be changed in a client with this setting.

- **No changes to repository objects**
  Objects of the SAP repository can't be maintained in a client with this setting.

- **No changes to repository/cross-client customizing objects**
  Combination of both previous restrictions: neither cross-client Customizing objects nor objects of the SAP repository can be changed in a client with this setting.

- **CATT and eCATT Restrictions**
  This setting either allows or restricts the Computer-Aided Test Tool (CATT) and enhanced CATT (eCATT), which are scripting utilities used for automated testing. This setting either permits these scripts to run or prevents them from doing so.

- **Restrictions**
  This setting outlines other restrictions that can be made to the client. The options are:

  - **Locked due to client copy**
    This checkbox will indicate when the client is locked against logon. It's used during a client copy to prevent data changes during the copy. It's not a selectable box because it only indicates status.

  - **Protection against SAP Upgrade**
    This checkbox will prevent an upgrade from taking place on this client when the system itself is being upgraded. It's only used in exceptional cases.

4.1.2   Suggested Client Settings

Table 4.1 through Table 4.4 list the suggested client settings for typical use cases. To summarize, production and test clients shouldn't be open to changes. However, development clients should be because their purpose is to implement changes. As always, client 000 should also be protected from changes because it's the SAP-delivered reference client.

Settings	Client 000, Any System
Client role	SAP reference
Changes to client-specific objects	No changes allowed

Table 4.1 Suggested Client Settings for Client 000 in All Systems

Changes to cross-client objects	No changes to SAP repository or Customizing
Client copy protection	Protection level 1: no overwriting

Table 4.1 Suggested Client Settings for Client 000 in All Systems (Cont.)

Settings	Productive Clients
Client role	Production
Changes to client-specific objects	No changes allowed
Changes to cross-client objects	No changes to SAP repository or Customizing
Client copy protection	Protection level 1: no overwriting

Table 4.2 Suggested Client Settings for Productive Clients

Settings	Testing Clients
Client role	Test
Changes to client-specific objects	No changes allowed
Changes to cross-client objects	No changes to SAP repository or Customizing
Client copy protection	Protection level 0: no restrictions

Table 4.3 Suggested Client Settings for Testing Clients

Settings	Development Clients
Client role	Customizing
Changes to client-specific objects	Changes are automatically recorded
Changes to cross-client objects	Changes allowed to SAP repository or Customizing
Client copy protection	Protection level 1: no overwriting

Table 4.4 Suggested Client Settings for Development Clients

4.1.3   Changing Client Settings

Now, let's walk through how to change client settings. Follow these steps:

1. Navigate to Transaction SCC4.

2. In the upper-left menu, click **Table View**, then select **Display • Change** (Figure 4.4).

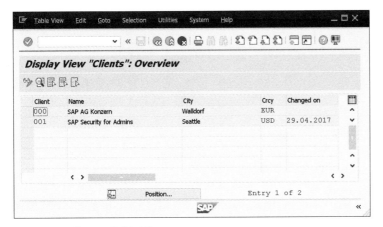

Figure 4.4 Change Table View

3. The system will prompt you with a warning about the table being cross-client (Figure 4.5). Click the check button ✔ to proceed.

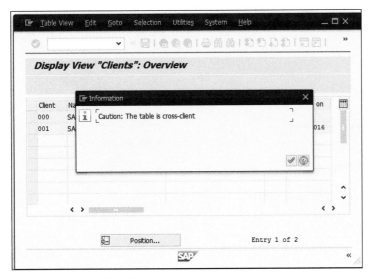

Figure 4.5 Cross-Client Warning

4. Double click on the row of the client you'd like to change settings for (Figure 4.6).

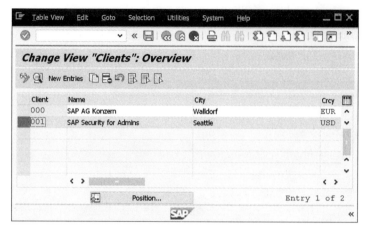

Figure 4.6 Select Client to Change Settings

5. The system will now display, in change mode, the settings for the client you have selected (Figure 4.7).

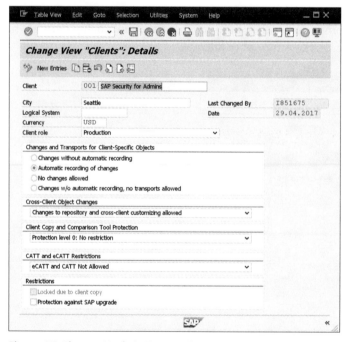

Figure 4.7 Change Mode in Transaction SCC4

6. Once you've made your changes, click the **Save** icon ![save icon].

Depending on your chosen client settings, you may see a transport request. This is to ensure that your settings can be move to any other systems you choose. If you don't want to transport your client settings, delete the transport that you create to contain this change.

4.2   Client Logon Locking

Occasionally, you'll need to lock a client. This may be for an upgrade or a system maintenance activity. Locking the client will prevent users from logging into the client that is locked. A similar effect can be gained by locking all users in a client using Transaction SE10, but the method described in this section is more quickly implemented. Locking using Transaction SE10 will be covered in Chapter 6.

> **Remote Locking**
>
> This procedure can be done in any client, to any client, or with an RFC connection to a remote system with the proper authorizations.

To lock a client and prevent logon, follow these steps:

1. Navigate to Transaction SE37.
2. Enter the **Function Module** name "SCCR_LOCK_CLIENT" and click the **Test/Execute** button ![button] in the toolbar (Figure 4.8).

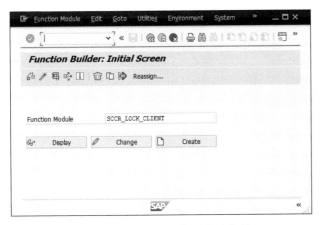

Figure 4.8 Enter Lock Client Function Module Name

3. Enter the number of the client for which you'd like to prevent logon (Figure 4.9). Click the **Execute** button 🔵 in the toolbar.

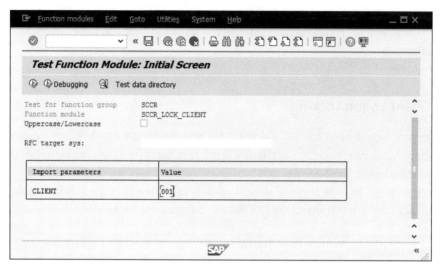

Figure 4.9 Enter Number of Client to Lock

Now, if a user attempts to access the locked client, he will receive the notification seen in Figure 4.10.

Figure 4.10 Client Locked against Logon Notification

To unlock a client, follow these steps:

1. Navigate to Transaction SE37.

2. Enter the **Function Module** name "SCCR_UNLOCK_CLIENT" and click the **Test/Execute** button 🖳 in the toolbar (Figure 4.11).

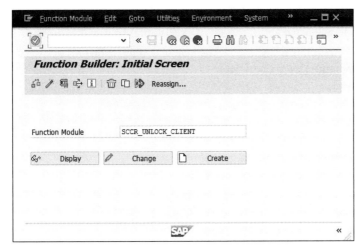

Figure 4.11 Enter Unlock Client Function Module Name

3. Enter the number of the client you'd like to unlock for logon (Figure 4.12). Click the **Execute** button 🕀 in the toolbar.

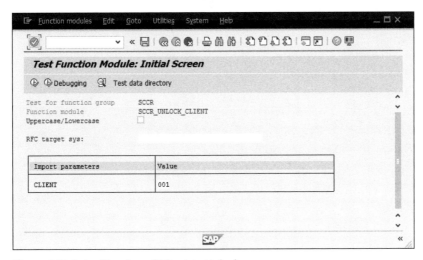

Figure 4.12 Enter Number of Client to Unlock

4.3   Summary

In this chapter, you learned about client settings and how they're used to control what's allowed in each client. We covered what settings are appropriate in specific client roles and what the production client should be set to. You also learned how to lock users out of a client and how to reverse that lock.

In the next chapter, you will learn about the set of executables that make up the SAP NetWeaver AS ABAP system, called the kernel. The kernel is an integral part of the system that administrators must keep up to date.

Chapter 5
Securing the Kernel

Before reading this chapter, you should understand the basics of work processes and how to navigate the filesystem of your SAP system. We also recommend that you be familiar with SAP Support Portal, reading SAP Notes, and the Product Availability Matrix.

As a security administrator, you'll often be expected to have a solid understanding of the kernel and when it's appropriate to patch it. Although kernel patching can fix vulnerabilities and system issues, it can also open the door to unknown issues and should be approached with abundant caution. A security administrator will always need to weigh the pros and cons before modifying such a critical portion of the system.

One of the most common approaches to attacking an SAP system is to target systems with components that are out of date. No matter how well-written code may be, it's always possible for a vulnerability to be discovered or even created. Knowing your kernel component versions and support pack versions is the key to staying up to date. Because SAP NetWeaver is proprietary software (the source code is only known and maintained by SAP), it's harder for nefarious parties to exploit kernel executables because they don't have access to the source code to analyze it for vulnerabilities. This is a positive feature of a closed-source system, but we mustn't rely on the code being private as a means of security. As with any system, closed- or open-source, vulnerabilities will eventually be found. We must plan for when they're found and adapt properly.

Therefore, given that old, unpatched systems are often the target of nefarious hackers, it's critical that we keep our systems up to date, especially on the kernel level. This chapter will give you a fundamental understanding of the kernel and equip you with the toolset required to check and update the kernel.

5.1   Understanding the Kernel

One of the most critical components of the overall SAP NetWeaver application server is the kernel. The *kernel* is best defined as the set of executable files and shared libraries required to run a dialog instance of SAP NetWeaver Application Server. We're interested in these executables because they're the basis (as in, Basis layer) of how the system works. It's important for a security administrator to understand what versions of each part of the kernel are installed on his SAP system.

Someone could exploit vulnerabilities in these executables to capture data or even take over a system. It's the security administrator's job to secure these executables and make sure they aren't compromised by a nefarious party or forced to act in a way that risks downtime or loss of data integrity or privacy.

The kernel requires three core parts to function (illustrated in Figure 5.1):

- **Dispatcher and work processes (disp+work)**
  The disp+work executable for dispatcher and work processes. This executable does much of the ABAP processing. You'll find multiple instances of this executable running on each application server.

- **Internet Connection Manager (icm; icman)**
  The ICM executable is the communication server for SAP, most commonly for Internet traffic. This is a critical component from both functionality and security perspectives.

- **Gateway (gwrd)**
  The gateway executable enables communication between work processes and external programs, as well as communication between work processes from different instances or SAP systems. The gateway is also a critical concern of a security-minded administrator.

These three components are required for the application server to function. The technical reason for this is that they provide the input and output functionality for the system's work processes. These three executable files use shared memory for interprocess communication. Therefore, SAP recommends that they only be updated together because they form a working unit. Think of this as the "core" of the kernel. This core is often referred to by SAP as the *DW package*. It's important to make the distinction between the singular disp+work executable and the DW package. The DW package contains all three of the components that make up the core parts of the kernel, discussed earlier. Most often, the DW package is simply called *DW.SAR* because that's the filename available in SAP Support Portal (*support.sap.com*) for download.

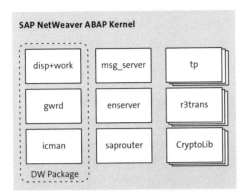

Figure 5.1 SAP NetWeaver ABAP Kernel

The kernel also contains following major components (see Figure 5.1):

- **msg_server**
  This is the executable for the message server. The message server is responsible for communication between application servers. Each SAP system will have one message server.

- **enserver**
  This is the enqueue server, which is the locking system for SAP.

- **tp**
  This is the transport mechanism.

- **R3trans**
  This executable controls tp.

- **SAPXPG**
  This utility is used to start programs on the application server (not shown in Figure 5.1).

- **Common Cryptographic Library (CommonCryptoLib)**
  This library provides encryption functions to the kernel. This is covered in depth in Section 5.2.

- **Monitoring tools**
  Such tools include dpmon, msmon, and ensmon (not shown in Figure 5.1).

There are many more components to the kernel—too many to mention exhaustively. Each plays a specific part in the operation of SAP NetWeaver ABAP. Each part is also a potential threat vector that should be updated appropriately. We'll talk about updating the kernel in the next section.

5.1.1   Kernel Patching

As with any software, from time to time the kernel will need to be updated. Because of the criticality of the kernel, SAP is very careful only to update the kernel when absolutely necessary.

SAP typically issues a kernel correction for one of the following three reasons:

- **Function error**: The kernel contains a function error for which no convent work-around exists. For example, perhaps a business user's normal input to a program causes a work process to crash. Work processes shouldn't ever crash, so SAP would issue a kernel correction for this issue.

- **Enhancement**: An enhancement is available that improves performance, stability, or maintainability—for example, adopting the kernel to a new processor multi-threading technology in the internal work process code. This isn't an error in the existing kernel, but an adoption of newer technology to improve the performance of the system.

- **Security issue**: A security issue is discovered. Security weaknesses that are discovered that might lead to unauthorized access, disclosure, disruption, modification, or destruction of the customer's data are fixed with kernel corrections. For example, if a new SSL vulnerability is discovered in the ICM or CommonCryptoLib, a kernel patch may be released to upgrade one or both components.

Clearly, a security administrator is most interested in kernel security patches. Security administrators will need to be vigilant for kernel patches that are created for this reason. This information is released alongside the new kernel in what are called *kernel release notes*. These notes can be found on SAP Support Portal with the kernel files themselves.

Something that should also be kept in mind is that kernel corrections are always cumulative. What's corrected in the kernel at one point in time also will be corrected in any kernel correction issued afterward. Therefore, if you discover an issue with a particular function in the kernel you're currently using and that issue is corrected in a later version of the kernel, you can safely upgrade to the *latest* available kernel and be assured that your issue will have been fixed. This assumption also applies to security updates.

With this in mind, you might think that it always would be prudent to adopt the latest version of the kernel quickly. This approach is generally discouraged by SAP, however, because of the added risk of undiscovered issues with a newly released kernel. Because a newly released kernel hasn't stood the test of time, it may contain issues that could negatively affect the system and shouldn't be used unless deemed necessary. SAP has issued some general guidance for administrators regarding the prospect of kernel updates.

SAP Guidance on Kernel Updates

Unless there's explicit demand, either due to a kernel error or a known existing or potential security issue, there's absolutely no need to update the kernel of an SAP system.

One key aspect to note about kernel upgrades is that the process of upgrading the kernel is completely and easily reversible: you can upgrade and downgrade with no effect to the underlying business data in your system. We'll discuss this in detail in Section 5.3. However, using a kernel that has issues could lead to downtime, which could be a critical factor to your business, even if it's easy to back out of the changes.

A security administrator's task often will be to decide if a vulnerability that affects a certain version of the kernel or it's individual tools warrants either a patch of those specific tools or an upgrade to a newer kernel entirely. Upgrading to the latest patch level of the kernel is usually the recommendation from SAP, but the responsibility will fall on the security administrator to analyze the issue. It's also a security administrator's task to evaluate the risk in patching a vulnerability now versus when the next support stack kernel package is released. Often, a vulnerability will be important to address, but not so important that the stability and consistency of the system should be put at risk.

Finally, the kernel contains no business logic, only the tools required to process the code written in the application that runs on SAP NetWeaver AS ABAP. Therefore, the testing requirements for a kernel upgrade are almost completely technical because the SAP system hasn't changed in any meaningful business specific way. Because of this, business regression testing, which is a large part of an SAP support package or system upgrade, isn't normally performed when a kernel update is applied.

5.1.2   Kernel Versioning

As with all SAP software, the SAP kernel is versioned. The first component of versioning is the *kernel release level*, the general version of the entire kernel. In Figure 5.2, we're on release level 7.45. Kernel release levels are supported for various SAP NetWeaver levels. You can check the Product Availability Matrix (PAM) to find out what kernel levels your SAP NetWeaver system is compatible with.

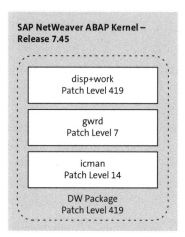

Figure 5.2 DW Package and its Components' Kernel Versions

Every executable in the kernel will have its own patch level (PL). The PL is distinct for each version of each executable that makes up the kernel. Therefore, disp+work, msg_server, and tp each will have its own distinct patch levels. In Figure 5.2, the patch levels for disp+work, gwrd, and icman are all different.

The DW Package

Within a release, each core group (DW or disp+work) will be labeled with a distinct number, called a *kernel patch level*. In Figure 5.2, we're on DW patch level 419. Within this core group, we have various patch levels for the three main components. The disp+work patch level will usually set the patch level for the DW package because it's the main component of this group. Beyond the core DW group, each executable has its own patch level.

SAP Guidance on Applying the DW Package

Apply a kernel patch such as DW.SAR that's newer than the latest available SP stack kernel only if you're experiencing a serious error that will be fixed by this kernel patch but not by the latest SP stack kernel.

SP Stack Kernel Release Package

SAP packages what are called support package (SP) *stack kernels*, which are tested groups of kernel components that are safe to run in production. These kernel releases are bundled in parts I and II. You'll find more information about these parts in Section 5.3.2.

In Figure 5.3, all components have the same patch level in an SP stack kernel. SP stack kernels are published along with ABAP support packages about four times a year and are generally regarded as well tested and ready for production use.

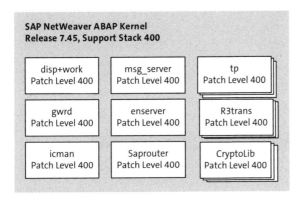

Figure 5.3 Kernel Release SP Stack 400

Note that kernel versions only apply to the kernel of the SAP system. The SAP NetWeaver system and its add-ons will have their own releases and support package levels. We'll cover this more in Chapter 9.

Matching Kernel Versions

Your kernel release doesn't need to match your SAP NetWeaver release version or product release version. Typically, the documentation or the PAM will specify which kernel level is required for your product.

Individual Kernel Executables

As we saw in Figure 5.2, each individual kernel executable can have its own version. Within SAP Support Portal, you can find single executables for download. This leads to the following question: "Do I update parts, or use the whole kernel package?"

In general, it's preferred to update the entire kernel package to a specific stack level. The individual executables available are intended to fix issues discovered in specific versions of each tool between kernel releases. For example, if you run into a bug with SAProuter, SAP support may direct you to replace the SAProuter executable with a newer version available on SAP Support Portal. For quick response to a security issue that may be critical, this might sometimes be required. However, you should only update individual kernel components when directed by SAP support. The risk of an undiscovered issue arises when using non-thoroughly tested kernel components together.

5.1.3   Checking the Kernel Version

You can check the current kernel version in your system by using SAP GUI. Follow these steps:

1. First, in the menu bar, click on **System · Status**. You'll see the screen in Figure 5.4.

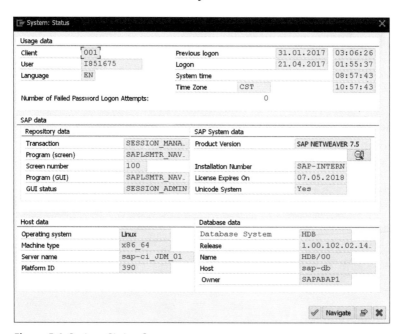

Figure 5.4 System Status Screen

2. Then, click the **Other Kernel Information** button to access the screen in Figure 5.5.

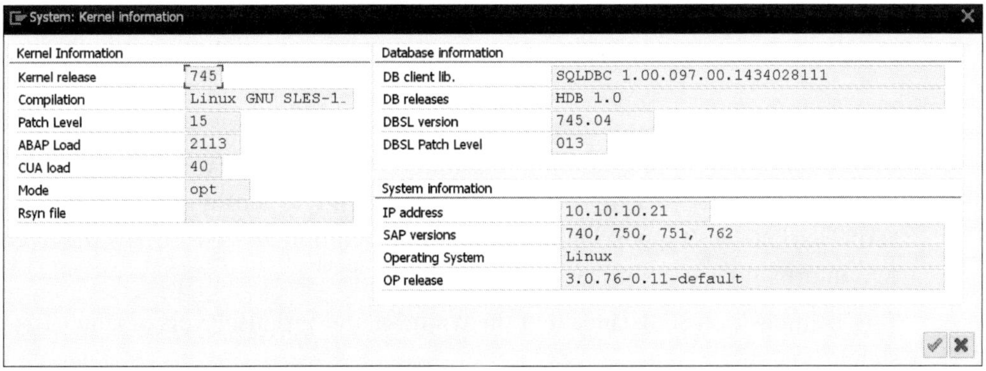

Figure 5.5 Other Kernel Information Screen

5.1.4   Checking the Kernel Version from the Operating System Level

You can also check the kernel version through OS commands.

```
sap-ci:jdmadm 52> cdexe
sap-ci:jdmadm 53> disp+work -v

Fri Apr 21 09:02:31 2017
Loading DB library '/usr/sap/JDM/SYS/exe/run/dbhdbslib.so' ...
Library '/usr/sap/JDM/SYS/exe/run/dbhdbslib.so' loaded
Version of '/usr/sap/JDM/SYS/exe/run/dbhdbslib.so' is "745.04", patchlevel (0.13
)

--------------------
disp+work information
--------------------

kernel release             745

kernel make variant        745_REL

DBMS client library        HDB_1.00.95.00.1429086950

DBSL shared library version 745.04

compiled on                Linux GNU SLES-11 x86_64 cc4.3.4 use-pr150807 for
linuxx86_64

compiled for               64 BIT

compilation mode           UNICODE

compile time               Oct 12 2015 18:19:42

update level               0

patch number               15

source id                  0.015

RKS compatibility level    0
```

Figure 5.6 Kernel Version Display from OS Level

Open a terminal window as the SIDADM user and type the following:

```
cdexe
./disp+work -v
```

Once you execute the second command, the system will display version information about the `disp+work` package, a main part of the kernel, as shown in Figure 5.6. Most kernel executables support being run with the `-v` option and will display their version information.

This example is on SUSE Linux, but the Windows and various flavors of Linux/Unix should be similar.

> **Checking Versions of Various Kernel Components**
>
> The `-v` flag works on every executable within the kernel. You can use this command to find each version easily from the OS level.

5.2   Common Cryptographic Library

The CommonCryptoLib is the container that delivers cryptographic functionality to an SAP system. The CommonCryptoLib is an important tool in a security administrator's toolbelt because it controls the methods used for encryption. Therefore, it's important to have a fundamental understanding of this portion of the kernel.

There are many important settings that control how cryptography and encryption work in SAP, as we'll cover in detail in Chapter 13. For now, you need to know what version of the CommonCryptoLib you have installed. Let's walk through how to determine that now.

5.2.1   Checking the CommonCryptoLib in SAP GUI

You can find CommonCryptoLib version information via SAP GUI, using Transaction STRUST. In the menu, select **Environment • Display SSF Version** (Figure 5.7).

The screen that opens will display version details, as shown in Figure 5.8.

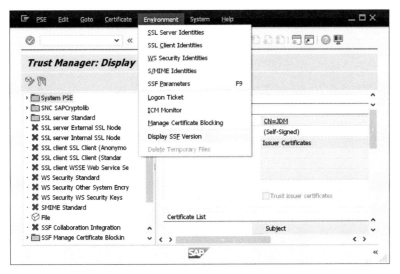

Figure 5.7 Transaction STRUST Menu

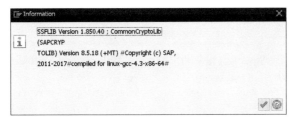

Figure 5.8 CommonCryptoLib Version Information

5.2.2   Checking the CommonCryptoLib on the OS Level

On the OS level, you can execute the following commands to check your version of the CommonCryptoLib (Figure 5.9):

```
cdexe
sapgenpse cryptinfo
```

Upgrading CommonCryptoLib is as simple as copying the relevant libraries into the kernel directory. CommonCryptoLib is no different than any other kernel file you may need to update. A list of important SAP notes to read before upgrading your CommonCryptoLib can be found in Table 5.1.

```
> sapgenpse

Loaded CommonCryptoLib from sapgenpse folder
"/usr/sap/JDM/SYS/exe/uc/linuxx86_64/libsapcrypto.so"

Platform:    linux-gcc-4.3-x86-64   (linux-gcc-4.3-x86-64)
Versions:    SAPGENPSE    8.4.43 (Oct  8 2015)
             CommonCryptoLib (SAPCRYPTOLIB) Version 8.4.43 pl40 (Oct  8 2015) MT-safe
                Build change list: 213937
```

Figure 5.9 Checking CommonCryptoLib on OS Level

Title	SAP Note Number
Common Cryptographic Library Central Note	1848999
CommonCryptoLib in dw_utils.sar	2125088
Setting up SSL on Application Server ABAP	510007

Table 5.1 Important SAP Notes for CommonCryptoLib

A Tip on Upgrading CommonCryptoLib

CommonCryptoLib fixes can be patched independently from SAP kernel packages. They don't rely on any specific version of the kernel.

5.3   Kernel Update

Typically, kernel activities will be performed by a system administrator or Basis administrator, though in some organizations the security administrator will be charged with the task of updating the kernel. It's important to understand the general process to ensure the stability and security of an SAP NetWeaver system.

The simplest explanation of a kernel update procedure is as follows: a new kernel is copied into place over the old one. Simple, right? However, we're also concerned with the following points:

- Minimizing downtime
- Maintaining a high level of uptime

- Proper testing
- The cruciality of the system to the business

To address these concerns, a general procedure must be adopted.

5.3.1   Overall Kernel Update Process

It's of the utmost importance to properly plan a kernel update. Determine the scope of the upgrade. Ask yourself the following questions:

- Can I just update the DW.SAR portion of the kernel, or do I need to update the kernel to the latest patch level?
- What's the desired end state of my kernel versions?

The preactivities discussed in the following sections are crucial for a successful kernel upgrade.

Reading Notes

A listing of release notes can be found by executing the version check mentioned in Section 5.1.4. A list of SAP Notes that contain the bugs fixed in each kernel version will be listed. Also, see Table 5.2. Although each SAP Note may not specifically list your version number, each will contain valuable information about the kernel update process, which applies closely to modern versions of SAP NetWeaver as the process has remained nearly identical for each SAP NetWeaver release.

Title	SAP Note Number
Downloading SAP kernel patches	19466
Release Roadmap for Kernel 74x and 75x	1969546
Versions and Kernel Patch Levels	2083594
Kernel Upgrade on Windows Cluster	1929379
Rolling Kernel Switch	953653
Installing a 7.20 kernel in SAP Web AS 7.00/7.01/7.10/7.11	1636252

Table 5.2 Important SAP Notes for Kernel Installation

Checking the PAM

The PAM will list which support package stacks and versions of SAP NetWeaver are compatible with the products installed on your system. Take care not to install a non-supported combination of product, SAP NetWeaver, and kernel.

Having a Backout Plan

In the event that a kernel upgrade breaks your system, it is essential to have a plan to back out the change and revert to the original version of the kernel. Fortunately, as discussed earlier, a kernel upgrade is a completely reversible process. Because the kernel contains no business logic, it has no effect on the business data of your system. You will simply need to copy the old kernel back and restart the system. However, this requires downtime, so you must take care to minimize the number of interruptions to the end users.

Backup

Be sure to copy the existing kernel in each system and take a backup of it. You may never know when you'll need to roll back to an earlier version, even months later, to test an issue. Often, this will require copying the old kernel to a sandbox, so keeping clear and accurate records of your backups is important.

Testing

Sometimes, it's impossible to determine where an issue with the kernel may come from. Keep this in mind during your testing period. Any error in the system may potentially be caused by the kernel. Be on the lookout for any odd activity. If you identify an issue, test with both the old and new kernels and compare the results. You can find common testing procedures in Table 5.3.

Three-Tier Approach

We recommend applying your chosen kernel to a sandbox system for initial testing. This sandbox system should have a copy of your production kernel and be working correctly before you begin. After upgrading the kernel, and once you've made sure your system starts and operates normally, you can plan the rest of your deployment. Be sure to use the exact same kernel on each system in your landscape. The best way to ensure this is to copy the new kernel from each system to the next. This will make sure that each is identical. You'll also want to compare your production kernel to your nonproduction systems. Before and after the kernel upgrade, all should be identical.

5.3.2   Downloading the Kernel

The kernel can be found in the **Downloads** section of SAP Support Portal. The procedure in this subsection will walk you through each step to select the correct kernel package for your application.

SAP's Recommendation for Which Kernel to Select

SAP's recommendation is to always use the most recent SP stack kernel. A more recent patch level should be implemented if an error occurs in the kernel that you currently use.

Selecting the Correct Kernel Packages from SAP Support Portal

You'll need to decide if you're going to use an SP stack kernel, the DW package, or just individual parts of the kernel.

To select the correct kernel packages from SAP Support Portal, you'll need to know four things about your SAP system: processor architecture, codepage, OS, and database. We'll walk through each item next.

Processor Architecture

You'll need to know the architecture of your processor. Typically, you'll be picking between 32-bit and 64-bit systems. In your SAP system, you can find the required architecture in the **Machine Type** box of the **Host data** section of the system status screen (see Figure 5.4).

Codepage

Unicode, or UTF-8, is an expanded character set that allows more characters than the historical standard codesets. At the time of writing, many existing and almost every newly installed SAP system is Unicode. Non-Unicode encoding is typically used on older systems that have legacy requirements. If the system you're working on is not Unicode, you'll need to take special steps when you download updates. You can find information on Unicode in SAP Note 1322715. In your SAP system, you can find the required code page in the **Unicode System** box of the **SAP System data** section of the system status screen (see Figure 5.4).

Operating System

The SAP kernel is compiled for several different OSs. You'll need to be sure to select the operating system of your system. In your SAP system, you can find the required OS in the **Operating system** box of the **Host data** section of the system status screen (see Figure 5.4).

Database

In your SAP system, you can find the required OS in the **Database System** box of the **Database data** section of the system status screen (see Figure 5.4).

EXT Kernel

You'll often find an EXT kernel on SAP Support Portal. EXT stands for *extended kernel maintenance*. The EXT kernel is used when specific versions are important for regulatory compliance and support.

When a kernel is created by SAP, the kernel source code is compiled on a specific supported version of the OS the kernel is intended for. For example, if you're using Solaris 11 on your application servers, the kernel for Solaris 11 is compiled on a system at SAP with a supported version of both Solaris 11 and the tools that compile your kernel.

Sometimes, the tools used by SAP to compile the kernel fall out of support and must be updated. In these situations, the OS vendor will certify a newer version of these tools and SAP will use these newer tools to compile a new kernel. The kernel compiled with these tools is called the *EXT kernel*.

Why is this important? Some regulatory rules like the Sarbanes-Oxley Act, or the Food and Drug Administration regulations and, to a further extent, some IT policies require strict adherence to supported versions when it comes to software compatibility and the OS. Therefore, SAP provides this version of the kernel to support adherence to these rules.

Downloading Files

Once you've determined the key system information, you'll need to select the correct files.

If you intend to replace your entire kernel with an SP stack kernel, you'll need two files. SAP labels these files in a consistent manner to avoid confusion:

- **Kernel Part I**
  This database-independent part contains all database-independent components for the SAP kernel.

- **Kernel Part II**
  Database-specific kernel patches are provided under the database version (e.g., SAP HANA or Oracle).

If you intend to replace only the core DW package components, you'll only need DW.SAR. If you intend to replace individual executables, you can find those within the download area as well.

To download your files, follow these steps:

1. In your web browser, go to *support.sap.com/patches*.
2. Select **Software Downloads**.
3. Select **Support Packages & Patches**.
4. Select **By Alphabetical Index**.
5. Select **K**.
6. Select the processor architecture you require.
7. Select the release level that you require.

At this point, you'll see a dropdown box that specifies your OS and database. First, select your OS and processor architecture. Download any database-independent files you need—usually either the disp+work package or the SAPEXE.SAR package. This package is referred to in the description as **Kernel Part I**.

Next, select your database. You'll be presented with database-dependent files for the selected database. Typically, you'll need SAPEXEDB.SAR, with a description of **Kernel Part II**.

Once you've downloaded your files, extract and store them. Various needs may arise for which you'll be required to roll back to a specific kernel version. Having the kernel files well-organized in an archive will save you much time and effort in the future.

In addition, if you need to upgrade the CommonCryptoLib, you can find it in the **Kernel Utilities** package, DW_UTILS.SAR.

5.3.3   Installing the Kernel

Installation of the kernel can vary by system type. Therefore, we recommend checking SAP Support Portal for the specific installation requirements for your application. In general, the installation process is similar for all platforms.

The general process for a kernel upgrade is as follows:

1. Copy the new kernel in place of the old kernel.
2. Restart your system.

This is a very simple process, but a prudent security administrator will take steps to make sure he or she is able to easily revert to the old kernel in the case of an issue. Let's dig deeper into the process step by step.

Kernel Location

First, you need to understand where in the OS the kernel resides. In SAP NetWeaver 7.5, the kernel exists in two locations. The first location is called the central directory for executables and is shared between each application server: *sapmnt/<SAPSID>/ exe*.

The location of this directory is set by the profile value DIR_CT_RUN.

The second location is called the local directory for executables and is specific to each application server: *usr/sap/<SAPSID>/sys/exe/<codepage>/<platform>*.

A copy of the shared kernel should be copied here each time the application server starts. This path is set by the profile value DIR_EXECUTABLE.

sapcpe

The sapcpe kernel program is an important part of how the kernel is deployed between the central instance and application servers. When a dialog instance is started, a line within the profile calls sapcpe and copies the kernel from the sapmnt share (DIR_CT_RUN) to each application server's local kernel directory (DIR_EXECUTABLE).

The sapcpe program checks that the local executables are up to date at each startup of an SAP NetWeaver instance that uses local executables. It compares the local executables against the central directory and copies new executables for which the date or size has changed.

Always check that sapcpe is making its copy during startup. The best way to do this is to check the version of each application server's kernel manually. You can do this either by checking on the OS level as described in Section 5.1.4 or by using Transaction SM51 to log on to each server with SAP GUI and check via the method in Section 5.1.3.

Technical Kernel Upgrade Steps

Perform the following steps to upgrade the kernel:

1. Copy your downloaded SAR files into a temporary directory on your system.
2. Copy or download and extract your new kernel.
3. Backup your old kernel.
4. Stop the SAP system. (In Windows, you may also need to stop the SAP services using the Control Panel).
5. Stop all running parts of the SAP system on all application servers.
6. Copy your new kernel to the *sapmnt/<SAPSID>/exe* directory.
7. Perform any post-kernel-install steps, such as running saproot on Linux systems.
8. Start the SAP system.

The next step is to test the system after the kernel upgrade to make sure there are no errors.

Testing after a Kernel Upgrade

The common tests you should perform after upgrading the kernel are detailed in Table 5.3.

Transaction	What to Look For
SICK	Check the general health of the system.
ST22	Look for kernel-related short dumps.
SM50	Look at your processes: Are they running? Have they restarted a significant number of times?
SM51	Log onto each dialog server in your system and verify that sapcpe executed correctly.
SM21	Look at the system log for any abnormal kernel related errors.

Table 5.3 Common Testing Steps after Kernel Upgrade

Once you've performed testing and everything looks good, you can allow users to use the system. If you wish, program SGEN can be run to compile programs for the new kernel. If you notice issues or log entries that indicate errors related to the kernel, you should consider implementing your back out plan.

SGEN

To run program SGEN, follow these steps:

1. Go to Transaction SGEN. You'll see the **SAP Load Generator** screen, as shown in Figure 5.10.

Figure 5.10 Transaction SGEN Selection Screen

2. On this screen, select the **Regenerate already existing loads** checkbox and the **Regenerate only invalid loads** radio button. Click the **Continue** button ✔.

3. On the next screen, make sure the checkbox for at least one of your application servers is selected, as shown in Figure 5.11. Click **Continue**.

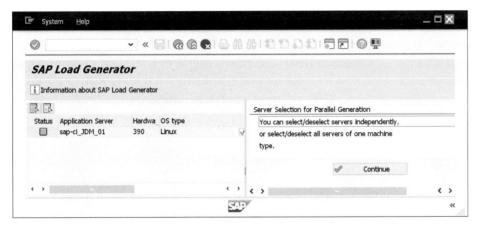

Figure 5.11 Server Selection Screen of Transaction SGEN

4. On the **Job Monitor** screen that appears next, click the line matching your job, then click the **Start Job Directly** button 🔧 (Figure 5.12). Depending on the size, number of app servers selected, and resources available to your system, program SGEN may take a few hours to complete.

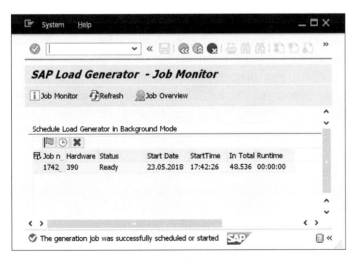

Figure 5.12 Job Monitor in Transaction SGEN

The execution of Transaction SGEN is completely optional because if a program hasn't yet been generated, the system will generate it when it's first executed. Once the program has been generated the first time, no further generation will be required. Therefore, Transaction SGEN just generates everything at once, saving users the time it would take for their programs to generate when using the system.

You'll need to weigh the pros and cons of either getting the system back to end users as quickly as possible or giving end users the best possible performance. Many organizations time system maintenance to run on nights or weekends, so giving a user access to the system an hour earlier may not matter—but users waiting for a program to compile the next morning may, so plan accordingly.

Rolling Kernel Switch

The rolling kernel switch (RKS) is a new feature from SAP that allows you to upgrade your kernel while your SAP system runs. The prerequisite for this is that you are using a high availability (HA) cluster for ABAP Central Services (ASCS) and enqueue and have more than one dialog instance. The general approach is that each instance is brought down and upgraded one by one so that the system encounters no downtime. If you want to use the RKS procedure to minimize system downtime when replacing the kernel, refer to SAP Note 953653.

5.4   Summary

In this chapter, you learned about kernel versioning. You learned about the DW package and how it should be applied to the kernel as a group. You also learned about individual kernel executables and how they work with the kernel. Next, you learned how to check which version and patch level of the kernel and components you're running. Next, you learned about the CommonCrypto Lib and its use within the kernel. We will further explore the CommonCryptoLib in Chapter 12 and Chapter 13. You also learned strategies and things to look out for when deciding to upgrade your kernel, and we discussed how to plan for, prepare, execute, and test a kernel upgrade.

In the next chapter, you'll learn how to secure and maintain user accounts. This is important because in order for your SAP NetWeaver AS ABAP system to be effective, users must be able to log in to it, and malicious parties must be kept out.

Chapter 6
Managing Users

The user ID grants access to the SAP system and has the ability to perform certain functions based on its authorizations. Managing different types of users and understanding their capability is a key part of a security administrator's job.

To log on to the SAP system, you need a user ID, also called a *user master record*. The user master record contains all the necessary information to successfully log on and execute transactions in an SAP system. Authorizations are granted by authorization profiles, which are assigned either through roles or profiles.

This chapter discusses the management and handling of user accounts and covers what measures to take to securely configure your system.

6.1 What Is a User ID in SAP?

A user master record contains authorization objects that can allow the user to view, update, or delete relevant data in the SAP system. The SAP NetWeaver AS ABAP system follows a *positive authorization* concept, which means you must explicitly specify which functions can be executed by a user.

User IDs are client-dependent and stored in table USR02. To access different clients, the user must be created in each client separately. Passwords are also client-dependent and must follow the password rules.

6.2 Different User Types

An SAP system has five different types of users that can be created and authorized. These users are listed in Table 6.1.

User Type	Dialog Logon	Multiple Logon	RFC Logon	Password Expires	Password Change by User	Back-ground Job Execution
Dialog	Yes	No	Yes	Yes	Yes	Yes
System	No	Yes	Yes	No	No	Yes
Communication	No	Yes	Yes	Yes	Yes (RFC function module)	No
Service	Yes	Yes	Yes	No	No	Yes
Reference	No	Yes	No	No	No	No

Table 6.1 Overview of Properties of Users for Different User Types

6.2.1   Dialog User: Type A

The dialog user is the most common user type in an ABAP system. A dialog user can log on to SAP via SAP GUI or equivalent logon methods (such as the SAP NetWeaver Business Client). The dialog user always represents a natural person and can't be shared with other natural persons due to licensing compliance. During a dialog logon, the SAP system checks if the password is expired or initial, and if so asks the user to set a new valid password. Multiple dialog logons are checked and logged if necessary. The user can change her own password.

6.2.2   System User: Type B

The system user is used for technical, system-related processing like background processing or workflows. Specific applications like the TMS and Central User Administration (CUA) use the system user. The system user is excluded from password validity settings. Unlike for a dialog user, multiple logons are permissible. The password can only be changed by the administrator.

6.2.3   Service User: Type S

A service user is a dialog user that's available to several anonymous users. Service users are authorized restrictively because the system doesn't check whether the password has expired, nor does it check whether the password has been used. Also, make sure that the maintenance of service users is restricted. A typical example of a service user is the firefighter ID, which is used in SAP GRC Access Control. The firefighter ID is available to a predefined set of users so that they can log on and perform emergency activities, which mostly contain highly sensitive access. Although SAP GRC Access Control tracks the usage of the firefighter ID, all the activities are performed in the context of the firefighter ID (a service user).

6.2.4   Communication User: Type C

The communication user is used for dialog-free communication between systems using Remote Function Call (RFC) or Common Programming Interface for Communication (CPIC). Dialog logon using SAP GUI isn't possible. The password can be changed by the user and expires. However, to change the password during the dialogs, the caller system must use an RFC function module (USR_USER_CHANGE_PASSWORD_RFC).

6.2.5   Reference User: Type L

The reference user is like a service user that isn't assigned to a specific person. Dialog logon isn't possible. The reference user was introduced to assign additional authorizations to users, when the authorization profile limit of 312 was reached. The SAP kernel performs the authority check always against the reference user first and then, only if it fails, against the dialog user that has the reference user assigned.

6.3   The User Buffer

As mentioned earlier, the SAP system follows a positive authorization concept, which means that authorizations must be assigned to a user to execute certain transactions in the system. To assign authorizations to a user, roles and profiles must be assigned. Historically, SAP only used profiles to handle user authorizations. Roles were introduced later to simplify the maintenance process. Therefore, each role contains at least one authorization profile once the role is generated. These profiles, when assigned to a user through a role, are then loaded into the user buffer during the logon procedure. Whenever the SAP system performs an authority check against the user, it does so against the user buffer. The user buffer holds all authorization objects with its corresponding values. You can display the user buffer in Transaction SU56.

> **Tip**
>
> When assigning roles to a user who's currently logged on, the user buffer must be refreshed to reflect the changes to the authorizations. To refresh the user buffer, the user must log off and on. When assigning profile SAP_ALL, the user buffer is refreshed automatically.

6.4   Creating and Maintaining a User

The central transaction to create and maintain a user is Transaction SU01 (User Master Record). With Transaction SU01, an administrator can create, maintain, and delete users, as well as change their properties and parameters, assign roles and profiles, change logon data, and more.

On the initial screen (Figure 6.1), you can select or define a user based on the **User** ID or **Alias**. Once selected, you can create, change, display, copy, delete, lock/unlock, or reset the password.

To create a user, you have to define a user ID of no more than 12 characters in length. User IDs should follow a naming convention (see Section 6.8) so that identifying them later is possible. This is especially important when searching for users, such as for mass changes. Also, you should be able to distinguish between technical users and dialog users.

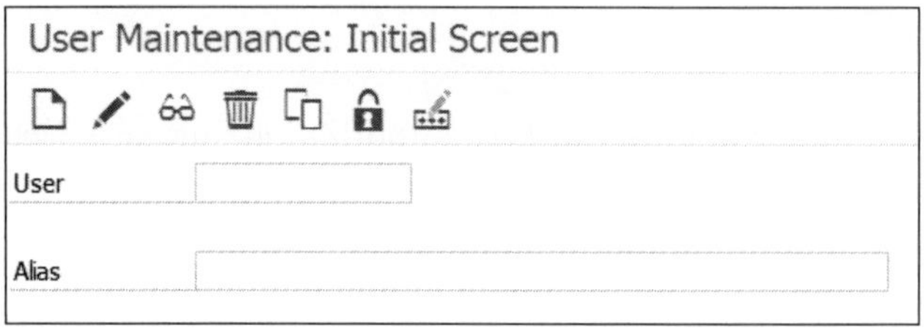

Figure 6.1 Initial Screen of Transaction SU01

The user master record consists of different tabs that can be maintained through Transaction SU01. Table 6.2 gives a quick overview of the tabs that are available.

Tab	Description
Documentation	Free-form text to capture documentation regarding the user
Address	Information about the user and how to contact them
Logon Data	Password, user type, and validity for the user
SNC	SNC parameters
Defaults	Default values for the user
Parameters	Standard field defaults
Roles	Role assignments to the user
Profiles	Profile assignments to the user
Groups	Assignment to user groups
Personalization	Person-related settings for personalization purposes
Lic. Data	Classification for measurement
DBMS	Database management for SAP HANA databases

Table 6.2 User Maintenance Tabs

6.4.1   Documentation

With SAP NetWeaver 7.50, the **Documentation** tab (Figure 6.2) was introduced to document changes to a user. Changes to a user can only be detected by the change documents, but those don't contain any explanations. Therefore, the **Documentation** tab lets you document the reason for a change and document technical users like RFC users. You can also define a person responsible for the user.

To delete the documentation of selected user, you can use report RSUSR_DELETE_USERDOCU. This report is a clean-up report; it allows you to massively delete documentation of several users, such as after a system copy.

Documentation	Address	Logon Data	SNC	Defaults	Parameters	Roles	Profiles

Description	Technical User for RFC interface between SAP ERP and SAP GRC
Person Responsible	ABANZER

Documentation for User:

26.03.2018 21:21:16 ABANZER:
01/01/2018 ABANZER: created the user with RFC authorization according to ticket number 12345.
01/02/2018 ABANZER: added missing authorization for BAPI_USER_CHANGE. Ticket 67890.

Figure 6.2 Documentation Tab in Transaction SU01

6.4.2 Address

When you create a user, the system asks for two mandatory fields. One of those fields is **Last name**, which is maintained in the **Address** tab (Figure 6.3).

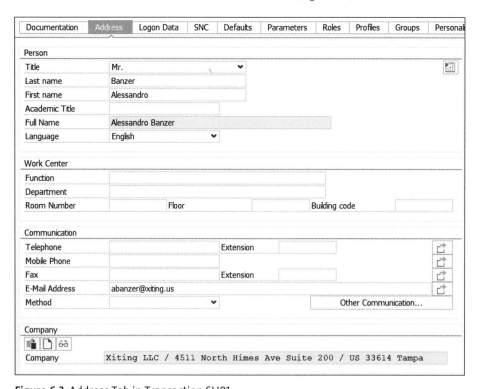

Figure 6.3 Address Tab in Transaction SU01

In the **Address** tab, you maintain personal information about the user himself (in the **Person** section), the **Work Center** the user works for, **Communication** methods, and a **Company** assignment. For example, when using workflows and automated system emails, most of the default programs work with the email address that is maintained in Transaction SU01. Therefore, you want to make sure that those fields are maintained accordingly.

Company addresses can be maintained in Transaction SUCOMP.

6.4.3   Logon Data

In the **Logon Data** tab (Figure 6.4), you can maintain the second mandatory field for the user master record: the **New Password**. Without an initial password, you can't create a user. In the **Logon Data** tab, you also define the **User Type**, as well as a specific **Security Policy**, if desired. Also, you can define a user **Alias** which can be used to identify the user ID with a longer (up to 40 characters) and more descriptive name.

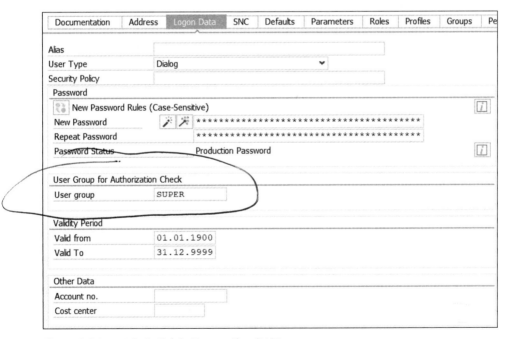

Figure 6.4 Logon Data Tab in Transaction SU01

The initial password can either be typed manually or be automatically generated by the system based on the system password rules. Also, it's possible to deactivate the password so that the user can't log on to the system with a password. If deactivated, an alternative logon method through SSO (X.509 certificate or logon tickets) must be used. When using SSO methods, we recommend deactivating passwords to increase security because most passwords usually remain initial because they aren't used and hence aren't changed.

An important field here is **User Group for Authorization Check**, which is used to protect user maintenance through Transaction SU01, Transaction SU10, Transaction PFCG, etc. If you decide to divide user maintenance among several user administrators, you can segregate the authorizations by the user group, for example, in authorization object S_USER_GRP.

> **Tip**
>
> If you want to make **User Group for Authorization Check** a mandatory field, check and implement SAP Note 1663177 (SU01: User Group as Required Entry Field).

With **Validity Period**, you define the validity period of the user. If the validity period is in the past, the system doesn't allow the user to log on regardless of whether the user is locked.

It's important to remember that the user group for authorization check should always be maintained. If the user group isn't assigned, every administrator with access to S_USER_GRP and the corresponding activities will be able to administrate the user.

> **Tip**
>
> You can configure automated emails that are encrypted to send out the initial password to the maintained email address of the user. For more information, check and implement SAP Note 1750161 (User Administration: Saving Additional Information).

6.4.4   Secure Network Communication

The **SNC** tab (Figure 6.5) lets you define an external security product, such as SAP Single Sign-On, to secure the communication between SAP GUI and the application server. Prior to SAP NetWeaver 7.40, the **SNC** tab was shown only when you'd activated the snc/enable profile parameter. As of version 7.40, the tab is always shown.

Figure 6.5 SNC Tab in Transaction SU01

Tip

SAP Single Sign-On is beneficial not only to the end user but also to the security administrator because it lessens the burden of user administration tasks such as password resets. It doesn't completely eliminate password resets but it reduces them to a minimum. At the same time, SAP Single Sign-On increases overall security because user passwords can be deactivated; it therefore reduces the likelihood of abusing user IDs.

6.4.5   Defaults

In the **Defaults** tab (Figure 6.6), you can define default settings for a user. Each user can change the defaults via Transaction SU3 for her own user ID. You can define the **Start menu** for a user if it's different than the default start menu of the system. To find the default start menu of the system, or to set one, use Transaction SSM2.

Logon language can be preset for a user, but the user can change the language during logon on the logon screen in SAP GUI. Date format, time format, and decimal notation can be set using the system proposals. Also, you can define an output device for a user and a time zone.

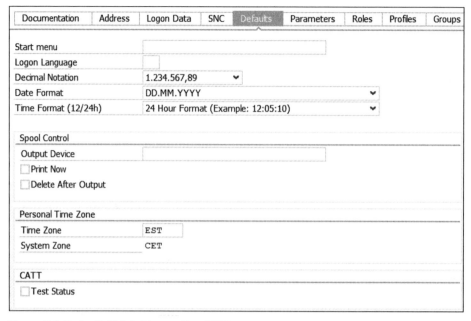

Figure 6.6 Defaults Tab in Transaction SU01

6.4.6   Parameters

In the **Parameters** tab (Figure 6.7) you can define certain default parameters for a user. For example, you can define the company code (BUK in this example) for a user. The parameters are usually set by the user via Transaction SU3.

If you set the **Company code** (as shown in Figure 6.7), the user won't have to enter the company code in input fields (it will be automatically populated by the system) each time the system requires that input field.

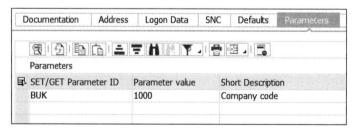

Figure 6.7 Parameters Tab in Transaction SU01

6.4.7   Roles

In the **Roles** tab (Figure 6.8), you assign and maintain the roles assigned to a user. Roles are assigned with a **Start Date** and **End Date**. Each role can be assigned directly or indirectly. The last column **Indirect User-Role Assignment** indicates whether it's directly assigned or assigned through a composite role or a reference user.

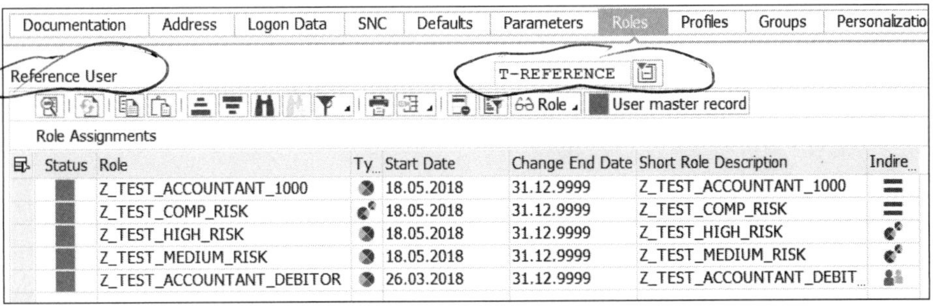

Documentation	Address	Logon Data	SNC	Defaults	Parameters	Roles	Profiles	Groups	Personalizatio

Reference User — T-REFERENCE

User master record

Role Assignments

Status	Role	Ty	Start Date	Change End Date	Short Role Description	Indire
	Z_TEST_ACCOUNTANT_1000		18.05.2018	31.12.9999	Z_TEST_ACCOUNTANT_1000	=
	Z_TEST_COMP_RISK		18.05.2018	31.12.9999	Z_TEST_COMP_RISK	=
	Z_TEST_HIGH_RISK		18.05.2018	31.12.9999	Z_TEST_HIGH_RISK	
	Z_TEST_MEDIUM_RISK		18.05.2018	31.12.9999	Z_TEST_MEDIUM_RISK	
	Z_TEST_ACCOUNTANT_DEBITOR		26.03.2018	31.12.9999	Z_TEST_ACCOUNTANT_DEBIT	

Figure 6.8 Roles Tab in Transaction SU01

As of SAP NetWeaver 7.40, you can display assignments that come through a reference user directly in Transaction SU01.

> **Tip**
> Check SAP Note 2110144 (SU01: Display of Reference User Roles) to display the role assignments that come through a reference user directly in Transaction SU01.

6.4.8   Profiles

In the **Profiles** tab (Figure 6.9), you can see the authorization profiles of the assigned roles and directly assigned profiles. You can assign and remove profiles from here. We recommend authorizing users via roles, not via manual profiles.

Prior to SAP NetWeaver 7.40, it was possible to manually add authorization profiles to the **Profiles** tab. However, when you run Transaction PFUD (User Master Data Reconciliation), those assignments will be removed automatically. Therefore, always assign roles to a user and not the authorization profile of the roles.

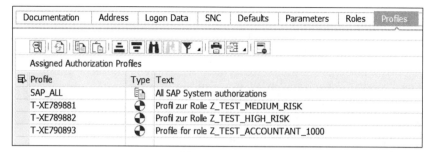

Documentation	Address	Logon Data	SNC	Defaults	Parameters	Roles	Profiles

Assigned Authorization Profiles

Profile	Type	Text
SAP_ALL		All SAP System authorizations
T-XE789881		Profil zur Rolle Z_TEST_MEDIUM_RISK
T-XE789882		Profil zur Rolle Z_TEST_HIGH_RISK
T-XE790893		Profile for role Z_TEST_ACCOUNTANT_1000

Figure 6.9 Profiles Tab in Transaction SU01

6.4.9   Groups

In the **Groups** tab (Figure 6.10) you can create groupings of users. It's very important to understand that these groups are different from the user groups maintained in the **Logon Data** tab. The **Groups** tab is primarily used for grouping purposes and doesn't control any authorizations. Only the user group on the **Logon Data** tab is checked during an authorization check.

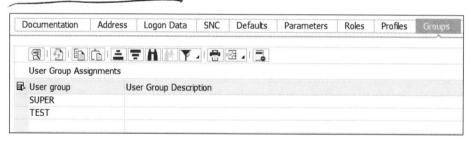

Documentation	Address	Logon Data	SNC	Defaults	Parameters	Roles	Profiles	Groups

User Group Assignments

User group	User Group Description
SUPER	
TEST	

Figure 6.10 Groups Tab in Transaction SU01

For example, the grouping can be used in Transaction SU10 (User Mass Maintenance) or Transaction SUIM (User Information System) to select users based on groups.

6.4.10   Personalization

In the **Personalization** tab (Figure 6.11), you can define person-related settings using personalization objects (SAP has not made full use of this tab just yet). The same tab is also available in the role maintenance in the Profile Generator (Transaction PFCG). As an example, you can define certain settings that control the output of certain programs, like the number of entries to be displayed.

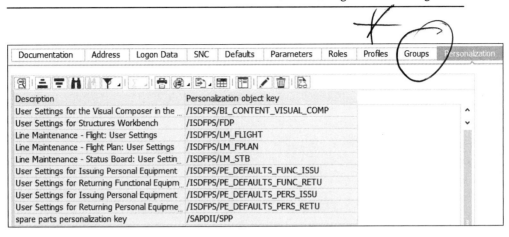

Figure 6.11 Personalization Tab in Transaction SU01

6.4.11 License Data

In the **Lic. Data** tab (Figure 6.12), you can define the contractual user type of the user being used in the licensing classification. Each user can be assigned to one classification.

Documentation	Address	Logon Data	SNC	Defaults	Parameters	Roles	Profiles	Groups	Personalization	Lic. Data

Contractual User Type ID
Development Workbench User

Figure 6.12 License Data Tab in Transaction SU01

For more information about the user classification, Section 6.13.

6.4.12 DBMS

In the latest SAP NetWeaver releases, a dedicated database management system tab (**DBMS**) has been introduced (Figure 6.13). In this tab, you enable the application service to manage users and their privileges in the database. Currently, only the SAP HANA database is supported.

With SAP S/4HANA, there are certain use cases that require a user to have a database user on the database also (SAP HANA). To simplify administration, SAP introduced the **DBMS** tab to create and maintain the database user and its privileges from within Transaction SU01.

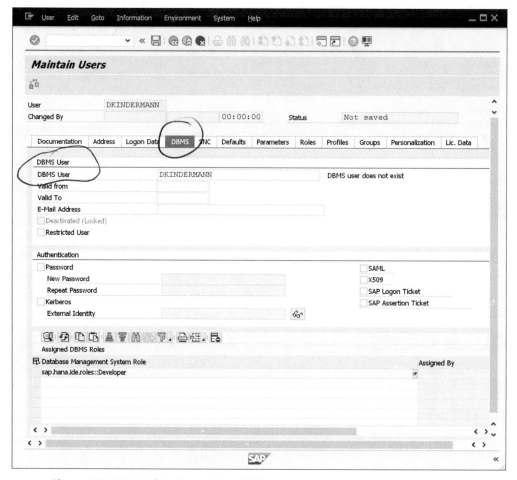

Figure 6.13 DBMS Tab in Transaction SU01

6.5 Copy a User

In Transaction SU01, you can copy an existing user and create a new user ID. To copy a user, enter the user ID that you want to copy and click the **Copy** icon on the toolbar.

After you click **Copy**, the system will open a pop-up (Figure 6.14) with the user you want to copy from in the **From** field and the new user ID in the **To** field. The **To** field must be changed accordingly. You then define which attributes of the user you want to copy. By default, the system suggests everything but the **Address Data** and **Documentation**, which are very user-specific. Based on what you're trying to achieve, you can select or deselect some of the attributes.

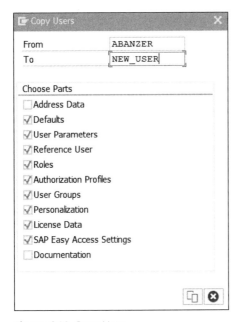

Figure 6.14 Copy User

After you click the **Copy** button, you'll see the regular Transaction SU01 screen with the selected attributes prepopulated. You can always make a change there; the attributes you've selected only serve as a suggestion.

6.6   Change Documents for Users

There are several ways to access to the change documents for users. The most common way is through Transaction SU01 and the menu option **Information • Change Documents for Users**.

In the selection screen of the change documents, you can select the user(s), as well as several other parameters such as who performed the change, when the change was made, and so on (Figure 6.15).

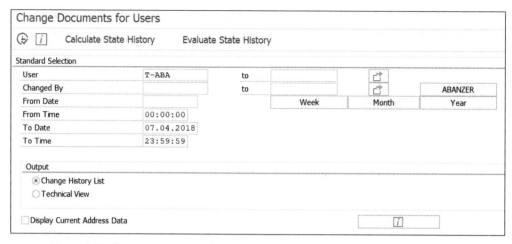

Figure 6.15 Change Documents for Users

Once the standard selection has been set, you can narrow down more selection criteria in regard to the user, the roles and profiles, and the CUA systems, roles, and profiles (Figure 6.16).

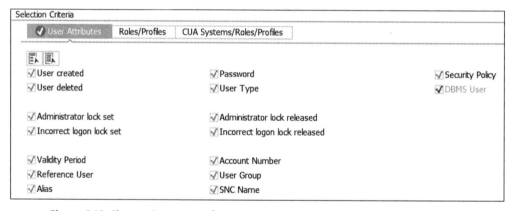

Figure 6.16 Change Documents for Users

The output will be in an ALV list that can offer default sorting and filtering. In the output, you'll see all the change documents that are recorded for the user (Figure 6.17).

The change documents offer a good audit trail to find out who changed what when. Also, they help to identify role and profile assignments, as well as user locks and unlocks.

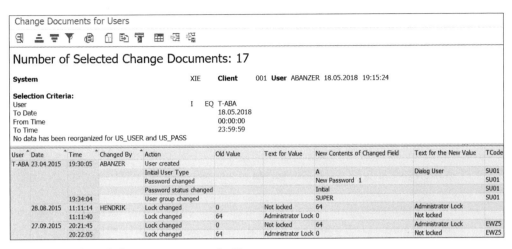

Figure 6.17 Selected Change Documents for User

6.7   Mass User Changes with Transaction SU10

Unlike Transaction SU01, which allows you to change one user at a time, with Transaction SU10 you can change multiple users in one shot. Transaction SU10 allows you to create, change, and delete users, as well as change roles and profile assignments. Although Transaction SU10 allows mass processing, it also has its limitations. With Transaction SU10, you have to perform the change for all users in the selection. Individualization is not possible, nor can you assign a different set of roles to several users. For example, say that you want to assign ROLE_1 to Users 1–10 and ROLE_2 to Users 1, 2, 3, and 4. To perform that change, you have to use Transaction SU10 twice: once to assign ROLE_1 to all 10 users, and a second time to assign ROLE_2 to Users 1–4. Uploading a template set isn't possible.

Transaction SU10 works in a two-step approach. First you make your user selection, then you make your adjustments to the users. In the initial screen, shown in Figure 6.18, you have to define the set of users you want to maintain.

The user table in the initial screen is limited in such a way that you can't insert many users from your clipboard (you have to scroll down and insert a subset), you can use one of the user selection options available.

Figure 6.18 Initial Screen of Mass User Maintenance in Transaction SU10

From the **Address Data** area, you can find users based on attributes related to the user master (Figure 6.19). If you have a list of usernames, you can use the multiple selection for the **Users** field. In the **Multiple Selection** prompt, you can insert values from your clipboard to select users in mass.

Users by address data

Names

First Name		
Last Name		
Users		

Communication Paths

Company	
City	
Buildings	
Room	
Extension	

Other Data

Department	
Cost Center	

Format List

Title	
Layout	

Figure 6.19 Search Users by Address Data

From the **Authorization Data** area, you can find users based on different attributes belonging to the users (Figure 6.20). Common options include user groups, lock status, all unlocked users, users within validity data, users based on user language, or users with a specific role, transaction, profile, or authorization.

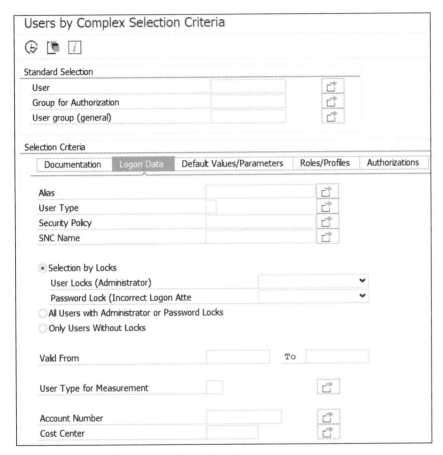

Figure 6.20 Search Users by Authorization Data

From the **Logon Data** area (Figure 6.21), you can find users based on logon information from the users. Those options include the validity of the user, selection by locks or by login attempts, user types, and the status of the password.

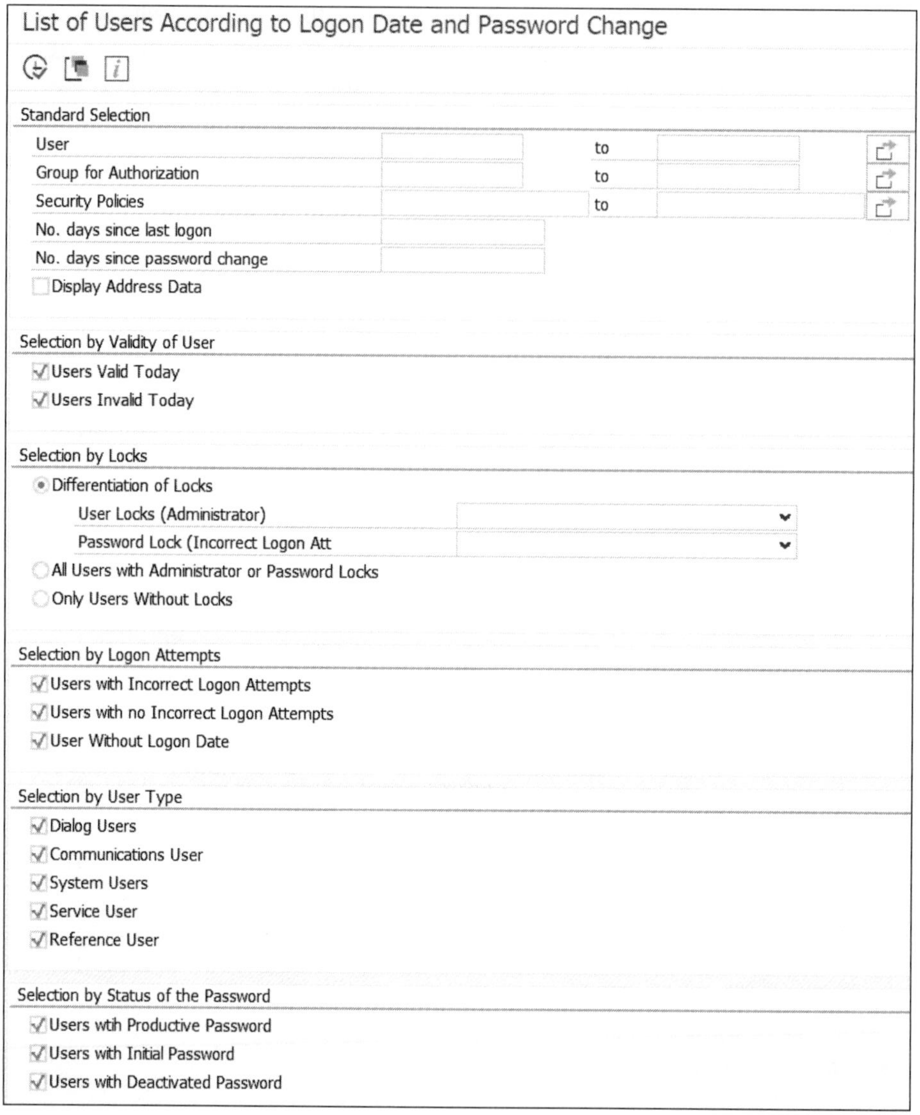

List of Users According to Logon Date and Password Change

⊕ [▣] [i]

Standard Selection

User		to		⤢
Group for Authorization		to		⤢
Security Policies		to		⤢
No. days since last logon				
No. days since password change				
☐ Display Address Data				

Selection by Validity of User

☑ Users Valid Today
☑ Users Invalid Today

Selection by Locks

◉ Differentiation of Locks
    User Locks (Administrator)   ⌄
    Password Lock (Incorrect Logon Att   ⌄
◯ All Users with Administrator or Password Locks
◯ Only Users Without Locks

Selection by Logon Attempts

☑ Users with Incorrect Logon Attempts
☑ Users with no Incorrect Logon Attempts
☑ User Without Logon Date

Selection by User Type

☑ Dialog Users
☑ Communications User
☑ System Users
☑ Service User
☑ Reference User

Selection by Status of the Password

☑ Users wtih Productive Password
☑ Users with Initial Password
☑ Users with Deactivated Password

Figure 6.21 Search Users by Logon Data

For each of the selection screens, once you run the report the system will show you the users that match the selection criteria. From this report, select the users that you want to transfer to Transaction SU10 and click the **Transfer** button (Figure 6.22).

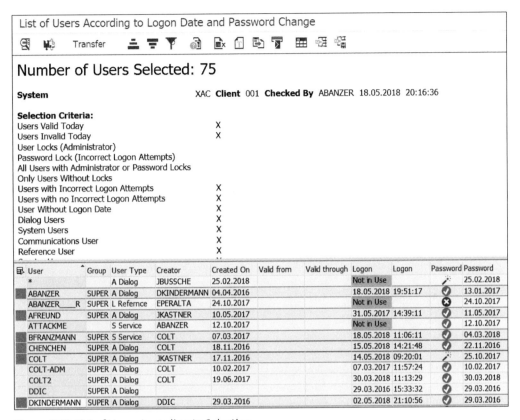

List of Users According to Logon Date and Password Change										

Number of Users Selected: 75

System   XAC **Client** 001 **Checked By** ABANZER 18.05.2018 20:16:36

Selection Criteria:

Users Valid Today	X
Users Invalid Today	X
User Locks (Administrator)	
Password Lock (Incorrect Logon Attempts)	
All Users with Administrator or Password Locks	
Only Users Without Locks	
Users with Incorrect Logon Attempts	X
Users with no Incorrect Logon Attempts	X
User Without Logon Date	X
Dialog Users	X
System Users	X
Communications User	X
Reference User	X

User	Group	User Type	Creator	Created On	Valid from	Valid through	Logon	Logon	Password	Password
*		A Dialog	JBUSSCHE	25.02.2018			Not in Use			25.02.2018
ABANZER	SUPER	A Dialog	DKINDERMANN	04.04.2016			18.05.2018	19:51:17	✓	13.01.2017
ABANZER___R	SUPER	L Refernce	EPERALTA	24.10.2017			Not in Use		✗	24.10.2017
AFREUND	SUPER	A Dialog	JKASTNER	10.05.2017			31.05.2017	14:39:11	✓	11.05.2017
ATTACKME		S Service	ABANZER	12.10.2017			Not in Use		✓	12.10.2017
BFRANZMANN	SUPER	S Service	COLT	07.03.2017			18.05.2018	11:06:11	✓	04.03.2018
CHENCHEN	SUPER	A Dialog	COLT	18.11.2016			15.05.2018	14:21:48	✓	22.11.2016
COLT	SUPER	A Dialog	JKASTNER	17.11.2016			14.05.2018	09:20:01		25.10.2017
COLT-ADM	SUPER	A Dialog	COLT	10.02.2017			07.03.2017	11:57:24	✓	10.02.2017
COLT2	SUPER	A Dialog	COLT	19.06.2017			30.03.2018	11:13:29	✓	30.03.2018
DDIC	SUPER	A Dialog					29.03.2016	15:33:32	✓	29.03.2016
DKINDERMANN	SUPER	A Dialog	DDIC	29.03.2016			02.05.2018	21:10:56	✓	29.03.2016

Figure 6.22 List of Users According to Selection

Once transferred, you'll see the set of users in your initial screen in Transaction SU10. Now you can decide what operation you want to perform. Available options are listed here and shown in Figure 6.23, starting from the left:

- User Creation
- Change All the Users
- Change Users Individually
- Delete the Users
- Lock the Users
- Unlock the Users
- Unlock the Users Globally (if CUA)
- Change Password

- Change Role Assignments
- Select All Users
- Deselect All Users
- Remove Users from Selection
- Display Saved Logs

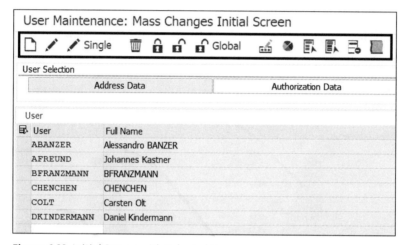

Figure 6.23 Initial Screen with Selected Users

Warning

One of the most common and costly mistakes is to click the **Delete** button (the trash can icon) to remove users from the selection. The **Delete** button will immediately and irreparably delete all users that are in the selection. No return or revert button is available. If the users are deleted, they must be recreated manually. Previous role assignments are only viewable from the user change log, and recreating them is a time-consuming task.

To change role assignments for users, you can choose either the **Change** or **Change Role Assignment** button. If you choose **Change**, you can navigate to the exact same screen as used in **Change Role Assignment**. In the **Roles** tab, you can add or remove roles from a user. It isn't possible to add and remove roles at the same time, but you can perform these actions one at a time.

When removing roles from a user, it's important to define the **Start Date** as early as the first assignment of that role to capture the validity.

For example, user T-ABA has the role Z_TEST_SINGLE_ROLE assigned with a validity of May 18, 2018 (Figure 6.24).

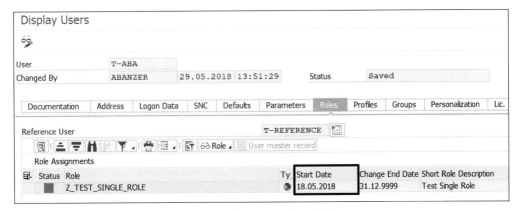

Figure 6.24 Role Assignment of User T-ABA in Transaction SU01

Let's perform a role change for user T-ABA and role Z_TEST_SINGLE_ROLE in Transaction SU10 with the default values. You can see that the system automatically sets the start date to the current date, which in the example shown is May 29, 2018 (Figure 6.25).

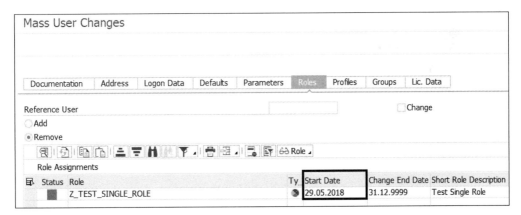

Figure 6.25 Remove Role Assignments in Transaction SU10

Once you save the change, the system will tell you that no change was made to the user. The system couldn't find a role assignment within the time frame given, as shown in Figure 6.26.

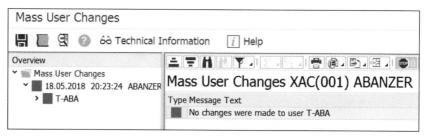

Figure 6.26 Mass User Change Status Notification after Save

Let's try again with validity data that captures the actual role assignment. If you want to remove the roles regardless of the validity, then define a date such as **01.01.1900** (Figure 6.27).

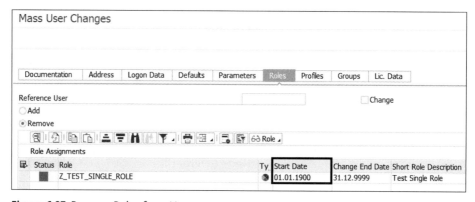

Figure 6.27 Remove Roles from Users

Once you save the change, you'll see a notification that the user has been changed. Also, the role was removed successfully (Figure 6.28).

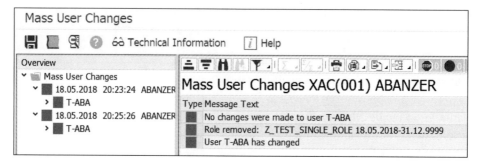

Figure 6.28 Mass User Change Successful Status Information after Save

6.8   User Naming Convention

Defining a naming convention for your users is very important and helps reduce complexity in the long run. With a proper naming convention, you can easily identify your users, which allows you to use the selection criteria more precisely.

As a rule of thumb, you want to define the naming convention to group certain sets of users. For example, technical users should have the same identifier so that you can distinguish them from your dialog users. Some examples include the following:

- RFC users should be identifiable by the calling system and the to-be-called system with a naming convention such as RFC_<calling system SID>_<called system SID>—for example, RFC_ERP_CUA or RFC_GRC_CUA.

- Dialog users should start with the letter A and then a mix of last and first name. For example, the first six characters of the last and the first 4 of the first name: A_BANZERALES, A_MARKGRJOE.

SAP user IDs can be up to 12 characters long. Using the full length makes it easier to identify users—not only for you as an administrator, but also for end users when it comes to change logs and the like. Proper naming, as in the preceding examples for dialog users, gives good identification of who (in the sense of which person) performed a change in the system. Cryptic user IDs, such as combinations of numbers, are difficult to connect to real people. Cryptic user IDs are sometimes required for legal reasons or because the company wants to have the user IDs be the same across the landscape (LAN, SAP Enterprise Portal, SAP, etc.).

User naming conventions are important. Therefore, the goal of your naming convention should be to:

- Reduce complexity
- Help identify users (i.e., user type, purpose, etc.)
- Enhance legal or organizational requirements—for example, the use of a personnel number or random number to obscure a user's identity (this is sometimes a legal requirement)

Your user naming conventions should be consistent across your entire landscape wherever possible. A properly designed user naming convention will ensure that one user doesn't have different user IDs across the SAP landscape, or in non-SAP applications.

Naming conventions are unique to each company; there really is no best practice. Commonly seen user naming conventions include the following:

- *<Initials>_<last 4 of personnel number>* (e.g., ABA_0987)
- *<User Type>_<Random Number>*:
  - Dialog user: A_12345678
  - Reference user: R_12345678
  - Batch user: B_12345678
  - System user: S_12345678
  - Guest user: G_12345678
- *<First Initial><Last Name>* (e.g., ABANZER, JMARKGRAF, etc.)
  For duplicate users (e.g., Alessandro Banzer and Andre Banzer), you can always add a number or middle initial in the naming convention.
- *<First Initial><First 4 Characters of Last Name><2 digit number>* (e.g., ABANZO1, ABANZO2, JMARKO1, JMARKO2, etc.)

A naming convention should also apply for test users so that you can clearly separate them from your productive users. This is especially important when you have to measure your user base for licensing costs, as you will want to distinguish between test and productive users.

There isn't a right or wrong choice nor are there common best practices when it comes to naming conventions. It's only important to define a naming convention that suites your organization; it might differ based on the organization's size, systems in use, and other factors

6.9   Security Policies

With the security policies in Transaction SECPOL, SAP offers the capability to flexibly define security policies for certain users. Although security parameters like password complexity are defined globally within the profile parameters, Transaction SECPOL allows you to more granularly define security parameters for a set of users. For example, say that you want to increase the password complexity for your high-privileged accounts, like administrators. To increase that for a set of users, you can define a security policy in Transaction SECPOL (Figure 6.29).

The security policy is a set of attributes and their values, which can be configured in Transaction SECPOL. Once assigned to a user, the system will always evaluate the security policy and not the default parameters from the profile parameters. Profile parameters are only relevant to the user without a security policy assigned. One user can only have one security policy. It's important to understand that the security policy will replace the values that are valid for the user. Also, if you maintain a security policy for a user, make sure to include all the parameters that are set in the profile parameters. By design, the SAP system will otherwise evaluate the kernel values and not the ones from the profile parameters.

What does that mean? Let's assume you define a security policy for administrators and you want to increase some of the complexity by defining the minimum characters higher than the standard profile parameter value. If you do so, you have to include all the other values as well.

In Transaction SECPOL, you define a security policy and its attributes. To create a new policy, click **New Entries** in the change view (Figure 6.29).

Figure 6.29 Initial Screen of Transaction SECPOL

Name the policy by entering a name in the **Security Policy** field and a description in the **Short Text** field (Figure 6.30).

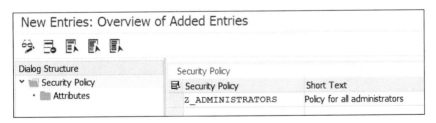

Figure 6.30 Create Security Policy in Transaction SECPOL

Once defined, select the policy and double-click the **Attributes** field. To add new attributes to the policy, click **New Entries**. Each attribute comes with a classification:

- 1: Password rules
- 2: Password change policies
- 3: Logon restrictions

Use the match code search to see all available attributes and their classifications (Figure 6.31).

Type	Policy Attribute Name	Long Field Label	Default
	Technical Name of a Security Policy Attribute 21 Entries		
1	CHECK_PASSWORD_BLACKLIST	Check the Password Blacklist	1
1	MIN_PASSWORD_DIGITS	Minimum Number of Digits	0
1	MIN_PASSWORD_LENGTH	Minimum Password Length	6
1	MIN_PASSWORD_LETTERS	Minimum Number of Letters	0
1	MIN_PASSWORD_LOWERCASE	Minimum Number of Lowercase Letters	0
1	MIN_PASSWORD_SPECIALS	Minimum Number of Special Characters	0
1	MIN_PASSWORD_UPPERCASE	Minimum Number of Uppercase Letters	0
2	MIN_PASSWORD_CHANGE_WAITTIME	Minimum Wait Time for Password Change	1
2	MIN_PASSWORD_DIFFERENCE	No. of Different Chars When Changing	1
2	PASSWORD_CHANGE_FOR_SSO	Password Change Req. for SSO Logons	1
2	PASSWORD_CHANGE_INTERVAL	Interval for Regular Password Changes	0
2	PASSWORD_COMPLIANCE_TO_CURRENT_POLICY	Password Change After Rule Tightening	0
2	PASSWORD_HISTORY_SIZE	Size of the Password History	5
3	DISABLE_PASSWORD_LOGON	Disable Password Logon	0
3	DISABLE_TICKET_LOGON	Disable Ticket Logon	0
3	MAX_FAILED_PASSWORD_LOGON_ATTEMPTS	Maximum Number of Failed Attempts	5
3	MAX_PASSWORD_IDLE_INITIAL	Validity of Unused Initial Passwords	0
3	MAX_PASSWORD_IDLE_PRODUCTIVE	Validity of Unused Production Passwords	0
3	PASSWORD_LOCK_EXPIRATION	Automatic Expiration of Password Lock	0
3	SERVER_LOGON_PRIVILEGE	Logon if server_logon_restriction=1	0
3	TENANT_RUNLEVEL_LOGON_PRIVILEGE	Logon for Each Tenant Runlevel > 0	0

Figure 6.31 Available Attributes for Security Policy

From the match code, you can also see the default value from the profile parameters. Pick the attributes and define the values that you want to enforce with the policy (Figure 6.32).

Policy Attribute Name	Attrib.Value
Attributes	
MIN_PASSWORD_LENGTH	30
MIN_PASSWORD_DIGITS	4
MAX_PASSWORD_IDLE_INITIAL	1
MAX_FAILED_PASSWORD_LOGON_ATTEMPTS	2

Figure 6.32 Example Attributes of Security Policy

In the **Attributes** window, you can check the effectiveness of the policy, as well as items that are similar to the profile parameters, as shown in Figure 6.33.

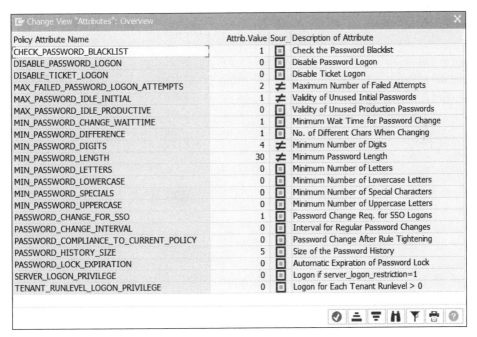

Figure 6.33 Effective and Superfluous Entries in Transaction SECPOL

To check the effectiveness, click the **Effective** button and check the values in comparison to the profile parameters (Figure 6.34). This will give you a good indication of whether your policy is stricter than the default or if you should just maintain what's already defined on a global level via the profile parameters.

Policy Attribute Name	Attrib.Value	Sour.	Description of Attribute
CHECK_PASSWORD_BLACKLIST	1		Check the Password Blacklist
DISABLE_PASSWORD_LOGON	0		Disable Password Logon
DISABLE_TICKET_LOGON	0		Disable Ticket Logon
MAX_FAILED_PASSWORD_LOGON_ATTEMPTS	2	≠	Maximum Number of Failed Attempts
MAX_PASSWORD_IDLE_INITIAL	1	≠	Validity of Unused Initial Passwords
MAX_PASSWORD_IDLE_PRODUCTIVE	0		Validity of Unused Production Passwords
MIN_PASSWORD_CHANGE_WAITTIME	1		Minimum Wait Time for Password Change
MIN_PASSWORD_DIFFERENCE	1		No. of Different Chars When Changing
MIN_PASSWORD_DIGITS	4	≠	Minimum Number of Digits
MIN_PASSWORD_LENGTH	30	≠	Minimum Password Length
MIN_PASSWORD_LETTERS	0		Minimum Number of Letters
MIN_PASSWORD_LOWERCASE	0		Minimum Number of Lowercase Letters
MIN_PASSWORD_SPECIALS	0		Minimum Number of Special Characters
MIN_PASSWORD_UPPERCASE	0		Minimum Number of Uppercase Letters
PASSWORD_CHANGE_FOR_SSO	1		Password Change Req. for SSO Logons
PASSWORD_CHANGE_INTERVAL	0		Interval for Regular Password Changes
PASSWORD_COMPLIANCE_TO_CURRENT_POLICY	0		Password Change After Rule Tightening
PASSWORD_HISTORY_SIZE	5		Size of the Password History
PASSWORD_LOCK_EXPIRATION	0		Automatic Expiration of Password Lock
SERVER_LOGON_PRIVILEGE	0		Logon if server_logon_restriction=1
TENANT_RUNLEVEL_LOGON_PRIVILEGE	0		Logon for Each Tenant Runlevel > 0

Figure 6.34 Check Policy Effectiveness in Transaction SECPOL

If you click the **Superfluous Entries** button, you'll see a list of parameters that are similar to the profile parameters (Figure 6.35).

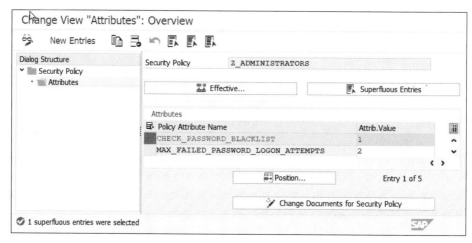

Figure 6.35 Superfluous Parameters in Transaction SECPOL

Once the security policy is defined, save your entries and assign the policy to a user. To do so, go to Transaction SU01 or Transaction SU10 and assign the policy in the **Logon Data** tab (Figure 6.36).

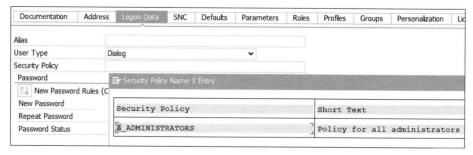

Figure 6.36 Assign Security Policy to User in Transaction SU01 or SU10

Once assigned and the user has been saved, the new policy will be enforced.

6.10   Maintain User Groups

User groups are used to categorize users into common logical groups. You can use the user group to segregate user administration, but also to search and sort users by a common grouping. To create and maintain user groups, use Transaction SUGR (Figure 6.37). In this transaction, you can create, edit, display, and delete user groups from the system. Also, you can assign multiple users to a user group. Note that assigning a user to a user group from Transaction SUGR will add the user to the user groups that can be utilized for grouping (via the **Groups** tab in Transaction SUO1). It doesn't assign the user to the user groups used for the authority check (**Logon Data** tab in Transaction SUO1).

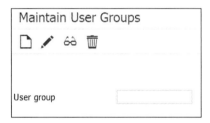

Figure 6.37 Initial Screen of Transaction SUGR

To maintain and change the assignment of user groups, enter the name and click on the respective save icon (Figure 6.38). Changes will be effective immediately once saved.

Maintain User Groups

User group		
User group	USER_ADMINS	
Text	User Administrators User Group	

User Assignment		
User Name	Full Name	Assignment comes from HR Organizati...
ABANZER	Alessandro Banzer	

Figure 6.38 Maintain User Groups in Transaction SUGR

In the user master record in Transaction SUO1, you can see that the user group has been added to the **Groups** tab, as shown in Figure 6.39.

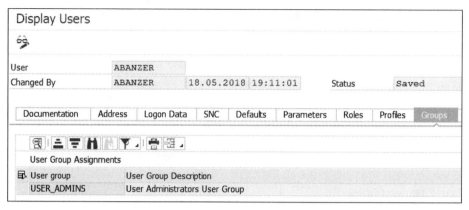

Figure 6.39 Grouping of Users in Groups Tab in Transaction SU01

The user group used for authority checks in the **Logon Data** tab remain untouched (Figure 6.40).

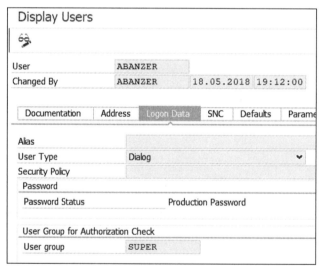

Figure 6.40 User Group for Authorization Check in Logon Data Tab of Transaction SU01

Remember, if a user isn't assigned to a user group, every administrator with access to Transaction SU01 or Transaction SU10 and S_USER_GRP with the respective authorization activity can maintain that user. Therefore, we recommend assigning each user to a user group. To make this a required field, you can set a customizing option to make the user group for authorization check mandatory. Before you change the customizing, make sure that all users are assigned to a user group. Then, create a default user group and maintain it for the USER_GRP_REQUIRED parameter in the customizing table USR_CUST through Transaction SM30. If a user administrator wants to have a different user group per default, she can define user parameter S_USER_GRP_DEFAULT that overrides the default user group from table USR_CUST.

Note

Check SAP Note 1663177 (SU01: User Group as Required Entry Field) for more information.

6.11 Central User Administration

In complex system landscapes, you have to manage users and their attributes, like roles and profile assignments, locally in each system. With CUA (Figure 6.41), you can manage users globally from one central system and distribute its changes to all connected child systems. You can also maintain the users in a single place and make sure they stay in sync across different clients and systems in different landscapes.

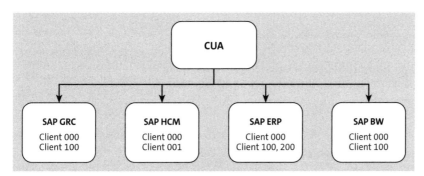

Figure 6.41 CUA Schema

The user master record is client-specific and hence needs to be maintained in each system independently. With CUA, you can simplify that process by distributing the user master records to several systems at the same time. You can distribute changes from a central system, which indeed is a central client, to all connected child systems. The child systems must be connected through an RFC connection used to transfer the data back and forth. The RFC interfaces must have a system user with the authorizations needed to perform the changes. SAP predelivers a set of roles that can be utilized for this purpose. The predelivered roles start with SAP_BC_USR_CUA* and are as follows:

- SAP_BC_USR_CUA_CENTRAL
  Authorizations for RFC Service User in CUA Central System

- SAP_BC_USR_CUA_CENTRAL_BDIST
  Authorizations for RFC Service Users in CUA Central System (Back)

- SAP_BC_USR_CUA_CENTRAL_EXTERN
  Authorizations for RFC Users in CUA Central System (for External Users)

- SAP_BC_USR_CUA_CHDOC_READ
  To read the local change documents for the CUA landscape from the child systems

- SAP_BC_USR_CUA_CLIENT
  Authorizations for RFC Users in CUA Child System

- SAP_BC_USR_CUA_CLIENT_BATCH
  Authorizations for RFC Users in CUA Child System (Background Processing)

- SAP_BC_USR_CUA_CLIENT_PFCG
  Authorizations for RFC Users in CUA Child System (for Calling PFCG)

- SAP_BC_USR_CUA_CLIENT_RFC
  Authorizations for RFC Users in CUA Child System (for RFC)

- SAP_BC_USR_CUA_SETUP_CENTRAL
  Authorizations for RFC Users in CUA Central System (for CUA Configuration)

- SAP_BC_USR_CUA_SETUP_CLIENT
  Authorizations for RFC Users in CUA Child System (for CUA Configuration)

In an Application Link Enabling (ALE) network, data exchange takes place by exchanging intermediate documents (IDocs) via RFC. Therefore, you require logical systems for the ALE distribution to work. Logical systems follow the naming convention:

<SID>CLNT<Client> (e.g. CUACLNT100, GRCCLNT001, ERPCLNT100)

You can also provision SAP Enterprise Portal through the User Management Engine (UME). With the UME in place, you can authorize roles or groups in the SAP Enterprise Portal through SAP authorization roles in the ABAP system. The SAP authorization roles are linked with the groups in the UME.

Once the RFC connection and the users are defined, you can continue with the configuration of the CUA landscape.

6.11.1   Distribution Parameters for Fields (Transaction SCUM)

In the configuration of the CUA, you can define which fields will be distributed and how they're being managed. In Transaction SCUM, you can define the distribution parameters of each field available in the user master record. The distribution parameters listed in Table 6.3 are available.

Option	Description
Global	The field can only be maintained in the central system and is automatically distributed to the child system. In the child system, the field cannot be changed.
Local	The field can only be maintained in the child system. Changes aren't distributed to other systems.
Proposal	The field can be maintained in the central system and the change is automatically distributed to the child system when the user is created. Changes are maintained in the child system. The central system does not distribute changes to existing users.
Redistribution	The field can be maintained in the central and child system. Changed fields in a child system will be synchronized back to the central system and then distributed to all child systems.
Everywhere	The field can be maintained everywhere. However, only changes to the central system will be distributed. Local changes might be overwritten when the field is changed in the central system.

Table 6.3 CUA Distribution Parameters in Transaction SCUM

The user distribution fields can be defined individually. In Figure 6.42, you can see the distribution settings for the **Logon data** tab. The initial password can be defined everywhere, whereas the security policy will be maintained locally only.

The same applies for roles and profile assignments. With the CUA master system, you can not only create and maintain the users but also manage the role assignments if that option is set to **Global** (Figure 6.43).

| Documentation | Address | Logon data | Defaults | Parameters | Profiles |

Field Attributes for Central User Admin.

Fld Name	Global	Local	Proposal	Redist	Evrywhr	
User group	●	○	○	○		
Validity period	●	○	○	○		
Account no.	●	○	○	○		
Cost center	●	○	○	○		
User type	●	○	○	○		
Alias	●	○	○	○		
Initial password	○	○	○	○	●	
Security Policy	○	●	○	○		

Figure 6.42 User Distribution Field Selection for Logon Data in Transaction SCUM

| Profiles | Roles | SNC | Lock | Groups | Personalization | LicenseData |

Field Attributes for Central User Admin.

Fld Name	Global	Local	Proposal	Redist	Evrywhr	
Role Assignment	●	○	○	○		
Reference user	●	○	○	○		

Figure 6.43 User Distribution Field Selection for Roles in Transaction SCUM

6.11.2 Background Jobs

The CUA requires a few background jobs to run frequently to ensure changes are processed seamlessly. The central system has to know the roles and profiles from the child systems so that you can assign them through the CUA. You can therefore schedule the text comparison job SUSR_ZBV_GET_RECEIVER_PROFILES.

To immediately process the changes in the child systems, set the IDoc processing to **Immediately**. To ensure that all IDocs are processed, you can schedule the job RBDAPP01 in all connected child systems.

Since the CUA processes a huge number of IDocs, make sure that you reorganize them regularly. You can delete IDocs of type CCLONE and USERCLONE.

6.11.3   CUA-Related Tables

In every CUA system, you can find helpful tables to slice and dice data. It's important to understand which tables are available in case you want to quickly check something through the table browser. Table 6.4 provides a list of CUA-related tables.

Table	Description
USRSYSACT	Roles in distributed systems
USRSYSACTT	Roles text in distributed systems
USRSYSLNG	User's language in distributed systems.
USRSYSPRF	Profiles in distributed systems
USRSYSPRFT	Profiles text in distributed systems
USERSYSUPL	Price list in distributed systems
USERSYSUPPL	Assignment of user types to price list
USLA04	Assignment of users to roles

Table 6.4 CUA-Related Tables

CUA offers an easy way to simplify user administration. Regardless of the number of systems and clients you have, you might profit from using CUA. It's also possible to install CUA in a dedicated client in one of your systems.

6.12   User Lock Status

In the user master table (table USR02) there are different lock statuses of a user in the UFLAG field. The following statuses are known to an SAP system:

- 0: User is not locked
- 32: User is locked globally by an administrator
- 64: User is locked locally by an administrator
- 128: User is locked due to incorrect logons

The different lock statuses let you identify how the user was locked. Also, the lock status is cumulative; hence, you might see a lock status such as 160, which means the user was locked globally by an administrator (32) and is also locked due to incorrect logons (128).

You might ask yourself: Why is this important? The answer is simple. If you use tools like SAP GRC Access Control or SAP Identity Management that offer password self-service capabilities to unlock users independently, then the lock status is very important. With password self-service, the user can only unlock if the lock status is 128 (locked due to incorrect logon). The user can't unlock a local or global lock.

If a user's locked out due to incorrect logon but also locked globally by the administrator, the user can remove the 128 lock with the password self-service tool but will remain locked with 32 (global lock by the administrator). In this case, the lock status in USR02-UFLAG will be reduced from 160 to 32 (160 − 128 = 32).

6.13   User Classification

On a periodic basis, SAP requests a measurement of the system landscape to determine license costs. You as an administrator have to provide the list of users along with their classifications. Based on the number of users for each classification, the license cost is calculated. You can be under- or over-licensed depending on changes in your number of users and transactions/reports used.

Until the end of 2017, SAP measured the license cost based on historical usage data in the system. The classification of a user was calculated based on the transactions and reports used. As of 2018, SAP is changing the licensing model to a new approach that considers the authorizations assigned to a user (see Figure 6.44). For a user to be classified for a certain license type, the assigned roles are considered. This applies to your organization as soon as you renew the contract that includes the new classification type.

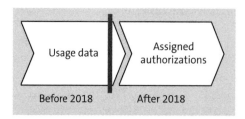

Figure 6.44 Change of License Classification in 2018

> **Warning**
>
> Keep in mind that with the change of the license classification, many customers will need to recalculate the cost of their license, because users who executed certain transactions and reports were authorized to do so. However, in addition to users that require certain transactions and reports, there may also be users that have the authorization to execute these transactions and reports but don't. With the new model, these users would be classified as well, resulting in more licenses than are actually required.

With the new method of classifying a user, it's very important to set authorizations to avoid unnecssary license costs. Following a least-privilege principle and/or redesigning your roles might be in order.

6.14   User-Related Tables

User-related tables offer an easy way to get access to data directly. Although most data can be accessed through Transaction SUIM (User Information System), security administrators tend to use the table browser (Transaction SE16) to access data. Therefore, it's very handy to know the most common tables that are available, as listed in Table 6.5.

Table	Description
USR01	Contains the runtime data of the user master record
USR02	Logon data of the user master record, such as passwords
USR03	User address data
USR04	User master authorizations
USR05	User parameter IDs
USR09	Contains the user menu
USR10	User master authorization profiles
USR11	User master texts for profiles
USR12	User master authorization values

Table 6.5 User-Related Tables

Table	Description
USR21	Assignment of a user master to the address data
USR40	List of blacklisted/forbidden passwords
USH02	Change history for logon data
USH04	Change history for user master authorizations
USER_ADDR	Generated table view for user address data
USRPWDHISTORY	User password history
ADRP	Personal address information like first name, last name, and so on
ADR2	User telephone numbers
ADR3	User fax numbers
ADR6	User email addresses
USR_CUST	Customizing settings for users/authorizations

Table 6.5 User-Related Tables (Cont.)

6.15   Securing Default Accounts

The SAP systems come with several default users that have extended access to the system. These users are created during the installation process and through the implementation and customization of certain functionality. When you install an SAP system, standard users like SAP*, DDIC, and EARLYWATCH are created. Table 6.6 provides their settings.

User	Description	Clients	Default Password
SAP*	SAP system super user	000, 001, 066, and all new clients	06071992 PASS
DDIC	ABAP Dictionary and software logistics super user	000, 001	19920706

Table 6.6 SAP Standard User Overview

User	Description	Clients	Default Password
EARLYWATCH	Dialog user for the SAP EarlyWatch Alert service in client 066	066	SUPPORT
SAPCPIC	User for remote connections	000, 001, and all new clients	ADMIN
TMSADM	User for TMS	000	Set during installation

Table 6.6 SAP Standard User Overview (Cont.)

Because these parameters are publicly known, it's very important to protect these users from unauthorized use. To protect the users, deactivate user SAP*, change all the default passwords, assign the users to user group SUPER, and lock users DDIC and EARLYWATCH. Assigning users to user group SUPER protects them from being changed by anyone other than administrators, who are authorized to change users in the user group SUPER.

To avoid the automatic creation of user SAP*, set the profile parameter `login/no_automatic_user_sapstar = 1` in the instance profile. It's important to set this parameter in the instance profile and not in the default profile (see SAP Note 68048). For emergency purposes, when the user SAP* is needed, set the parameter to 0, delete the user account, and restart the system. Once the system has been started, the SAP* user will be created with profile SAP_ALL automatically. The **Change Documents for Users** screen will show that the changes were performed by user SAP* through the kernel transaction, which means that the user was generated automatically (Figure 6.45).

User	Date	Time	Changed By	Action	Old Value	Text	New Value	Text	TCode
SAP*	29.03.2016	15:13:06	SAP*	User group changed			SUPER	SUPER	KRNL
				Password changed			New Password	1	KRNL
				Password status changed			Productive		KRNL

Figure 6.45 Example of Change Documents for User SAP*

Other standard users to check are TMSADM and SAPCPIC. TMSADM is required for the TMS and will only exist in client 000 of each system. Make sure that the default password for user TMSADM has been changed in client 000 and that the user is deleted in any other client. To change the default password for user TMSADM, follow SAP Note 1414256 and proceed as described. SAPCPIC must be locked in all clients or completely deleted. Also, change the standard password.

Report RSUSR003: Check Standard Users in All Clients

The standard report RSUSR0003 (Figure 6.46) displays standard users and their statuses across all clients in a system. It's important to execute this report in each system because users are client-dependent and hence different in each client and system.

Depending on your current release, report RSUSR003 might not report user TMSADM. Check SAP Note 1552894 to learn how to update the report to show the status of user TMSADM.

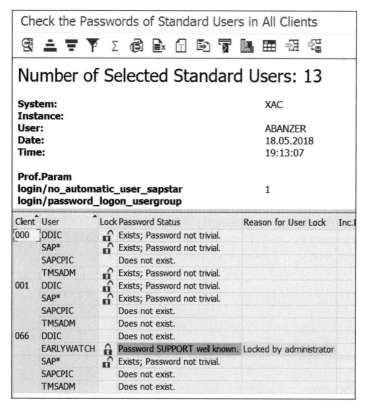

Figure 6.46 Example of Report RSUSR003

6.16   User Access Reviews

To effectively protect your SAP system, it's important to perform user access reviews of your users and their authorizations periodically. SAP GRC Access Control offers a workflow-driven user access review capability. However, regardless of the tools used or even when performed manually, most auditing firms request a user access review once per year. For some user groups, like high privileged accounts—such as security administrators—it's required more often.

User access reviews must include a thorough review of all roles and profiles assigned to a user with a proper sign-off procedure. The review must include all users in the system, regardless of whether they're active. For inactive users, we recommend removing the authorizations. During the approval procedure, role assignments are removed and new roles might be requested. In several cases, a user needs specific authorization but is assigned to a large set of roles that grant additional access that isn't required. Therefore, as a security administrator you might be contacted to create smaller roles with less of a surplus.

6.17   Inactive Users

In every SAP system, you can find users that haven't logged on for several months. It's important to define a process that describes how to deal with inactive users. For example, many companies lock users that haven't logged on for more than 30 days and delete them after 90 days.

To find users that have been inactive for a certain time, you can use report RSUSR200 (Figure 6.47). In the selection screen, you can define the number of days since last logon.

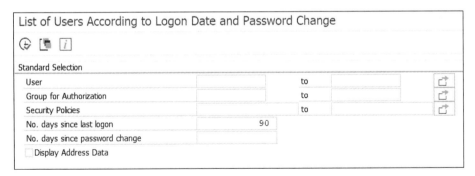

Figure 6.47 Report RSUSR200 to Find Inactive Users

Managing inactive users increases the security of your SAP system and might also have a positive impact on user classification and hence on your license costs. Inactive users pose a risk because they exist in the system with authorizations and aren't used by a specific user. Therefore, locking or even deleting those users reduces the risk of inappropriate use.

6.18   Password and Logon Security

Compromised passwords are among the most significant threats to an organization. With a compromised password, not only is the organization at risk, but an end user is personally vulnerable as well because someone else can abusively use his account. Therefore, secure passwords are required. Before we start looking at what secure passwords are and how you can enforce them, let's see how a password can be compromised.

Most often, passwords are compromised by one of the following events:

- Someone is able to guess the password; the password is neither complex nor random. Someone who knows the person can guess the password, which could be the name of the user's spouse or child, a hobby, or so on.
- Brute-force attacks are the go-to strategy to hack passwords. Brute-force compares sequentially generated password hashes with the password hashes from SAP. The comparison and testing is performed outside of SAP. Different freeware programs, like John the Ripper, HashCat, and others, are available. To expedite the process, most commonly an extended password list is used to test common passwords first.
- We've seen several data breaches lately in which user accounts along with their passwords are exposed. An exposed password is no longer safe because it can be mapped to a user. Also, password lists used in brute-force attacks will be updated with the exposed passwords from a data breach. Therefore, once your password is exposed, make sure to change it immediately.

As you can see, it's important to enforce secure passwords. Let's see how that can be achieved.

6.18.1   Where Does SAP Store Passwords?

An SAP system stores passwords in different tables and views. These tables are among the most vulnerable and hence require proper protection. Make sure these tables are securely protected and only visible to administrators who require access to these tables and views. Common tables that store passwords are USR02, USH02, USH02_ARC_TMP, and USRPWDHISTORY. The two main views are VUSER001 and VUSR02_PWD.

6.18.2   What Is the Code Version?

Passwords are stored as a hash value and not in cleartext. An algorithm generates the hash value from the cleartext password and stores its value in table USR02. The algorithm that generates that hash value is called the *code version*. The code version of the password can be seen in table USR02 from field CODEVN. In SAP NetWeaver 7.50, the values listed in Table 6.7 are possible.

Code Version	Description
A	Code Version A (Obsolete)
B	Code Version B (MD5-Based, 8 Characters, Upper-Case, ASCII)
C	Code Version C (Not Implemented)
D	Code Version D (MD5-Based, 8 Characters, Upper-Case, UTF-8)
E	Code Version E (Corrected Code Version D)
F	Code Version F (SHA1, 40 Characters, Case-Sensitive, UTF-8)
G	Code Version G = Code Vers. F + Code Vers. B (2 Hash Values)
H	Code Version H (Generic Hash Procedure)
I	Code Version I = Code Versions H + F + B (Three Hash Values)
X	Password Deactivated

Table 6.7 Code Version of Password Hash Algorithm in SAP NetWeaver 7.50 as seen in the SAP GUI

As a rule of thumb, the lower the letter of the code version in the alphabet, the weaker its algorithm and hence faster to crack.

6.18.3   Why Do I Have to Protect These Tables?

Because brute force attacks happen outside the SAP environment, you can't protect your system from these attempts. There is no profile parameter that can be set, for example, to lock a user. The attacks aren't detectable by the SAP kernel. Therefore, it's ultimately important to protect access to these tables not only in the SAP system itself, but also on the OS level. In the SAP system, the most common ways to access table USR02 (and the other tables) is through the data browser (Transaction SE16/SE17/SM30) and ABAP programs that can directly access tables through a SQL statement.

Chapter 7, Section 7.10 describes how you can protect these tables effectively. It's important to restrict access via table browser transactions like Transactions SE16, SE17, SM30, and the like and to have the authorization objects S_TABU_DIS/S_TABU_NAM under control.

6.18.4   Logon Procedure

To understand how the system verifies if a user can log on to the SAP system, it's important to be familiar with the steps involved in the logon procedure. With standard authentication by user ID and password, the system checks the following in series:

- Is the password activated? (Remember, you can deactivate passwords.)
- Is the user permitted to logon with the password?
- Is the user locked by an administrator?
- Is the user locked due to too many failed attempts?
- Is the password correct?
- Is the password expired or initial and needs to be changed?

Once all steps are successful, the user is logged on and the system will write the logon timestamp into the user master. As an end user, you can always check when you last logged on to the system (Figure 6.48). In the SAP GUI, go to **System • Status**.

System: Status				
Usage data				
Client	001	Previous logon	21.03.2018	10:08:31
User	ABANZER	Logon	26.03.2018	15:39:11
Language	EN	System time	28.03.2018	19:38:15
		Time Zone	EST	12:38:15
Number of Failed Password Logon Attempts:			0	

Figure 6.48 Last Logon Date and Time in System Status.

You can not only see when the previous logon took place, but also how many times you had a failed attempt due to a wrong password. That gives you an indication if someone else tried to logon with your user ID.

6.18.5   Password Change Policy

The password change policy may be set by your IT policy, or you may be setting the policy yourself. Just remember, when strong security isn't mandated, it's not used. Most users will do what's easiest, which can lead to easy-to-guess passwords that can result in serious security breaches. Therefore, make sure that you enforce strong passwords through the login parameters.

Configuration Parameters for Login

To enforce complex and secure passwords, several profile parameters can be set. Table 6.8 gives an overview of common parameters and their recommended values. All available profile parameters for logon and password start with login/*.

Parameter	Description	Recommended Value
login/min_password_lng	Minimum password length.	10
login/min_password_letters login/min_password_digits login/min_password_specials	Minimum number of letters, digits, and special characters in a password.	2
login/min_password_lowercase	Minimum lowercase letters.	1
login/min_password_uppercase	Minimum uppercase letters.	1
login/min_password_diff	Minimum characters that must be different from the previous password.	4
login/password_history_size	Sets the number of different passwords so that the same password can't be used again.	20
login/password_change_waittime	Sets the time in days until the password can be changed again.	1

Table 6.8 Login Profile Parameters

Parameter	Description	Recommended Value
`login/password_max_idle_productive`	Sets the validity in days for a productive password that isn't used before expiration.	30
`login/password_max_idle_initial`	Sets the validity in days for an initial password before expiration.	14
`login/password_compliance_to_current_policy`	Makes a user comply with the password rules and requires a password change if the password doesn't meet the rules.	1
`login/password_downwards_compatibility`	Allows or disallows old MD5 password hashes.	0
`login/password_expiration_time`	Defines the validity of the password in days.	120

Table 6.8 Login Profile Parameters (Cont.)

You can set parameter `login/password_downwards_compatibility` to value `0` to restrict that passwords are downward compatible. This forces the use of an iterated salted SHA1-hash (field `PWDSALTEDHAS` in table `USR02`). "Old" encryption methods are no longer used (field `BCODE`: `MD5`, field `PASSCODE`: `SHA1`). Once you change that parameter, also make sure to delete the old password hashes via report CLEANUP_PASSWORD_HASH_VALUES.

Use a Password Manager

We recommend using a password manager to store your complex passwords. Most modern password managers allow you to automatically fill out your login forms, which simplifies the logon procedure. With a password manager, you can increase the complexity and don't have to memorize your passwords.

Password Blacklist

In table USR40 (Figure 6.49), which can be maintained through Transaction SM30, you can define backlisted passwords that can't be used as productive passwords. To maintain table USR40, you can use two wildcards:

- ? stands for a single character.
- * stands for a sequence of any combination of characters of any length.

You can form patterns like the following:

- *123* prohibits anything that contains 123 in the password.
- Password? prohibits all passwords that start with Password and have one additional character—for example, Password1, PasswordB, and so on.

You can also define a password as case-sensitive, but mostly it doesn't make sense to force case-sensitivity because a blacklisted password shouldn't be possible to choose if a single character is set uppercase.

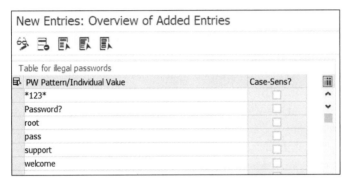

Figure 6.49 Table USR40 for Blacklisted Passwords

6.19   Segregation of Duties

SoD is the concept of separating tasks among more than one person. In an SAP system, SoD applies not only to business processes but also to administrative processes like user creation, role assignments, and so on.

In theory, an individual shouldn't have access to more than one function for a task that requires separation. A task consists of two or more functions. Here are some examples:

- Maintain users and maintain roles
- Create vendors and process payments to them
- Order goods and book goods received
- Change HR master data and perform payroll

SoD isn't always possible. This can be due to limited resources in your organization or simply because it would enlarge the process and hence slow down the organization. However, having SoD principles in place is beneficial for audits.

For security administrators, separating the security administration tasks sounds terrifying, and you might ask yourself how it could be possible. Let's look at an example in which you want to segregate user administration from roles/authorization administration. The user administrator maintains the user master record and the role assignments to users, while the authorization administrator maintains the roles and creates the authorizations and their profiles. The risk of one user maintaining both tasks is that an admin could potentially create a role and assign it to himself. Therefore, separating those tasks and having at least two different administrators have the authorizations will reduce the risk.

In some cases, as in the preceding example, the principal of dual control is sufficient. Depending on your organization and its risk appetite, you may want to increase the controls to get a higher level of security. In this case, you want to implement the principle of *treble control*—that is, have three persons involved to complete entire tasks. In our example, that means that we want to have a third person involved and we might want to further segregate the task of the authorization administrator. For example, an administrator maintains the authorizations in Transaction PFCG but doesn't have the rights to generate the authorization profile of a role. To generate the authorization profile, a third administrator is required.

Always keep in mind that SoD comes at a price, whether an increase in complexity or an increase in the time it takes to complete a task.

Standard Reporting in SAP Systems

SAP offers report RSUSR008_009_NEW that can be used to analyze users and roles for critical authorizations or critical combinations (Figure 6.50).

Figure 6.50 Report to Analyze Users or Roles with Combinations of Critical Authorizations

6.20 Summary

User IDs can be created and maintained in different ways. Whether you do it classically on a per-system basis or through a central system, understanding how they can be securely maintained is important. Security policies can be used to enforce strict security parameters for a certain set of users. Also, with the help of certain reports you can make it easier to find changes to a user, critical authorizations, and different types of change documents. Password and logon security is an important aspect to increase the overall security of your SAP system so that user IDs cannot be exposed by unauthorized persons.

In the next chapter we'll explore user authorizations in more detail.

Chapter 7
Configuring Authorizations

Authorizations control the functions a user can execute and which data can be displayed, changed, entered, deleted, etc. With a compelling authorization concept, you can ensure that your SAP system is compliant with common laws and regulations and protect it from fraudulent actions.

This chapter explains the broad topic of authorizations. It first discusses the general concepts behind authorizations and then describes how to perform the basic operations that a security administrator would be responsible for. We will also walk you through how to set and check roles and authorizations.

In the business world, authorizations are used to control access at the application level. There are several factors that come into play when authorizing business users. A company must meet certain legal requirements based on its country of operations, compliance regulations, and so on. These include, for example, data protection and privacy protection laws. To comply with current laws, a company must be able to adhere to these regulations. On the other hand, fraudulent actions and obstruction of business processes must be prevented. For example, public companies must comply with the Sarbanes-Oxley Act (SOX) and other SoD standards. In addition, cost-benefit relations must be in balance, and extensive security comes at a certain cost.

As a result, the challenge for a security administrator is to balance the requirements and at the same time ensure stable business processes and appropriate access for end users.

This chapter introduces the general authorization concepts of SAP NetWeaver AS ABAP systems and how to design them. It also provides an introduction to SAP Governance, Risk, and Compliance (SAP GRC) Access Control to comply with regulations like SOX, the General Data Protection Regulation (GDPR) from the European Union (EU), and so on.

7.1   Authorization Fundamentals

Before you learn how to configure authorizations, let's explore some basic concepts.

7.1.1   What is a Role?

In SAP, there are mainly two types of roles: single roles and composite roles. A *single role* contains all authorization objects and field values required for a transaction to be executed. You can derive single roles from their organizational values into derived roles. A *derived role* by its technical nature is still a single role that inherits its functional authorizations from a master role. A *composite role*, on the other hand, is a collection of single and derived roles that you can group into a common composite role menu.

Once a role contains at least one authorization object and gets generated, the system automatically creates an authorization profile for the role. The relationship between role and profile is *1:n*, which means a role can have more than one profile. A profile is limited to 150 authorization objects. Once that limit is reached, multiple profiles are generated automatically. You can see the generated profile in the **Authorizations** tab in the Profile Generator (Transaction PFCG).

> **Tip**
>
> Table AGR_1016 shows the generated profiles for a role. If a role has more than 150 authorization objects, you'll see two or more entries in the table. The COUNTER field will increase accordingly and show the number of profiles for the role.

7.1.2   What is a Profile?

Profiles existed long before roles. In versions before R/3, profiles were used to authorize users in the system. With the introduction of roles, the profile is the technical remainder required by the system. When a role is generated, it creates a profile that contains the actual authorization objects and its values. However, profiles are still available and can be used to authorize users. A common profile is SAP_ALL, as well as S_A.SYSTEM and S_A.DEVELOP. SAP_ALL is the most powerful authorization in an SAP system. It contains all authorizations.

7.1.3   Authorization Objects

Authorization objects are used to protect certain objects within the SAP system. SAP offers a wide range of authorization objects to protect and limit access to certain applications. Authorization objects contain at least one and a maximum of 10 fields with maintainable values. You can see all the available authorization objects in Transaction SU03 or Transaction SU21. With those transactions, you can also create and maintain customer-specific authorization objects. This, however, requires a developer key because it's a development-specific task.

In most cases, an authorization object consists of two fields: one is the activity field and the other the object to be protected.

> **Tip**
> Check table TOBJ to get a list of all authorization objects with the available authorization fields.

7.1.4   The Profile Generator

The Profile Generator (Transaction PFCG) is the central cockpit to create and maintain roles and authorization data. It allows you to create and change your own role, SAP standard roles, and any other roles that exist in the system. The Profile Generator also lets you assign users to roles.

7.1.5   Authorization Checks

The SAP system checks for a user's authorization at different levels (see Figure 7.1). The first check is at the start of the transaction, also referred as the *TSTC check*. In this first check, the system validates the transaction against table TSTC to check whether the transaction exists and that it isn't locked. In a second step, the system checks whether the user is authorized to start the transaction via the authorization object S_TCODE and the *TSTCA check*. Additional authorization checks are coded in the program. Whereas the S_TCODE and TSTCA checks decide whether a user can start the transaction or not, the authority checks in the program allow you to more granularly check what a user can display, maintain, execute, delete, and so on from the program.

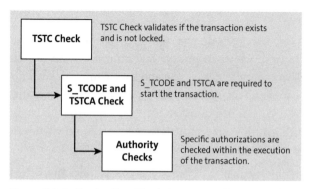

Figure 7.1 Authorization Check Sequence of Transaction

At Transaction Start

The common checks at the transaction start are TSTC, S_TCODE, and the TSTCA check. Whenever a user executes a transaction, the system automatically performs the TSTC check and validates if the transaction exists and isn't locked. If successful, it checks for the S_TCODE object. To increase the security of a transaction, Transaction SE93 (Figure 7.2) allows you to add further authorization checks at transaction start.

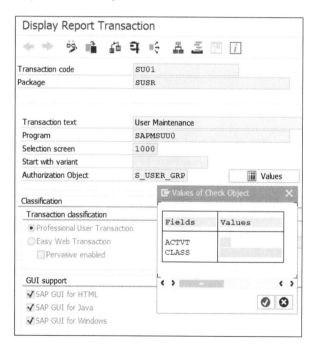

Figure 7.2 Display Transaction SU01 in Transaction SE93

Those additional checks are stored in table TSTCA. After S_TCODE is successful, the system automatically checks the authorization object TSTCA and its values. This non-mandatory check adds an additional level of security especially for sensitive transactions such as Transaction SU01 or Transaction PFCG. Both authorization checks, S_TCODE and TSTCA, must be successful to start the transaction.

In the Program

Once the S_TCODE and the TSTCA checks are successful, the program is executed. Depending on the level of complexity, the program can display certain fields, grey fields out, or hide them. Also, it allows you to distinguish among certain actions a user can perform within that program. To achieve different behavior, the outcome of the authority check decides whether a user can view, update, delete, execute, or perform other such actions.

> **Tip**
>
> You can analyze the source code of a program with report RSABAPSC; scan for AUTHORITY-CHECK commands.

Exceptions

As always, there are exceptions to every rule. When it comes to the authority check, there are two main exceptions that must be considered. First, SAP allows you to deactivate the authority check for all objects other than those starting with S* and P*. All other objects can be deactivated globally. Second, in Transaction SU24 you can deactivate the **Check Indicator** field for authorization objects that do not belong to Basis or human resources (HR) components.

7.1.6 Display Authorization Data

As security administrators, we often face the issue that a user can't execute certain transactions or gets authorization failures while running a specific transaction. Troubleshooting such issues sounds cumbersome, but with the proper tools it isn't. Investigating authorization failures for a user mostly starts with Transaction SU53, one of the basic transactions each user should have. With Transaction SU53, we can detect the failed authorization checks only, which is also the largest limitation of this transaction as it does not show which authorization checks were successful. Once a user experiences an authorization issue, he should immediately go to Transaction SU53 and forward a screenshot to you. For a security administrator, that information often leads to the problem and lets you correct a user's roles.

In Figure 7.3, the user was successfully able to start Transaction FK03 (Display Vendors) but got an authorization error when trying to access vendors from company code 0001.

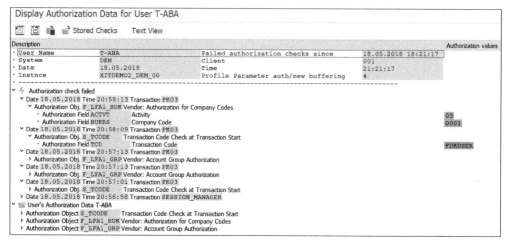

Figure 7.3 Example of Display Authorization Data in Transaction SU53

As an administrator with authorization to view users in the system (authorization object S_USER_GRP with ACTVT 03 and access to certain user groups), you can also check the authorization data from other users. Click the third button from the left (**Display for Different User**) in the toolbar of Transaction SU53 and enter the user name, as shown in Figure 7.4.

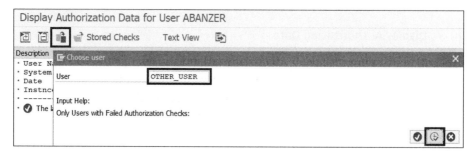

Figure 7.4 Display Authorization Data for Another User in Transaction SU53

We recommend that you advise users to immediately go to Transaction SU53 once they experience an authorization issue and to send a screenshot of the fully expanded failed authorization check to an administrator.

7.1.7 The User Buffer

The user buffer (Transaction SU56) contains all authorizations that a user is authorized for. The user buffer is filled during the logon procedure and remains active until the user logs out or restarts the SAP menu (command /n). In the user buffer, you can check all authorization objects and their values. As an administrator, you can also check the user buffer of other users in the system by clicking the **Display for other user/authorization object** button and entering the user ID, as shown in Figure 7.5.

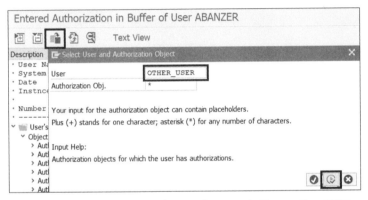

Figure 7.5 Display User Buffer for Another User in Transaction SU56

The user buffer is very helpful when you want to check if a user has certain authorization objects and values without checking each role assigned to the user.

7.1.8 Maintain Check Indicators: Transaction SU24

In prior chapters, you've seen different authorization checks that can be introduced. How does the security administrator know which authorizations must be maintained for a certain transaction? Certainly, there are security administrators out there that know all transactions by heart. But what about everyone else?

With Transaction SU24, you can maintain proposals for transactions, reports, function modules, and so on. In this transaction, you can maintain default values for authority checks that are proposed in the Profile Generator (Transaction PFCG) when a transaction is added to the role. That simplifies the maintenance of a transaction drastically, as it proposes standard values that must be maintained in any case to successfully execute a transaction. In addition, Transaction SU24 allows you not only to maintain authorization proposals but also to deactivate certain authorization checks for certain transactions by switching the check indicator to **Do Not Check**.

Let's look at Transaction SU01 and see what's been maintained in Figure 7.6.

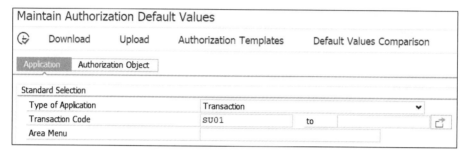

Figure 7.6 Maintain Authorization Default Values in Transaction SU24 for Transaction SU01

In Transaction SU24, you can see that a whole list of authorization objects are maintained for Transaction SU01, as shown in Figure 7.7. What information here is important to know?

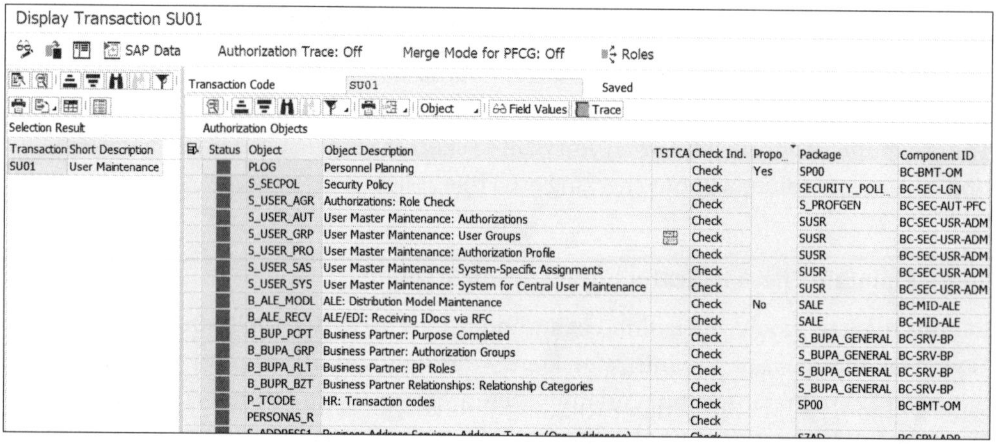

Figure 7.7 Authorization Proposals for Transaction SU01

In the sixth column (**Proposal**), we can see which objects are mandatory and hence must be maintained to successfully use the transaction. Those proposals come with the proposal status as **Yes**. In the fourth column (**TSTCA**), we see the proposal for the mandatory object that has been maintained in Transaction SE93, which is checked at transaction start.

If we double-click an authorization object, we can also define its values, if known. For example, you can see in Figure 7.8 that the authorization object **S_USER_GRP** proposes activity 03 (display) and 08 (execute) but no **CLASS** (user group). If the transaction is added to a role via Transaction PFCG, the system automatically proposes **S_USER_GRP** with **ACTVT** 01, 02, 03, 05, 06, 78. The administrator then only has to maintain the **CLASS** (user groups).

Default Authorization Values (S_USER_GRP)			
Object	Field name	From To	Display
S_USER_GRP	ACTVT	01	👓
		02	👓
		03	👓
		05	👓
		06	👓
		78	👓
	CLASS		👓

Figure 7.8 Value Proposals for S_USER_GRP

It's important to understand that simply adding an authorization object to Transaction SU24 doesn't mean it's being checked. All checks other than S_TCODE and TSTCA must be implemented in the code with the AUTHORITY-CHECK statement. However, if you want to deactivate an AUTHORITY-CHECK from the code, you can do that with the **Check Indicator** column by changing to **Do Not Check**. It's only possible to change the **Check Indicator** for objects other than those for HR and Basis.

7.1.9 System Trace

If a user has problems accessing a transaction or program, missing or inappropriate authorizations are usually the cause. To analyze missing authorizations, an administrator can activate the system trace to see what authority checks the system performs. The system trace is considered a short-term trace and should only be activate for a certain time. In Transaction ST01, the administrator can switch on the system trace for authorizations (along with other traces) on the local application server. If a system consists of more than one application server, the trace only records findings when the user (for whom the trace has been activated) is logged on to the same application server as the administrator. In later SAP NetWeaver versions (check SAP Note

1603756 to see which ones), Transaction STAUTHTRACE was introduced, which allows you to switch on the system trace globally. As an additional benefit, the reporting has been increased and now allows you to filter, remove duplicates, and more.

> **Tip**
>
> Use Transaction STAUTHTRACE for system-wide traces. With its increased reporting capabilities, not only is it easier to analyze the log files, but it offers an ALV view to drill down into the source.

In Transaction STAUTHTRACE (Figure 7.9), the administrator can activate the trace for specific users only. For the evaluation, the report allows you to filter duplicate entries and use some other filter criteria.

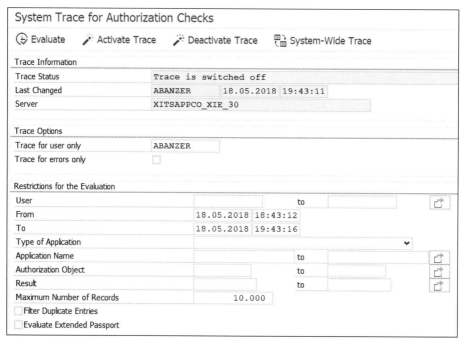

Figure 7.9 System Trace for Authorization Checks in Transaction STAUTHTRACE

Once the trace is switched on, as shown in Figure 7.10, the system will automatically log the authorization checks for the defined user(s). Depending on whether **Trace for errors only** has been selected, the trace file may only contain failed authorization checks. In Figure 7.11, we can see successful and unsuccessful checks.

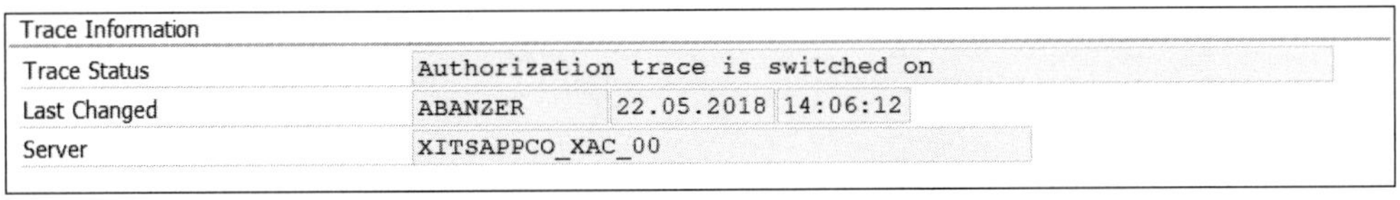

Trace Information	
Trace Status	Authorization trace is switched on
Last Changed	ABANZER 22.05.2018 14:06:12
Server	XITSAPPCO_XAC_00

Figure 7.10 Authorization Trace Switched On

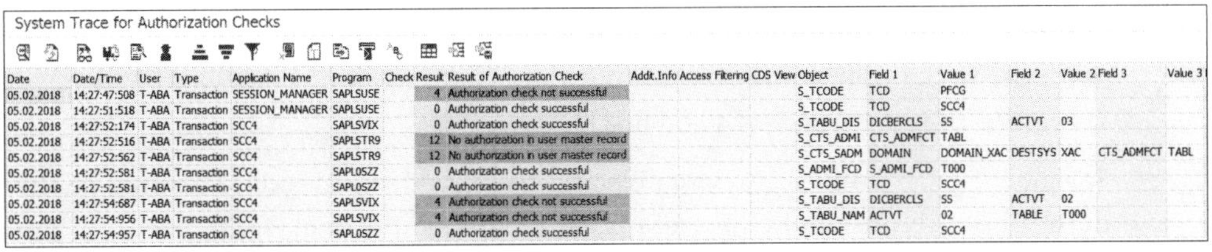

Figure 7.11 Example Trace: User T-ABA Logged on and Started Transaction SCC4

Figure 7.11 shows that some authorization checks passed whereas others failed. Particularly interesting are the ones marked in red, which are those that failed.

The return code of an authority check defines why and what was missing. Any return code greater than 0 indicates that the authorization check failed, and it will provide more details of what was missing.

Table 7.1 lists the return codes and their descriptions.

Return Code	Description
0	Authorization check successful.
4	Authorization check not successful. However, the user has the authorization object but not the expected value.
12	Authorization check not successful because the user does not have the authorization in the user master record.
40	The checked user does not exist.

Table 7.1 Authorization Check Return Codes

Let's take a closer look at an example with the S_TABU_DIS object, as shown in Figure 7.12.

177

User	Type	Applic.	Program	Che...	Result	Result of Authorization Check	Object	Field 1	Value 1	Field 2	Value
T-ABA	Transaction	SCC4	SAPLSVIX		0	Authorization check successful	S_TABU_DIS	DICBERCLS	SS	ACTVT	03
T-ABA	Transaction	SCC4	SAPLSVIX		4	Authorization check not successful	S_TABU_DIS	DICBERCLS	SS	ACTVT	02

Figure 7.12 Authorization Check for S_TABU_DIS Object

Figure 7.12 shows that the first check on the S_TABU_DIS object was successful. The second check indicates that the user clicked on a button that requested activity (**ACTVT** field) **02**, which means change. The return code gets value 4, because activity 02 does not exist in the user master record, but the object exists with activity 03 (display). Therefore, the return code is 4 and not 12.

For the S_CTS_ADMI and S_CTS_SADM objects, we received return code 12 because neither of the objects is present in the user master record, as shown in Figure 7.13.

User	Type	Applic.	Program	Che...	Result	Result of Authorization Check	Object	Field 1	Value 1	Field 2	Value	Field 3	Value
T-ABA	Transaction	SCC4	SAPLST		12	No authorization in user master record	S_CTS_ADMI	CTS_ADMFCT	TABL				
T-ABA	Transaction	SCC4	SAPLST		12	No authorization in user master record	S_CTS_SADM	DOMAIN	DOMAIN_XAC	DESTSYS	XAC	CTS_ADMFCT	TABL

Figure 7.13 Authorization Check for S_CTS ADMI and S_CTS_SADM Objects

Transaction STAUTHTRACE also allows you to extend the system trace with data from the system kernel (Transaction STAD). To do so, select the **Evaluate Extended Passport** option from the initial screen. This option enriches data especially for inbound RFC calls and adds the following fields at the end of the output list:

- **Initial Component**
  Adds the calling system and its instance and client

- **ActionType**
  Adds the type of action, such as transaction call, batch processing, and so on

- **Initial Action**
  Adds the transaction or job name

Figure 7.14 shows these three additional columns at the far right. With the **Initial Component** column, you can identify where the call initiated. In this example, it was an inbound RFC from another system.

System Trace for Authorization Checks

User Name	Type of Application	Application Name	Result	Result of Authorization Check	Object	Field 1	Value 1	Field 2	Value 2	Field 3	Value	Initial Component	ActionType	Initial Action
GRC_RFC	RFC Function Module	BAPI_USER_DISPLAY	0	Authorization check successful	S_RFC	RFC_TYPE	FUGR	RFC_NAME	SU_USER	ACTV	16	XIE/XITSAPPCO_XIE_30/001	Transaction	SE37
GRC_RFC	RFC Function Module	BAPI_USER_DISPLAY	0	Authorization check successful	S_USER_GRP	CLASS	SUPER	ACTVT	03			XIE/XITSAPPCO_XIE_30/001	Transaction	SE37
ABANZER	Transaction	STAUTHTRACE	0	Authorization check successful	S_ADMI_FCD	STOR						XAC/XITSAPPCO_XAC_00/001	Transaction	STAUTHTRACE
ABANZER	Transaction	STAUTHTRACE	0	Authorization check successful	S_ALV_LAYO	ACTVT	23					XAC/XITSAPPCO_XAC_00/001	Transaction	STAUTHTRACE

Figure 7.14 Transaction STAUTHTRACE with Extended Passport Data from Transaction STAD

Reuse Trace Data in Transaction PFCG

With SAP ERP Enhancement Package (EHP) 6, SAP introduced another handy feature to reuse data from the authorization trace in your role maintenance process. Whether you use Transaction ST01 or Transaction STAUTHTRACE, the trace data can be loaded into Transaction PFCG. In Transaction PFCG, you have two options to use the trace data. The first option is to import the trace when you build your roles' menu (Figure 7.15). When you create the menu from the trace, the system adds the objects that show up in the fields **S_TCODE**, **S_SERVICE**, and **S_RFC** to your menu.

Figure 7.15 Import from Trace in Transaction PFCG

In the import evaluation pop-up, as shown in Figure 7.16, you can evaluate the trace and choose which objects you want to insert into your roles. Select the objects you want to have in your role and click the **Transfer** button. Once the objects are selected and visible in the left window, insert them into your role by clicking **Insert as List**, or alternatively click **Insert as SAP Menu** or **Insert as Area Menu**.

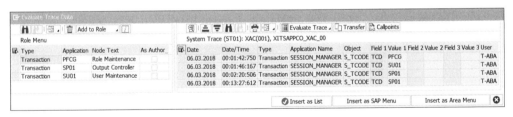

Figure 7.16 Evaluate Trace Data in Transaction PFCG

If you want to enrich your authorizations with trace data, you can use the functionality in the authorizations maintenance screen, as shown in Figure 7.17. Click the **Trace** button and load your trace data. Once loaded, you can select authorizations that you want to transfer to your role. Choose an authorization object that you want to check, evaluate the trace, and decide whether you want to move those values from the trace into the role.

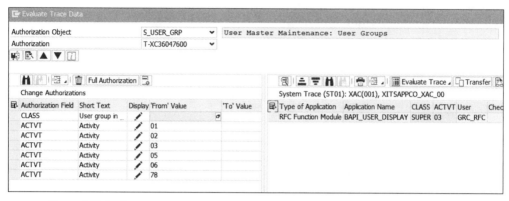

Figure 7.17 Evaluate Trace Data in Authorizations in Transaction PFCG

The trace import functionality is a handy feature to move findings based on a trace into Transaction PFCG. Not only can you build your role menu, you can also enrich the authorization values that need to be maintained based on the trace.

Other Traces

An *authorization trace* (Transaction STUSOBTRACE) is a long-term trace that collects data from all clients. The data is stored in database table USOB_AUTHVALTRC. You can reuse the trace data in Transaction PFCG, as described in the previous subsection.

The *user trace for authorization checks* (Transaction STUSERTRACE) is also a long-term trace that collects data from the client when it's activated. Trace data is stored in table SUAUTHVALTRC. The trace saves the checked authorizations during the execution of a program. It doesn't save duplicates because it only keeps the first record with the very first timestamp.

7.2   SAP Role Design Concepts

This section compares three common SAP role design concepts and explains the pros and cons of each approach: single roles, composite roles, and enabler roles. Each of the concepts can either follow a task- or job-based approach to authorize end users.

7.2.1 Single Roles

A single role contains all the authorization objects and field values (organizational and nonorganizational) required for the transactions that the role contains. In SAP, authorization objects are represented by two types of fields: the so-called activity field and the organization value field. Technically, you can't separate the two fields, because the SAP kernel evaluates them together during an authority check, and hence they must be in the same role. However, a single role can have multiple individual authorization instances to depict different combinations of the field values when they can't be merged into one authorization instance to be evaluated by the check. Therefore, a single role can also be a composite of authorization instances.

Typically, when people talk about a *single role* concept, they're referring to a job- or position-based role design. In such cases, all required authorizations for a user's job/position are contained in a single role. A user might, however, have more than one job/position. Such a user will be assigned multiple single roles, such as purchaser and contract manager—each of these single roles will contain a complete authorization set to execute transactions, so that the roles are functional on their own. There are no dependencies.

However, many "single role" designs don't contain all of a user's required authorizations. It's not uncommon to create a "basic authorization" role that contains transactions and authorizations that are common for all users. For example, the ability to print or to get to the SAP Business Workplace. Likewise, some employees might have additional authorizations to execute special tasks. As a result, such employees may get a "special task" single role assigned to them—for example, the ability to close accounting periods or approve purchase requisitions.

7.2.2 Derived Roles

You can also use single roles for role derivation. Derived roles consist of a so-called master or parent role and additional child roles that differ from the master and each other only in their organizational values. Note that there are limitations to this approach. If you try to promote nonorganizational fields to organizational fields, then the values must all be the same within one role, regardless of which authorization object is using the field. In other words, you shouldn't use different nonorganizational fields in combination with derived roles because the values across all child roles will always be the same as the master role and will affect all objects.

7.2.3   Composite Roles

A *composite role* is a collection of single roles that you can group into a common composite role menu. As a result, you can indirectly assign multiple single roles to a user by assigning only the composite role that contains the single roles. That makes the temptation greater to build smaller single roles without considering required user assignments while doing so.

Many SAP customers leverage composite roles to reduce the number of single roles that are assigned directly to users. However, this often leads to less transparency, higher effort needed to maintain more roles, and an increased risk of cross-pollination from a single role to multiple composites. The ability to change the single roles rapidly reduces the side effect of having more single roles.

Technically, a composite role is a bundling of single roles to map a task-level single role or, in the worst-case scenario, a single role per transaction to a composite role. The aim is that the assignment to the user can be a functional unit or position in the organizational structure. In addition to the number of single roles that result from this, the organizational structure and its changes also play a part in the choice of concept.

7.2.4   Enabler Roles

In recent years, we've seen role concepts in which the SAP standard has been broken. These are often called *enabler* or *value role* concepts. In these concepts, you separate the organizational authorization values from their functional authorizations. That results in needing two roles to successfully execute a transaction.

In these concepts, the functional role gets all the authorization objects and values, but not the organizational level. A second, required enabler role that contains the "missing" organizational values enlarges the users' authorization. Therefore, to successfully execute a transaction, a user requires the functional role and a corresponding enabler role.

The idea behind enabler roles is mostly to isolate the organizational fields and simplify the user assignments when it comes to organizational distinction. However, any organizational type of field, which also has an activity field in the same authorization object, can't be separated into a different role.

That's almost always the case in SAP authorization objects. Because of this disadvantage, enabler roles can't work as they're sometimes envisioned. The typical result is a proliferation of authorizations in the enabler roles and the number of enabler roles, which often exceeds the number of users.

An enabler role concept sometimes looks tempting in PowerPoint presentations, and some customers might expect enabler roles to behave similarly to organizational management in the SAP ERP Human Capital Management (HCM) module. However, you can't apply it to authorization objects and role-based authorization concepts nor to the modern menu-based visibility access concepts such as SAP Fiori applications and SAP Enterprise Portal/SAP Business Warehouse (BW) reporting.

7.2.5 Comparison of the Role Design Concepts

Table 7.2 gives a detailed overview of the pros and cons of each role design concept. The table is a product of years of experience and best practices by SAP consulting. The traffic lights show how well each concept supports the listed requirements: WS means well-supported, PS means partly supported, NS means not supported, and NA means not applicable.

Requirements	Enabler Roles	Single Roles (with Optional Derivation)	Composite Roles
Effort of initial role definition	WS	WS	PS
Possibility to optimize grouping of functions	PS	WS	PS
Possibility to individualize role assignments	NS	WS	PS
Reduction of functional/organizational redundancies	PS	WS	PS
Effort of functional role maintenance	NS	WS	NS
Effort of organizational role maintenance	PS	PS	PS
Effort of user assignment maintenance	NS	PS	PS
Compliance in data protection at role level	WS	WS	WS

Table 7.2 Comparison of Different Role Designs

Requirements	Enabler Roles	Single Roles (with Optional Derivation)	Composite Roles
Compliance with SoD	PS	WS	WS
Possibility of role mining	PS	PS	NS
Cascading of SAP role design	NA	WS	NS
Reporting (auditing, transparency)	NS	WS	PS
Upgrade capability (e.g., enhancement packages, SAP S/4HANA)	NS	WS	NS
Post-maintenance	NS	WS	NS

Table 7.2 Comparison of Different Role Designs (Cont.)

As you can see, single roles (with optional derivation) are considered the best practice for SAP role design. They offer the greatest flexibility, transparency, and the broadest support of requirements and changes with upgrades. On the other side of the spectrum, we have enabler roles, which are the least flexible and have several design and maintenance disadvantages.

7.2.6   Why Not Use Enabler Roles?

An enabler role concept is a nonstandard approach to role design. Its origin comes from the assumption that it isn't possible to create a role that can display all items but only change a subset. This is because an authorization object with two or more fields will check all of them and require that they're present in the same role authorization.

Let's look at a simple example of an enabler role for Transaction FK03 (Display Vendors) in Figure 7.18.

The transactional single role contains Transaction FK03 with all its authorization objects and values. The organizational level (BUKRS in this example) for object F_LFA1_BUK is left empty.

A second role, the so-called enabler role, contains the organizational values for object F_LFA1_BUK only, as shown in Figure 7.19.

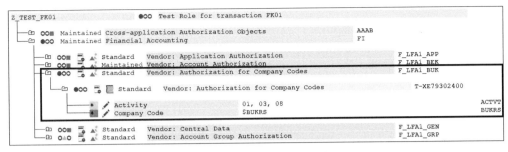

Figure 7.18 Example of Transactional Role for Transaction FK03

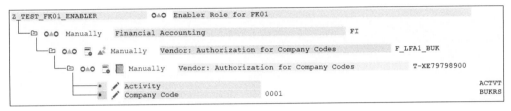

Figure 7.19 Example of Enabler Role for F_LFA1_BUK Object

In the user buffer (Transaction SU56), you can see the two authorization profiles assigned to the user (Figure 7.20).

```
∨ 🗔 User's Authorization Data T-ABA
  > Object Class AAAB          Cross-application Authorization Objects
  > Object Class BC_A          Basis: Administration
  > Object Class BC_C          Basis - Development Environment
  > Object Class BC_Z          Basis - Central Functions
  ∨ Object Class FI            Financial Accounting
    > Authorization Object F_LFA1_APP Vendor: Application Authorization
    > Authorization Object F_LFA1_BEK Vendor: Account Authorization
    ∨ Authorization Object F_LFA1_BUK Vendor: Authorization for Company Codes
      ∨ Authorizat. T-XE79302400
        · Profl. T-XE793024    Profile for role Z_TEST_FK01
        · Role Z_TEST_FK01 Transaction Role for FK01
        ∨ Authorization Field ACTVT Activity
          ·                                                              01, 03, 08
        ∨ Authorization Field BUKRS Company Code
          ·                                                              ' '
      ∨ Authorizat. T-XE79799000
        · Profl. T-XE797990    Profile for role Z_TEST_FK01_ENABLER
        · Role Z_TEST_FK01_ENABLER Enabler Role for FK01
        ∨ Authorization Field ACTVT Activity
          ·                                                              ' '
        ∨ Authorization Field BUKRS Company Code
          ·                                                              0001
    > Authorization Object F_LFA1_GEN Vendor: Central Data
    > Authorization Object F_LFA1_GRP Vendor: Account Group Authorization
  > Object Class HR            Human Resources
```

Figure 7.20 Example of Authorizations for User with Both Roles Assigned

You can see that the two authorizations are in different authorization profiles. Each time the SAP kernel performs an authority check, it checks the values in one authorization profile. Let's see if Transaction FK03 works for the user who has both roles assigned (Figure 7.21).

Figure 7.21 Example of Executing Transaction FK03

The user can successfully execute the transaction but is unable to view vendors in company code 0001, even though the enabler role contains the company code. However, because the SAP kernel checks the activity and the company code in the same authorization profile, the authorization check is unsuccessful. Therefore, it isn't possible to have the activity in one role and the organizational field in another and expect that the check will be successful as a whole. This type of enabler role design also leads to several other issues:

- It breaks the SAP standard. Transaction SU24 is used to propose required authorization objects in Transaction PFCG. Breaking this standard and manually inserting objects will impact upgrades, security patches, complexity, where-used-list reporting, and so on.

- With enabler roles, role administrators must use manually inserted objects instead of relying on solid Transaction SU24 proposals for the activity-type fields. However, applications need Transaction SU24 proposals, and they're visible in the user's menu. Over time, when the role requirements change, this typically leads to obsolete authorization values and a mess that no longer matches the original intention to "enable" the transaction.

- Post-maintenance of roles is typically more labor-intensive than in a derived role design due to the lack of automation. The number of enabler roles explodes such that there are more roles than there are users in the system.

- You can't run an SoD analysis on role level because most available tools (e.g., SAP GRC Access Control) check on the TCODE and AUTH object level. If the transactions, activities, and organizational authorization objects are separated, you'd need to simulate the correct pairing of roles to have the full set of authorizations to be assigned to a user. Note that SoD conflicts matter the most when assigned to a user. At this point, enabler role concept users are tempted to also use composite roles for the assignments, thus adding the additional disadvantages of composite roles on top of the enabler roles.

- It increases the complexity of role mining during the user provisioning process. For a requestor who has to request access, finding two roles is significantly harder than finding one—especially when using tools like SAP Identity Management or SAP GRC Access Control, because it forces the requestor to not only understand the concept but also identify and find the matching pair of roles.

- Role testing becomes exponentially more difficult because it requires testing a pair of roles. This is especially true if the organizational structure changes and the roles to be tested must reflect the changes.

Most of these issues arise because of missing Transaction SU24 content. Over time and by necessity, the manually inserted authorization objects become obsolete and overauthorize a user. Because manually inserted objects aren't attached to a transaction, there's no identification for which transaction they belong to and why they were added to the enabler role in the first place. This results in maintaining and upgrading the roles becoming a nightmare in the long run.

If composite roles are used for user assignments, then a cascading of the problem occurs and changing the enabler roles is nearly impossible—so the administrators typically create additional, new enabler roles.

7.2.7 What Impact Does a System Upgrade Have on Roles and Authorizations?

Due to new requirements and improvements, system landscapes change over time. Nowadays, many customers are planning to migrate to SAP S/4HANA. Others are upgrading to the latest Enhancement Packages. Every upgrade comes with new and enhanced authorizations and requires roles to be adjusted accordingly. When implementing new value proposals via Transaction SU25 into Transaction SU24, your roles need to be updated to include the latest changes. When using fewer single roles that are more closely aligned with job functions, the Transaction SU24 upgrade and impact analysis on the roles can be performed without any problems. For instance, say that a standard transaction gets a new organizational object that's required to use the transaction successfully. When performing Transaction SU25 and upgrading your roles from Transaction SU24, the role will have the new organizational object proposed automatically. Also, the roles carry the where-used list of an authorization object. This is especially important when performing SoD remediation tasks because it shows you which authorization object belongs to which transaction. Not having the where-used list means that you can only guess to which transaction the authorization object belongs.

However, if you're using enabler roles, upgrading roles can be a formidable task because you have no where-used list references and you typically have many more roles than you need.

7.2.8 Role-Naming Conventions

Before you start building your roles, we recommend spending some time to come up with a role-naming convention that suites your organization. It's a common mistake that roles are built without any convention, resulting in a messy design that's hard to maintain in the long run. Also, a lack of naming conventions increases the complexity of finding and assigning roles to an end user—especially when tools such as SAP Identity Management or SAP GRC Access Control are used for role provisioning through workflows in which a requester has to enter the roles to be assigned to a user.

Table 7.3 shows an example of a role-naming convention that's been implemented successfully with many clients. The table denotes which character or characters are used in which position in the role name. Character 1 is the first character in the name, character 2 is the second character in the name, and so on.

Character	Description	Examples
1	Fixed value "Z" for customer namespace	
2	Identifier for the system level	P: Production D: Development T: Test S: Sandbox Q: Quality I: Integration
3	Fixed underscore (_) character for separation	
4	Identifier for role type	S: Single role C: Composite role M: Master role
5	Identifier for user group	C: "Common" role for basic functions for all users E: End user role for job function I: IT roles for administrators, developers, and so on T: Technical roles for RFC, batch, web services, and so on R: Reference user roles
6	Fixed underscore (_) character for separation	
7 - 8	Identifier for business area or SAP module	BC: Basis BI: Business Intelligence CR: Customer Relations CO: Controlling EC: SAP ERP component FI: Finance

Table 7.3 Example of Role-Naming Convention

Character	Description	Examples
7 - 8 (Cont.)		HR: Human Resources MM: Material Management PI: Process Integration PS: Project Systems SD: Sales and Distribution SM: SAP Solution Manager SR: Supplier Relations
9	Fixed underscore (_) character for separation	
10	Identifier for leading organizational element	A: All N: None C: Company code P: Purchasing organization S: Sales organizations P: Plant D: Division
11	Fixed underscore (_) character for separation	
12 - 15	Organizational value for the organizational element	A–GLOB: All N–GLOB: None C–$BUKRS: Value from company code S–$VKORG: Value from sales organization P–$WERKS: Value from plant
16	Fixed underscore (_) character for separation	

Table 7.3 Example of Role-Naming Convention (Cont.)

Character	Description	Examples
17 - 19	Identifier for activity group in regard to the user group	COM: Common authorizations REP: Reporting with display-only authorization EAM: Emergency access authorizations KEY: Key user authorizations MDM: Master data authorization ADM: Administration authorization HPU: High-privileged user authorizations
20	Fixed underscore (_) character for separation	
21 and beyond	Free text	

Table 7.3 Example of Role-Naming Convention (Cont.)

Based on Table 7.3, here are a few examples of how such a naming convention might apply:

- **ZP_SI_BC_N_GLOB_HPU_OPEN_CLIENT**
  A single role for a productive system that doesn't include any organizational data and is considered a high-privileged user role to open clients.

- **ZP_CE_FI_C_1000_REP_ACCOUNTANT**
  A composite role for a productive system that includes organizational values for company code 100 with display-only access for reporting purposes for an accountant.

- **ZD_SI_BC_N_GLOB_HPU_DEVELOPER**
  A single role for a development system that doesn't include any organizational data and is considered a high-privilege user role for developers.

With the role-naming conventions described in this section, it's possible to both find roles easily and to understand what each role does—for both an administrator and an end user. Also, because the identifiers are defined and follow a specific pattern, role analysis can be simplified. For example, a role that contains "REP" in characters 17 to 19 is a reporting-only role, which shouldn't contain any insert, change, update, or delete authorizations. For role quality and sustainability purposes, a strictly enforced role-naming convention is therefore mandatory.

7.3   The Profile Generator

For role maintenance, we use the Profile Generator from Transaction PFCG. The Profiler Generator differentiates between single and composite roles that must be selected before any action can be taken. The Profile Generator automatically creates authorization data based on the selected objects from the role menu. It's therefore important that transactions, function modules, Web Dynpro applications, and so on are added to the role via the role menu. Only then can the Profiler Generator utilize Transaction SU24 authorization proposals and build a where-used list.

With the Profile Generator, you can create and maintain several types of roles—single and composite roles, as well as master and derived roles from a single role. Derived roles only differ in the organizational level from their master roles.

7.3.1   Create a Single Role

To create a role, you have to define a role name, which can be up to 30 characters long, and then click the type of role. For this example, select **Single Role**, as shown in Figure 7.22. Ideally, you'll have defined your role-naming convention before you start building your roles. The role definition is saved to table AGR_DEFINE.

Figure 7.22 Create Role in Transaction PFCG

Each role requires a **Role** name and a **Description**, as shown in Figure 7.23. Once entered, the role can be saved. The role description is saved to table AGR_TEXTS.

Role	
Role	Z_TEST_SINGLE_ROLE
Description	Test Single Role
Target System	

Figure 7.23 Define Role Description

In the **Description** tab, you should document the purpose of the role and give more information about what functionality is authorized, as shown in Figure 7.24. You can also use this area to document the history of changes to the role.

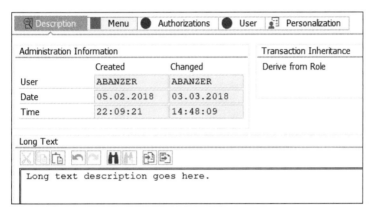

Figure 7.24 Role Description Tab

The **Transaction Inheritance** area will show the imparting master role that can be used as a reference. The master role propagates the functional authorizations to its child roles. The child roles only differ in their organizational levels, which must be maintained.

Visiting the **Menu** tab (Figure 7.25) is the first step when creating and defining a role. In the menu, you define the transactions, function modules, Web Dynpro applications, and so on to be authorized with a particular role. Defining objects from the menu is important because it considers the Transaction SU24 authorization proposals. For example, if you want to authorize a user for Transaction SU01, you don't know which authorization objects are required. Therefore, SAP has predelivered authorization proposals that can be used in the Profile Generator.

Figure 7.25 Available Objects to Be Added to Role Menu

You can also copy menus (Figure 7.26) from other objects, like another role, the SAP menu, or even from a trace. This option allows you to quickly define a menu based on another object.

Menu Options (Figure 7.27) allows you to define certain attributes of the role, such as whether the menu will show up in the SAP Easy Access menu or in SAP NetWeaver Business Client.

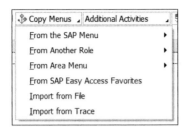

Figure 7.26 Available Options to Copy Menu

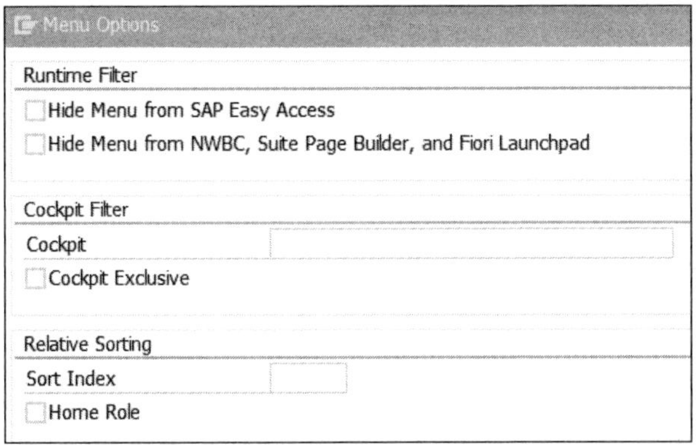

Figure 7.27 Menu Options in Profile Generator

The **Role Menu** (Figure 7.28) also allows you to create a hierarchy with folders to increase the visibility of objects in the users' menu. We recommend that you create a company menu and use that throughout your roles. Only then will users have a common menu that they can rely on to simplify the finding process of transactions and objects.

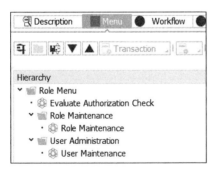

Figure 7.28 Role Menu Hierarchy in Transaction PFCG

In the **Authorization** tab (Figure 7.29), you can see who created and changed the role, as well as the profile name that was generated. To maintain the authorization data and to generate the profile, there are two buttons available. The first, **Change Authorization Data**, is the quick and dirty way to maintain a role and is not recommended because it doesn't consider Transaction SU24 values. Instead, use **Expert Mode for Profile Generation** to properly maintain the roles.

Figure 7.29 Authorization Tab in Profile Generator

If you click the **Expert Mode for Profile Generation** button, the system will ask you what action you want to execute, as shown in Figure 7.30.

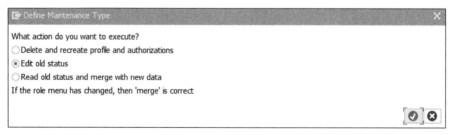

Figure 7.30 Available Maintenance Types in Profile Generator

The three available maintenance types work as follows:

1. **Delete and recreate profile and authorizations** is used to delete all the authorizations from the role and pull new data from Transaction SU24. Remember, this will delete all data that has previously been maintained.

2. **Edit old status** is the same as the not-recommended **Change Authorization Data** option, which doesn't consider Transaction SU24 when you make changes to the role.

3. **Read old status and merge with new data** is the recommended way to create and update your authorizations. In this mode, the Profile Generator pulls the authorization proposals from Transaction SU24 and merges them into the role.

Once you're in the authorizations, you'll see a screen similar to Figure 7.31. Here, you can maintain your authorization data related to the transactions that you've added in the role menu.

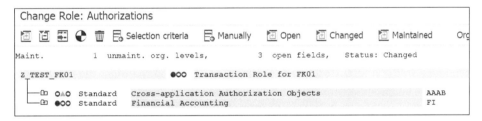

Figure 7.31 Change Authorizations for Role in Profile Generator

Each authorization object comes with two statuses that will indicate if and how the object was maintained. The traffic light (red, yellow, green) marks whether the object is completely maintained (green), maintainable values are missing (yellow), or organizational values are missing (red). The second status indicator, which tells you how the object was maintained, marks one of four different statuses for an authorization object:

- **Standard**
  The object and its authorizations come from Transaction SU24.

- **Maintained**
  The object and its authorizations come from Transaction SU24, and open authorizations that aren't maintained in Transaction SU24 were maintained by the administrator.

- **Changed**

  The object and its authorizations comes from Transaction SU24, but the administrator changed the automatic proposals.

- **Manually**

  The object was manually introduced to the role. There is no reference to which object it belongs.

Figure 7.32 shows the four different type of statuses a role can have.

Maintained	Old	Customer: Application Authorization	F_KNA1_APP
Standard	Old	Vendor: Application Authorization	F_LFA1_APP
Changed	New	Vendor: Account Authorization	F_LFA1_BEK
Manually	New	Vendor: Authorization for Company Codes	F_LFA1_BUK

Figure 7.32 Different Status of Authorization Objects in Transaction PFCG

The best practice approach is to maintain Transaction SU24 proposals and then use Transaction PFCG to propose the required authorizations for a transaction. The authorization proposals only work if the transaction is added via the role menu.

To maintain a role and build it sustainably, only the **Standard** and **Maintained** statuses should be used. If a proposal from Transaction SU24 needs to be changed, don't change it in the role; instead, go to Transaction SU24 and maintain the value properly. Once you update your Transaction SU24 values and merge the changes into the role, the role will get the latest Transaction SU24 proposals only if the authorization objects have the **Maintained** or **Standard** status.

Read Old, Merge New

With the read old, merge new data functionality, we can ensure that the role gets the latest updates from Transaction SU24. The authorization object status therefore is important to know. We'll discuss those in the next sections.

Status Standard

This status tells you that your role uses the data maintained in Transaction SU24. In Figure 7.33 authorization object F_LFA1_APP is pulled from Transaction FKO3.

Figure 7.33 Example of Authorization Object with Standard Status

If you update Transaction SU24 and merge the change into the role, it will automatically adjust the values. Let's assume we add the activity with value 08 (**Display Change Documents**) for Transaction FK03 in Transaction SU24 and merge the changes into the role, as shown in Figure 7.34.

Figure 7.34 Example of Updated Standard Authorization Object

We now can see an additional status, **Updated**, which tells us that the standard object has been updated with new values from Transaction SU24. Having standard values simplifies the role maintenance process and reduces risks during an upgrade because you can introduce new values automatically into the roles.

Status Maintained

An object gets the status **Maintained** (Figure 7.35) if the value of an authorization object in Transaction SU24 isn't maintained. This status tells you that you have to take care of the value because it couldn't be defined in Transaction SU24. Open values in Transaction SU24 are common and considered best practice because they allow the administrator to define the missing values during role maintenance.

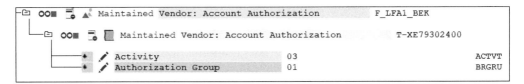

Figure 7.35 Example of Maintained Authorization Value

Status Changed

An object gets the status **Changed** if you manually change the proposed value of the authorization object (Figure 7.36). Changing value proposals is not recommended because it causes conflicts during upgrades and reduces the maintainability of the roles. If you consider a value proposal to be wrong, update Transaction SU24 accordingly or leave the field value open in Transaction SU24 so that you can maintain the field.

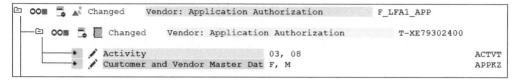

Figure 7.36 Example of Changed Authorization Value

If you use the read old, merge new functionality, the changed object will be reintroduced to the role. Next to the changed status, you'll see an indication that there has been a **New** value introduced. If you expand the object, you'll see which values are new and which are old (Figure 7.37).

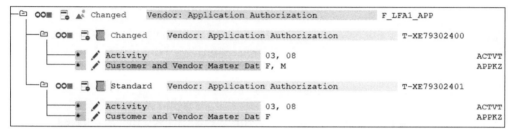

Figure 7.37 Example of Read Old, Merge New with Changed Object

Changing value proposals is not recommended because you'll have duplicated objects in your roles, as well as a decrease in maintainability.

Status Manually

Manually inserting objects (Figure 7.38) is the worst thing that you can possibly do. Not only is there no reference to a transaction (because it doesn't get pulled from Transaction SU24), but most likely manually inserted authorizations will result in orphaned and unmanageable roles and authorizations.

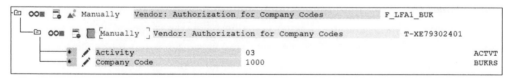

Figure 7.38 Example of Manually Introduced Authorization Object

Manually inserted objects cause issues during upgrades and reduce the maintainability of the roles. Also, you lose the reference to a transaction, which increases the complexity when removing transactions from a role later down the road. Avoid inserting objects manually whenever possible. If an authorization is required to successfully execute a transaction, then it should be maintained in Transaction SU24. Once maintained, use the read old, merge new functionality and the authorization object will be introduced to the role properly.

Organizational Values

Organizational values, or *org values*, authorize a user based on organizational belonging. Therefore, several business transactions require certain org values to function. All org values are authorization fields, but not all authorization fields are org values. Org values are maintained as a header-like set of data that is valid for the whole role. Once maintained, all authorization objects that require an org field will get the data proposed from the header.

To maintain the org values in a role, click the **Organizational Levels** button in the **Authorizations** screen of Transaction PFCG, as shown in Figure 7.39.

Figure 7.39 Change Role Authorizations Organizational Levels

Org levels are linked to the enterprise structure of your system and may vary depending on your customizing. As a security administrator, you don't create and maintain org levels in your system; you use them to protect certain areas of your organization. For example, SAP ERP has org values like **Company Code** (BUKRS), **Purchasing Organization** (EKORG), **Controlling Area** (KOKRS), **Sales Organization** (VKORG), **Plant** (WERKS), and so on (Figure 7.40).

If an org level isn't maintained, the corresponding fields in the role have a red status indicator (for unmaintained org levels) and the technical name of the org level (Figure 7.41).

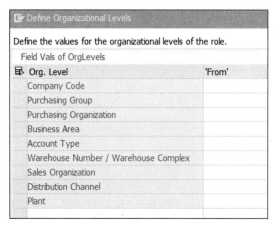

Figure 7.40 Example Organizational Levels

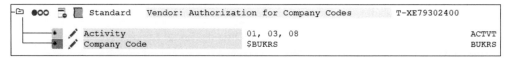

Figure 7.41 Open Org Values in Transaction PFCG

Once maintained, the value will change according to the header information and the status will become green (maintained field), as shown in Figure 7.42.

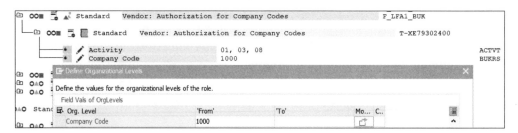

Figure 7.42 Maintained Org Level Company Code in Transaction PFCG

The advantage of org levels is that you can centrally maintain them once for the entire role. Therefore, you can build roles based on organizational restrictions and apply the derivation concept. It is possible to manually change instances of the maintained org fields, however, so that certain org fields don't match the org levels. If you change the field, as shown in Figure 7.43, the system automatically sets the authorization object as inactive and adds a new instance with the **Changed** status that contains the changed fields.

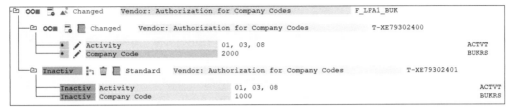

Figure 7.43 Manually Changed Org Field in Transaction PFCG

If you decide to change the org levels, the manually changed fields will remain. The system updates the inactivated org value instead.

Apart from using the standard org levels that can be customized, it's also possible to promote authorization fields to org levels. Promoting fields is mostly done to increase security, but it must be thoroughly analyzed because it can impact existing roles and authorizations. SAP delivers this capability with report PFCG_ORGFIELD_CREATE. We recommend reading SAP Note 323817 before using the report.

Where-Used Lists

The where-used list of a role is a very handy feature to sustainably maintain the roles. It not only tells you which objects belong to which transaction, it also helps you for remediation purposes when changing roles.

The where-used list is built based on Transaction SU24 proposals that come with a transaction. Only if the authorization object is proposed through Transaction SU24 can the Profile Generator build the where-used list. The where-used list can be pulled for an authorization object by clicking the button showing two triangles, highlighted in Figure 7.44.

In the pop-up, you can see that authorization object F_LFA1_AEN comes from Transaction FK03. If you change the authorization proposal for this authorization object in Transaction SU24, the Profile Generator will introduce that change through the read old, merge new functionality. Also, when removing transactions from a role, the Profile Generator will automatically remove the related authorizations objects from the role to avoid orphaned authorizations.

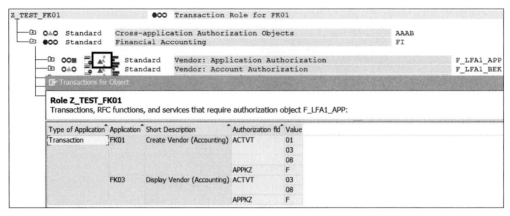

Figure 7.44 Example of Where-Used List in Profile Generator

7.3.2   Create a Composite Role

Composite roles were invented to simplify the assignments of single roles to a user. A composite role is a container that consists of one or more single roles. Once assigned to a user, the system automatically assigns the associated single roles indirectly to the user.

To create a composite role, you have to specify a name and click the **Composite Role** button in Transaction PFCG to start the creation (Figure 7.45).

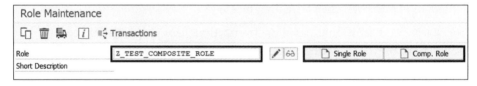

Figure 7.45 Create Composite Role in Transaction PFCG

Define a role **Description** and save the role. The composite role is then created and can be assigned to users (Figure 7.46).

To define the single roles to associate with the composite, go to the **Roles** tab and add the required roles (Figure 7.47). You can use the match code or input help ⌨F4 to search for single roles, or simply type them into the input list. You can also deactivate single roles from a composite. However, for readability purposes, we recommend removing a single role if not required any longer.

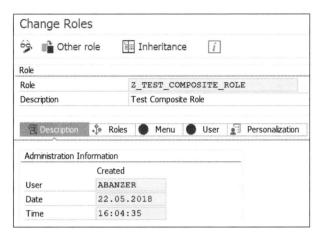

Figure 7.46 Created Composite Role in Transaction PFCG

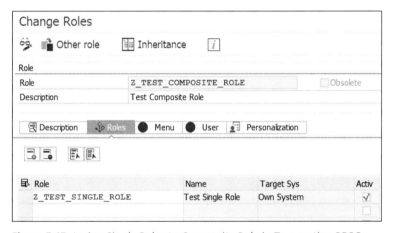

Figure 7.47 Assign Single Roles to Composite Role in Transaction PFCG

In the **Menu** tab, you can create the menu for composite roles. To read menus from the associated single roles, simply click on the **Import Menu** button (Figure 7.48), and the system reads the menu.

If you have different menu structures in your associated single roles, the system will merge them and display the results accordingly. In Figure 7.49, you can see a menu that is synchronized from the associated single role. If you wish, you can also create a menu structure manually. However, we recommend building it through the single roles because they contain the objects that belong to a menu.

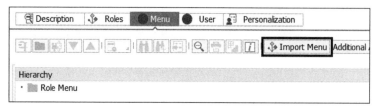

Figure 7.48 Role Menu in Composite Role

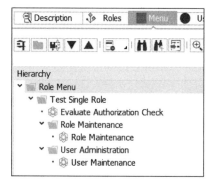

Figure 7.49 Example Role Menu of Composite Role

In the **Users** tab, you can add and remove assignments to users (Figure 7.50). Once the users are assigned, you have to run the **User Comparison** so that the assignments become active.

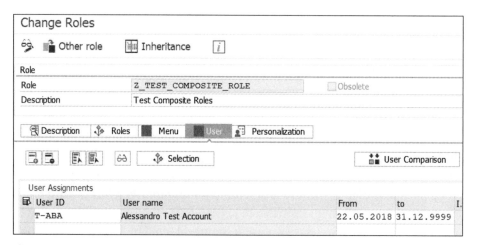

Figure 7.50 User Assignments in Composite Role

7.3.3   Create a Master and Derived Role

In a master (parent) and derived (child) role concept, the child role differs from its parent only in the organizational levels. The child role will inherit all objects and their values except the values of the organizational level fields from the parent.

The creation of a master role is similar to the creation of a single role, because a master role is a single role. Basically, you can create a child role from any single role. For an example, let's create a master role for finance that contains some organizational levels. To create the role, use the **Role Menu** to assign the necessary transactions to the role (Figure 7.51).

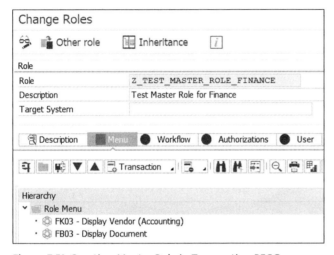

Figure 7.51 Creating Master Role in Transaction PFCG

In the **Authorizations** tab, skip the first screen that asks you to maintain the org levels. The org levels should remain empty in the master role because you want to maintain them in the child role (Figure 7.52). It is also possible to maintain a character symbol (e.g. a dollar sign [$]) so that the objects turn to status maintained (green). However, we will maintain all the other values so that the role is functionally ready to be used.

Once you've maintained all the open authorizations, you should only see red status lights to indicate that the org level is not maintained (Figure 7.53). All the other fields are green and hence properly maintained.

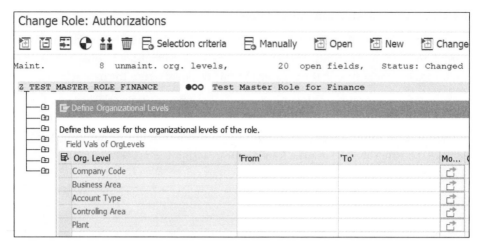

Figure 7.52 Empty Org Levels in Master Role

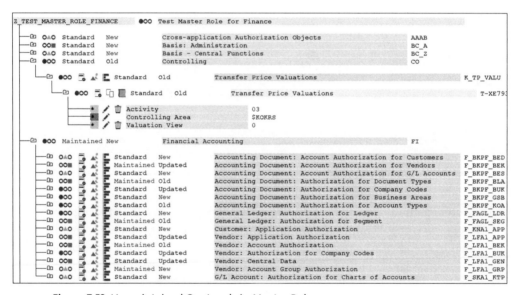

Figure 7.53 Unmaintained Org Levels in Master Role

When you generate the profile, the system tells you that you have open org levels. You can ignore this warning and generate the profile (Figure 7.54).

Figure 7.54 Profile Generation Warning for Open Org Levels

Once the profile is generated, return to the initial screen of Transaction PFCG and create the derived role. Give the derived role a name and click the **Single Role** button. (A derived role is also a single role.)

In the **Description** tab, define the **Role Description** and set the inheritance of the child role to inherit all the objects from its parent, as shown in Figure 7.55.

Figure 7.55 Create Derived Role from Master Role

Once you've saved, you can see that the **Menu** tab indicator turns green as the objects are inherited from the parent. In the **Authorizations** tab, go ahead and maintain the org levels (Figure 7.56). The system will immediately prompt you to define the org levels.

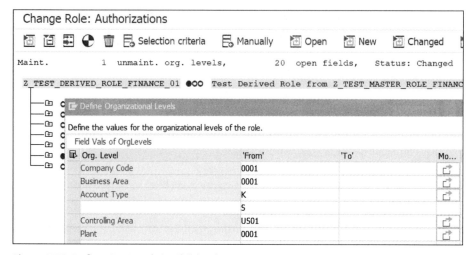

Figure 7.56 Define Org Levels in Child Role

Once defined, you can see in Figure 7.57 that the org levels are maintained and all other objects inherited their values from the parent. The child role is ready to be generated and assigned to users.

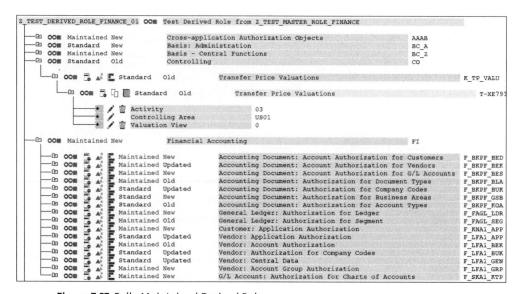

Figure 7.57 Fully Maintained Derived Role

As a best practice, never change objects in a derived role because those changes will be overwritten when changes to the master role are pushed to all the child roles.

Update and Maintain Master Role

The advantage of a derived role concept is that changes to a master can be distributed to all its children. In organizations with multiple org level differentiations, that simplifies the process of maintaining roles in the long run.

To change a master and all its child roles, simply go to the master role and perform changes. For example, you can add new transactions, change authorizations, and so on.

In Figure 7.58, we're changing the authorization of the authorization object F_BKPF_ BED from an asterisk (*), denoting full authorization to the field, to display-only.

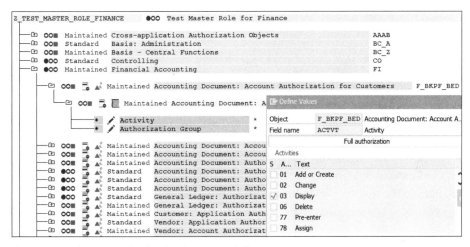

Figure 7.58 Change Authorization in Master Role

Once that change is saved and the profile is generated, you'll want to distribute the changes to derived roles. To do so, click the **Generate Derived Roles** button (Figure 7.59).

Figure 7.59 Generate Derived Roles from Master

The resulting pop-up (Figure 7.60) will give you some more information about what happens with this function and which authorizations are required to perform this task. Acknowledge by clicking **OK**.

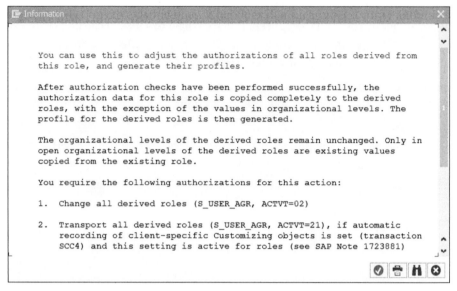

Figure 7.60 Information Pop-Up to Distribute Changes to Child Roles

If you go to the derived role, you can immediately see that a change happened based on the **Changed** field in the role description. The changed **Date** and **Time** reflect the changes to the master role. In the **Authorizations** tab, you can see that the change to object F_BKPF_BED was pushed through (Figure 7.61).

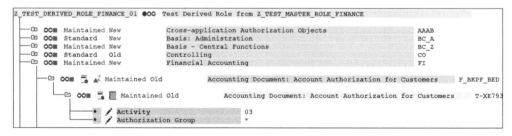

Figure 7.61 Inherited Change from Master Role in Its Child

7.3.4   Overview Status

The Profile Generator lets you analyze the status of your roles. Start the report from the menu under **Utilities · Overview Status** and make your role selection (Figure 7.62).

Status overview

Selection of roles

| Role | Z * | to | |

☑ Only Display Roles with Errors and Warnings
☐ Check assignment of workflow tasks

Figure 7.62 Status Overview in Profile Generator

The program will report the following characteristics that may occur with your selected roles:

- The role has a menu
- The role is distributed
- The corresponding profile(s) is generated
- The role is assigned to users
- The role is assigned to a composite role
- The role is indirectly assigned
- The profile comparison is current

Figure 7.63 shows the status overview of a set of roles with different findings. We can see that some roles don't have objects in the role menu, others are not assigned to users, and some don't have a current authorization profile.

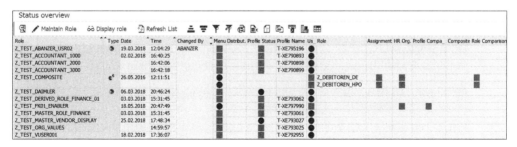

Figure 7.63 Status Overview in Profile Generator

213

With this report, you can increase the quality and stability of your roles. Make sure that all roles have a menu and the profile is properly generated.

7.3.5   Mass Generation of Profiles

Another handy feature is to generate and update profiles en mass for your roles. You can start the mass generation of profiles either via **Utilities · Mass Generation** in Transaction PFCG or directly from Transaction SUPC. The mass generation program (Figure 7.64) allows for initial selections and whether you want to generate the profiles automatically or not. If not, the program will only display the findings and you can manually decide if you want to generate the profiles.

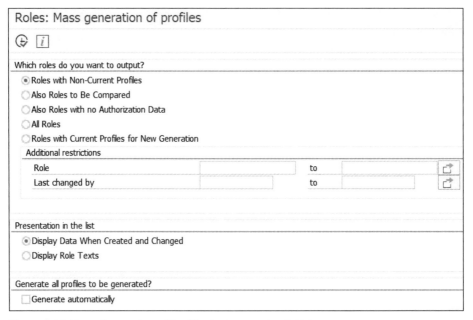

Figure 7.64 Mass Generation of Profiles in Transaction SUPC

Once you execute, the system will show you a list with different findings. Some roles don't have a profile generated, or the profile isn't current (Figure 7.65).

Select the role that you want to update and either generate the profile or change the authorization data. If the profile isn't current, then check the authorization data of the role to see what's been changed but wasn't generated. Also, with the merge functionality you can see if the role will get new proposals from Transaction SU24 (Figure 7.66).

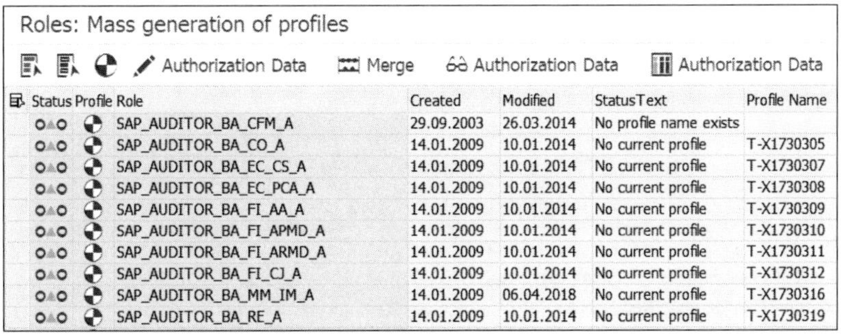

Status	Profile	Role	Created	Modified	StatusText	Profile Name
		SAP_AUDITOR_BA_CFM_A	29.09.2003	26.03.2014	No profile name exists	
		SAP_AUDITOR_BA_CO_A	14.01.2009	10.01.2014	No current profile	T-X1730305
		SAP_AUDITOR_BA_EC_CS_A	14.01.2009	10.01.2014	No current profile	T-X1730307
		SAP_AUDITOR_BA_EC_PCA_A	14.01.2009	10.01.2014	No current profile	T-X1730308
		SAP_AUDITOR_BA_FI_AA_A	14.01.2009	10.01.2014	No current profile	T-X1730309
		SAP_AUDITOR_BA_FI_APMD_A	14.01.2009	10.01.2014	No current profile	T-X1730310
		SAP_AUDITOR_BA_FI_ARMD_A	14.01.2009	10.01.2014	No current profile	T-X1730311
		SAP_AUDITOR_BA_FI_CJ_A	14.01.2009	10.01.2014	No current profile	T-X1730312
		SAP_AUDITOR_BA_MM_IM_A	14.01.2009	06.04.2018	No current profile	T-X1730316
		SAP_AUDITOR_BA_RE_A	14.01.2009	10.01.2014	No current profile	T-X1730319

Figure 7.65 Examples in Mass Generation of Profiles

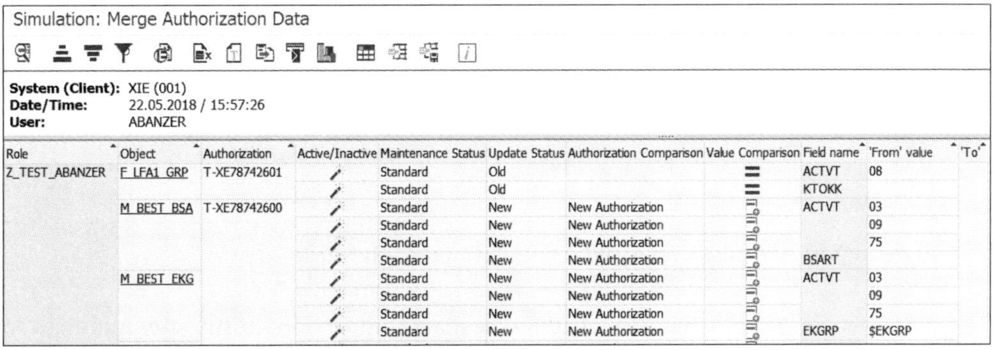

Role	Object	Authorization	Active/Inactive	Maintenance Status	Update Status	Authorization Comparison	Value Comparison	Field name	'From' value	'To'
Z_TEST_ABANZER	F_LFA1_GRP	T-XE78742601		Standard	Old			ACTVT	08	
				Standard	Old			KTOKK		
	M_BEST_BSA	T-XE78742600		Standard	New	New Authorization		ACTVT	03	
				Standard	New	New Authorization			09	
				Standard	New	New Authorization			75	
				Standard	New	New Authorization		BSART		
	M_BEST_EKG			Standard	New	New Authorization		ACTVT	03	
				Standard	New	New Authorization			09	
				Standard	New	New Authorization			75	
				Standard	New	New Authorization		EKGRP	$EKGRP	

Figure 7.66 Merge Authorization Data in Transaction SUPC

In the merge simulation, you can see which objects and fields will be changed. Prior to merging the new data into the role, we recommend checking and validating whether the change is correct.

7.3.6 Mass Comparison

Another feature of the Profile Generator is the mass user comparison (Figure 7.67). To make changes to authorizations of a user effective, the comparison must be run. The comparison will not only make a new assignment effective, it will also remove profiles that are no longer current from the user master. You can start the mass comparison either from the menu in Transaction PFCG under **Utilities • Mass Comparison** or directly from Transaction PFUD.

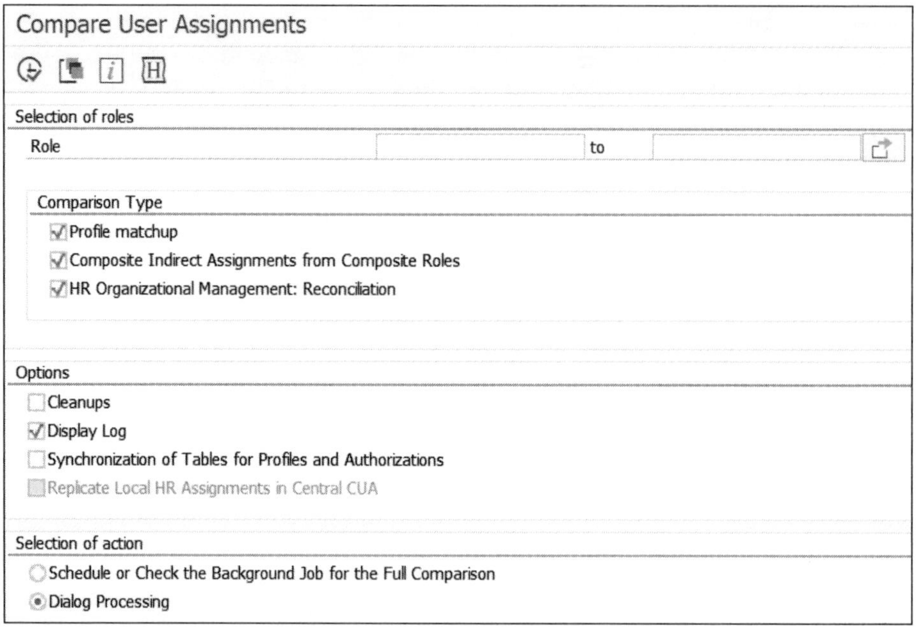

Figure 7.67 Compare User Assignments in Transaction PFUD

It is recommended that you schedule the mass comparison shortly after midnight so that the validity date of the roles is considered. The reason behind this is that the authorization profile doesn't know a validity date, only the role does. Since the authorization profile grants access to a user, the profile must be assigned and removed from the user master, according to the validity date. That's when Transaction PFUD or the program `PFCG_TIME_DEPENDENCY` comes into play. `PFCG_TIME_DEPENDENCY` calls the program `RHAUTUPD_NEW` which is the program behind Transaction PFUD. To schedule the program in the background, you can create a variant for program `RHAUTUPD_NEW` that only considers your roles. `PFCG_TIME_DEPENDENCY` does not allow for role selection and runs against all roles.

7.3.7   Role Menu Comparison

The role menu comparison allows you to compare and adjust role menus in the local system, as well as via RFC in a remote system. You can start the role menu comparison in Transaction PFCG from **Utilities • Role Menu Comparison**. In the selection, choose the two roles you want to analyze and click the **Compare** button (Figure 7.68).

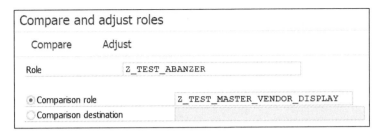

Figure 7.68 Role Menu Comparison in Transaction PFCG

7

The report tells you that certain transactions exist in one role but not in the other (Figure 7.69). Some transactions are in common and shown in green.

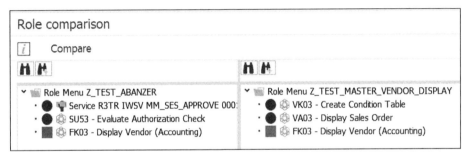

Figure 7.69 Example of Role Menu Comparison

It's important to understand that this report only compares the menu, not the authorizations.

7.3.8   Role Versioning

SAP introduced role versioning with SAP NetWeaver 7.31. To start role versioning, you can either use report RSUSR_AUTH_DATA_VERSION directly or navigate through Transaction PFCG. To navigate to the report from Transaction PFCG, open a role in **Change** mode and open the authorization data. In the **Authorization data**, you can start the report from the menu item **Utilities • Versions**. Since this report is part of the Profile Generator and requires authorizations for Transaction PFCG it is not part of the User Information System (Transaction SUIM).

On the initial screen (Figure 7.70), you get an overview of all the versions that are available for the role. You can see who changed the role and when.

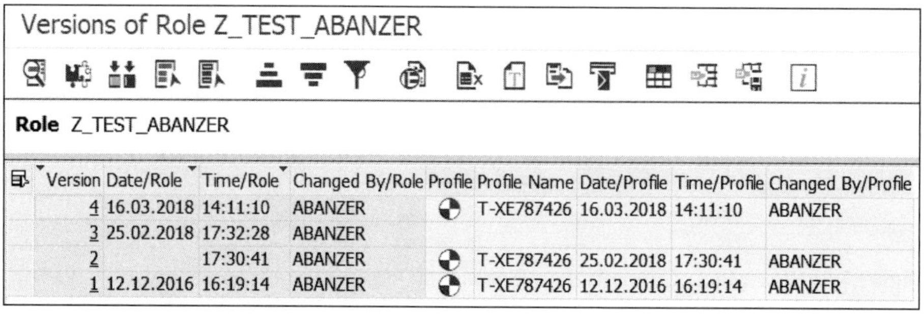
Versions of Role Z_TEST_ABANZER

Role Z_TEST_ABANZER

Version	Date/Role	Time/Role	Changed By/Role	Profile	Profile Name	Date/Profile	Time/Profile	Changed By/Profile
4	16.03.2018	14:11:10	ABANZER		T-XE787426	16.03.2018	14:11:10	ABANZER
3	25.02.2018	17:32:28	ABANZER					
2		17:30:41	ABANZER		T-XE787426	25.02.2018	17:30:41	ABANZER
1	12.12.2016	16:19:14	ABANZER		T-XE787426	12.12.2016	16:19:14	ABANZER

Figure 7.70 Versions of a Role

The report allows you to compare two versions of a role with each other, and display the authorization data of a particular version. To display the authorization data, simply double-click on the desired role version or click the **Display Details** button [F9] and a new screen will open (Figure 7.71).

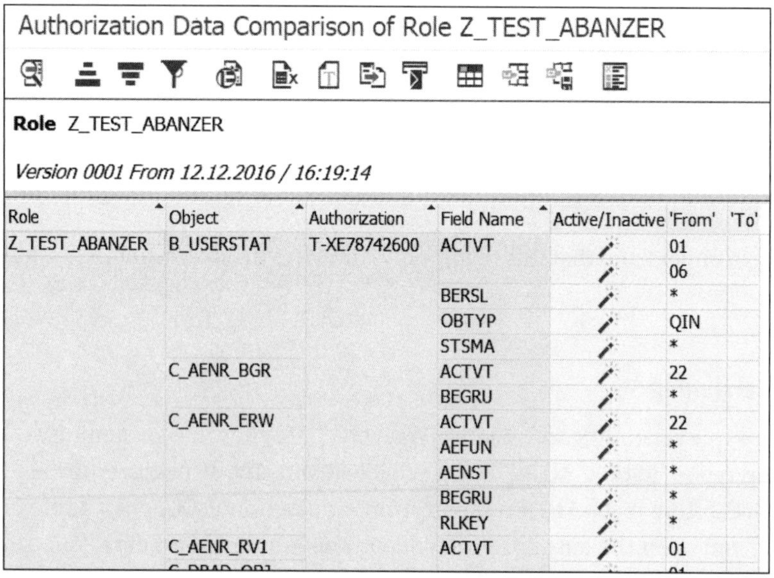
Authorization Data Comparison of Role Z_TEST_ABANZER

Role Z_TEST_ABANZER

Version 0001 From 12.12.2016 / 16:19:14

Role	Object	Authorization	Field Name	Active/Inactive	'From'	'To'
Z_TEST_ABANZER	B_USERSTAT	T-XE78742600	ACTVT		01	
					06	
			BERSL		*	
			OBTYP		QIN	
			STSMA		*	
	C_AENR_BGR		ACTVT		22	
			BEGRU		*	
	C_AENR_ERW		ACTVT		22	
			AEFUN		*	
			AENST		*	
			BEGRU		*	
			RLKEY		*	
	C_AENR_RV1		ACTVT		01	

Figure 7.71 Authorization Data Details of a Role

To compare two versions, select two different line items and click on the **Compare** button. The report will display both authorization data and how they compare to each other in the **Value Comparison** column (Figure 7.72).

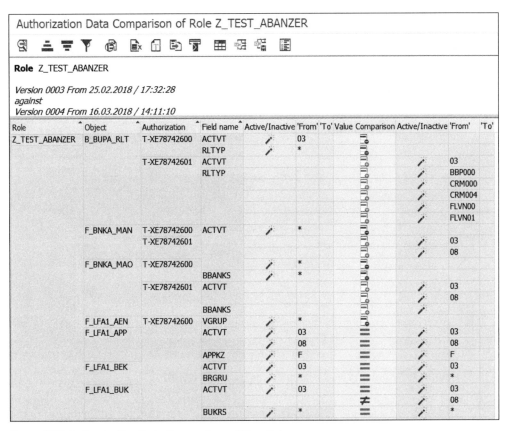

Figure 7.72 Authorization Data Comparison of Two Roles

The **Value Comparison** column indicates how the values of the two versions relate to each other. They can either be newly added, removed, identical or changed. This allows you to easily understand what has been changed in a role.

If you start report RSUSR_AUTH_DATA_VERSION directly from Transaction SA38, you can also analyze roles that do no longer exist in the system. If you don't have the report available, check and implement SAP Note 2248464.

7.4   Assign and Remove Roles

An SAP system knows multiple ways to assign and remove roles to and from users. To assign and remove roles in a local system, three methods are available. Most commonly, Transaction SU01 is used to assign and remove roles to and from individual users. If mass assignments are required, Transaction SU10 can be utilized. The third option to assign and remove roles to and from users is to go through Transaction PFCG. Open the role and change the assignments under the **Users** tab.

In Transaction SU01 and Transaction SU10, you can add and remove roles in the **Roles** tab. To add a new role to a user, simply select or enter the roles in an empty line. To remove a role, select the line item and click on the **Remove** button (Figure 7.73).

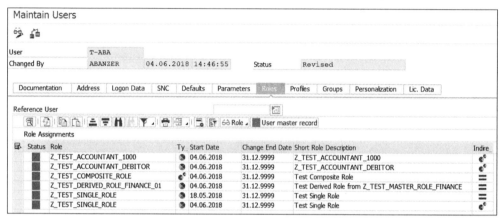

Figure 7.73 Maintain Role Assignments in Transaction SU01

To change role assignments in Transaction PFCG, open the role and navigate to the **Users** tab. In the **Users** tab, you can add users to the role or remove them accordingly (Figure 7.74).

Figure 7.74 Change User Assignments of a Role

7.5   Lock and Unlock Transactions

The SAP system lets you lock transactions so that no user can execute and start those transactions. Prior to SAP NetWeaver 7.5, Transaction SM01 was used to lock and unlock transactions. As of SAP NetWeaver 7.5, the lock transactions functionality was replaced by Transactions SM01_CUS and Transaction SM01_DEV, as we discussed in Chapter 3. Remember, when a user starts a transaction, the kernel first performs the TSTC check, which validates whether the transaction is locked. If locked, an error message will be displayed to indicate that the transaction has been locked.

With the enhanced functionality, you can distinguish between a global lock of the workbench object and a local lock as a customizing setting. With Transaction SM01_ DEV, you can globally lock a transaction. Transaction SM01_CUS allows you to locally lock a transaction in the client you are logged on to. If you log on to client 000 and start Transaction SM01_CUS, you can choose if you want to lock the transaction in all clients or for a specific client only.

SAP Note 2234192 explains the enhancements made to the application start lock.

7.6   Transaction SUIM: User Information System

You can use the User Information System (Transaction SUIM) to obtain an overview of the authorizations and users in your SAP system at any time using search criteria that you define (Figure 7.75). In particular, you can display lists of users to whom authorizations classified as critical are assigned. There are several entry points to slice and dice the information from different angles.

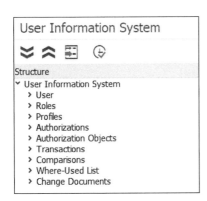

Figure 7.75 Initial Screen of the User Information System (Transaction SUIM)

Transaction SUIM offers comprehensive reporting based on different entry levels. In a nutshell, the following options are available:

- User
- Roles
- Profiles
- Authorizations
- Authorization objects
- Transasctions
- Comparisons
- Where-used lists
- Change documents

In this section, we'll provide an overview of each option to show you what information you can obtain.

7.6.1 User

The first option is to find users (Figure 7.76). You can analyze users based on different objects—for example, which user has access to system A, which user has access to transaction B, which user has authorization to C, and so on. You can also find users based on unsuccessful logins, critical authorizations, logon date, and password changed date.

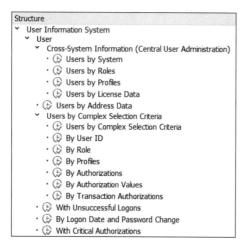

Figure 7.76 Transaction SUIM: Search for Users

7.6.2   Roles

In this option, you can search roles based on different critiera (Figure 7.77). For example, which roles are assigned to user A, which roles contain transaction B, which roles contain authorization object C, and so on. You can also find roles based on change dates and other complex selection crtieria.

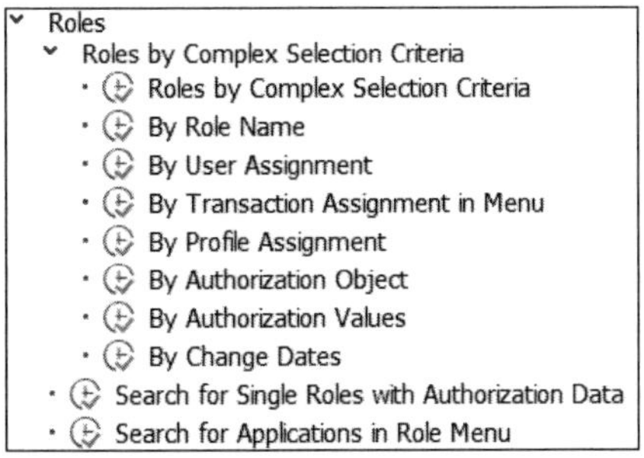

```
˅  Roles
   ˅  Roles by Complex Selection Criteria
      ·  ⊕  Roles by Complex Selection Criteria
      ·  ⊕  By Role Name
      ·  ⊕  By User Assignment
      ·  ⊕  By Transaction Assignment in Menu
      ·  ⊕  By Profile Assignment
      ·  ⊕  By Authorization Object
      ·  ⊕  By Authorization Values
      ·  ⊕  By Change Dates
   ·  ⊕  Search for Single Roles with Authorization Data
   ·  ⊕  Search for Applications in Role Menu
```

Figure 7.77 Transaction SUIM: Search for Roles

7.6.3   Profiles

In this option, you can search for profiles based on different criteria (Figure 7.78). For example, which profile contains authorization object A, which profile contains authorization value B, and so on. Also, you can find profiles by roles and last change date.

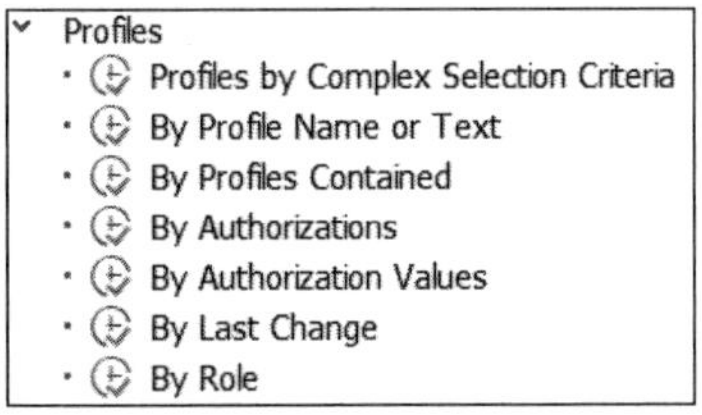

```
˅  Profiles
   ·  ⊕  Profiles by Complex Selection Criteria
   ·  ⊕  By Profile Name or Text
   ·  ⊕  By Profiles Contained
   ·  ⊕  By Authorizations
   ·  ⊕  By Authorization Values
   ·  ⊕  By Last Change
   ·  ⊕  By Role
```

Figure 7.78 Transaction SUIM: Search for Profiles

7.6.4   Authorizations

In this option, you can search for authorizations (Figure 7.79). In an SAP system, authorizations are defined as the combination of the authorization object and its values.

```
⌄  Authorizations
   ·  ⊕  Authorizations by Complex Selection Criteria
   ·  ⊕  By Object
   ·  ⊕  By Values
   ·  ⊕  By Last Change
```

Figure 7.79 Transaction SUIM: Search for Authorizations

7.6.5   Authorization Objects

In this option, you can search for authorization objects (Figure 7.80). For example, you can search all authorization objects that start with a partciular letter or search authorization objects by name, text, or class.

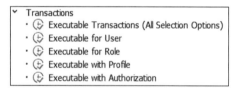

```
⌄  Authorization Objects
   ·  ⊕  Authorization Objects by Complex Selection Criteria
   ·  ⊕  By Object Name, Text
   ·  ⊕  By Object Class
   ·  ⊕  By Field, Text
```

Figure 7.80 Transaction SUIM: Search for Authorization Objects

7.6.6   Transasctions

In this option, you can search for transaction codes (Figure 7.81). For example, you can see which user can execute which transactions, which roles can execute which transactions, and so on.

```
⌄  Transactions
   ·  ⊕  Executable Transactions (All Selection Options)
   ·  ⊕  Executable for User
   ·  ⊕  Executable for Role
   ·  ⊕  Executable with Profile
   ·  ⊕  Executable with Authorization
```

Figure 7.81 Transaction SUIM: Search for Transactions

7.6.7   Comparisons

In this option, you can combare objects with each other (Figure 7.82). For example, you can compare two users, two roles, two profiles, or even two authorizations. You can also compare objects across different systems—for example, to compare a user in two systems. The comparison on the user level works on an authorization object level. It doesn't compare role assignments.

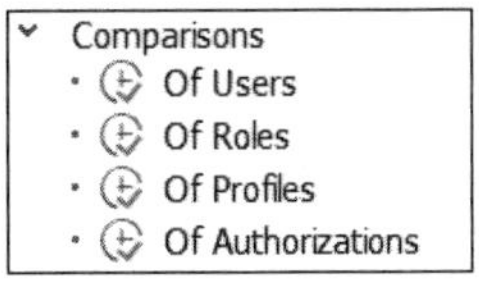

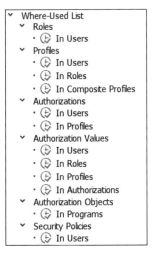

Figure 7.82 Transaction SUIM: Comparison Options

7.6.8   Where-Used Lists

In this option, you can find a where-used list of objects—for example, which role is assigned to which users, which profile is assigned to which users, which authorizations are assigned to which users, and so on (Figure 7.83). Most of the reports are also available in some of the other options.

Figure 7.83 Transaction SUIM: Where-Used Lists

7.6.9   Change Documents

In this options, you can search for change documents (Figure 7.84). For example, change documents for users, roles, profiles, role assignments, and so on.

225

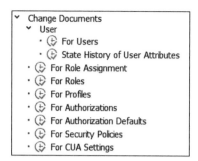

Figure 7.84 Transaction SUIM: Search for Change Documents

7.7   Role Transport

In a traditional three-tier system landscape, roles are created in the development system. Once built, the security administrator transports the roles to quality to undergo quality and user acceptance testing. Once approved, the final role definition is transported to production and assigned to end users. The Profile Generator (Transaction PFCG) offers two capabilities, single role transport and mass role transport, to move roles through the landscape. The single role transport allows you to add one role at a time, whereas the mass transport functionality allows you to add roles en masse to a transport request via wildcards, ranges, and so on.

To transport a single role, go to Transaction PFCG and select the role that you want to transport. Then either click the **Role Transport** button (Figure 7.85) or choose **Role · Transport** from the menu.

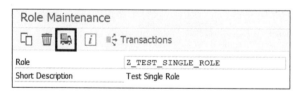

Figure 7.85 Role Transport in Transaction PFCG

In the screen that opens, shown in Figure 7.86, you can decide whether you want to transport direct user role assignments, the generated profile of the role, or personalization data. We recommend transporting the generated profile and the personalization data. User assignments might be different in the target system(s) and hence roles should be assigned to the users after transport. It's recommended that you not transport user assignments as you are usually transporting from a development system to a productive system. Development systems have different user assignments than productive systems. Also, in a productive system you have to follow your change management process with respective approvals, etc.

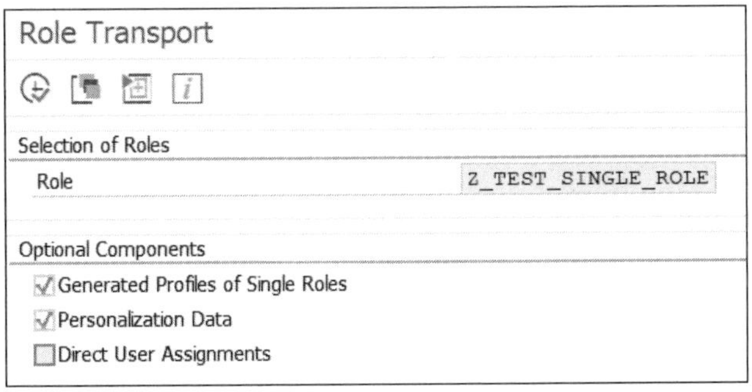

Figure 7.86 Role Transport in Transaction PFCG

Once you execute the role transport, the system will prompt for a transport request. An additional option for **Single Roles in Composite Roles** will be available when transporting composite roles (see Figure 7.87).

To massively transport roles, go back to the initial screen of Transaction PFCG and choose **Utilities · Mass Transport** from the menu. The selection screen is similar to the one from the single transport, but it offers the capability of multiple selection so that you can define your set of roles using ranges, wildcards, or even copy and paste (Figure 7.87).

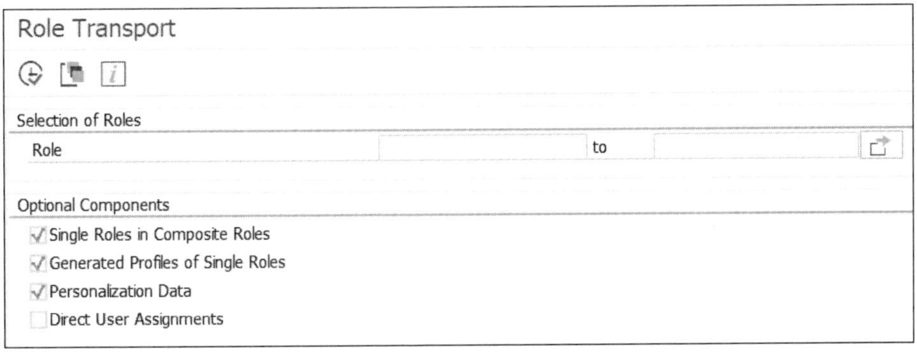

Figure 7.87 Mass Role Transport in Transaction PFCG

227

Once the roles are selected, choose from the available options for which components to transport. The option **Single Roles in Composite Roles** is available because composite roles can be transported, too. If you select this option, all single roles that are part of a composite role will be added to the transport so that the full set of roles is transported. Once you click **Execute**, the system will prompt you for a transport request.

7.8   Common Standard Profiles

With any SAP installation, standard profiles are created automatically. Such standard profiles grant broad access to the system and are considered critical. During IT audits, the auditors will always check if standard profiles are assigned to users, not only in productive systems. Make sure to assign the profiles on a per-user basis and avoid spreading profiles among multiple users.

The following lists some common standard profiles and their purpose:

- SAP_ALL is the most common standard profile, and it contains almost all authorizations that exist in an SAP system. With SAP_ALL, the user gets access to Basis administration, application and component maintenance, customizing, table maintenance, and so on.

- SAP_NEW contains all new authorizations that are introduced with the latest release. This profile is helpful after upgrading the system to a new release because it contains all the changed authorizations. Keep in mind that this profile also grants extended access to the system because, for example, all organizational values are prefaced with an asterisk (*). In later releases, the profile SAP_NEW was replaced with the role SAP_NEW. For more information see SAP Note 1711620 - Role SAP_NEW replaces profile SAP_NEW.

- S_A.SYSTEM contains Basis authorizations that allow a user to create and change users, create and change roles and profiles, and so on. Although not as powerful as SAP_ALL, this profile does allow a user to assign roles and profiles to another user and hence it can be a backdoor for SAP_ALL.

- S_A.DEVELOP contains authorizations for the developer that allow her to access almost everything in the system. Like all the other standard profiles, this shouldn't be assigned to anyone in a productive environment.

You can also read SAP Note 2548064 and understand how to use the common standard profiles like SAP_ALL and SAP_NEW.

7.9   Types of Transactions

In SAP, there are different types of transactions to execute certain commands and programs. The end user enters the transaction code in the command box or starts them from his favorites or from the SAP menu. To authorize a transaction, the security administrator can define necessary authorizations in Transaction SE93 and maintain them via Transaction SU24.

In this section, we'll provide an overview of the different types of transactions that are available in an SAP system and how to use them. To create and maintain transactions, you can use Transaction SE93 (Figure 7.88). The following types of transactions are available:

- Dialog transactions
- Report transactions
- Object-oriented transactions
- Variant transactions
- Parameter transactions

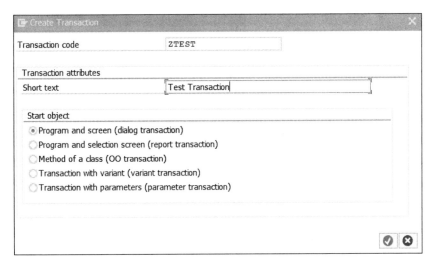

Figure 7.88 Create Custom Transaction in Transaction SE93

Let's take a closer look at each of the transaction types that are available and what they're used for. Some are particularly interesting for security administrators.

7.9.1   Dialog Transactions

Dialog transactions (Figure 7.89) start a program that has different screens. In Transaction SE93, you have to define the initial screen that will start when someone executes the transaction code.

An example of a dialog transaction is Transaction PFCG, which starts a certain screen number of the program it's executing.

Figure 7.89 Example of Dialog Transaction PFCG

7.9.2   Report Transactions

Report transactions (Figure 7.90) start an executable program that's used to display data in an output list. Report transactions are commonly used to display data in a simplified form after processing or performing some calculations.

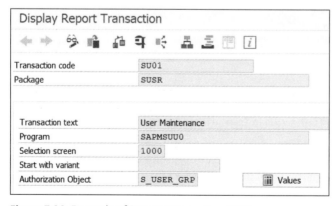

Figure 7.90 Example of Report Transaction SU01

An example of a report transaction is Transaction SU01, which starts a program with a selection screen.

7.9.3 Object-Oriented Transactions

Object-oriented transactions (Figure 7.91) start a class method directly. An example is Transaction SCOT, which is used to configure outgoing email. When the user enters Transaction SCOT, the system starts the START method of the CL_BCS_ADM_NODES class.

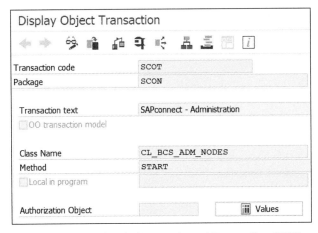

Figure 7.91 Example of Object-Oriented Transaction SCOT

7.9.4 Variant Transactions

Variant transactions let you preassign values to fields within a transaction, define field attributes, or hide certain screens.

With variant transactions, you can create variants from transactions to prevent a user from accessing functionality that you can't protect with an authorization object. Therefore, in Transaction SHD0, the system offers the flexibility to create transaction and screen variants to inactivate certain fields or buttons on a screen. For example, you can create a transaction variant to lock and unlock users without the other buttons and functionality shown on the screen. If you restrict the authorization object S_USER_GRP to activity 05, which allows you to lock and unlock users, the security admin still sees all the other buttons, even though he isn't authorized to execute them. Therefore, with the transaction variant, you can limit the visibility of the initial screen and only show the **Lock/Unlock** button.

In Transaction SHDO, create a transaction variant for Transaction SU01. Give the variant a name and click on the **Create** button (Figure 7.92).

Transaction and Screen Variants

□ ✏ With processing   ✏ 🔍 🖅 ⬛ 🗑 🗐 ⓘ

| Transaction Code | SU01 | User Maintenance |

| Standard Variants | Transaction Variants | Screen Variants |

| Transaction Variant | ZSU01_LOCK_UNLOCK |

Figure 7.92 Create Transaction Variant in Transaction SHDO

If you click **Create**, Transaction SU01 will start; you can enter a user ID and click any button. Transaction SHDO will interrupt and ask you to confirm the screen entries. From here, you can mark certain fields **Invisible**, **Required**, and so on (Figure 7.93). To hide menu functions, click the **Menu functions** button.

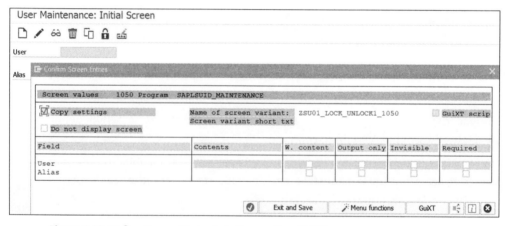

Figure 7.93 Define Screen Variants in Transaction SHDO

In the menu functions, to hide options from the screen, simply double-click the options that you want to hide and click the **OK** button. In Figure 7.94, the selected options to hide are shaded in yellow (the darker shading in the figure). We've left only **Display** and **Locks** available.

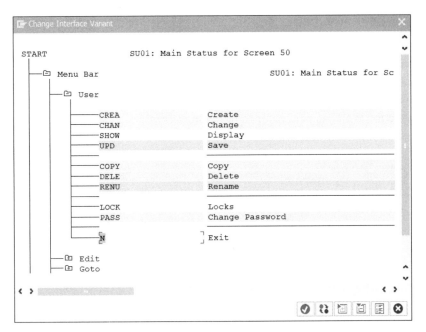

Figure 7.94 Change Menu Options in Transaction SHD0

Once the transaction variant is saved, go to Transaction SE93 and create a custom transaction of type **Transaction Variant**. If defined, you maintain Transaction SU24 values and the transaction is ready to be added to roles. If a user now executes that variant transaction, the screen will only have the buttons that we allowed (Figure 7.95).

User Maintenance: Initial Screen	
👓 🔒	
User	T-ABA
Alias	

Figure 7.95 Transaction Variant of Transaction SU01

Transaction variants are a handy feature to suppress sensitive data or data that isn't required from screens.

7.9.5   Parameter Transaction

Parameter transactions (Figure 7.96) allow you to preassign values to the fields in the initial screen. Moreover, you can skip the first screen and proceed with the predefined values automatically so that the user can't change or enter her own selection data. An example of a parameter transaction is client administration Transaction SCC4. Transaction SCC4 is a parameter transaction of Transaction SM30; it skips the initial screen to proceed directly to table T000.

Figure 7.96 Example of Parameter Transaction SCC4

When a user executes Transaction SCC4, the system automatically starts Transaction SM30 with table T000. The user can't enter another table or change fields in the initial screen because it's skipped automatically.

Parameter transactions allow you to properly define the authorization proposals in Transaction SU24. Parameter transactions also offer an elegant remediation alternative for table access transactions like Transaction SE16, Transaction SM30, and so on.

For example, say that an end user requires table access to table USR02. Rather than authorizing Transaction SE16 and manually adding authorization object S_TABU_NAM with the value for the table USR02 to a role, consider using a parameter transaction. The parameter transaction calls Transaction SE16; you can predefine the default values for table USR02 and skip the initial screen. In Transaction SU24, you can maintain S_TABU_NAM with the respective values. When you add the customer parameter transaction to your roles, you get standard authorization objects and values, which are traceable back to your transaction.

In Transaction SE93, create a new transaction and choose the **Start Object Transaction with Parameters** (parameter transaction). In the default values, set Transaction SE16 and select the **Skip Initial Screen** checkbox. In the **Default Values** section, choose the table name and set it as "USR02" (Figure 7.97).

Figure 7.97 Parameter Transaction for Transaction SE16 and Table USR02

In Transaction SU24, for parameter transactions you might consider breaking the inheritance from its parent (in our example, Transaction SE16). The inheritance comes by default. For Transaction SE16, the system proposes authorization object S_TABU_NAM and S_TABU_DIS for the parameter transaction because those proposals are maintained for Transaction SE16 itself. Because a properly defined parameter transaction for Transaction SE16 only calls one table, we can set that table name as an authorization proposal. With that, whoever adds the parameter transaction to a role gets fully proposed authorizations and doesn't have to figure out which values to maintain.

> **Tip**
>
> Inheritance of authorization proposals for parameter transactions isn't always desired. If deactivation of the inheritance is not available, check and implement SAP Note 1577135.

If the inheritance is active, click on the **Deactivate Inheritance** button (Figure 7.98). Once deactivated, add the object that you want to be proposed manually.

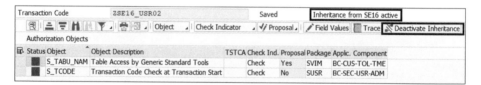

Figure 7.98 Inherited Authorization Proposals for Parameter Transactions

In our example, we add S_TABU_NAM with table USR02 as this parameter transaction only allows to access table USR02 (Figure 7.99).

> **Tip**
>
> Use parameter transactions to remedy critical authorizations conflicts with Transactions SE16, SE16N, SM30, and so on and benefit from best practice approaches. Parameter transactions also allow you to specifically define authorization proposals via Transaction SU24 to build stable roles, according to SAP best practices.

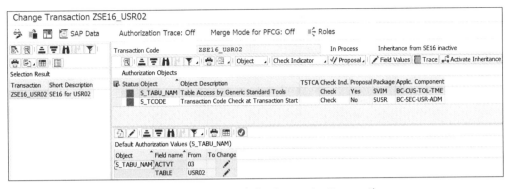

Figure 7.99 Maintained Authorization Proposals for Parameter Transactions

7.9.6 Call Transaction in Transaction SE97

In SAP, we often see transactions that call another transaction via the CALL TRANSAC-
TION ABAP command. Those calls sometimes perform an authorization check and
sometimes do not. As we know, when a user starts a transaction the system checks for
the S_TCODE object and value. With call transactions, you must define whether that
check is executed or not. In Transaction SE97 (Figure 7.100), you can control not only
if the check is being performed but also what happens if the authorization check fails.

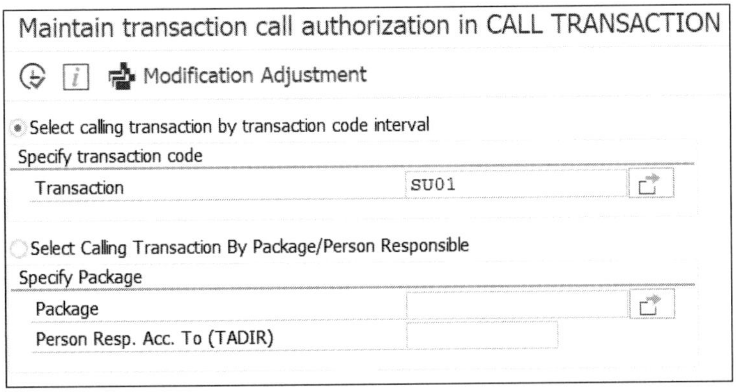

Figure 7.100 Transaction SE97: Initial Screen

Once you execute the report for a transaction, such as Transaction SU01, you'll see a
list of all called transactions along with the check indicator and its message type. The

Check Indicator column indicates whether the S_TCODE check and the TSTCA check (additional authorization check from Transaction SE93) for that transaction is performed. The value can be one of the following:

- **YES**

  The system checks the authorization when the CALL FUNCTION ABAP statement is executed.

- **NO**

  No authorization check is performed.

- **SPACE or empty**

  In current releases, no authorization check is performed. However, this might change in future releases.

For each call transaction, you can also define the message type for which message the system shows when the authorization checks fail. The values listed in Table 7.4 are possible options.

Value	Action
I	Information message but program continues
E	Error message but the user remains in the transaction
A	Termination message and the user returns to the SAP Easy Access menu
W, X, or space	Warning message and the user returns to the SAP Easy Access menu

Table 7.4 Transaction SE97: Overview of Message Types

Most SAP standard call transactions that check for authorizations come with the default value of a space character, which offers the best security. If a user isn't authorized, the system will show a warning message and stops the execution of the program.

Figure 7.101 shows the called transactions for Transaction SU01 and their check indicators.

Tip

The values shown in Transaction SE97 are stored in table TCDCOUPLES.

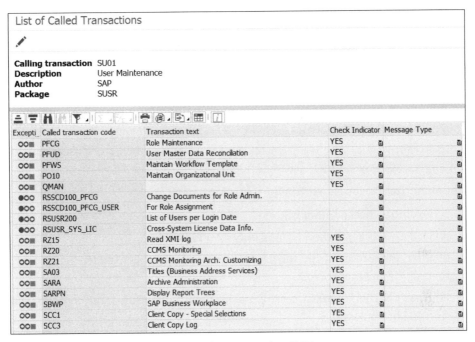

Figure 7.101 List of Called Transactions for Transaction SU01

Transaction SE97 is somewhat similar to Transaction SU24, as you can control if an authorization check is performed. However, it's also important to understand that maintaining a call transaction in Transaction SE97 alone doesn't perform the authorization check. It must be included in the code of the program; only then can you can control its behavior in Transaction SE97, like in Transaction SU24.

As a security administrator, you'll mostly likely only use Transaction SE97 for custom transactions. To add a called transaction to the list, simply use the **Add Transaction** button in edit mode. Changes will be recorded in a workbench transport and must be transported. For more information, see SAP Note 358122 (Function Description of Transaction SE97).

7.10   Table Authorizations

At the end of the day, all data that exists in an SAP system is stored in its database. Therefore, it's highly important to protect sensitive business data with proper table authorizations. For example, table PA0008 contains payroll information if the HR module is used, table USR02 stores a user's password; and so on. These and many other tables are worth protecting from unauthorized and abusive access.

There are several ways to access data from a table. Although SAP standard transactions read data through its frontend applications and are protected with authority checks, you can also access the tables directly with tools like Transactions SE16, SE16N, SE17, SM30, SM31, and so on. Those kinds of transactions allow you to view and maintain tables. By default, those tools check for authorization object S_TABU_DIS, and, if not successful, for S_TABU_NAM. If the table is client-independent and a user wants to modify it, it also checks for S_TABU_CLI.

The authorization checks work in the following order:

- S_TABU_DIS is checked (always!).
- If failed, S_TABU_NAM is checked (and only if *_DIS failed!).
- If either was successful and the user wants to modify a client-independent table, then S_TABU_CLI is checked.
- If S_TABU_CLI check is unsuccessful, the user will still be able to display the table since DIS or NAM passed.

The following sections outline each authorization object in more detail.

7.10.1   Table Group Authorizations via S_TABU_DIS

S_TABU_DIS checks authorization with an activity (field ACTVT) in combination with a table authorization group (field DICBERCLS). The table authorization group is a container of several tables that are like each other. Table authorization groups are maintained in Transaction SE54, or alternatively directly in Transaction SM30 for view V_DDAT_54. It's important to understand that not all tables are assigned to a table group. SAP uses a generic group called &NC&, which stands for "not classified." In an SAP ERP system (SAP NW 7.5 EHP 8) only about 20% of the tables are assigned to an actual table authorization group; the rest belong to &NC&. Therefore, assigning &NC& gives broad access to multiple tables and it must be used very carefully.

Table TDDAT for Quick Analysis

Check table TDDAT from Transaction SE16 and watch out for field CCLASS. Table TDDAT contains all table authorization group assignments for tables. This information is very helpful to identify the entire set of tables that is being authorized with a table group.

When authorizing S_TABU_DIS, please keep in mind that you always grant access to *all* tables that are assigned to a specific table authorization group. To more granularly authorize specific tables, take a closer look at S_TABU_NAM, which allows you specifically to authorize individual tables.

7.10.2   Table Authorizations via S_TABU_NAM

S_TABU_NAM is only checked if a previous check on S_TABU_DIS failed. If S_TABU_DIS was successful, there's no further check for S_TABU_NAM. Therefore, S_TABU_NAM doesn't replace S_TABU_DIS but allows you to more specifically grant access to tables. Like S_TABU_DIS, S_TABU_NAM checks for an activity (field ACTVT) and a table name (field TABLE). The TABLE field can contain wildcard values, but at the end only. For example, you can enter full table names like USRO2 or TDDAT, or use USR* or TD*. However, you can't use *02 or T*DAT.

7.10.3   Cross-Client Table Authorizations via S_TABU_CLI

If a table is client-independent and you want to maintain it, the SAP system checks for an additional object called S_TABU_CLI. Most of those tables are customizing and Basis tables and hence only required for Basis and security personnel. When a table is client-independent, its changes can have side-effects for other clients and hence require further protection. To identify a table as client-independent, you can check if the field MANDT (client) exists. If a table contains MANDT, it's a client-dependent table and hence doesn't check for S_TABU_CLI. As an example, client-independent tables include TDIR and TDDAT, whereas USRO2 is a client-dependent table.

S_TABU_CLI is a complimentary authorization check after S_TABU_DIS or S_TABU_NAM was successful. S_TABU_CLI is only checked when a user wants to modify data; display access is granted without checking S_TABU_CLI. S_TABU_CLI only knows one field, CLIIDMAINT.

7.10.4   Line-Oriented Table Authorizations via S_TABU_LIN

S_TABU_LIN is used to protect the content of a table with line-orientedd authorizations. The system checks S_TABU_LIN in addition to the table authorizations mentioned earlier, like S_TABU_DIS and S_TABU_NAM. Before S_TABU_LIN is checked, all the preceding checks must be successful. Also, note that S_TABU_LIN is only checked in standard table maintenance transactions like Transactions SE16, SM30, and so on. It

7

won't be checked automatically in your customer programs. However, to increase security in your custom programs, a developer can implement S_TABU_LIN checks through the authority check statement.

S_TABU_LIN only works after some configuration. The first step is to create an organizational criterion that's used within the authorization object. Let's make an example with table USR02 and the user group field CLASS. Say that we want to further protect table USR02 and its content so that a user who can access that table can't see all user groups. Rather than authorize access to table USR02, we'll authorize the users for view VUSER001. In Transaction SPRO, navigate to **SAP NetWeaver · Application Server · System Administration · User and Authorizations · Line-oriented Authorizations** and click **Define organizational criteria** (Figure 7.102).

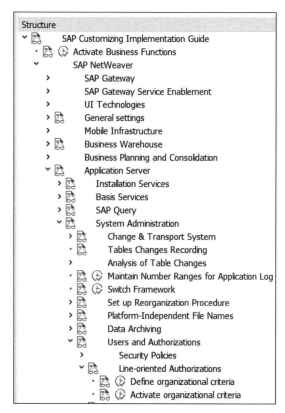

Figure 7.102 Display IMG in Transaction SPRO

You have the option to use existing organizational criteria or creating your own. For protecting table USR02, let's call our criterion "ZCLASS" and name it "User Group". The **Table Indicator** column lets you make the criteria available to all tables. In our example, let's leave it unchecked: we only want that criterion be available in tables maintained by us (Figure 7.103).

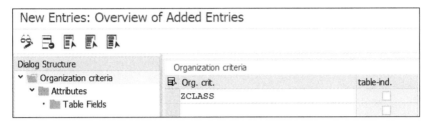

Figure 7.103 Create Organizational Criterion ZCLASS

Once the object is defined, select its line and switch to the **Attributes** view (Figure 7.104). Here, define the attribute (**Attrib.**) as "CLASS" with the **Name** "User Group". In total, SAP allows you to create eight attributes for the same criterion. However, in our example we'll only use the first.

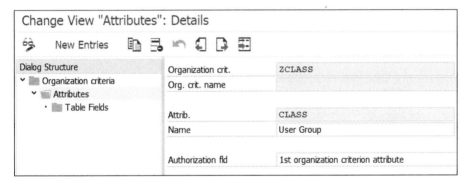

Figure 7.104 Define Attributes for Organizational Criterion

Finally, define the **Table Fields** that will be checked with this criterion. Set **View/Table** "VUSER001" with **Field Name** "CLASS" (Figure 7.105).

Once you save the change, the system will ask for a transport request. Once saved, go one step back in Transaction SPRO (Figure 7.106) and activate the org criterion by selecting the **Activ** checkbox so that you can use it with S_TABU_LIN.

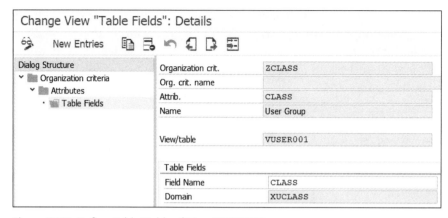

Figure 7.105 Define Table Fields of View VUSER001

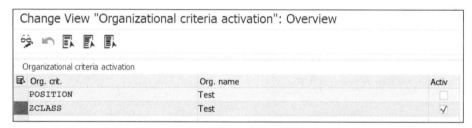

Figure 7.106 Activation of Newly Created Organizational Criterion ZCLASS

Once the line-oriented authorization is activated, it's important to update your roles so that the authorization check works. In Transaction PFCG, treat S_TABU_LIN (Figure 7.107) like any other authorization object. Make sure it's properly maintained and generate the profile.

Remember, S_TABU_LIN is an additional authorization check performed after S_TABU_DIS or S_TABU_NAM is successful. In the authorizations, you can define the **Activity** either as display (**03**) or change (**02**). Choose the organizational criterion and define the attribute. In our example, we'll grant display authorization to the user group (CLASS) SUPER.

> **Warning**
> Note that only key fields of a table/view can be defined as organizational criteria. Check the column of the table/view via Transaction SE11 first.

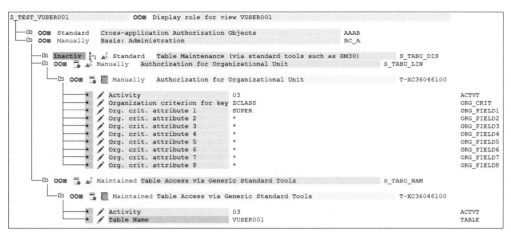

Figure 7.107 Example of S_TABU_LIN in Transaction PFCG

7.10.5   Table Authorizations and Auditors

During an SAP security audit, auditors are very well-known for checking table authorizations and reporting any potential weaknesses if such are not properly taken care of. Common checks include asterisk or ranges for S_TABU_DIS and S_TABU_NAM, as well as the generic table authorization group &NC&. If &NC& is given to users, all tables that aren't assigned to a table group are authorized. Customers mostly forget that customer-specific tables (Y* and Z*) aren't automatically assigned to a table group. Make sure that your customer tables are assigned to a table authorization group if they contain sensitive information. That's the task of the developer; if it's forgotten, it needs to be addressed.

7.10.6   Table Views for Database Tables

In previous sections, you learned that to protect a table you can use S_TABU_DIS and S_TABU_NAM, as well as S_TABU_CLI and S_TABU_LIN. Those authorization objects allow us to control the access to a table and to specific rows—but columns can't be protected with those authorization objects. To protect specific columns of a table, table views of any database table can be created.

The concept behind table views comes from the relational database, whereas a database administrator can create virtual tables (called *table views*) for physical tables directly in the database (on the database layer). With Transaction SE11, SAP allows us to create such table views on the application layer.

Let's return to our example with table USR02. We know how to protect rows with S_ TABU_LIN, but let's assume we want to grant access to table USR02 but don't want users to see the hash value and the code version of the password. As we discussed in Chapter 6, password hash values can be compromised by brute force attacks and therefore should be protected.

> **Warning**
>
> Creating table views is a developer task and requires a developer key. However, as a security administrator it's important to understand the possibility to further protect the system.

In Transaction SE11, you can create a table view for table SE11 and restrict the view to fields we don't want to show. Let's create a custom view called Z_LIMITED_USR02 in Transaction SE11, as shown in Figure 7.108.

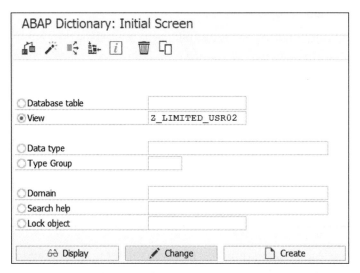

Figure 7.108 Initial Screen of Transaction SE11 to Create Database View

After you click the **Create** button, the system will ask for the type of view. For this example, define the view as a **Database view** (Figure 7.109).

Figure 7.109 Define View Type of Custom View in Transaction SE11

In the first screen, define a **Short Description** and the table you want to use. Note that with table views you can also build joins and display data from different tables. To keep the example short, let's use table USR02 to display certain fields (Figure 7.110).

Figure 7.110 Create Custom View in Transaction SE11

In the **View Flds** tab (Figure 7.111), you can define which field(s) from which table(s) will be shown. For our example, we use some fields from table USR02, but not the hash value of the password (field BCODE) and not the code version (field CODV1).

Once you save and activate the view, you can access it from the table browser (Transaction SE16). You'll only be able to see the fields that were defined in the previous steps (Figure 7.112).

Dictionary: Change View

Database View   Z_LIMITED_USR02   Inactive
Short Description   Limited Database View on Table USR02

| Attributes | Table/Join Conditions | View Flds | Selection Conditions | Maint.Status |

Table fields

View field	Table	Field	Key	Data elem.	Mod	DTyp	Length	Short description
MANDT	USR02	MANDT	✓	MANDT	☐	CLNT	3	Client
BNAME	USR02	BNAME	✓	XUBNAME	☐	CHAR	12	User Name in User Master Record
GLTGV	USR02	GLTGV	☐	XUGLTGV	☐	DATS	8	User valid from
GLTGB	USR02	GLTGB	☐	XUGLTGB	☐	DATS	8	User valid to
USTYP	USR02	USTYP	☐	XUUSTYP	☐	CHAR	1	User Type
CLASS	USR02	CLASS	☐	XUCLASS	☐	CHAR	12	User group in user master maintenance
LOCNT	USR02	LOCNT	☐	XULOCNT	☐	INT1	3	Number of failed logon attempts
UFLAG	USR02	UFLAG	☐	XUUFLAG	☐	INT1	3	User Lock Status
ACCNT	USR02	ACCNT	☐	XUACCNT	☐	CHAR	12	Account ID
ANAME	USR02	ANAME	☐	XUANAME	☐	CHAR	12	Creator of the User Master Record
ERDAT	USR02	ERDAT	☐	XUERDAT	☐	DATS	8	Creation Date of the User Master Record
TRDAT	USR02	TRDAT	☐	XULDATE	☐	DATS	8	Last Logon Date
LTIME	USR02	LTIME	☐	XULTIME	☐	TIMS	6	Last Logon Time

Figure 7.111 Create Custom View in Transaction SE11

Data Browser: Table Z_LIMITED_USR02 Select Entries   75

Check Table...

Table: Z_LIMITED_USR02
Displayed Fields: 13 of 13   Fixed Columns:

	MANDT	BNAME	GLTGV	GLTGB	USTYP	CLASS
☐	001	*	00.00.0000	00.00.0000	A	
☐	001	ABANZER	00.00.0000	00.00.0000	A	SUPER
☐	001	ABANZER____R	00.00.0000	00.00.0000	L	SUPER
☐	001	AFREUND	00.00.0000	00.00.0000	A	SUPER
☐	001	ATTACKME	00.00.0000	00.00.0000	S	

Figure 7.112 Data Browser for Custom Database Table View Z_LIMITED_USR02

To make the table available to an end user, we recommend that you create a variant transaction for Transaction SE16 that only allows a user to display that particular table/view.

7.11   Printer Authorizations

The SAP system has its own spool system to print documents and reports. In the spool system, you can manage output devices (e.g., printers), as well as the authorizations to access the spools. The authorization object to access spool devices is S_SPO_DEV. This authorization object controls which user can access which output device. To authorize users for S_SPO_DEV, you can use wildcards. With S_SPO_PAGE, you can control the number of pages a user can print on each output device. This authorization is dependent on the parameter rspo/auth/pagelimit, which must have a value of 1 in the system profile.

For a user to be able to select jobs from other users, the basic required authorization is S_ADMI_FCD with the value SPOR. To be able to select the spool from another user, you need S_SPO_ACT for the action (SPOACTION) BASE and DISP for the user (SPOAUTH) you want to see the spool. To see your own spool, you can leave the SPOAUTH field empty because the system assumes that the user is accessing his own spool. With Transaction SPO2, a user can access his spools; Transaction SPO1 with the desired authorizations allows someone to access spools of other users.

Check SAP Note 119147 to learn more about spool authorization and how to use them.

7.12   Other Important Authorization Objects

In an SAP ERP system, there are more than 3,000 authorization objects that control different applications of the system. Knowing them all is a daunting task, so we focus on the most important ones here. Also, SAP Help offers an explanation for each object, so we won't cover the whole list. Table and printer authorizations were covered in previous chapters. In this chapter, we'll only cover authorization objects of the system administration component, which start with S*. Module-specific authorizations are not covered.

7.12.1   Upload and Download Authorizations

Uploading and downloading data from an SAP system poses a potential risk because sensitive data can easily leave your organization. Within SAP GUI, the system checks authorization object S_GUI with activity 61 when downloading data to the frontend, and activity 60 when uploading data to the SAP system. Unfortunately, the authorization object doesn't support any protection for what's being downloaded. It either allows or disallows the download but doesn't differentiate between types of data. The same applies for the upload.

> **Tip**
>
> To enhance the security of downloads, SAP offers two user exits that can be implemented with custom logic. The first user exit (SGRPDL00) handles data that isn't tied to HR, and the second user exit (HRPC0001) handles data that comes from HR. Learn more in SAP Note 28777.

7.12.2   Report Authorizations

Reports and executable programs can be protected with S_PROGRAM through the program authorization group. The program authorization group is maintained in the program attribute, which can be checked in Transaction SE38 (Figure 7.113).

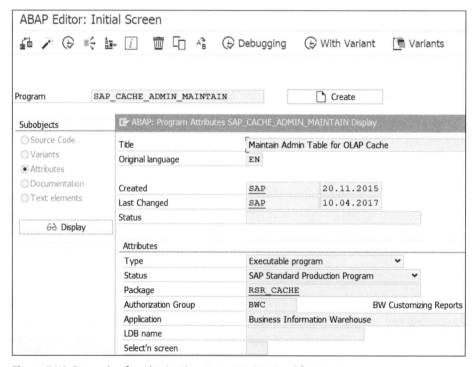

Figure 7.113 Example of Authorization Group Maintained for Program

> **Tip**
> Available program authorization groups can be checked in table TPGP.

7.12.3   Background Jobs

With Transaction SM36 to create background jobs and Transaction SM37 to view background jobs, users have the ability to schedule jobs not only for themselves but also for other users. We recommend running periodic background jobs in the context of a technical user because such users comply with different user policies. The basic object of background jobs is S_BTCH_JOB. As an administrator, you need S_BTCH_ADM to administer jobs created by other users. To schedule jobs in the context of another user, such as a technical user, you require authorization S_BTCH_NAM.

7.12.4   ABAP Workbench

To create development objects and to debug them, authorization S_DEVELOP is required. S_DEVELOP is one of the most powerful authorization objects in the entire system and hence authorized and assigned very carefully. If you assign S_DEVLOP with activity 02 to change variables at runtime, you pretty much give a user full access to your system because each and every return code can be manipulated.

7.12.5   Batch Sessions

With batch input sessions, data can be loaded into an SAP system. To monitor these sessions, Transaction SM35 is used. S_BCD_MONI controls the sessions and allows restriction on certain process activities, like lock and delete.

7.12.6   Query Authorizations

In any SAP system, the SAP Query component allows you to create simplified query reports without actual coding. Similar to the QuickViewer (Transaction SQVI), SAP Query offers more powerful tools to access data in the system. Hence, it's the security administrator's responsibility to protect SAP Query accordingly. SAP Query knows three main transactions to create, maintain, and execute queries: Transactions SQ01, SQ02, and SQ03. The queries don't access tables directly; they use an *info set*, which is defined as a table join or a logical database.

With Transaction SQ01, you can create queries that read data from the info sets maintained in Transaction SQ02. Transaction SQ03 is used to assign users to so-called query user groups. Unlike most of the other SAP components, queries are not only authorized through roles and authorizations. For a user to access a query, he must be assigned to the query user group, which is also assigned to the query and the info set. Those assignments are maintained in Transaction SQ03. Note that query user groups are not related to the user groups in the user master record. To create and maintain SAP queries, the authorization object S_QUERY is used.

To authorize end users who use SAP Query to run reports, you would authorize Transaction SQ00. Per default, Transaction SQ00 pulls S_QUERY with activity 02 for change; however, to only run reports, actual change authorization isn't required.

7.12.7   Remote Function Call Authorizations

Remote Function Call (RFC) is a communication interface for SAP systems. SAP systems communicate with each other via RFC. RFCs are also possible to receive from non-SAP systems. RFCs are grouped into two types: trusted RFCs and untrusted RFCs. With trusted RFCs, the calling system is a trusted source and hence doesn't require authentication. In an untrusted RFC, the calling system must authenticate itself with logon credentials (user and password) against the destination system. RFC connections are maintained within Transaction SM59.

When authorizing remote function calls, three main authorization objects are being used. Two objects control access from and to a system, and another controls access within the destination system on a function module level.

In the calling system, before the remote function call takes place, the system checks the S_ICF authorizations for the user who performs the remote function call. S_ICF grants access to the destination of the remote function call. Once granted, S_RFC and S_RFCACL are checked in the destination system.

For untrusted RFCs, authentication happens with the RFC user and its password. If successful, the called function modules are checked with authorization object S_RFC of the calling RFC user which is stored in the RFC destination in Transaction SM59 of the calling system.

For trusted RFCs, the interface is already authenticated and the RFC user doesn't have to log on. Instead, the system will perform an authority check against the dialog user who is calling the RFC. The authorization check is performed against S_RFCACL, which grants access to the system (destination) for the calling dialog user in combination with the desired RFC user. Once successful, the destination system checks for S_RFC for the calling RFC user.

To properly and securely authorize RFC destinations, make sure to follow the least-privilege principle. When you create your RFC authorization concept, distinguish between technical service users and normal dialog users. Each RFC destination must have its dedicated user ID and password. Only then can you determine from which system an RFC has originated. It also allows you to granularly authorize systems individually. Also, activate and review the security audit log for your RFC users to get required authorizations for the RFC interfaces.

> **Tip**
>
> To avoid missing authorizations in RFCs, most security administrators tend to authorize the RFC user with SAP_ALL. With SAP_ALL, the interface can be exploited to also call critical functions. Therefore, properly authorizing RFC users is a cumbersome but very important aspect of a secure SAP system. Read SAP Note 1682316 - Consulting: Optimizing RFC User Authorizations to learn how SAP consulting recommends optimizing RFC users.

7.13   Transaction SACF: Switchable Authorizations

With the switchable authorization concept, SAP delivers authorization checks based on scenarios. One of the key drivers for switchable authorizations is upgrades to higher support packages. With every upgrade, SAP introduces new authorization objects that are required to run certain functions. With each upgrade, the security administrator has to update the authorizations to reflect the latest changes and introduce missing authorizations into the roles; otherwise, users won't have access to execute the functions. Not only dialog users are affected by changes; RFC interfaces also might be interrupted if new authorizations aren't added accordingly. Most companies help themselves by granting SAP_ALL to interfaces, which is considered a high-risk decision.

To avoid interruptions, SAP delivers authorization changes as inactive scenarios within the switchable authorizations. What does that mean? Let's assume SAP introduces a new authorization object into one of its programs with an enhancement pack. To successfully execute that program, the newly introduced authorizations must be reflected in the roles. This task is time-consuming and cumbersome. With

Transaction SACF, SAP delivers an inactive scenario definition. This means that so long as the scenario is inactive, the old authorizations will still work. The security administrator now can check the inactive scenarios, update the roles, and test them before activating them in production.

Switchable authorization checks are delivered with an SAP Note. The SAP Note corrects the SAP code (to implement the new check mechanism), and adds a scenario definition as well as a description of the scenario. With its logging functionality, the scenario can be activated but fails to pass authorization checks. After the logged authorization checks are reviewed and corrected, the scenario can be activated.

Switchable authorizations checks look different in the code than traditional authorization check statements. Rather than performing the AUTHORITY-CHECK statement, an API is called. Figure 7.114 shows an authority check that was replaced with a switchable authorization check. On line 10 to 17, you can see the traditional AUTHORITY-CHECK statement and on line 19 and following you can see the API that is being used.

```
10▶ ⊟ *AUTHORITY-CHECK OBJECT 'S_TABU_NAM'
11▶  *          ID 'ACTVT' FIELD '03'
12▶  *          ID 'TABLE' FIELD 'USR02'.
13▶  *IF sy-subrc <> 0.
14▶  *   WRITE: / 'S_TABU_NAM - Authority check passed'.
15▶  *ELSE.
16▶  *   WRITE: / 'S_TABU_NAM - Authority check failed'.
17▶ └ *ENDIF.
18
19▶ ⊟ IF 0 = cl_sacf=>auth_check_spec( EXPORTING  id_name = 'Z_TEST_SCENARIO'
20                                                id_suso = 'S_TABU_NAM'
21                                                id_fld1 = 'ACTVT'
22                                                id_val1 = '03'
23                                                id_fld2 = 'TABLE'
24                                                id_val2 = 'USR02' ).
25
26    WRITE: / 'S_TABU_NAM - Authority check passed'.
27  ⊹ ELSE.
28    WRITE: / 'S_TABU_NAM - Authority check failed'.
29 └ ENDIF.
```

Figure 7.114 Example Code for Switchable Authorizations

The return code of the switchable authorization check is validated and processed in the API. Based on the scenario and the settings, the return code is handled differently.

7.14   Customizing Entries in Tables PRGN_CUST and SSM_CUST

Tables PRGN_CUST and SSM_CUST allow an administrator to define certain parameters to change the behavior of certain transactions and functionalities. Both tables are easily maintainable via the table maintenance in Transaction SM30. To get the full list of available parameters, open the input help (press F4) and check the available parameters.

As a security administrator, you can define certain behavior—such as how S_USER* authorization objects are checked—with table PRGN_CUST. Therefore, those parameters are helpful for understanding why the system reacts in a certain behavior.

The settings listed in Table 7.5 are recommendations for table PRGN_CUST.

Parameter	Default Value	Recommended Value	Description
ADD_ALL_CUST_OBJECTS	YES	YES	Controls the generation of custom authorization objects in the profile SAP_ALL. Once set to YES, generating the profile will include all Y* and Z* authorization objects and its values.
ADD_OLD_AUTH_OBJECTS	NO	YES	Controls the generation of obsolete objects in profile SAP_ALL. Obsolete authorization objects are part of class AAAA.
ADD_S_RFCACL	NO	YES	Gives full authorization to S_RFCACL in SAP_ALL.
ASSIGN_ROLE_AUTH	CHANGE	ASSIGN	Controls the required authorization to assign roles to users. If set to CHANGE, then the administrator requires S_USER_GRP with activity 02 for change and S_USER_AGR with activity 22 to assign. If set to ASSIGN, only S_USER_AGR with activity 22 for assigning is required.
AUTO_USER_COMPARE	YES	YES	Automatic user master record reconciliation in Transaction PFCG, SU01, and SU10.

Table 7.5 Recommended Values for Table PRGN_CUST

Parameter	Default Value	Recommended Value	Description
CUA_PARAMETER_CHECK	W	W	When CUA distributes a user to a child system and a parameter doesn't exist, the system shows a warning but performs all the other changes to the user master.
PFCG_EASY_MODE_ON	NO		Activation of Transaction PFCG_EASY.
PFCG_NAME-SPACE_CHECK	YES		Namespace check when creating roles in Transaction PFCG. This parameter checks that roles are in the customer name space.
PFCG_RFC_CONNECT	YES		Allows a user to import roles via RFC. See more information in SAP Note 511918.
REF_USER_CHECK	W	E	Checks the user type when assigning a reference user to a user. Reference users shall be of type Reference. Parameter E forces the reference user type and otherwise shows an error that the user isn't type Reference.
PROFILE_TRANSPORT	YES	YES	Allows a user to transport generated role profiles when transporting roles.

Table 7.5 Recommended Values for Table PRGN_CUST (Cont.)

The settings listed in Table 7.6 are recommendations for table SSM_CUST.

Parameter	Default Value	Recommended Value	Description
CONDENSE_MENU	NO	YES	Eliminates redundancies in the role menu.
SORT_USER_MENU	NO	YES	Alphabetically sorts user menu.
DELETE_DOUBLE_TCODES	NO	YES	Deletes duplicates from the role menu.

Table 7.6 Recommended Values for Table SSM_CUST

7.15   Mass Maintenance of Values within Roles

With Transaction PFCGMASSVAL, you can change the authorization values of multiple roles in one shot. You can change organizational levels, field values of authorizations for an object, and field values of authorizations for a field.

The transaction allows three different change modes:

- **Simulation**
  Simulate the changes before you perform an actual change. During this step, the system automatically locks all the roles so that no one else can interfere with the change.

- **Execution with Previous Simulation**
  Simulates the changes and offers the option to push the changes to the roles. During the simulation, the system locks all the roles automatically.

- **Direct Execution**
  The changes are immediately effective and displayed in a result list.

In the initial screen, shown in Figure 7.115, select the roles that you want to change and choose the change mode.

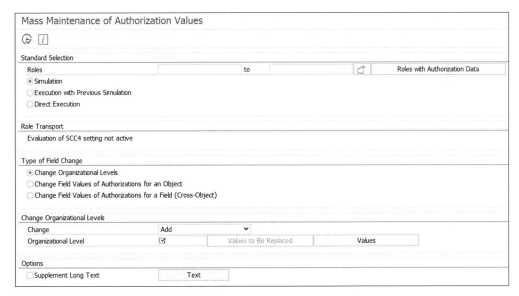

Figure 7.115 Initial Screen of Mass Maintenance of Authorization Values in Transaction PFCGMASSVAL

In the **Type of Field Change** section, you have to decide what change you want to perform. The following three types of changes are available:

- **Change Organizational Levels**
  You can change the global maintenance of all org levels of the selected roles. This doesn't affect authorization objects for which org levels have been changed manually.

- **Change Field Values of Authorizations for an Object**
  You can change all the fields and their values for an authorization object. Note that when you change an authorization object that contains org levels, the system will show a warning icon. If you proceed and change org levels, the authorization object will have the **Changed** status. This doesn't change the values of the global maintenance of the org levels.

- **Change Field Values of Authorizations for a Field (Cross-Object)**
  You can change the field values of a specific authorization field. For example, you can change the activity to O3 in all the selected roles regardless of the authorization object. Note that changes to an org level will show a warning and the status of the object will become **Changed**.

In the following example, we want to add a new company code to the org levels (Figure 7.116).

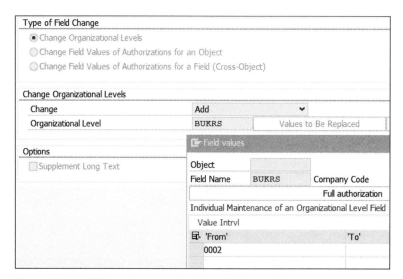

Figure 7.116 Add New Company Code to All Selected Roles

Let's assume company code 0002 was introduced and we want to add it to all our roles based on our selection. Selection is very important because it defines where the new company code gets added.

If we execute the report in simulation mode, we can see that the org level is introduced to the selected roles if BUKRS (company code) exists. In our example, role Z_TEST_DERIVEC_ROLE_FINANCE_01 has already a value (0001) for BUKRS. The **Value Comparison** shows that the value 0002 is added (Figure 7.117).

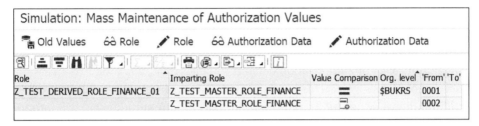

Figure 7.117 Simulation of Org Level Mass Maintenance

If, in the previous step, we decide to replace an existing value with a new one, the result looks slightly different. Let's assume we want to replace value 0001 with 0002. The simulation tells us that value 0001 is removed and value 0002 is introduced (Figure 7.118).

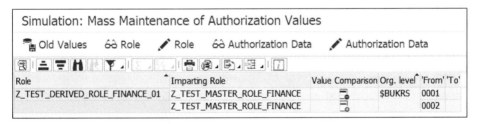

Figure 7.118 Replace Org Levels in Mass

To change field values of authorizations you can proceed in a similar fashion. Enter the fields and values to be changed; as a precaution, simulate your desired changes first.

Transaction PFCGMASSVAL is a handy feature and extends the mass maintenance capability of Transaction PFCG. With this transaction, you can save time when organizational changes must be reflected in roles.

7.16   Upgrading to a New Release

For an SAP system, a support package upgrade is a recurring event in any organization. With every support package, SAP releases new functions and applications, as well as corrections to existing ones. What does that mean to a security administrator? New functionalities and applications must be authorized to function properly, and changed applications might require new or changed authorizations. If an existing application used by your end users gets new authorization checks, then it's important to assign those new authorizations to the end users who use the application. So how do you know what's changed and what needs to be changed in your roles?

SAP delivers a set of authorization defaults in tables USOBT and USOBX. To access the data of those tables, you can use Transaction SU22, which contains the default values that were delivered by SAP. As a customer, you can modify and extend those authorization proposals. Your custom authorization defaults are stored in tables USOBT_C and USOBX_C. To check and maintain custom authorization proposals, Transaction SU24 is used.

> **Tip**
>
> Never change Transaction SU22 data manually because it's overwritten with each upgrade. Instead, use Transaction SU24 to define custom authorization proposals and use Transaction SU22 as a reference to compare custom data with SAP data.

With Transaction SU25, SAP provides a tool that allows security administrators to compare delivered Transaction SU22 data with Transaction SU24 and to update and modify custom authorization proposals in Transaction SU24 (Figure 7.119).

After an upgrade, there are certain steps in Transaction SU25 that are recommended and some that shouldn't be used. Step 1, the initial filling of customer tables, must be run only after installation, but not after an upgrade. Step 1 overwrites all customer tables with SAP-standard values and hence will destroy your Transaction SU24 values.

The first postupgrade task is running step 2A, in which the system compares the SAP default values with your custom values. Basically, it compares tables USOBT and USOBX with tables USOBT_C and USOBX_C. In this step, the system determines whether the default values can be copied to the customer values or if it requires manual modifications to the customer values. Manual modification is required when the custom values are different than the default values and hence automatic comparison would overwrite custom data.

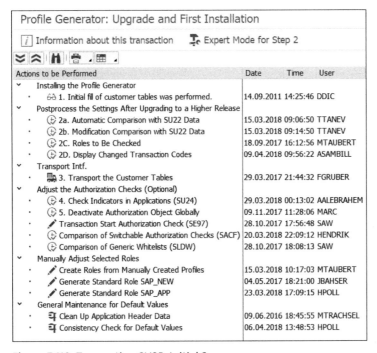

Figure 7.119 Transaction SU25: Initial Screen

When executing step 2A, it's recommended to run in test mode (select the **Test Mode** checkbox shown in Figure 7.120) first to get an overview of what's being changed.

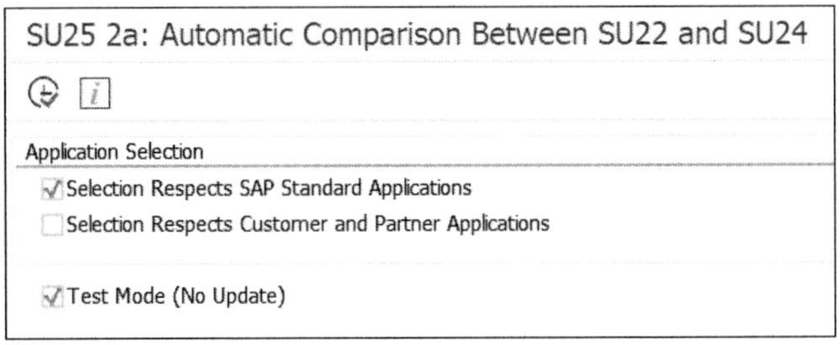

Figure 7.120 Step 2A: Automatic Comparison between Transactions SU22 and SU24

In the overview, the system tells you which objects can be updated automatically and which need to be manually updated (Figure 7.121).

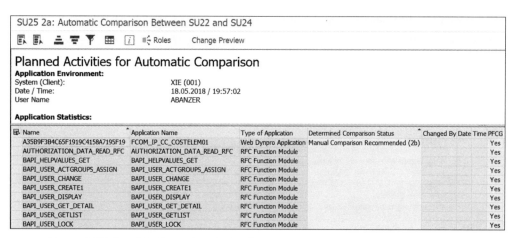

Figure 7.121 Step 2A: Planned Activities for Automatic Comparison

If you agree with the automatic changes, go back one step and execute the report without the **Test Mode** option selected.

Once step 2A is complete, continue with step 2B (Figure 7.122). In this step, you manually compare the list of transactions and decide whether you want to adopt the recommendations from SAP or continue with the custom values. This step can be time-consuming because it's best to check each transaction one by one.

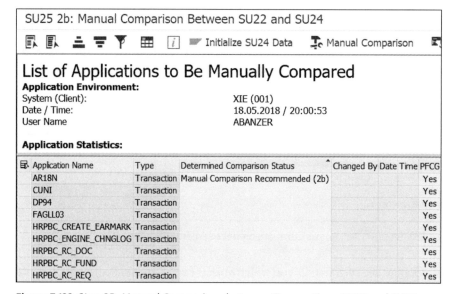

Figure 7.122 Step 2B: Manual Comparison between Transactions SU22 and SU24

To manually update a transaction, double-click the correct entry in the **Application Name** column (Figure 7.122) and check the authorization objects that are being proposed (Figure 7.123).

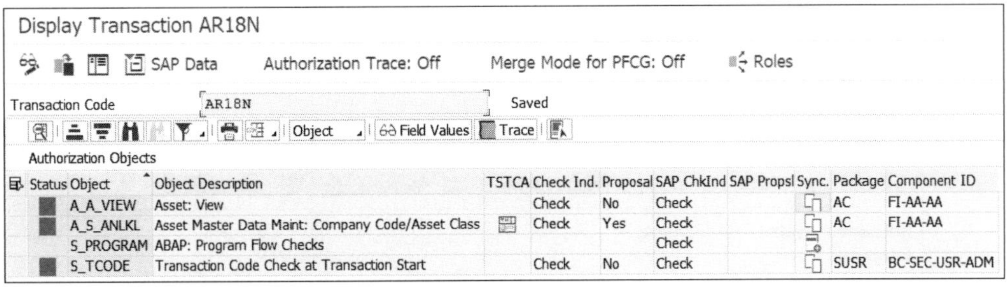

Figure 7.123 Manual Comparison of Example Transaction

In Figure 7.123, you can see which authorization objects will be introduced to Transaction SU24. The **Sync.** column allows you to manually insert the object into Transaction SU24. For the very first row, you can copy the SAP data to Transaction SU24, which will tell you that you currently have the authorization object maintained and this will overwrite the existing values. Same applies for the second and fourth row. For the third row, the values will be newly introduced as they don't exist in SU24 yet.

Deciding whether an object should be introduced is tough. In general, we recommend keeping the customer values unless there's a good reason to change them. Most likely, if you updated your Transaction SU24 proposals, you did so based on findings and usage of the transaction. Blindly adopting the changes from SAP and overwriting custom data isn't recommended. In some important cases, for example, SAP proposes to introduce a check—whereas you have it set as **Do Not Check**, as it increases the security of the transaction. In such cases it is recommend that you adopt the change from SAP. Also, SAP might introduce new authorization objects with new releases that are required for a transaction.

> **Tip**
>
> Before making any updates to your customer values in Transaction SU24, we recommend taking a backup of tables USOBT_C and USOBX_C. To download and upload data from Transactions SU22 and SU24, use reports RSU22DOWN and RSU22UPLD. In the options, choose **SAP Data** or **Customer Data**. SAP data represents Transaction SU22 and customer data Transaction SU24.

Once step 2B is complete, continue with step 2C (Figure 7.124), which provides an overview of all roles that need to be changed to get the latest updates from Transaction SU24. Remember that changing Transaction SU24 proposals only has an impact when they're merged into a role. Also, Transaction SU24 proposals only apply to objects that have been added via the role menu. Manually added objects (e.g., S_TCODE) won't consider your Transaction SU24 proposals.

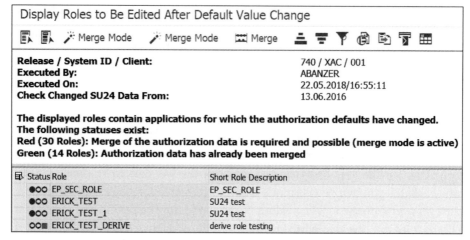

Figure 7.124 Display Roles to Be Edited after Default Value Change

The last step, 2D (Figure 7.125), is mainly used to check whether SAP has introduced new transactions that might replace an existing transaction. Transactions can become obsolete and need to be replaced with new ones. Therefore, check the list of the changed transactions and decide whether you want to adopt the new transactions for your roles.

As a final postupgrade step, run step 3 and transport the customer tables to all successive systems in your landscape. Once the customer tables are transported, we recommend transporting all your roles that were generated during the execution of step 2C.

Step 4 brings you to Transaction SU24, to check and update the custom specific authorization proposals. In step 5, you can globally deactivate authorization checks on certain authorization objects. You can also start the report with Transaction AUTH_SWITCH_OBJECTS directly. In this report, as shown in Figure 7.126, you can deactivate the objects by clicking on the checkbox to the left. Deactivated authorization objects will turn red.

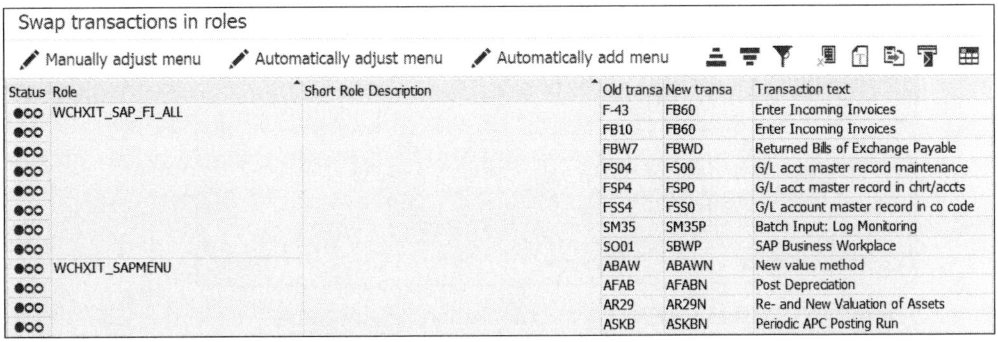

Figure 7.125 Swap Transactions in Roles

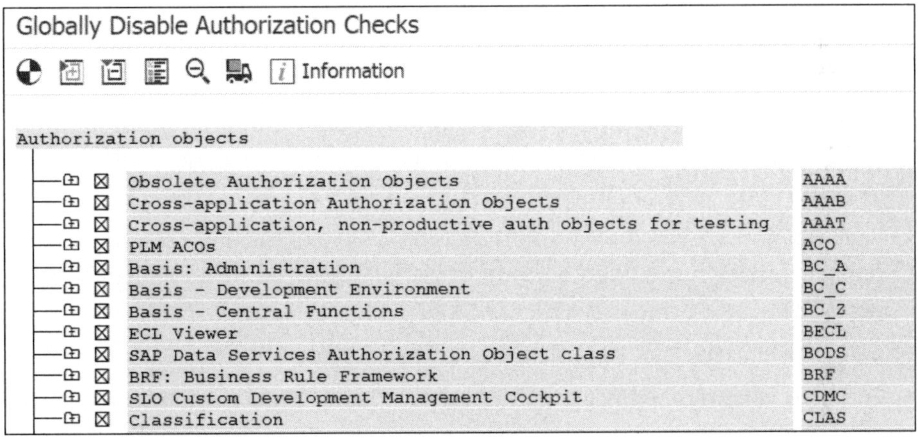

Figure 7.126 Globally Deactivate Authorization Checks

The last two steps involved in an upgrade are general maintenance for default values. In these two steps, you can clean up application header data and check the consistency of the default values. The clean-up of application header data registers services for Transaction PFCG and Transaction SU24, which are otherwise not always available in the input help [F4] when adding a service to a role.

To check the consistency of your default values, SAP provides a report that can either be started from Transaction SU25 or directly with report SU2X_CHECK_CONSISTENCY. This report runs against your Transaction SU24 data and checks the consistency of the selected authorization objects and organizational levels. Use this report, as shown in Figure 7.127, to identify any incorrect default values and correct them using forward navigation in the result screen.

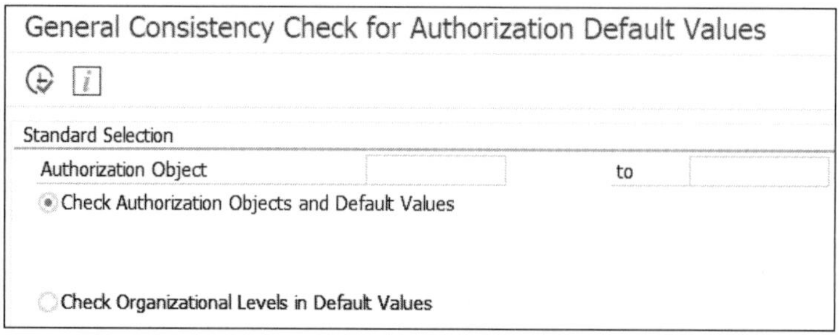

General Consistency Check for Authorization Default Values

⊕ [i]

Standard Selection

| Authorization Object | | to | |

⦿ Check Authorization Objects and Default Values

○ Check Organizational Levels in Default Values

Figure 7.127 Consistency Check for Authorization Default Values

To clean up inconsistencies in your default values, SAP provides report SU24_AUTO_ REPAIR. This report allows to detect inconsistencies and automatically correct them. If you want to correct your Transaction SU24 data as part of an upgrade, make sure to run it before executing step 2C. The auto repair report, as show in Figure 7.128, allows different selections:

- Delete Transaction SU24 default values for which there is no corresponding check indicator
- Repair bad fields based on the information from Transaction SU21 and add or remove missing respectively add authorization fields that are missing in Transaction SU24
- Delete invalid check indicators such as unknown values
- Complete missing modification flags so that the SU24 data indicates that it has been changed
- Delete invalid default values like <SPACE> or an asterisk (*) with another explicit value
- Remove incorrectly defined organizational levels like User Group ($CLASS)
- Add missing transaction start authorizations from Transaction SE93

Once you completed all the steps in Transaction SU24, your system has been upgraded from a security point of view and the next step is to test impacted business processes. From this point on, each time you add an object to a role via the role menu, the latest Transaction SU24 values will be considered and you will have upgradable roles in the future.

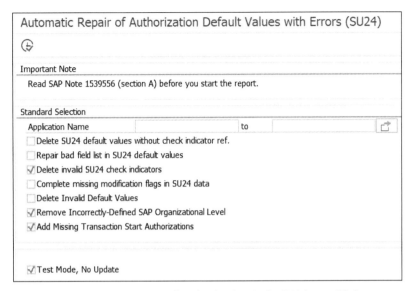

Figure 7.128 Automatic Repair of Authorization Default Values with Errors

7.17 ABAP Debugger

As a security administrator, it's important to understand some of the fundamentals of programming—especially how to use the ABAP debugger to debug code and to find and check authority checks.

Figure 7.129 shows an authority check for object F_KNA1_BED. The code checks the object with field values for the material group (field BEGRU) and for the activity (field ACTVT) with value 03 (display). In a second check, the system checks for authorization object F_LFA1_BEK.

For any authority check, it's most important that the return code is handled. Therefore, the program checks for IF SY-SUBRC <> 0, which checks the return code of the authorization check. The following return codes are available:

- 0: The user has an authorization with all the required values
- 4: The user does not have authorization
- 8: The number of specified authorization fields is incorrect
- 12: The specified authorization object does not exist

```
ABAP Editor: Display Include MF05LI00

Include                    MF05LI00                              Active
   561
   562  □       IF bseg-koart = 'D'.
   563            AUTHORITY-CHECK OBJECT 'F_KNA1_BED'
   564                        ID 'BRGRU' FIELD bsec-begru
   565                        ID 'ACTVT' FIELD '03'.
   566  □      IF sy-subrc <> 0.
   567            CLEAR ok-code.
   568            MESSAGE s450(f5a).
   569            EXIT.
   570         ENDIF.
   571       ELSEIF bseg-koart = 'K'.
   572            AUTHORITY-CHECK OBJECT 'F_LFA1_BEK'
   573                        ID 'BRGRU' FIELD bsec-begru
   574                        ID 'ACTVT' FIELD '03'.
   575  □      IF sy-subrc <> 0.
   576            CLEAR ok-code.
   577            MESSAGE s450(f5a).
   578            EXIT.
   579         ENDIF.
   580       ENDIF.
   581     ENDIF.
```

Figure 7.129 Example Code of Authority Check Statement

If the return code is greater than 0, that means that the authorization check failed. The program will return with a message saying that the user has no authorization to perform the desired action. It's also important to understand that most programs check for more authorization than is actually required by the user. In the previous example, the program doesn't terminate if the user has no authorization for one of the company codes that are available; it simply doesn't show values for that particular company code.

To start the debugger, you require authorizations for object S_DEVELOP with object type (field OBJTYPE) and value DEBUG. In addition, a breakpoint must be set so that the code knows when to stop and to start the debugging session. Breakpoints can either be hard-coded or set in the session. To switch on the debugger, enter "/h" in the command box (Figure 7.130).

Figure 7.130 Switch on Session Debugger

Although the ABAP debugger is a nice feature, it possesses potential danger to your system. With certain authorizations, you can change variables within the debugger and hence influence the behavior of a program. For example, if you have S_DEVELOP with activity (field ACTVT) and value 02 (change), you can change the return code (field SY-SUBRC) to value 0 after the authorization check fails. Also, you can avoid authorization checks by jumping or skipping certain steps of the program. Therefore, make sure that the authorization for debugging is restricted and only granted when needed. For productive environments, we also recommend assigning debugging authorizations via an emergency user that's monitored and approved.

7.18   Authorization Redesign and Cleanup

Authorization cleanup is a common but time consuming and cumbersome task for a security administrator. Authorization clean-up projects are commonly called role redesign, security redesign, RFC redesign, RFC hardening, or role remediation projects. The goal is to reduce maintenance and, at the same time, increase the quality and security of your authorization design. However, such projects come with a significant change to the SAP roles that impact the authorizations of your SAP users.

Authorization redesign projects are triggered for various reasons, such as:

- Changes in the organizational structure
- Use of SAP standard roles
- System upgrades
- Migrations to SAP S/4HANA
- Over-authorized users
- Segregation of duty (SoD) conflicts
- Legal requirements
- The desire to simplify role administration

Often it is a combination of some of the above factors, which together trigger the need for a complete role redesign project. On the plus side, a properly executed role redesign project often provides multiple benefits, including:

- Simplified role administration
- Remediation of SoD conflict
- Properly authorized users

7.18.1   Business Impact of Security Redesign

The main reason some organizations shy away from or delay role redesign projects is that such projects can be time consuming and expensive. This is true not only for the SAP security teams but also for business users. Traditional role redesign projects heavily involve business users and analysts during both the design and testing phases. By involving business users, you pull them from their day-to-day job, which takes a toll on their productivity.

Additionally, the business is likely going to take a second hit when it is time to go live with the new roles. Any gaps or missing authorizations that testers overlooked during acceptance testing will disrupt the workflow of business users, leading to more lost productivity and work for role administrators.

Many organizations have either accepted the cost of a role redesign and the impact on its business, or they have delayed such projects and decided to accept the risk that comes with incorrectly authorized users.

The good news is, there is a middle ground. In other words, you can successfully execute a role redesign project with only minimal or no impact on your business.

7.18.2   Reducing the Business Impact of a Role Redesign Project

Traditionally, roles in SAP contain the following authorizations data:

- Organizational fields with organizational values (i.e., company code, purchasing organization, etc.)
- Authorization objects (i.e., transactions, function modules, etc.)
- Authorization fields with is values (i.e., activity 03 for display)

As a result, a role could authorize a user to have display access (activity 03) to Transaction VA03 for company code 1000. Of course, this is a simplified view on a role design, but it helps to illustrate the concept.

When your organization tasks you with redesigning roles, business analysts often provide answers to such questions as:

- What transactions does user XYZ need access to?
- What authorizations does the user need? Display or change?
- What company code is the user booking to?

The answers to these and other questions often build the base of your role design concept. The problem is that obtaining that information for a large group of users is time consuming and error-prone. Additionally, business users tend to err on the side of requesting more authorizations when providing input to business analysts.

What many security admins don't or only partially realize is that the answers to all of the above questions are available in the database of your SAP system. You just have to know where to look. In other words, by retrieving the required information directly from SAP, you minimize the disruption caused by designing new roles on your business users.

Of course, once you have built the new roles or made changes to existing ones, you have to test them. User acceptance testing (UAT) is another time consuming phase of traditional role redesign projects that has the potential to negatively impact the productivity of your business users.

7.18.3   Gathering Authorization Data

Let's explore where to find authorization data in the SAP system.

Statistical Trace Data: Transaction ST03N

One treasure trove of information related to transaction execution activity is the Workload Monitor. You can access it via Transaction ST03N. Among many other things, it shows you user transaction execution activity. Using that information, you can analyze what transactions your users executed over the past few months. The exact timeframe depends on your system configuration. By default, your SAP system retains three months' worth of usage data, unless you changed the configuration.

We generally recommend accumulating between three to six months' worth of usage data to get a good overview of what transactions your users use. If you have SAP GRC Access Control, you can get the same information from SAP GRC's Action Usage Report (table GRACACTUSAGE).

The next step is to optimize your roles by merging Transaction SU24 proposals. If you haven't maintained your authorization proposals yet, it's recommended to optimize Transaction SU24. By bringing in Transaction SU24 proposals, you have taken the first step to populate your roles with authorization fields and values. Unfortunately, not all the objects you need in your roles are available via Transaction SU24. So, the next step is to find out what fields and values you need to properly authorize your users, including organizational values.

Authorization Fields and Values

Transaction STO3N does not include authorization objects below the transaction (TCODE) level. As a result, we have to leverage other trace sources, such as Transaction STO1, to get an idea of what authorization fields and values are required for the roles we are trying to build. Additionally, you will have to determine the proper organizational fields and values for each user. For the latter, you can retrieve the necessary information from a variety of tables, based on the type of data you need.

For instance, if you are building a role to authorize users to change purchasing documents, you can look at table EKKO for information about which users made changes to purchasing documents and what the associated org fields were.

Using that information, you can fine-tune your roles and make sure your users are properly authorized based on the relevant organizational values.

7.18.4   Testing Role Changes in Production

Once you have built new roles as part of your redesign project you have to test them. Unfortunately, SAP offers very limited tools to automate that process beyond individual trace files. Analyzing those traces for hundreds or thousands of users without proper reporting and gap analysis is not feasible. Instead, you can leverage the productive test simulation (PTS), which is part of the Xiting Authorizations Management Suite (XAMS), as described in SAP Note 1682316 - Consulting: Optimizing RFC User Authorizations.

Using this technology, you, as a role administrator, can test new roles in a production environment without negatively affecting end users. To accomplish this, XAMS leverages standard SAP reference users (user type Reference).

Let's say you want to test the new roles you created for user Dave. Via the XAMS, in production, you would create a reference user, assign the new roles to that reference user and then assign the reference user to Dave.

Why use a reference user? The answer is simple: anytime the SAP kernel performs an authority check, it does so against the reference user first—if there is a reference user assigned. If that authority check fails, then the SAP kernel performs the same authority check against the dialog user. If that authority check succeeds, SAP logs a return code 0. With the help of the XAMS, you can analyze these return codes and quickly export roles containing the missing authorizations. Using the exported roles, you can fine-tune your new roles in development and transport the changes up to production.

7.18.5   Automate Role Creation and Testing

While the steps discussed thus far about the creation of new roles help you to gather the required information to build proper roles in SAP, they are time-consuming and error-prone. As a result, the steps are impractical if your goal is to build roles for more than a handful of users. However, you don't have to perform the steps manually. To automate and simplify all the tasks we have described above, you can leverage XAMS.

With the XAMS, you can:

- Streamline the analysis and processing of trace data
- Instantly identify missing Transaction SU24 proposals
- Enable role administrators to build roles based on statistical trace data and via a drag-and-drop interface
- Automatically enrich the created roles with business data, including the required organizational fields and values
- Simulate new roles based on user activity in production to identify any missing authorization fields and values with the PTS
- Replicate individual roles across organizational units

7.19   Introduction to SAP GRC Access Control

This section provides an overview of SAP GRC Access Control and its four modules. The key benefits of SAP GRC Access Control are (1) to prevent and identify access and authorization risks in cross-enterprise SAP systems to prevent fraud and (2) to reduce the cost of continuous compliance and control. With its integrated risk analysis and workflow engine, it reduces the time required to detect, remediate, and approve access across different IT systems. It offers a centralized request and approval process with integrations to HR systems (such as SAP ERP HCM) to support the user life cycle process from hire to retire. If evaluated access is required for a short time, temporary access can be checked out and evaluated and checked by a supervisor.

7.19.1   Access Risk Analysis

As you learned in Chapter 6, Section 6.19, it's important to separate and control authorizations a user gets to be compliant with Sarbanes-Oxley (SOX) and other laws and regulations. The Access Risk Analysis (ARA) modules let you identify and detect access violations in the entire enterprise. It can check for SoD violations, critical transactions and authorizations, and critical roles and profiles. To check these violations, the ARA module uses a rule set that contains the definition of the critical authorizations. The system compares the defined rules from the rule set with the authorization in scope (e.g., a user, a role, a profile) and reports any violation that might occur.

7.19.2   Access Request Management

In a traditional organization, access is granted after completing paper forms that were sent through the organization and finally made their way to IT security. The IT security administrator then grants the access manually. Checking for compliance and traceability were both limited. During the manual approval process on paper, how can the signee identify possible threats that an assignment would create? Also, the approval process typically takes several days to complete, depending on the size and complexity of the organization,

With Access Request Management (ARM), a user can request access through a workflow based module. When an access request is submitted, it takes a predefined path and allows for multiple approvals and security checks. Because the ARM module is tied into the ARA module, the approver can execute compliance checks in the form of an access risk analysis to identify possible threats before they even occur. You can customize the workflow to reflect your company's policies. Roles and authorizations are automatically logged when the access requests are approved for future reference and audit purposes. ARM ensures corporate accountability and compliance with SOX, along with other laws and regulations.

7.19.3   Business Role Management

With Business Role Management (BRM), an enterprise can implement certain steps involved in the lifetime of a role. From role creation, for which BRM allows you to apply naming conventions, performing role updates with the approval from a role content approver, all the way to providing the attributes for role provisioning, BRM supports the life cycle of a role.

BRM empowers role owners to be involved in the role-building process, to run risk analysis before the role's deployed, and to document role testing.

With its business role concept, BRM offers the ability to create system-independent virtual roles to simplify the technical role assignment in the backend system. The concept is similar to that of composite roles, but it isn't restricted to a single system. The business role construct is only known in SAP GRC Access Control, but it can be shared with SAP Identity Management in an integrated provisioning scenario. When a business role is assigned to a user, the system distributes the technical role assignments to various backend systems, either via the CUA or directly. The backend system, however, doesn't know that the role assignment comes from a business role.

7.19.4 Emergency Access Management

With Emergency Access Management (EAM), a user can perform emergency activities outside his or her standard roles. The user performs the emergency activities in a controlled and fully auditable environment by checking out a firefighter ID. The application allows for a firefighter ID that grants the user (firefighter) broad yet regulated access. All activities that are performed in the context of the firefighter ID are logged and can be reviewed.

The firefighter ID usually comes into play in emergency situations in which it's imperative to execute certain tasks. These tasks are mostly irrespective of SoD violations and access risk violations. Integration with the ARM module allows you to control the assignment of firefighter IDs and the log report review workflow.

7.19.5 Segregation of Duties Management Process

The goal of the SoD management process is to eliminate or at least reduce the possibility of errors and fraud. Because a single user won't have access to several phases of a certain business process, the management of such risks is important. To achieve separation of duties, a business process must be divided, distributed, and allocated among various individuals. All this is carried out in three separate phases, and SAP GRC Access Control is an ideal tool to support this process:

1. **Phase 1**
   - *Risk recognition*
     In this first step, you define a high-level list of applicable SOD conflicts that allow fraud or generate significant errors. The outcome of this step is that your business has determined what is an unacceptable risk that they want to report

on and manage via remediation or mitigation. This step is carried out outside the system and includes a fundamental understanding of business processes and its vulnerabilities.

– *Rule building and validation*
In the second step, you build the technical rule set based on the recognized risks from step 1. The outcome of this step is the technical rule set that allows you to analyze and identify risks on users, roles, or profiles. The technical rule set is built in the ARA module.

2. **Phase 2**

– *Risk analysis*
The first step in phase 2 is to analyze the result of the risk analysis. The ARA module allows you to perform a risk analysis against users, roles, profiles, and even HR objects (positions, jobs, etc.). The result of the risk analysis will identify if a single user, a single role, a single profile, or a job/position has the ability to perform any of the conflicting functions defined in step 1. As a security administrator, you can use the results to provide the business insight into alternatives for correcting or eliminating discovered risks.

– *Remediation*
This is one of the most important steps in the process. The goal is to remediate the occurrence of the conflict on a user level. Please note, the occurrence of an SoD conflict happens the most when assigned to a user. Therefore, evaluate whether the conflicting tasks can be separated to another user. In this step, role changes and reassignment of roles becomes necessary because only then is a hard remediation of access violations possible. The result of this step is to reduce the number of conflicts to a minimum so that only a few must be mitigated.

– *Mitigation*
If remediation isn't possible, the remaining risks must be mitigated. Mitigation requires a formal description and action to appropriately mitigate the risk. In most cases, mitigation is achieved by implementing additional monitoring procedures that ensure to compensate the risk after an action happened. Mitigating actions are in most cases performed after an event happened. Therefore, it's recommended to use mitigations as little as possible.

3. **Phase 3**

   - *Continuous compliance*
   In this final phase, it's important to establish a continuous process wherein every access request is reviewed against the SoD conflict matrix prior to provisioning. In addition, make sure that all role changes undergo the risk analysis and are remediated before becoming available to end users. The result is that your system remains clean from violations.

7

7.20   Summary

Authorizations are an important aspect in any SAP system as they control what a user can see and do. Understanding the capabilities of authorizations and how they can be used to your advantage, is a mandatory skill for any SAP security administrator. With this chapter you gained informative knowledge about how authorizations work at its root and how you can use different tools to master them.

Chapter 8
Authentication

Before reading this chapter, you should have a basic understanding of how X.509 certificates work, as well as familiarity with SAP GUI setup on the Windows OS.

Authentication is the process of verifying that a user is who they claim to be. The process can vary based on what type of system you are using and the system's configuration. The simplest method used today is password authentication. This means that a user types a username and password into a login dialog box and, if their information match what the system has in its database, they are granted access.

Authentication can be much more advanced than a username and password mechanism. For example, a method like two-factor authentication (2FA) uses a hardware device or text messaging system to verify that a user knows the correct password, and has control of a secure device, increasing security.

SAP NetWeaver AS ABAP supports a wide range of different authentication methods. In this chapter, we'll dive into some of the options you have to enhance both your system's security and its ease-of-use when authenticating to different systems.

8.1 What Is Single Sign-On?

For as long as computers have been around, users have had user accounts with passwords associated with them. Although easy to quickly setup and manage, the username/password scenario becomes increasingly difficult when you have multiple enterprise systems that you'll need to use on a day-to-day basis. To address this issue, we use a single authentication authority to authenticate users and allow them to sign on to multiple enterprise applications without the need for multiple passwords. The use of a single authentication authority in the enterprise is commonly known as SSO.

SSO is an approach to standardizing authorization for end users. In many organizations, users have different usernames and passwords for each system in the organization. This becomes quite difficult to manage both for the end user and the administrator. Given the typical three-tier SAP landscape that most organizations adopt, an end user may have quite a difficult time keeping user credentials straight for their SAP accounts. Add in other systems that a user might use, email, non-SAP applications, and other organizational tools, and a user will become overwhelmed quite quickly with so many usernames and passwords. This difficulty is compounded if a rigid, prudent security policy that mandates strong and frequently changed passwords is adopted. Users will begin writing passwords on sticky notes or reusing the same simple password over and over again in different systems.

The solution to this challenge is adoption of a well-thought-out SSO strategy. SSO gives the administrator and organization a single source for credential management. The risk of users having multiple passwords or credentials in several disparate systems is eliminated, replaced with a single password (or even no password at all) in a centrally managed system.

Passwords are often a weakest link in enterprise security. Preventing the usage of passwords by implementing standards such as SAML, X.509 certificates, or Kerberos can go a long way to strengthening this weak link. Once an SSO strategy has been implemented, deficiencies in password complexity, change frequency, and reusability can be addressed. Moving to require a single, more secure password can help make organizational security stronger overall.

Beyond SSO with a simple username and password, many different authentication methods exist in the enterprise. Certificate authentication, smart cards, biometric authentication, and 2FA are all implementable with SAP. Regardless of the type of authentication used, the basic methods of SSO are identical.

SSO is more than just convenience for the end users. By restricting users to a single authentication platform, administration of user accounts can be greatly simplified and the risk of complexity and an increased attack surface can be greatly mitigated. The fewer accounts that users have traditional passwords for, the lower the likelihood of an exploit.

In addition, the use of SSO solutions allows the enforcement of a consistent authentication policy from a single centralized authentication system. Contrast that with non-SSO situations in which many different systems could have varying levels of security policy, which may put certain systems more at risk than others. It's easier for an attacker to find a system that has a lenient authentication policy and focus on exploiting that system. Once compromised, that system could lead to the attack of systems with more strict authentication policies.

8.1.1   Common Components of SSO

The basic components of any SSO solution are similar in nature. Technical workings of any specific SSO solution may differ. It's important to understand the basic building blocks and how they're used in each solution. Figure 8.1 shows common SSO components and their role in SSO solutions.

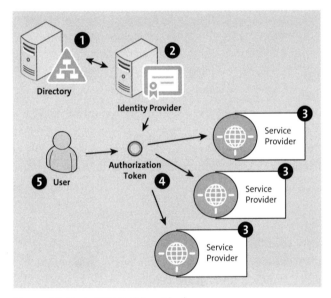

Figure 8.1 Basic SSO Building Blocks

Let's look at these components in more detail.

- **Directory service systems**

    A common starting place for SSO is the *user directory*, a central store in which an organization keeps information about its users, services, and systems. Directory services systems ❶ are ubiquitous in the enterprise. Such systems commonly communicate with other applications in the enterprise using the Lightweight Directory Access Protocol (LDAP). Microsoft's Active Directory is a common enterprise tool used for user and credential management, which can communicate using the LDAP protocol.

- **Identity provider systems**
  These systems ❷ obtain and provide proof in the form of a token or certificate of the user's identity. They sometimes are referred to as *authentication servers*. Often, but not always, these systems provide directory services. They also can be integrated with directory service systems, while staying separate; the directory service system manages the users, while the identity providing system will broker authentication. Examples of identity provider systems include Microsoft's Active Directory Federation Services and Kerberos authentication servers.

> **Other Forms of Authentication Using an Identity Provider Server**
>
> There are many ways to provide proof to an identity provider server. A username and password setup is the most common, but other methods can include biometrics, 2FA, mobile device authentication, and smart cards using X.509 certificates.

- **Service providing systems**
  These systems ❸ are systems that a user needs to log into to perform work. Traditionally, each of these systems kept their own usernames, passwords, and possibly authorizations within the application themselves. These systems make up most of the systems in an organization's IT landscape and often introduce security and administrative challenges for the security administrator. SAP NetWeaver–based systems running SAP's business applications are examples of systems that provide services to an end user.

- **Methods of proving identity to enterprise systems**
  There are several methods of proving identity, and this is the main way that SSO methods will differ. Some of the most common are as follows:

  - *Certificates*
    Certificates use a public key infrastructure (PKI) to prove that they were issued by a trusted authority. This can imply trust to service providers. With that trust, a service provider can grant or deny access to a user with a valid, proper certificate.

  - *Tokens or assertions*
    Most tokens ❹ also use certificates but contain more information about the user and her request or access levels within an application. They are usually time-sensitive and are issued (and reissued) by an identity provider. They can be validated by service providers and show valid proof of identity to a system.

Examples of tokens used in SSO solutions include a Kerberos token or a SAML assertion.

- **End users**
  The end user ❺, who is the person being verified, is the key portion of the SSO scenario. It's important to note that an end user is always assumed to be a single end user with a login name or credentials distinct from any other user's. End users can also be considered *service users*, or users that don't exist in real life but logically exist to do some sort of work on a system—for example, batch users or web service users. It's very important to take these scenarios into account when designing an SSO solution because they are both critical business functions and security vulnerabilities.

8.1.2   Establishing a Plan for SSO Adoption

Implementing SSO can be a complex and technically challenging project. It's important to address the following steps when planning an SSO adoption project:

1. Identify the most critical systems. It's important to safeguard your most critical data first. Identifying which systems contain your organization's most sensitive business information is an important step to deciding which systems to work on enabling SSO for first.

2. Within these critical systems, determine how many people have access to them. Define your overall SSO strategy and start with these critical business systems.

3. Understand the different modules of SAP Single Sign-On and analyze your system landscape to determine which SSO standards can be used.

4. Consider disabling user name/password authentication in critical business systems. Replace it with SSO using available technologies in which credentials are automatically determined and issued. This prevents users from logging into a system as users other than themselves.

5. Once you've implemented SSO, start enforcing SSO or at least strong passwords in the related systems (service or user accounts).

6. Finally, make sure your SSO identity provider systems are highly available. Your organization will rely on them to log onto multiple systems, so they need to be highly available to prevent business interruption.

8.2 Single Sign-On Technologies

There are many approaches, provided by both SAP and third-party vendors, to accomplish SSO. In this section, we'll cover a select number of the most commonly implemented technologies. Table 8.1 shows the access methods for which SSO is available on SAP NetWeaver AS ABAP systems.

Method of Access	SSO Available
SAP GUI	X.509 Certificate Kerberos SAP Logon Tickets *(Deprecated)*
Web-Based (Transaction SICF, SAP NetWeaver Business Client, SAP Fiori)	SPNEGO/Kerberos SAML 2.0

Table 8.1 SSO Methods for SAP NetWeaver AS ABAP

The Future of SSO

SAP S/4HANA's user interface is SAP Fiori-based, meaning that implementing SAML 2.0 will cover the majority of end users, considering SAP's current roadmap.

8.2.1 X.509 Digital Certificates

SSO using X.509 certificates uses the X.509 standard created by the International Telecommunications Union's standardization sector (ITU-T). X.509 is widely used by many Internet protocols and authentication mechanisms. In the X.509 standard, subjects (users, servers, anything that you may want to authenticate) are identified using a X.509 digital certificate, which includes a public key for cryptography. These certificates are passed from party to party and can establish identity to the certificate holder. X.509 is one of the most widely used standards and a security administrator will be working with it daily. It's imperative to have a good understanding of its function. The X.509 certificate request, response, and encryption procedures are covered in depth in Chapter 13. One widely known example of an X.509 certificate is the SAP Passport, which enables the holder to login to SAP Support Portal without having to enter his password. Instead of password authentication, the previously generated X.509 certificate is sent to the server, which authenticates the user.

8.2.2   Kerberos

Kerberos is an authentication protocol that allows users and servers to authenticate using tickets administrated by a central server. It was created by the Massachusetts Institute of Technology (MIT) and is widely used in computing as of the writing of this text.

Kerberos uses a client-server model, in which users request a ticket from a central *key distribution center* server. This ticket, called the *ticket-granting ticket* (TGT), is used by the client to request additional tickets for any service that the user will need to logon to. Tickets for requested services are granted to the end user: for as long as she has a ticket, she's granted logon without transmitting a password over the network. Kerberos relies on cryptography to ensure that each ticket is legitimate, establishes identity, and cannot be tampered with even if the network traffic is intercepted. Kerberos tickets require trust to be established between the user and the key distribution center, as well as trust between any other entities that the user will need to be authenticated in order to use.

Kerberos is the basis of Microsoft's Active Directory Server. Active Directory will often serve as the key distribution center when working with SAP Single Sign-On and SAP GUI.

SAP Secure Login Client enables the SSO login using a Kerberos token. It's licensed as part of the SAP Single Sign-On product.

8.2.3   SPNEGO

The Simple and Protected GSS-API Negotiation Mechanism (SPNEGO) is a standard that helps negotiate the cryptographic standard used to communicate between a client (usually the end user) and a server. In SAP's SSO applications, SPNEGO is used to negotiate which encryption and authentication protocols are used during web-browser-based SSO. Most often, SPNEGO enables a web browser to authenticate to an SAP NetWeaver AS ABAP system using a Kerberos token.

8.2.4   SAP Logon Tickets

SAP Logon Tickets are an SSO standard in which user credentials are shared between SAP NetWeaver AS Java systems, typically the SAP Enterprise Portal application and SAP NetWeaver AS ABAP systems. Tickets issued by the SAP NetWeaver Java AS system to the user can be used to log on to SAP GUI or other Java systems. SAP Logon Tickets require trust to be established between both ABAP and Java systems.

Historically, SAP Logon Tickets have been the primary SSO mechanism throughout SAP's product offerings through SAP Enterprise Portal. Due to a shift in SAP's approach regarding SAP NetWeaver AS Java, SAP Logon Tickets are no longer a good strategy to accomplish SSO. Furthermore, SAP Logon Tickets have the following deficiencies, which should be noted:

- The cryptography behind SAP Logon tickets is not strong.
- User IDs have to be identical in all systems; user mapping is not possible.
- All connected systems have to be within the same DNS domain.

SAP's recommendation is to use newer SSO technologies such as Kerberos/SPNEGO, X.509 certificates, and SAML tokens where technically possible. For more information, consult SAP Note 2117110.

8.2.5 SAML

Security Assertion Markup Language (SAML) is an XML-based open set of standards for authentication among multiple applications. Currently, SAML 2.0 is one of the most commonly implemented SSO standards because businesses are adopting SAP's next-generation UI, SAP Fiori, which is web-based. SAML will be covered in depth in Section 8.4.

8.3   SAP GUI Single Sign-On Setup

There are two main steps for setting up SAP GUI–based SSO: setting up SNC in Transaction SNCWIZARD and setting up Kerberos.

Notes

These steps apply for SAP Single Sign-On with Kerberos and SPNEGO.

The following prerequisites must be met before you start:

1. CommonCryptoLib must be installed and configured. For more information about configuring CommonCryptoLib, see Chapter 5.
2. For Kerberos and/or SPNEGO, Active Directory must be set up.
3. For SAP GUI logon using SSO, you must set up the secure login client on the workstations you wish to sign on with.

4. Each workstation must be joined to the Active Directory domain you wish to use SSO with.

Now we can begin setting up SAP GUI-based SSO.

8.3.1 Setting up Secure Network Communications in Transaction SCNWIZARD

To configure SNC parameters, proceed as follows:

1. Navigate to Transaction SNCWIZARD.

2. The wizard shown in Figure 8.2 will launch. The wizard will assist you in the configuration of the SNC identity, profile parameters, system restart, and credentials.

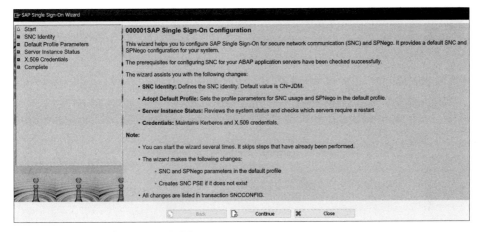

Figure 8.2 Transaction SNCWIZARD

Tip: Back up Your Profile

It is a good idea to take a manual backup of your profile directory. The wizard will use a new version of the profile in the database, but if your instance fails to start, you'll need to revert in the OS.

---

3. Click the **Continue** button.

4. The **SNC Identity** screen (Figure 8.3) will let you specify the identity string used to identify the SAP system. For this example, we'll use the SID of the demo system we're using (JDM). Once you've specified your SNC identity string, click the **Continue** button.

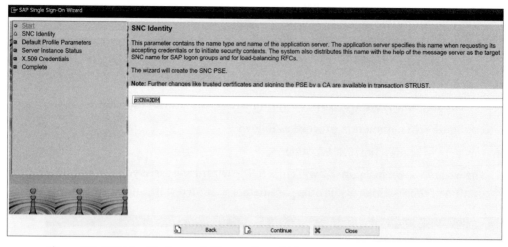

Figure 8.3 SNC Identity Screen in Transaction SNCWIZARD

5. The screen shown in Figure 8.4 will list the changes required to enable SNC and SPNEGO. These changes are performed in the default profile because they should be implemented identically for each application server in your SAP system. Click the **Continue** button.

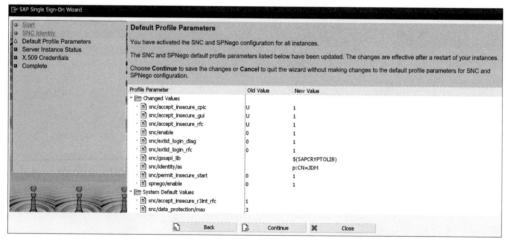

Figure 8.4 Default Profile Parameters Screen in Transaction SNCWIZARD

6. Figure 8.5 shows the **SNC Status** screen, which will show the current status of each application server in your system. Because the system in this example is a demo

system, it only has one application server. Be sure to check this list to make sure all your application servers are listed. When you're ready to continue, click the **Continue** button.

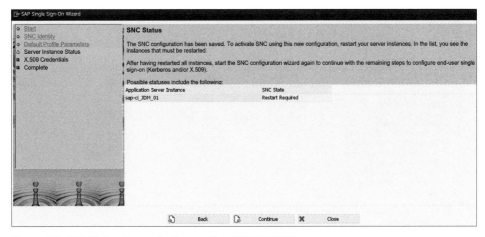

Figure 8.5 SNC Status Screen in Transaction SNCWIZARD

7. The screen shown in Figure 8.6 will show the currently listed trusted certificate issuers in your system. You'll need to import the root certificate of whatever trust provider is going to sign the certificate for this system. Click the **Continue** button to launch Transaction STRUST.

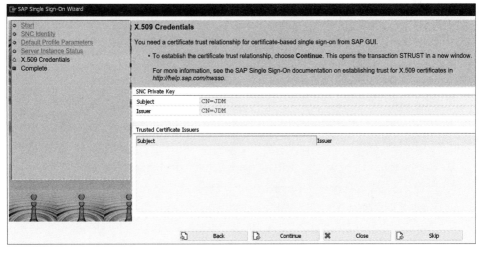

Figure 8.6 X.509 Credentials Screen in Transaction SNCWIZARD

8.   At this point, Transaction STRUST (Trust Manager) will open. Click the **SNC SAP-Cryptolib** folder (Figure 8.7). This will select the node for SNC in the right-hand pane.

Figure 8.7 STRUST Configuration during Transaction SNCWIZARD

9.   In the top menu bar, click **Edit • Create Certificate Request** (Figure 8.8).

10. The system will now generate a certificate signing request (CSR), as shown in Figure 8.9. This CSR will need to be provided to a certificate signing authority to be signed. Save this CSR to a file and provide it to your certificate signing authority.

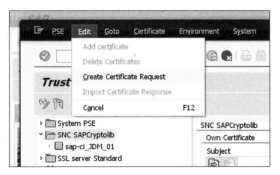

Figure 8.8 Creating Certificate Signing Request for SNC Personal
Security Environment (PSE)

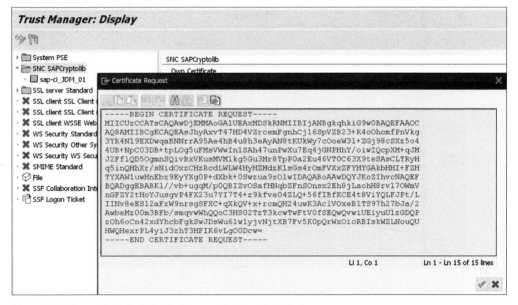

Figure 8.9 Generated Certificate Request in Pop-Up Window

Note: Signing CSRs

If you are using SAP Single Sign-On, it can act as the signing authority. If not, X.509
certificates can be signed by a number of sources depending on your application and
business requirements. Consult the documentation of your identity or certificate
provider software for instructions on how to sign X.509 certificates.

---

11. Once you've received your signed certificate, import it to the SNC SAPCryptolib PSE. To do so, navigate back to Transaction STRUST and select **SNC SAPCryptolib** in the left-hand column. Now, click the **Display <-> Change** (✐) button in the toolbar to switch into change mode.

12. In the top menu bar, click **Edit • Import Certificate Request** (Figure 8.10).

Figure 8.10 Importing Certificate Request in Transaction STRUST

13. A certificate response window will appear. Paste or import your certificate response into this input box (Figure 8.11).

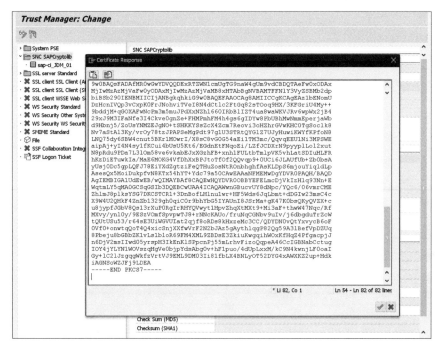

Figure 8.11 Certificate Response Dialog with Certificate Response Pasted In

Importing the Root Certificate for Your Signing Authority

If at this point you encounter an error, it's most likely that the system doesn't have a root certificate for the signing authority that signed your certificate. You will need to import the missing root certificate into the system. Importing a PKCS7 format certificate will include all certificates in the chain. If you do not have a PKCS7 format certificate, you must also import any intermediate (chain) and root certificates as well. To import additional certificates into the SNC SAPCryptoLib PSE, click **Certificate • Import** in the menu bar.

14. Your SNC SAPCryptoLib PSE should be similar to that shown in Figure 8.12. You should see a certificate under **Own Certificate** as well as **Issuer Certificates** that will complete the chain of trust. Click the **Save** button and exit Transaction STRUST.

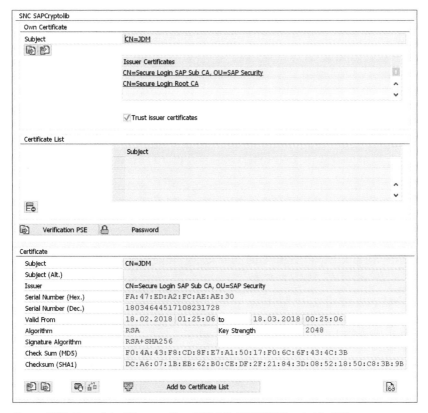

Figure 8.12 Completed Transaction STRUST: SNC SAPCryptoLib PSE

15. Execute Transaction SNCWIZARD. This should bring you back to the wizard start screen (Figure 8.13). Click **Next**.

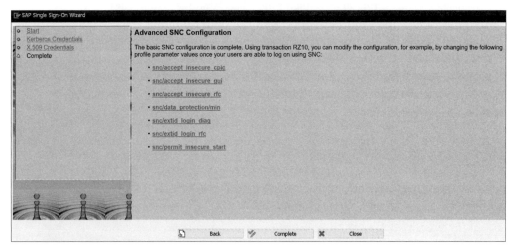

Figure 8.13 SNC Completion Screen

16. You will see a completion screen suggesting additional parameters. It's a good idea to set each of these parameters once you've successfully tested SNC.

17. Finally, restart your application server to activate the profile changes. When your system comes back up, you can continue.

Now that you've enabled SNC, you can test the encryption portion of SNC. Proceed as follows:

1. The root certificate for the system that signs your PSE must be installed on the workstation you're running SSO on. This is because the certificates exchanged must be trusted by the OS.

2. In your SAP GUI launchpad, right-click and select **Properties** for the connection to your SAP NetWeaver AS ABAP system.

3. Click the **Network** tab (Figure 8.14).

4. Set the settings as shown in Table 8.2.

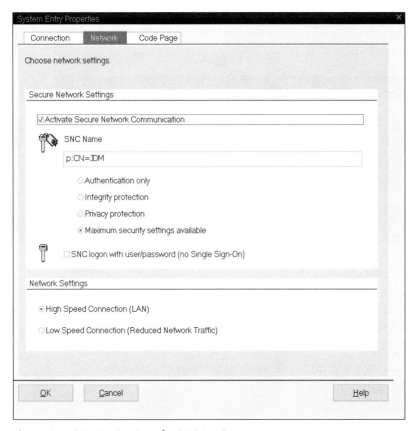

Figure 8.14 SAP GUI Settings for SNC Testing

Setting	Value
Activate Secure Network Communication	Checked.
SNC Name	Enter the SNC name you set in Transaction SNCWIZARD. This is listed in the default profile under the parameter snc/identity/as.
SNC Logon with User/Password	Checked.

Table 8.2 SNC Settings for SAP GUI

5. Double-click your connection to connect. You should see a logon screen (Figure 8.15) with a closed lock in the lower right-hand corner. This indicates the SNC encryption is active.

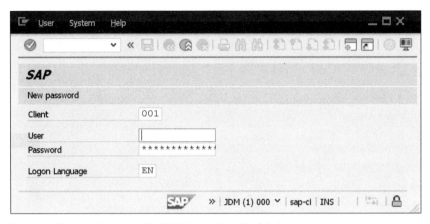

Figure 8.15 Login Screen with SNC Encryption Enabled

> **Debugging SNC**
>
> If you encounter issues, consult the following SAP Notes to debug SNC:
>
> - SAP Note 2491573 (How to Enable Trace of CommonCryptoLib)
> - SAP Note 2381157 (How to Create a Secure Login Client Trace in SAP Single Sign-On 3.0)

8.3.2   Setting Up Kerberos Single Sign-on with SAP GUI

Kerberos SSO is a part of SAP Single Sign-On. Kerberos SSO lets the end user use a Kerberos token, which he obtains when he logs into a Microsoft OS using Microsoft's Active Directory product. In this scenario, the Active Directory system acts as the Kerberos authentication authority and issues tickets. The Windows OS uses this technology by default as its primary authentication mechanism. Using this same Kerberos token, we can configure SAP GUI to pass the token to the SAP system, which will be configured to trust it. Therefore, along with SNC, we'll be adding authentication.

To set up Kerberos and SPNEGO, proceed as follows:

1. The steps in Section 8.3.1 need to be complete and the application server need to be restarted.

2. The secure login client must be installed on the workstation you'll using with SAP GUI.

3. The workstation you're testing with must be joined to the domain in which you're configuring Kerberos.

4. For SPNEGO, SSL must be configured on the SAP NetWeaver AS ABAP system.

5. In Active Directory, a service user must be created that represents the SAP Net-Weaver AS ABAP system.

Creating the SAP System User in Microsoft Active Directory

These steps have been performed on a Windows Server 2012 R2 machine with the Active Directory Domain Services role installed. These steps should be similar for most Windows Server versions. Consult Microsoft's documentation for steps specific to your Windows Server version.

Proceed as follows:

1. In the Server Manager, click **Tools** · **Active Directory Users** · **Computers**.

2. Create a new user for your service, as shown in Figure 8.16. You can put this user in any organizational unit (OU) you find sufficient. For this example, we created a separate OU named NETWEAVERSSO.

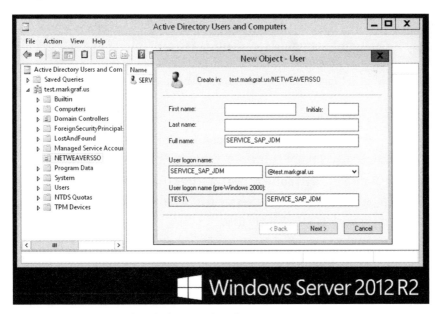

Figure 8.16 User Setup in Windows Active Directory

> **SAP Services in Active Directory**
>
> Create a service for each SAP system you intend on configuring SSO with. Use a strong password or passphrase. Set it to never expire (see Figure 8.17).

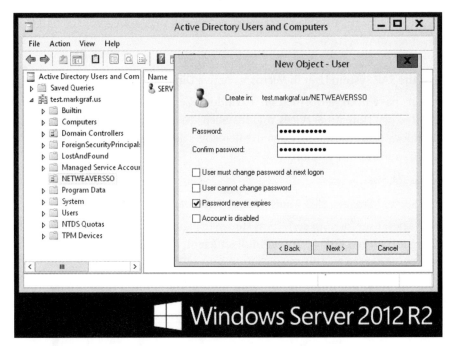

Figure 8.17 Password Settings for Service Users in Active Directory

Setting the SPN in Active Directory

A service principal name (SPN) is the unique identifier for a service that Kerberos will authenticate against. To set the SPN, perform the following steps:

1. In the Server Manager, click **Tools** • **Active Directory Users** • **Computers**.

2. Right-click the service user created for SSO and select **Properties**. In this example, we've named our user "SERVICE_SAP_JDM".

3. Select the **Attribute Editor** tab. If you do not see this tab, turn on **Advanced Features** in the **Edit** menu of the **Active Directory Users and Computers** window (Figure 8.18).

4. Double-click the **servicePrincipalName** entry. A multivalued string editor will pop up, as shown in Figure 8.19. You will need to specify two SPNs in this dialog box.

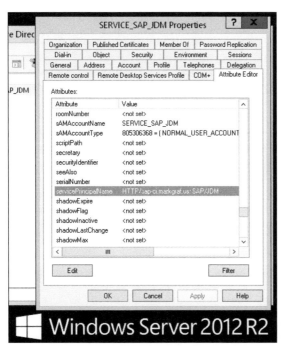

Figure 8.18 Attribute Editor Tab of SSO Service

Figure 8.19 Setting servicePrincipalName in Active Directory

You need to specify which SPNs are registered for SNC and SPNEGO. Your first SPN should follow this format:

SAP/<SID>

The prefix SAP/ is mandatory. The rest is up to you—but we recommend following a comprehensive and strict naming rule that always includes the ABAP system identifier (SID). The SPN must match the SNC name chosen for SNC. If they don't match, the secure login client won't be able to match the SPN with the server's SNC name and SSO will fail, but encryption will be successful. Your second SPN should follow this format:

HTTP/<FQDN of appserver>

Here appserver should be the fully qualified canonical domain name of the appserver server host or any alias of the appserver.

Enter each of your SPNs in the **Value to Add** box and click the add button. Once you have finished, click the **OK** button.

Configuring Kerberos Trust in SAP NetWeaver AS ABAP

The next part of the Kerberos process is setting up trust on the SAP NetWeaver system. This is done for both Kerberos-based SAP GUI SSO and SPNEGO-based browser SSO.

1. Navigate to Transaction SNCWIZARD
2. Notice that the status light for **Kerberos Credentials** is red (Figure 8.20). Click **Continue**.

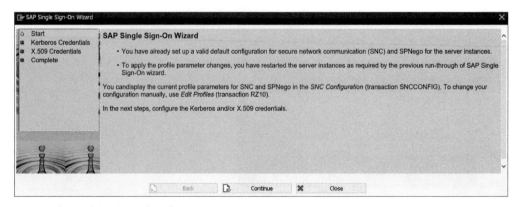

Figure 8.20 SSO Wizard

3. Click **Continue** again (Figure 8.21).

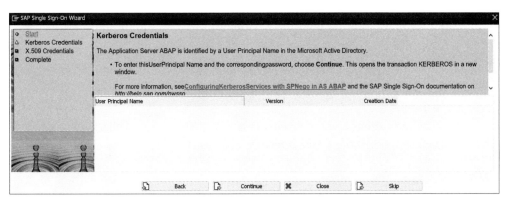

Figure 8.21 Kerberos Credentials Screen of Transaction SSOWIZARD

4. This will bring you to the **SPNEGO Configuration** page (Figure 8.22). Click the **Display/Edit** button .

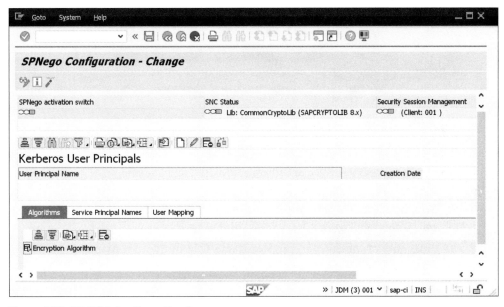

Figure 8.22 SPNEGO Configuration Screen

5. You'll see an information page that will warn you that you will need an SAP Single Sign-On license to continue. If your organization doesn't have a license, contact your SAP license sales representative before continuing.

6. On the **SPNEGO Configuration** screen, click the **Add** button.

7. Fill in the **User Principal Name** info and the **Password** created in Active Directory. Be sure to run a check of the username and password. Click the green checkmark, then **Save**.

8. Once the system saves the credentials, a test will be run to check the login functionality against the Active Directory (Figure 8.23).

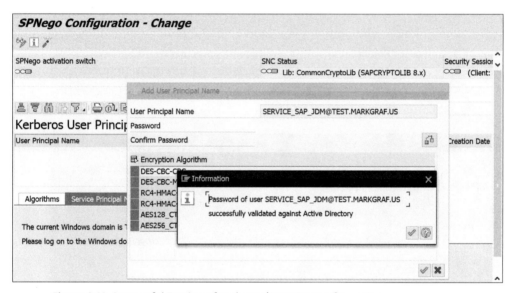

Figure 8.23 Successful Testing of Kerberos/SPNEGO Configuration

9. You should see the SPNs you created in Active Directory under the **Service Principal Names** tab (Figure 8.24).

10. Take note of the entry in the **SNC Name** field in the **User Mapping** tab (Figure 8.25).

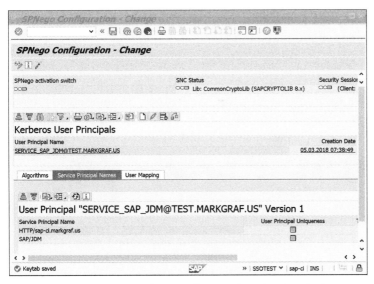

Figure 8.24 Service Principal Names from Active Directory System

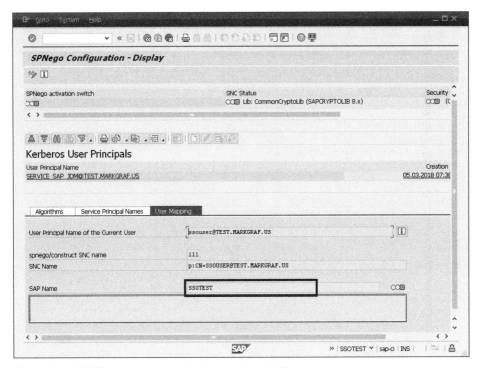

Figure 8.25 SNC Name Generated for Transaction SU01

Next, you'll need to map the SNC name to the ABAP user name:

1. Navigate to Transaction SU01.

2. Choose your test user and click the **Edit** button.

3. Choose the **SNC** tab. Input the **SNC Name** as set in the **User Mapping** tab of Transaction SPNEGO for this user and click the **Save** button. The name should follow this format: p:CN=<AD NAME>@<AD Domain>, where <AD Name> is the active directory user name and <AD Domain> is the full Active Directory domain name (Figure 8.26).

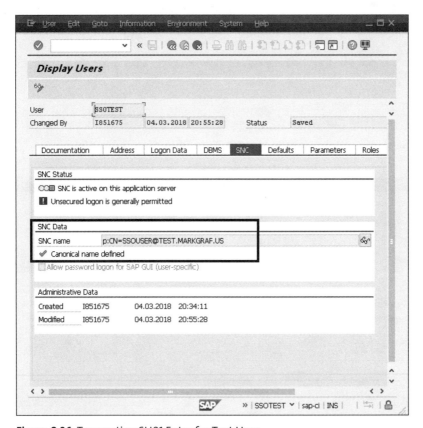

Figure 8.26 Transaction SU01 Entry for Test User

Managing SNC Data for Many Users

Do you have a lot of users that need SNC names mapped? Report RSUSR300 can be used to update the SNC names for all users. SAP Note 1898778 covers this operation in detail.

Testing Kerberos SSO

Testing Kerberos SSO is simple. To do so, execute the following steps on the workstation you're attempting to login with:

1. Configure your SAPLOGON client again as we did previously in Figure 8.14.

2. In the SAP Secure Login Client, right-click on the Kerberos token for your testing user and select **Use Profile for SAP Applications** (Figure 8.27).

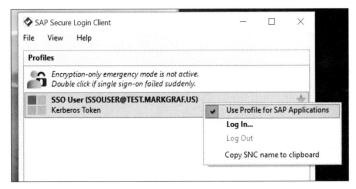

Figure 8.27 Selecting Kerberos Token in Secure Login Client

3. In SAP GUI, select your system entry, right-click, and select **SNC Logon with Single Sign-On**. The system will attempt to login using the available Kerberos ticket.

4. If SSO is successful, you should see the **Easy Access** screen of SAP GUI. If you click **System • Status** from the menu bar, you should see your test **User ID** and **SNC Name** (Figure 8.28).

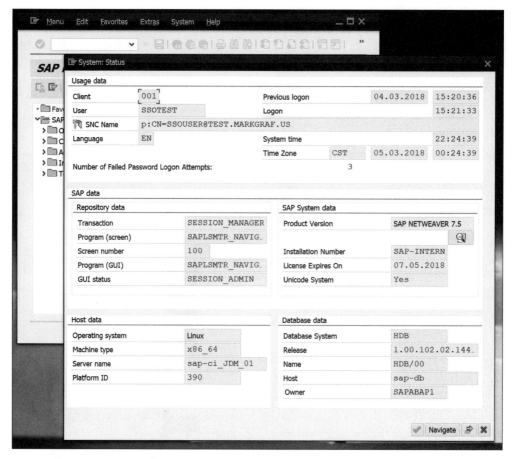

Figure 8.28 Successful Kerberos SSO

Troubleshooting Kerberos SSO

Due to the number of different configuration pieces involved, SSO may require some debugging to find out what went wrong. Don't feel bad: it happens to the best security administrators.

Be sure to double-check the following:

- Check your service user in Advanced Directory and SPN settings in Advanced Directory and Transaction SPNEGO.

- Check that your testing workstation is setup properly:
  - The SNC root certificate must be installed.
  - SAP Secure Login Client must be installed.
  - The workstation must be in the same Windows domain as the service user you set up in the Active Directory.
  - SNC-only encryption works.
- CommonCryptoLib should be up to date and working properly.
- There must be network connectivity (open firewall) for Kerberos:
  - Port 88/UDP, 389/TCP/UDP.
  - If you're using LDAP with SSL, port 389 changes to 636.

A good place to start debugging is with the SAP Secure Login Client. To enable debugging in SAP Secure Login Client on your workstation, proceed as follows (Figure 8.29):

1. Click **File • Options**. Select the **Tracing** tab.
2. Set the **Trace Level** to **Errors, Warnings, and Information**.
3. Click the **Apply** button.
4. Click the **Open Trace Folder** button. You can view the traces generated by SAP Secure Login Client. The entire SSO login process from the client side will be viewable in a text editor.

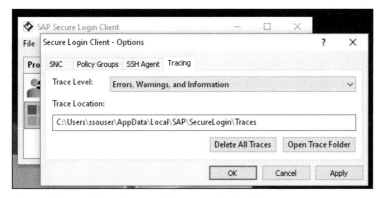

Figure 8.29 Enabling Trace in SAP Secure Login Client

Diagnosing Issues: Kerberos

If you encounter issues with your Kerberos SSO configuration, read the following notes to enable tracing to help you debug:

- SAP Note 2491573 (How to Enable Trace of CommonCryptoLib)
- SAP Note 2381157 (How to Create a Secure Login Client Trace in SAP Single Sign-On 3.0)
- SAP KBA 2564084 (SNC Kerberos Config for SAP GUI Troubleshooting)

Testing SPNEGO SSO

SPNEGO is used by the browser to select an SSO protocol for authentication. The SSO protocol that SPNEGO will be negotiating will be Kerberos, which you just set up.

To test SPNEGO SSO, you'll need to install and configure a web browser on your testing workstation. For this example, we'll use Mozilla Firefox because it's the easiest to configure for SPNEGO. Follow these steps:

1. In SAP GUI, make sure the Internet Communication Framework (ICF) service for the SAP Web GUI is activated. You can find it at the following ICF path:

   `/sap/bc/gui/sap/its/webgui`

2. On your testing workstation, open Firefox. In the **Address** field, type "about:config" and press ⌈Enter⌉.

3. In the **Filter** field, type "network.n".

4. Double-click **network.negotiate-auth.trusted-uris**. This preference lists the sites that are permitted to engage in SPNEGO authentication with the browser. Enter the FQDN of your SAP NetWeaver AS ABAP server.

5. Restart Firefox.

6. Navigate to the following URL:
   `https://<FQDN><SSLPORT>/sap/bc/gui/sap/its/webgui`, where `<FQDN>` is the fully qualified domain name of your server and `<SSLPORT>` is the SSL port you're running SSL on.

7. If you have everything configured correctly, the SAP Web GUI will launch and automatically log you in using SPNEGO and your Kerberos ticket. You should see your SSO user as the user that's logged on (Figure 8.30).

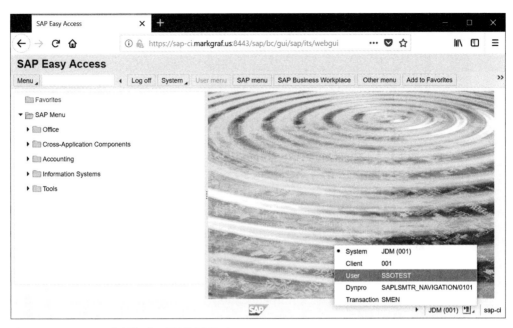

Figure 8.30 Successful Firefox SPNEGO Test

Diagnosing Issues: SPNEGO

Issues with SPNEGO can be diagnosed by consulting SAP Note 1488409.

8.4 SAML

Security Assertion Markup Language (SAML) enables applications, also known as *service providers*, to no longer deal with user account maintenance by using the SAML protocol for SSO. SAML is an open standard set by the OASIS Security Services Technical Committee. SAML is well-supported in many HTTP-based products as of the writing of this book. SAP's future implementation of products like SAP Fiori or SAPUI5 will include support for SAML.

SAML uses a structure similar to most other SSO technologies. What makes SAML unique is that it's XML-based, allowing it to be used cross-platform quite easily. In the following subsections, we'll cover the technical roles in a SAML SSO scenario, as well as how to set up SAML with SAP NetWeaver AS ABAP.

8.4.1   Principals

The *principal* in a SAML scenario is the end user. A principal is the entity that requires access to a service provider, which in turn trusts an identity provider to provide verification that a principal is authenticated.

8.4.2   Identity Providers

A SAML identity provider is the entity that provides the authentication service. This authentication is usually performed with a username and password but can use any number of different authentication mechanisms.

Examples of SAML identity providers include the following:

- SAP Cloud Platform Identity Authentication
- SAP Single Sign-On
- SAP NetWeaver AS Java
- Microsoft Active Directory Federation Services
- Microsoft Azure Active Directory

Once a user has been authenticated using an identity provider, the identity provider creates a SAML assertion, which is then sent back to the user. The user provides this SAML assertion, or a SAML token, to a service provider, which validates it and provides access to its services.

8.4.3   Service Providers

A SAML service provider uses an identity provider for authentication and provides a service to the user. For example, a user may authenticate using SAP Cloud Platform Identity Authentication to log in to an SAP NetWeaver AS ABAP system that's running SAP CRM.

Examples of SAML service providers include the following:

- SAP HANA
- SAP NetWeaver AS ABAP

- SAP NetWeaver AS Java
- Concur
- Cisco Webex
- Microsoft SharePoint
- Microsoft Office 365

8.4.4 SAML Assertions

A SAML assertion is a key part of how authentication occurs using SAML. The following list describes an assertion and its function within the SAML standard:

- An identity provider will provide the principal with a SAML assertion after authentication. An assertion contains information about the user, cryptographic proof of the assertion's source, and the principal's authentication, as well as information about access rights granted to the principal.
- Assertions are commonly referred to as tokens. You'll often find this in documentation produced by various vendors.
- Assertions have an expiry time. This protects against forgery.
- Assertions must be renewed or refreshed by the identity provider. This can be done automatically.
- Assertions do *not* contain password information.
- Assertions can be used to authenticate to other service providers or even to other identity providers in some situations.

8.4.5 Overall SAML Process

The process for a SAML logon is as follows (see Figure 8.31):

❶ The principal requests to use a service from the service provider. The user has not logged in and has no SAML assertion or token.

❷ The service provider redirects the principal to the identity provider.

❸ The principal authenticates to the identity provider using his credentials.

❹ The identity provider provides the principal a SAML assertion or token.

❺ The principal provides this token to the service provider, which in turn allows the user to access the application.

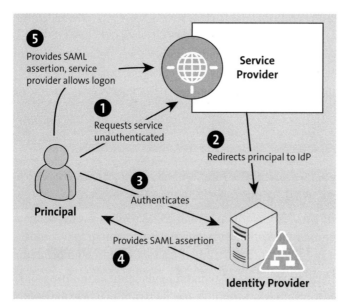

Figure 8.31 SAML Process

8.4.6   SAP NetWeaver AS ABAP Service Provider Setup

SAML setup involves the identity provider and the service provider exchanging information about each other via a metadata file. In this example, we'll exchange metadata between an SAP NetWeaver AS ABAP system in the role of service provider, and the SAP Cloud Platform Identity Authentication service in the role of identity provider. An exchange needs to occur from the service provider to the identity provider, as well as from the identity provider to the service provider.

Preparing SAML Services

Before you proceed through the following steps, your SAP NetWeaver AS ABAP system must have SSL set up:

1. Navigate to Transaction SICF.

ICF Services

You may not have all the required services activated in Transaction SICF. See SAP Note 517484 for a list of ICF nodes that need to be activated.

---

2. Click the **Execute** button.

3. Enter the following in the **Service Path** field: "/sap/public/bc/sec/saml2/".

4. Click the green **Execute** button 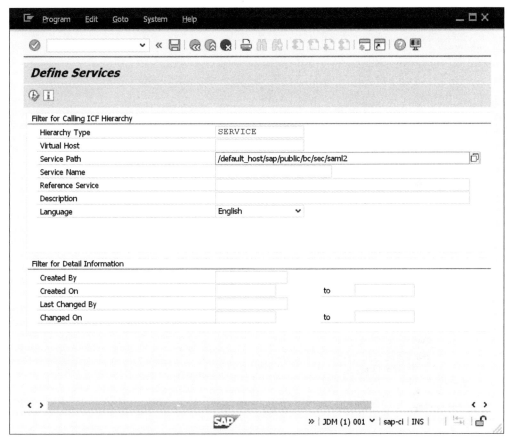 (Figure 8.32).

Figure 8.32 Transaction SICF Service Screen

5. Select the **saml2** entry and right-click it. Select **Activate Service** (Figure 8.33).

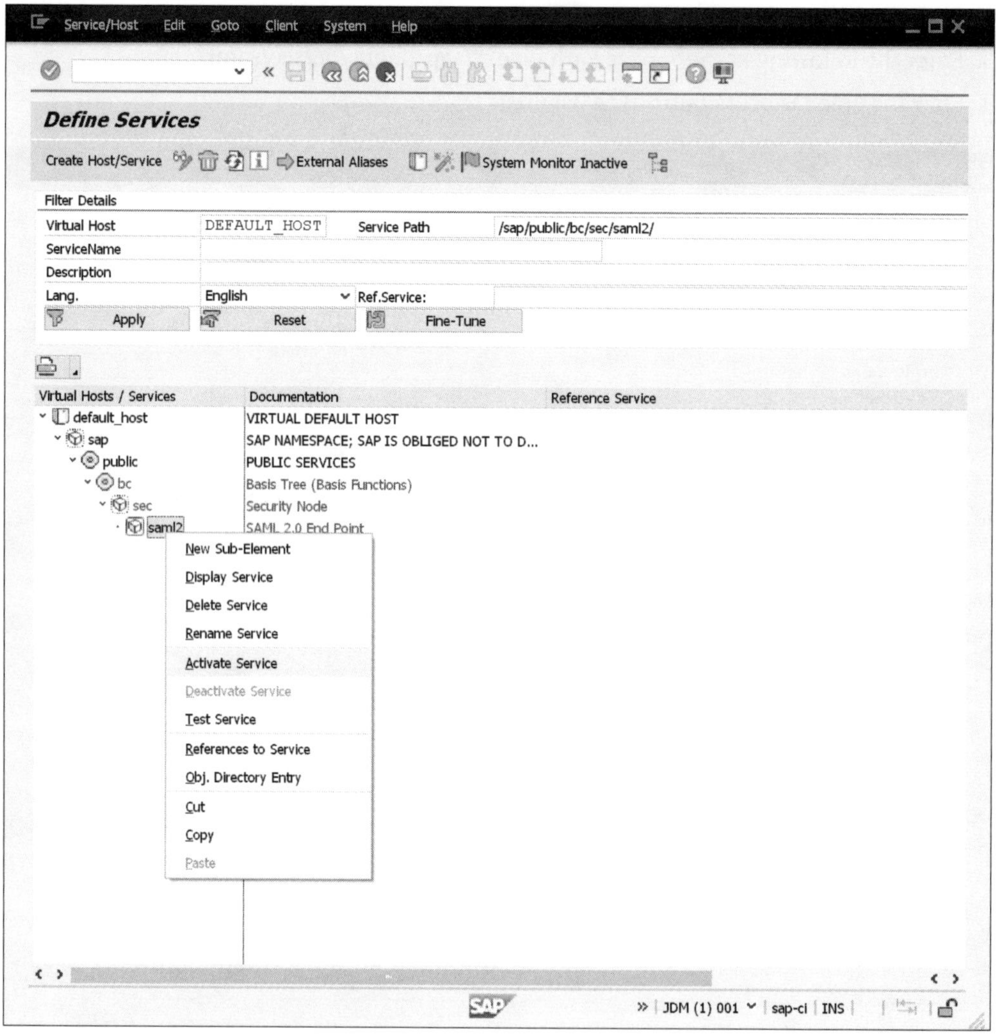

Figure 8.33 Activating SAML2 Service

6. When prompted, select the leftmost **Yes** button (Figure 8.34).

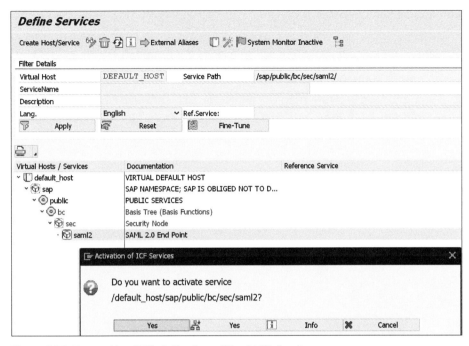

Figure 8.34 Transaction SICF: Activating of the SAML Service

7. The service will activate.

Execute the same steps for the following services:

- /sap/public/bc
- /sap/public/bc/ur
- /sap/public/bc/icons
- /sap/public/bc/icons_rtl
- /sap/public/bc/webicons
- /sap/public/bc/pictograms

- /sap/public/bc/sec/cdc_ext_ service/
- /sap/public/bc/webdynpro/
- /sap/public/bc/webdynpro/ mimes/
- /sap/public/bc/webdynpro/ssr/
- /sap/bc/webdynpro/sap/saml2

General Guidance: ICF Services

Only activate services you need. Activated services that aren't needed are a security attack vector.

Configuring SAML Services

SAML services must be configured in the SAP NetWeaver AS ABAP system in order to activate them. The following steps will enable SAML 2.0 support.

1. Navigate to Transaction SAML2. This will launch a web browser.

2. If prompted, log in. The system will render the page shown in Figure 8.35. Click the **Enable SAML 2.0 Support** button and select **Create SAML 2.0 Local Provider**.

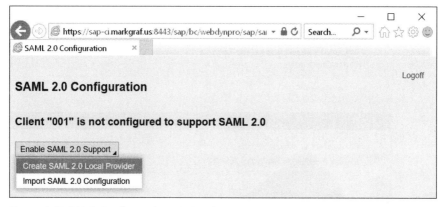

Figure 8.35 SAML Configuration ICF Service

3. Choose a meaningful name for your SAML service provider and click the **Next** button (Figure 8.36).

Figure 8.36 Name SAML Service Provider

4. The default **Clock Skew Tolerance** is usually acceptable. Click **Next** to continue (Figure 8.37).

Figure 8.37 Choose Clock Skew Tolerance

Up-to-Date Time!

Clock skew tolerance is the amount of time that the clocks of two servers can be off by before the SAML request is denied. In practice, all SSO solutions are sensitive to time to prevent replay attacks. It's very important to keep the OS clocks on your SAP NetWeaver AS ABAP system and database accurate. Alongside these clocks, it's equally important to have your identity provider's clock accurately set too. The SAP recommended solution to this issue is to use Network Time Protocol (NTP) synchronization. Note that an automatic time service—which automatically synchronizes the OS time of the server with a master time—should execute soft adjustments of the server time. This means that the time should never be reset suddenly. It must be reset gradually. A sudden time change can lead to a system hang or crash.

5. Unless you have a reason to change them, the default values for **Local Provider Configuration** should be sufficient (Figure 8.38). Click the **Finish** button.

6. The system will now display the configuration page (Figure 8.39). You should see the status as **Enabled**. Click the **Metadata** button.

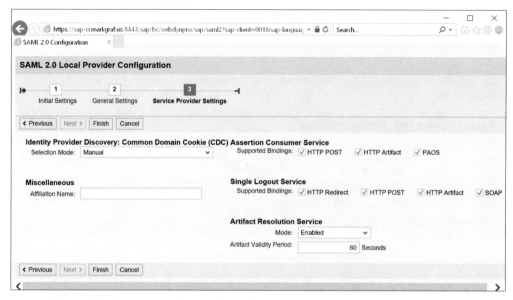

Figure 8.38 SAML 2.0 Local Provider Configuration

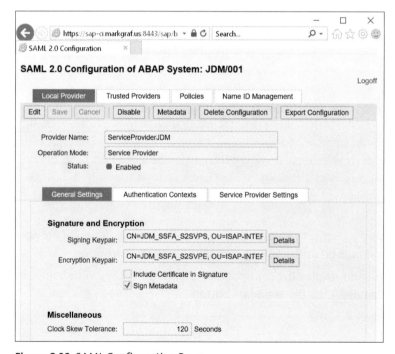

Figure 8.39 SAML Configuration Page

7. Make sure all three checkboxes are checked and click the **Download Metadata** button (Figure 8.40).

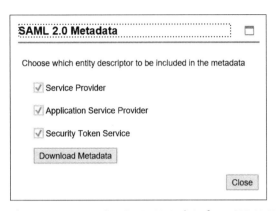

Figure 8.40 Exporting SAML Metadata from SAP NetWeaver AS ABAP

8. Finally, you will provide this metadata file to your SAML identity provider, which will import the configuration and enable your system as a service provider.

Configuring SAP Cloud Platform Identity Authentication for SSO with SAP NetWeaver AS ABAP

SAP Cloud Platform Identity Authentication can be used as a simple identity provider for SAP NetWeaver AS ABAP.

Please be aware that this service isn't based in SAP NetWeaver AS ABAP. It's a Java-based service running on SAP Cloud Platform. Its setup is included here because it's an easy and flexible solution that plays nicely with SAP NetWeaver AS ABAP.

Any SAML identity provider can be used in place of SAP Cloud Platform Identity Authentication. The basic steps for importing metadata will be very similar to the following steps:

1. Log in to the Administration Console of SAP Cloud Platform Identity Authentication. Click the **Applications** tile (Figure 8.41).

2. In the left-hand pane, click the **Add** button at the lower right. Add a new application with an appropriate name of your choosing. For our example, we'll use "NetWeaver AS ABAP" (Figure 8.42).

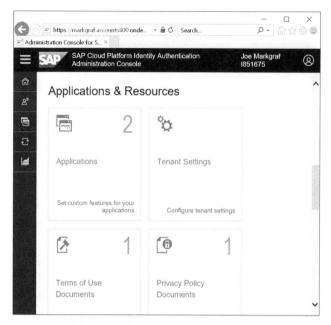

Figure 8.41 Administration Console

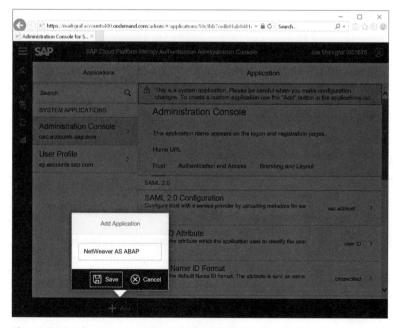

Figure 8.42 Administration Console for SAML 2.0 Trust Tab

3. Now, for your new application, select **SAML 2.0 Configuration**.

4. On the resulting screen, upload the metadata file that you generated in Transaction SAML2. This will automatically fill out all required fields on this screen. Once you've uploaded the file, click the **Save** button (Figure 8.43).

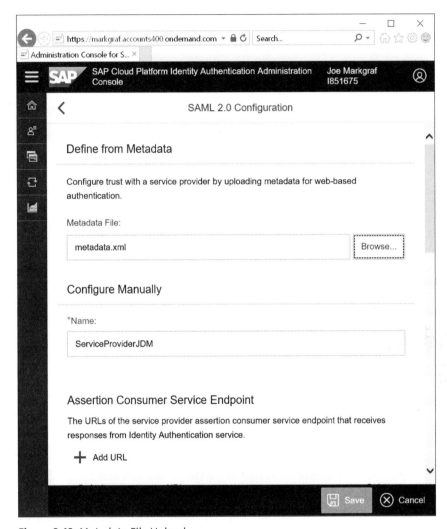

Figure 8.43 Metadata File Upload

Establishing Trust in SAP NetWeaver AS ABAP

At this point, your identity provider knows about your service provider. Now, you must generate another metadata file for your identity provider that you can import into your service provider:

1. In the Administration Console, click **Tenant Settings**.
2. Select **SAML 2.0 Configuration** (Figure 8.44).

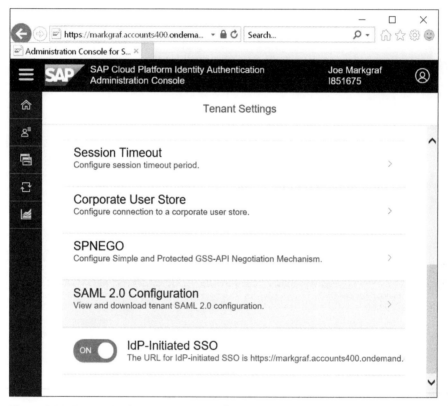

Figure 8.44 Tenant Settings: SAML 2.0 Configuration

3. In the lower left-hand corner of the right-hand pane, click the **Export Metadata** link. You'll be importing this metadata file into your service provider's (SAP Net-Weaver AS ABAP) SAML configuration (Figure 8.45).

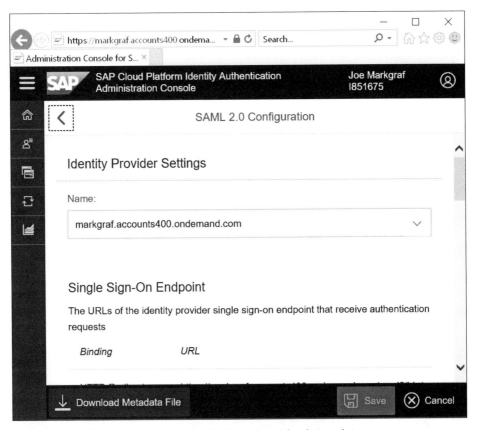

Figure 8.45 SAML 2.0 Identity Provider Settings: Download Metadata

4. Scroll down to the **Signing Certificate** section. Copy all the text in the **Insert as Text** text box. This is your signing certificate. Save this to a text file with a .crt extension. This will also need to be imported into your service provider.

Set the Service Provider options in SAP Cloud Platform Identity Authentication

For SAP NetWeaver AS ABAP to know which field to map for user IDs, you must specify this in SAP Cloud Platform Identity Authentication as follows:

1. In the Administration Console, click **Applications** (Figure 8.46). Select your ABAP service provider.

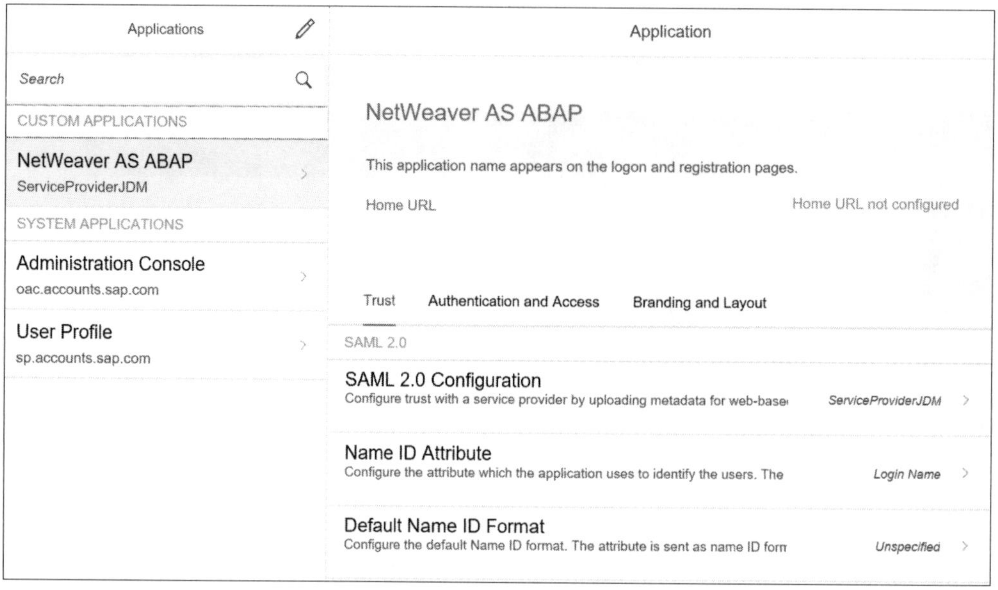

Figure 8.46 SAP Cloud Platform Identity Authentication Service Provider Settings

2. Set the **Name ID Attribute** to **Login Name**.

3. Set the **Default Name ID Format** to **Unspecified**.

Importing Identity Provider Metadata into SAP NetWeaver AS ABAP

The identity provider's metadata must be imported into the SAP NetWeaver system to establish trust so that when a user presents a valid SAML assertion, it is trusted and login is allowed.

1. In your SAP NetWeaver AS ABAP system, navigate to Transaction SAML2. This will launch a web browser. You will be prompted to log in using basic username/password authentication (Figure 8.47).

2. Click the **Trusted Providers** tab (Figure 8.48).

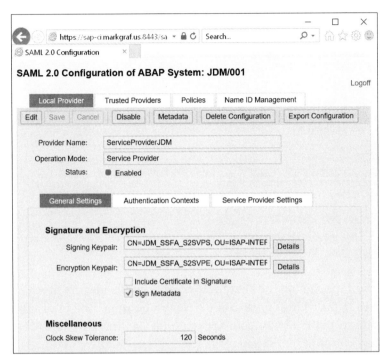

Figure 8.47 Transaction SAML2's Web-Based Configuration

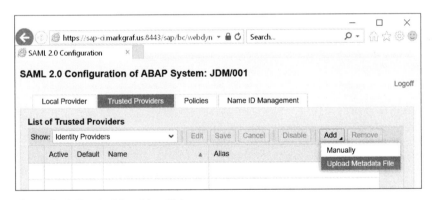

Figure 8.48 Trusted Providers Tab

3. Click the **Add** button, then select **Upload Metadata File** from the dropdown menu. Select your identity provider's metadata file. In our example, this is the metadata file we exported from SAP Cloud Platform Identity Authentication. Select your file

using the **Browse** button. Click the **Next** button at the bottom of the screen (Figure 8.49).

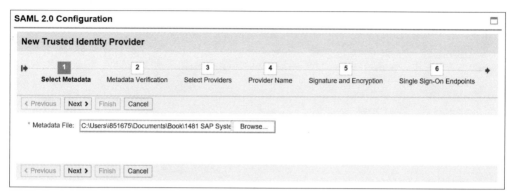

Figure 8.49 Identity Provider Metadata Upload

4. Import the copy of the signing certificate you saved from the identity provider. This will be saved in the address book. If you have trouble importing from a file, import the certificate to the address book and import it via the search functionality. Click the **Next** button at the bottom of the screen (Figure 8.50).

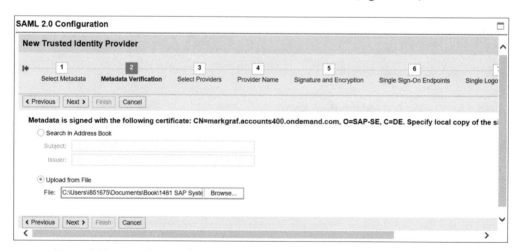

Figure 8.50 Importing Local Copy of Signing Certificate

5. Under the **Provider Name** step, if you want, input a meaningful name in the **Alias** field. This will show users a friendly name for your identity provider instead of its URL/hostname. Click the **Next** button at the bottom of the screen (Figure 8.51).

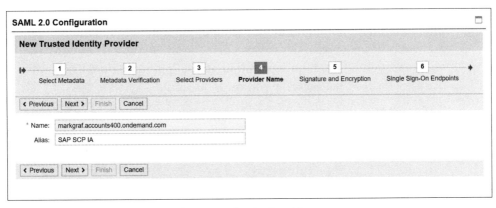

Figure 8.51 Configuration of Alias for SAML Identity Provider

6. On the next screen (Figure 8.52), advanced signature and encryption options are set. For the purposes of this example, all options are set at their defaults. However, most applications will require adjustments of these settings depending on your requirements. Click the **Next** button at the bottom of the screen.

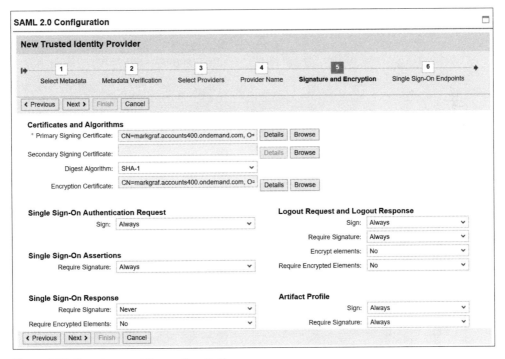

Figure 8.52 Signature and Encryption Options

7. The next screen of the workflow (Figure 8.53) is the **Single Sign-on Endpoints** settings screen. This will set the default binding of the SAP Cloud Platform Identity Authentication endpoint. This will be where the SAP NetWeaver AS ABAP system sends a request for SAML authentication. For our purposes, the defaults will suffice. Click the **Next** button at the bottom of the screen.

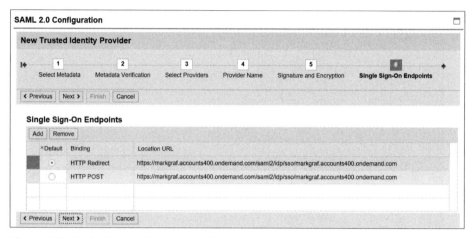

Figure 8.53 Single Sign-on Endpoints Settings

8. The next screen of the workflow is the **Single Logout Endpoints** settings screen (Figure 8.54).

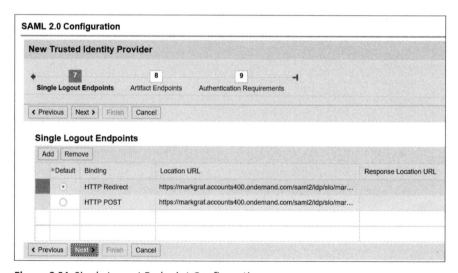

Figure 8.54 Single Logout Endpoint Configuration

This will set the default binding of the SAP Cloud Platform Identity Authentication endpoint for logout. This will be where the SAP NetWeaver AS ABAP system sends a request when the user clicks the **Logout** button. For our purposes, the defaults will suffice. Click the **Next** button at the bottom of the screen.

9. In our example, we have no need for artifact endpoints. Artifacts are a method by which SAML can initiate communication between the service provider and the identity provider without using the browser. This would be used in scenarios in which stronger security is required. Click the **Next** button at the bottom of the **Artifact Endpoints** screen (Figure 8.55).

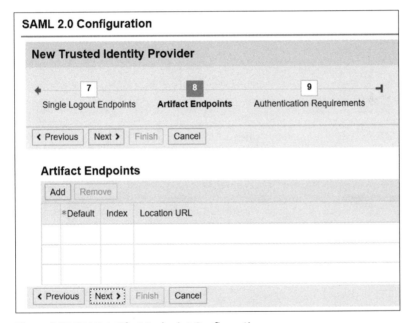

Figure 8.55 SAML Artifact Endpoint Configuration

10. Finally, the **Authentication Requirements** section (Figure 8.56) requires no changes from the defaults. At the bottom of the screen, click the **Finish** button.

11. Now, back at the **Trusted Providers** section of the SAML2 configuration, click the **Edit** button. Then add a **Supported NameID** format using the **Add** button. Select **Unspecified** and click the **OK** button (Figure 8.57).

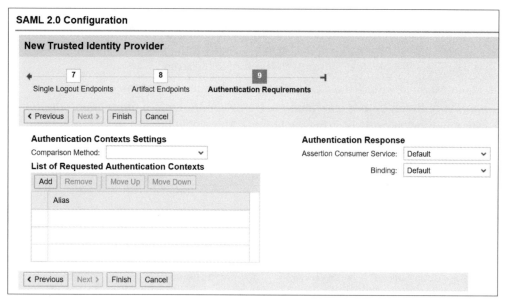

Figure 8.56 SAML Authentication Requirements Configuration

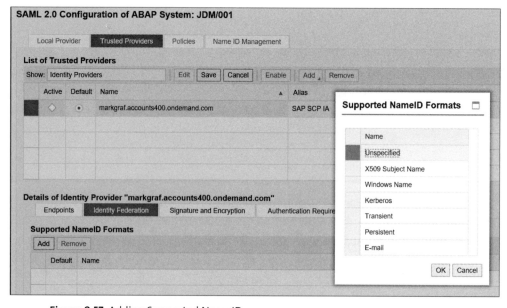

Figure 8.57 Adding Supported NameID

12. Click the **Save** button, then click the **Enable** button for your Identity Provider. Click the **OK** button on the **SAML2.0 Confirmation** popup (Figure 8.58). You should now see the **Active** column with a green status indicator.

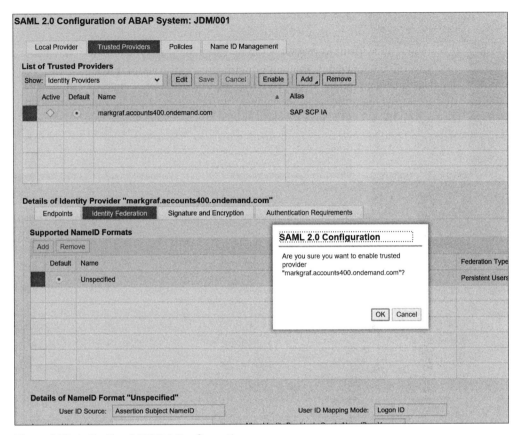

Figure 8.58 Activating SAML2.0 Configuration

Testing SAML SSO

To test SAML logon in SAP NetWeaver AS ABAP, we must create the same user in both SAP Cloud Platform Identity Authentication and the ABAP system.

SAP Cloud Platform Identity Authentication

In SAP Cloud Platform Identity Authentication, we'll need a test user to sign in using SAML.

1. In the Administration Console, click **User Management**. In the lower right-hand corner, select the **+ Add User** button. The screen shown in Figure 8.59 will open.

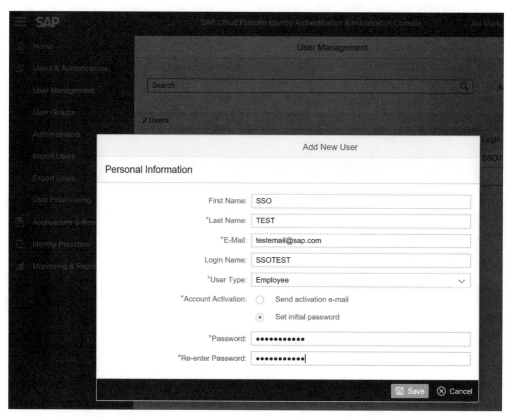

Figure 8.59 Creating Test User in SAP Cloud Platform Identity Authentication

2. Enter the credentials you'd like to test with. In the lower right-hand corner, click the **Save** button.

SAP NetWeaver AS ABAP

In the SAP NetWeaver system we'll also need a user to test SAML SSO.

1. Navigate to Transaction SU01 and create a new test user. Recall that we learned how to create users in Chapter 6. Be sure that you use the same user names for both your SAP Cloud Platform and your SAP NetWeaver user (Figure 8.60).

2. Be sure to select the exact same user name that you specified under **Login Name** in the Administration Console.

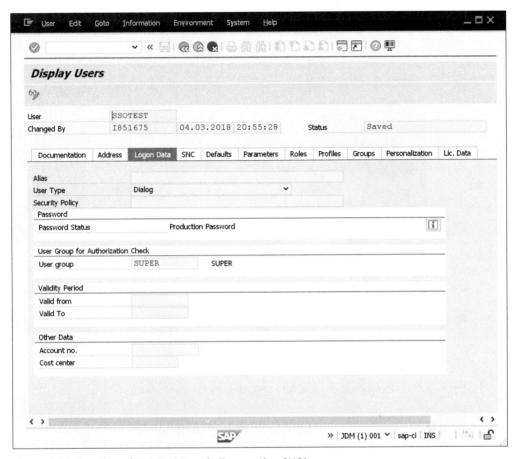

Figure 8.60 Creation of SSO Test User in Transaction SU01

Testing SAML Logon

At this point, you are ready to test. Proceed as follows:

1. Navigate to the following URL:
   `https://<FQDN><SSLPORT>/sap/bc/gui/sap/its/webgui`, where `<FQDN>` is the fully qualified domain name of your server and `<SSLPORT>` is the SSL port you're running SSL on.

2. The SAP NetWeaver AS ABAP system will then prompt you to select the identity provider you wish to use to login. Notice that the system displays the alias you set up in the SAML2 configuration. Select your identity provider and click the **Continue** button (Figure 8.61).

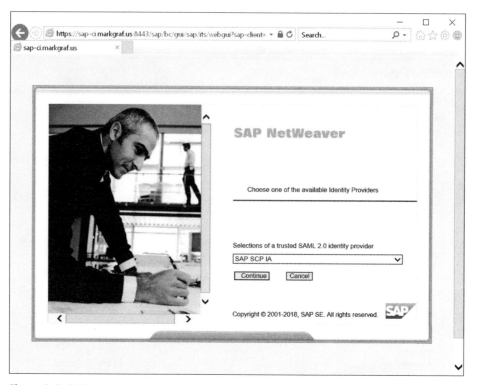

Figure 8.61 SAP NetWeaver AS ABAP SAML Identity Provider Selection Screen

3. The SAP NetWeaver system will redirect your request to SAP Cloud Platform Identity Authentication for login. You should see the SAP Cloud Platform Identity Authentication login page. Enter your SSOTEST user's credentials (Figure 8.62).

4. You should now be logged in to the ICF node as the SSOTEST user. You can verify this by clicking the **Status** button in the lower right-hand corner 🔳. You should see the SSOTEST user id as the logged in user (Figure 8.63).

Testing Tip: SPNEGO and SAML

If you've previously set up SPNEGO, you'll need to disable it in the logon procedure list for the service you're attempting to test with SAML. You can do this by selecting **SPNEGO** in the **Logon Procedure List** and clicking the **Remove** button 🔳. This is shown in Figure 8.64.

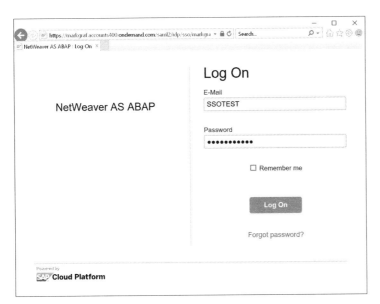

Figure 8.62 SAP Cloud Platform Identity Authentication Logon Page

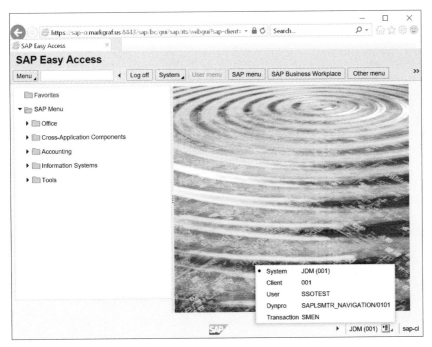

Figure 8.63 SAP Web GUI Screen after SAML Logon

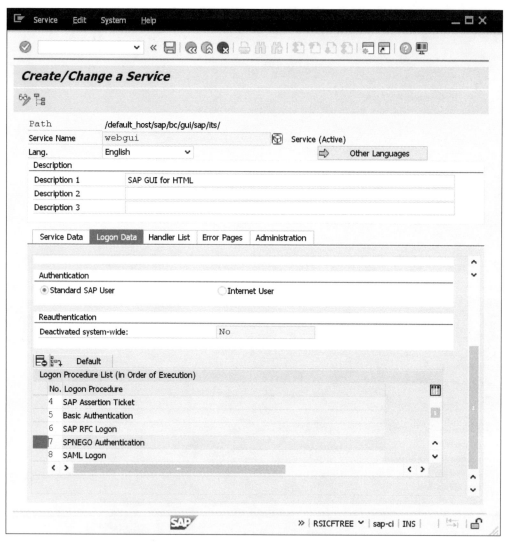

Figure 8.64 Disabling SPNEGO if Testing SAML

Disable the Use of SAML 2.0 Authentication Temporarily

Sometimes, it might make sense to disable SAML 2.0 authentication, possibly to login as another user that doesn't have SSO configured. To do so, call the ICF service with URL parameter `saml2=disabled`—for example: `https://<hostname>:<port>/sap/bc/gui/sap/its/webgui?saml2=disabled`.

Tracing SAML2

In the event of an issue, it's useful to use the security diagnostic tool to debug the SAML authentication process. To use this tool, proceed as follows:

1. Activate the following ICM service:
    /sap/bc/webdynpro/sap/sec_diag_tool

2. The following URL will launch the tool:

    <system hostname>:<ssl port>/sap/bc/webdynpro/sap/sec_diag_tool/

3. The tool will launch allowing SAML tracing/debugging to be switched on and off using the toolbar (Figure 8.65).

Figure 8.65 SAML Debugging Tool

4. Each time you attempt a SAML logn while tracing is turned on, a trace file entry will appear in the tool. Opening the trace file will show output that can be used to debug the SAML authentication process (Figure 8.66).

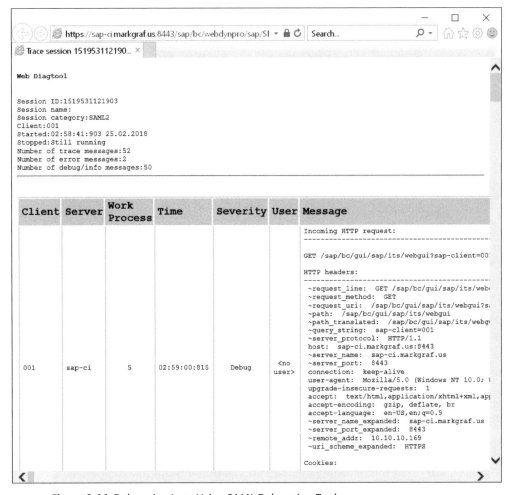

Figure 8.66 Debugging Logs Using SAML Debugging Tool

8.4.7   ICF Service Authentication and SAP Fiori

SAML authentication is enabled for all ICF services by default. Each ICF service in SAP NetWeaver AS ABAP is configured with a standard logon procedure consisting of eight authentication mechanisms. SAML authentication is in the seventh place. These mechanisms are sorted by priority.

If an incoming HTTP request delivers credentials for one of the six mechanisms before SAML, it will be processed by the corresponding mechanism. Otherwise, the system will select SAML as the mechanism and will begin the SAML token process with the identity provider. This enables things like certificate logon to take the place of SAML if the user has a certificate. If the user provides no certificate, SAML logon is attempted.

What If SAML Fails?

In the event of a SAML authentication failure, the system will attempt basic authentication (username/password) by default.

SAP Fiori, SAP's latest UX/UI product, runs on SAP NetWeaver AS ABAP as an addon and uses SICF services to serve the SAP Fiori user interface, similar to the SAP Net-Weaver Business Client or the SAP Business client. For this reason, setting up SSO with SAP Fiori is similar to SSO setup with any ICM service.

8.5 Summary

In this chapter, we covered the common components of SSO. You learned how each component is used in the role of an SSO system. You then learned how to plan an SSO implementation. Next, we covered the individual SSO technologies available for SAP NetWeaver AS ABAP.

You then learned how to set up SSO using SNC, with both Kerberos and SPNEGO for SAP GUI and browser-based SSO authentication using Microsoft Active Directory and Kerberos tokens.

Finally, you learned about SAML 2.0 and how to set it up on SAP NetWeaver AS ABAP, as well as using the SAP Cloud Platform Identity Authentication service as a simple identity provider for SAP NetWeaver AS ABAP. Our last topic was SAML and SAP Fiori, which we learned operates through ICF services.

In the next chapter you will learn about SAP's strategy for patching. This is important for a security administrator because security issues are often solved by applying new patches delivered by SAP.

Chapter 9
Patching

Before reading this chapter, you should be familiar with SAP Support Portal, the Change and Transport System (Transaction STMS), and basic SAP GUI navigation.

SAP applications require occasional patching to introduce new features and optimization and ensure that both security vulnerabilities and program errors are fixed. Patches fix newly-discovered vulnerabilities and keeping the system up to date on patches limits the system's exposure. However, all patches should be carefully evaluated—patching can have desired and undesired effects and an administrator should take care to determine the impact a patch will have.

In this chapter, you'll learn about evaluating and applying patches and you'll see how to check if new patches have introduced unintended vulnerabilities to the system.

9.1 Patching Concepts: SAP's Approach to Patching

SAP NetWeaver AS ABAP and SAP's business applications that run on top of it occasionally require patching. SAP approaches patching applications by several methods. In this section, we'll overview the most common patch-delivery methods.

The most common fix is an *SAP Note*, a numbered entry in SAP's online service system, the SAP Support Portal. These SAP Notes contain a description of a known issue, along with symptoms, considerations, information, detailed instructions, or even code corrections to fix the issues that the SAP Note describes.

Notes that are found by SAP to be applicable to all customers are grouped together as *support packages*. Support packages contain several notes and corrections. These packages are installed using either the Software Update Manager (SUM) or Transaction SPAM. In general, support packages will include several security fixes, many of which are not urgent but necessary.

Enhancement packages (EHPs) are corrections or enhancements to the business functionality of a system. This could include security functions but is mostly on a business level. This would affect roles and application-level security.

A *system upgrade* is a change to overall release level of the system. Often, this includes an upgrade of the underlying SAP NetWeaver system. Upgrades often provide good opportunities to review gaps in security because roles and business functions of the system are changing and must be addressed.

Upgrades, enhancement packages, and support packages are usually scheduled activities, planned in coordination with the business and IT support teams. SAP Notes, on the other hand, are often adopted at any time deemed necessary by security administrators.

9.1.1   SAP Notes

SAP Notes are SAP's method of delivering information, sometimes including fixes for issues you may encounter in an SAP system. They're released on the SAP Support Portal, SAP's customer portal for technical support. Each SAP Note has a unique number that serves as its reference. SAP Notes can be downloaded into an SAP NetWeaver ABAP system and, if they contain corrections, can be automatically implemented by a security administrator. We'll cover more on this functionality later in this chapter.

SAP Notes can have several general type classifications, as follows:

- **General SAP Notes**
  General SAP Notes contain fixes or coding corrections to help solve a problem with SAP software. These issues can be technical or business-related.

- **Performance-relevant SAP Notes**
  Performance-relevant SAP notes address issues with system performance. They often deal with technical portions of the system, like the enqueue server or message server, but can also be enhancements to business reports that allow them to run more quickly.

- **Legal change SAP Notes**
  Legal change SAP Notes address changing legal requirements across the world as they pertain to SAP software. This can often affect portions of the system that pertain to account, legal, or human resource areas.

- **Security SAP Notes**
  Security SAP Notes contain information about known security vulnerabilities. They will contain information or actual fixes applicable to the security issue they

cover. This can include correction instructions, configuration recommendations, service pack or upgrade recommendations, or manual measures such as kernel upgrade recommendations. These SAP Notes will be the primary focus of a security administrator.

SAP has a special listing for security SAP Notes on SAP Support Portal. You can access this listing at *support.sap.com/securitynotes*.

It's critical that the security administrator visits this portal regularly to review if any security SAP Notes apply to his or her systems. If an SAP Note is applicable, then a plan must be developed to implement it.

9.1.2 SAP Note Severity

Each SAP Note also has a severity or priority assigned to it. Table 9.1 outlines the different priorities.

Priority	Category	Description
Priority 1	Hot news	An urgent correction that should be implemented immediately
Priority 2	Correction with high priority	An important correction that should be implemented
Priority 3	Correction with medium priority	Optional; will be included in an upcoming support package
Priority 4	Correction with low priority	Optional; will be included in an upcoming support package

Table 9.1 SAP Note Priority Levels

SAP strongly recommends implementing security fixes flagged as priority 1 and 2. These fixes primarily remedy externally reported or publicly known issues. Priority 1 and 2 SAP Notes are used to fix a particular vulnerability without needing to update a system to a newer service pack. To reduce implementation effort for SAP's customers, priority 3 and 4 security SAP Notes will generally be delivered with the next applicable support package. However, if you determine that a priority 3 or 4 note is relevant to your system, you should strongly consider implementing it.

> **Support Packages**
>
> SAP strongly recommends that its customers apply support packages on their systems as soon as they're available. The reasoning behind this is that a support package will contain all priority 3 and 4 security SAP Notes.

9.1.3   Other Patching

Patches for third-party databases and operating systems should also be managed in conjunction with SAP patching. Often, SAP will release information about critical patches for third-party operating systems and non-SAP database vendors. It's important to keep in mind that SAP certifies each OS and DB combination, so be careful to apply patches that are certified with SAP. This information can usually be found in the respective SAP Note for each OS/database.

9.1.4   SAP Security Patch Day

SAP releases its monthly security patches on security patch day, which is generally the second Tuesday of every month. All critical patches that have occurred since the last security patch day will be released on the next security patch day. This falls in line with patch days of other vendors, such as Microsoft and Oracle. Because of this, security administrators can plan to review and potentially install security patches on a fixed schedule.

SAP categorizes security SAP Notes as *Patch Day Security Notes* and *Support Package Security Notes*. This is done to indicate the severity and urgency of specific issues that should be patched ad hoc or with the next support package upgrade.

Patch Day Security Notes

Security SAP Notes that solve vulnerabilities reported by sources that are external to SAP (third-party or public knowledge source) and security SAP Notes solving vulnerabilities that were found internally (only very high, priority 4, or Common Vulnerability Scoring System [CVSS] 9.0 and higher) are released to customers on security patch day.

When to Implement Security-Related SAP Notes

SAP recommends that you implement all security SAP Notes as soon as they are published. Once notes are published, both you and potential attackers become aware of the system vulnerability. It is very important to implement the fix as soon as you are able to.

Common Vulnerability Scoring System Scores

SAP has opted to use the CVSS framework to score and classify SAP security issues. This system is the industry standard for scoring and classifying security threats. CVSS helps convey the urgency and priority of discovered vulnerabilities so that security administrators can quickly gain an understanding of what vulnerabilities to focus on first. It's vendor-neutral and designed to unify how security threats are assessed industry-wide. As of the writing of this text, SAP supports CVSS version 3.0.

Each security SAP Note has a base CVSS value, as described in Table 9.2. These values give an indication of the priority at which the issue is rated on the CVSS base score scale.

SAP Note Priority	CVSS v3 Value
Hot news: very high priority	9.0-10.0
Correction with high priority	7.0-8.9
Correction with medium priority	4.0-6.9
Correction with low priority	0.1-3.9

Table 9.2 CVSS Score Reference

When a vulnerability is reported, a CVSS base score between 0.0 and 10.0 is produced using several metrics. The higher the score, the more severe the patched vulnerability. Thus, a CVSS score of 10.0 represents the most severe vulnerability. The corresponding SAP Note would be issued as *hot news*, which is a very high priority note and should be implemented as soon as possible.

Security SAP Notes that address an issue that is CVSS-rated will have a CVSS information heading with the relevant ratings. An example is shown in Figure 9.1.

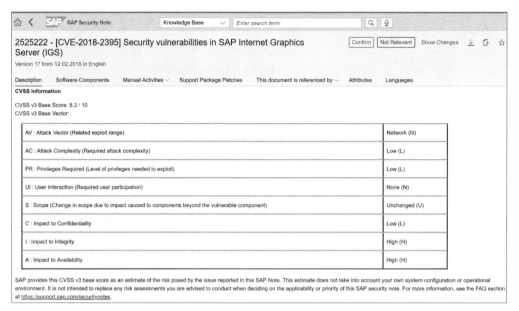

Figure 9.1 SAP Note with CVSS Rating

In the example SAP Note, the base CVSS score is 8.3, which makes the severity *correction with high priority*. Along with the base CVSS score, a detailed base vector listing is also included. This describes the ways in which the vulnerability described can be attacked and the threat level of each vector. Each piece of information can be used to evaluate the threat and urgency of response required by the security administrator.

> **Note**
>
> Your business requirements or system configuration may affect the priority or applicability of a security SAP Note. Be sure to conduct your own analysis before making the decision to implement any security SAP Note.

Support Package Security SAP Notes

Security SAP Notes that solve priority 2, 3, or 4 vulnerabilities that were not disclosed to SAP by a third party or are not public knowledge will typically be released as part of the next support package. In some cases, a support package SAP Note will be released to customers as an individual security SAP Note when a functional SAP Note is dependent on it.

9.2   Application of Security SAP Notes

In many organizations, the security administrator is tasked with coordination and management of security patching or security SAP Notes. This is a complex, challenging, and demanding position. Often, the security needs of an organization are balanced between the needs of the business and the risk associated with poor security. Figure 9.2 illustrates this dilemma.

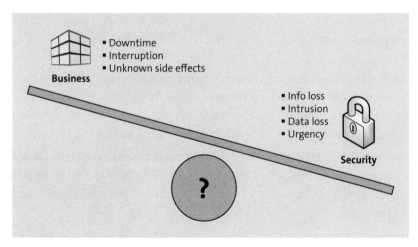

Figure 9.2 Challenges of Patching

At any point in time, multiple vulnerabilities are present and pose a risk to the business. The security administrator's task is to judge these risks using the tools and knowledge he or she has. Tools like CVSS scores and SAP Solution Manager help in the analysis, but it's also important to factor in the risks of disruption and damage to the business as result of making changes to the system. Make no mistake, security SAP Notes are system or configuration changes and do pose a risk to business stability if implemented recklessly. It's important to plan ahead and coordinate with your business users.

It's also important to have a policy set for patching that the business can agree on. In this policy, setting timeframes for each priority level of released SAP Notes can help manage a timeline for implementation for a security administrator. Determining the criticality of your SAP systems along with the criticality of a released security SAP Note is a good practice. You can find an example timeline in Table 9.3.

Business System Criticality	SAP Note Priority	Deadline for implementation
Very high	Very high	12 days
Very high	High	30 days
High	Medium	45 days
Medium	Medium	60 days
Low	Low	180 days

Table 9.3 Sample Patching Timeline

Along with a patching timeline, it's good to set ground rules on patching. For example, the business may ask that patching happen once a month on a Friday night. IT may insist that it happen within 72 hours of a critical patch being released. A balance between business needs and security objectives needs to be found.

Finally, there needs to be a policy for exceptions. It's inevitable that the business will need to delay fixes or change implementation timelines. Proper documentation and approval by the responsible parties is a critical part of keeping systems secure and passing an audit.

Once the decision has been made to patch, it's often up to the system or security administrator to apply the proper SAP Notes to the system. If an SAP Note has the implementation status **Can Be Implemented** and has corrections attached to it, it can be applied with Transaction SNOTE. The implementation status can be found in the header of the SAP Note along with the number of corrections that the SAP Note contains.

Reverting an SAP Note

The system can also revert Transaction SNOTE changes using the **Revert Code to Original State** option. To uninstall an SAP Note, select **Reset SAP Implementation Note** from the Transaction SNOTE menu. Although this may help when an issue is discovered, be careful. There are risks to this procedure. See SAP Note 518990 for more information about the risks of reverting SAP Notes.

Sometimes, SAP Notes may not have automatically implementable corrections within them. They may carry instructions on how to fix the issue instead. Often, SAP Notes will prescribe a kernel upgrade or a setting change or patch on the OS or database levels. Carefully read each SAP Note and apply its recommendations as prescribed by SAP.

Digitally Signed SAP Notes

As of the writing of this book, SAP has begun moving towards digitally signing all SAP Notes. Information about digitally signed SAP Notes can be found in the SAP Support Portal in SAP Note 2408073.

Applying Corrections Using Transaction SNOTE

The SAPOSS RFC connection in Transaction SM59 must be working to download SAP Notes from SAP Support Portal directly to your SAP NetWeaver AS ABAP system. See SAP Note 33135 for a guide to connecting to SAP via the SAPOSS RFC.

To apply SAP Note corrections, proceed as follows:

1. Navigate to Transaction SNOTE.
2. Click the **Download Note** button 🗎 in the toolbar.
3. In the dialog box (Figure 9.3), enter the number of the SAP Note you wish to download and click the **Execute** button 🕹.

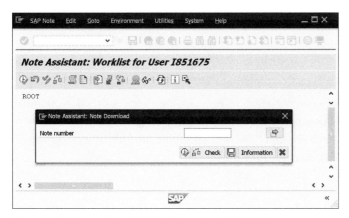

Figure 9.3 Transaction SNOTE: Download SAP Note

4. The system will connect to SAP and download the SAP Note. You'll see the status of the download in the lower left-hand corner of the SAP GUI window.

5. Once the SAP Note has downloaded, you'll see an entry created in the Transaction SNOTE main screen under the new tree entry (Figure 9.4). Double-click the text of the SAP Note you downloaded to enter the SAP Note view.

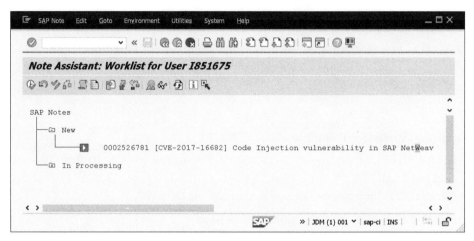

Figure 9.4 Transaction SNOTE: SAP Note Overview

6. This view will provide technical information about the SAP Note. Take care to read and understand the changes and effects of the SAP Note. Even though SAP Notes are generally reversible, it's a risk to rely on this functionality. If the SAP Note requires manual steps, that fact will be mentioned in the text for the SAP Note. If the SAP Note can be implemented using Transaction SNOTE, the implementation state (**Impl. State**) will read **Can Be Implemented**, as shown in Figure 9.5.

7. To implement the note, click the **Implement SAP Note** button ⊕ in the toolbar.

8. The system will display a confirmation screen. Double-check your SAP Note number and click the green **Download SAP Notes** checkmark ✔ when you're ready to continue (Figure 9.6). Be aware that if there are prerequisite SAP Notes required for this SAP Note to be implemented, they may appear in the list shown.

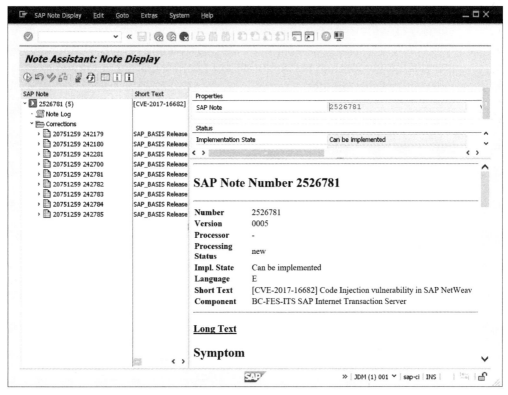

Figure 9.5 Transaction SNOTE: SAP Note Display

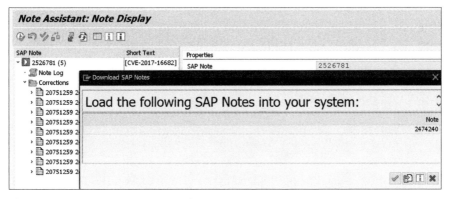

Figure 9.6 Transaction SNOTE: Confirmation Screen

9. The system will now download the SAP Note corrections. Once it's finished, it will display a confirmation box that asks if you understand all the steps required as per the recommendations listed in the SAP Note's text (Figure 9.7). Be sure to fully read and understand the text in the box before continuing. Click the **Yes** button when you are ready to continue.

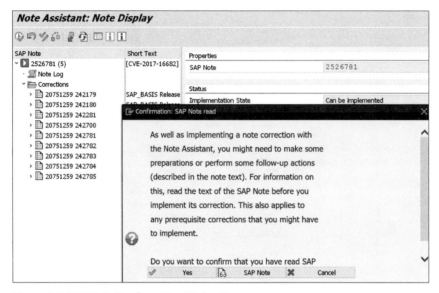

Figure 9.7 SAP Note Confirmation Dialog Box

10. At this point, depending on the type of change, the system will walk you through making the proper changes and packaging them in a transport to move them to other systems. Be aware that this process can be different for any specific SAP Note, depending on its corrections.

Transporting Security SAP Notes

SAP recommends transporting each security SAP Note separately through your landscape. Don't bundle multiple security SAP Notes into a single transport.

---

11. In this example, code is being changed in the system to fix an HTTP request vulnerability. Figure 9.8 shows a confirmation that changes will be made to a specific object within the SAP NetWeaver AS ABAP system. Again, the SAP Note's specific changes will affect what process Transaction SNOTE will follow for implementation.

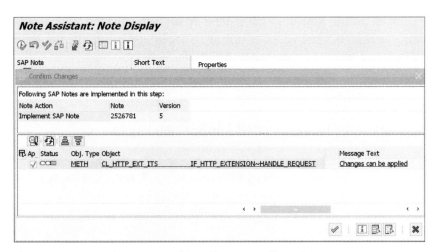

Figure 9.8 Transaction SNOTE: Object Change Confirmation

12. Once Transaction SNOTE has finished implementing the selected SAP Note, it will bring you back to the SAP Note display. If the SAP Note implementation is successful, **Impl. State** will have changed to **Completely Implemented** (Figure 9.9).

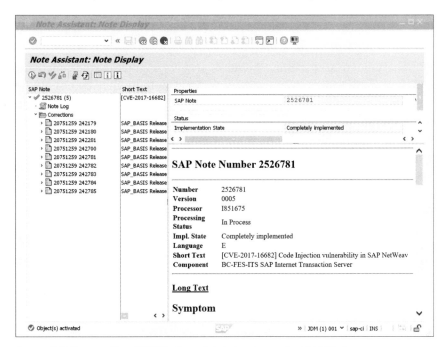

Figure 9.9 Transaction SNOTE: Completely Implemented SAP Note

13. After completing SAP Note implementation, we advise testing the functionality that the SAP Note has altered. Once testing has been performed, the transport containing the SAP Note can be released and considered for import into downstream systems.

9.3   Implications of Upgrades and Support Packages

Upgrades and support packages bring new code into an SAP system. They also may bring new or updated roles and authorization objects. Patch notes will be issued to help identify the changes, but it's always important to test for security-related implications or changes introduced after a note installation, support package import, or after a system upgrade occurs.

Regression testing should be performed by a security administrator after any significant changes to the system. Roles should be examined and tested for any key vulnerability by both the security administrator and the business users. It's common for a security administrator to oversee testing and record results for auditors. This can be as simple as checking authorization objects in Transaction SUIM or executing a testing script as a business user. The scope of regression testing should be determined using audit criteria such that regular regression testing will satisfy auditing requirements.

Once additional point to keep in mind is that when major upgrades to the underlying SAP NetWeaver application server stack are performed, there may be changes in security parameters or even changes to the overall system architecture; for example, consider changes to things like the CommonCryptoLib. Between two different versions of SAP NetWeaver, this functionally may change. It's important to read the SAP Notes and release documentation, which will most certainly call out these concerns.

9.4   Evaluating Security with SAP Solution Manager

SAP Solution Manager is an SAP product that assists in the management of SAP landscapes. It features tools, processes, and utilities that are beneficial to both IT support teams and the business. It's built with both business processes and application lifecycle management in mind. It's a valuable tool for both the implementation and operations phases of any SAP project. Best of all, it's delivered as part of SAP's annual maintenance fee. In this section, we'll highlight some of the tools that SAP Solution Manager has to offer.

SAP Solution Manager: Additional Reading

SAP Solution Manager is an important tool for security administrators to understand and use. Due to its complexity, we'll only be introducing some of its features in this chapter. We highly recommend that any system or security administrator become familiar with SAP Solution Manager by reading SAP Solution Manager-specific literature. A good resource is *SAP Solution Manager—Practical Guide* by Christian, Pytel, Swoboda, and Williams (SAP PRESS, 2017, *www.sap-press.com/4411*).

9.4.1   SAP EarlyWatch Alert Reporting

SAP EarlyWatch Alert reporting is an automated reporting capability that is one of the quickest and easiest return on investment activities that can be accomplished with SAP Solution Manager. SAP EarlyWatch Alert reports are system-generated reports that cover the status, health, performance, growth, and security of your SAP solutions. SAP EarlyWatch Alert reports can be reviewed internally and sent to SAP for expert analysis.

Specifically, SAP EarlyWatch Alert reports each have an excellent section dedicated to system security. A sample SAP EarlyWatch Alert report is shown in Figure 9.10.

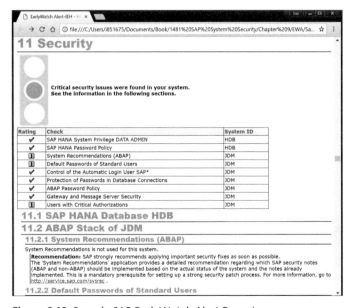

Figure 9.10 Sample SAP EarlyWatch Alert Report

Working through any issues determined by SAP EarlyWatch Alert reporting should be a security administrator's top priority. SAP EarlyWatch Alert reports will often call out critical SAP Notes and configurations that haven't been implemented and recommend that they be implemented.

> **More Information**
>
> SAP Note 863362 contains more information about the available security checks in SAP EarlyWatch Alert reports.

9.4.2   System Recommendations

SAP Solution Manager 7.2 has a built-in SAP Notes recommendation application. (Figure 9.11) This application pulls data from each of your SAP systems and checks SAP Support Portal for relevant SAP Notes.

This helps keep track of where SAP Notes might be within your landscape and what important SAP Notes you may be missing. It can also analyze the effect that implementing an SAP Note may have on your systems and business processes.

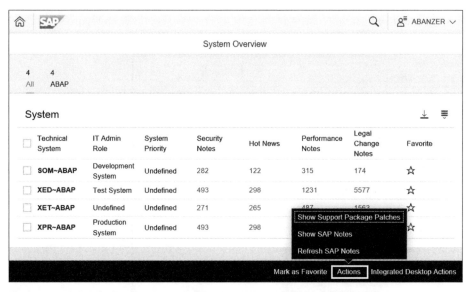

Figure 9.11 SAP Solution Manager: System Recommendations Application

9.4.3 Other Functionality

SAP Solution Manager has other functionality that can be leveraged to assist with security-related administration. Each of the following tools within SAP Solution Manager is optional—but each can add an exceptional amount of value to your day-to-day security and technical management activities, possibly saving a large amount of time and effort for both security administrators and the business:

- **Business Process Change Analyzer**
  Business Process Change Analyzer is a tool that can be used to identify which business processes system-level changes can affect. By running this tool, a security administrator can determine the business effect of security SAP Notes before they're implemented. This can help plan adoption and testing and mitigate threats to the business.

- **Usage and Procedure Logging**
  Usage and Procedure Logging is functionality in SAP Solution Manager that records object usage on connected systems. For example, if a report is run on an SAP ERP system that's connected to SAP Solution Manager, then SAP Solution Manager can capture statistics on the object being used or not used. Using these statistics, you can determine if what you're changing will affect a commonly used object or an entirely unused or seldom-used object.

- **Configuration Validation**
  SAP Solution Manager can be configured to report on the configuration of systems that it manages. This includes the implementation status of security SAP Notes in target systems. Using this functionality, security administrators can compare technical information, like which SAP Notes have been implemented in which systems or what kernel level each system is at, within their SAP environments.

- **Change Request Management**
  Change Request Management (ChARM) is a tool used to manage changes throughout your SAP environment. It uses a workflow and manages implementation, testing, and logistics for each change, including transportable security SAP Notes. It's a valuable tool that SAP Solution Manager offers, and it can help make your landscape more secure by strengthening the change process.

9.5   Summary

In this chapter, we explored how SAP releases changes to its customers using several different types of SAP Notes, including security SAP Notes. You learned about security patch day and the schedule to release hot news or priority 1 changes. You also learned about CVSS scoring and how a system administrator needs to be able to identify which patches may need to be considered for implementation immediately and which can wait until the next support package. Next, you learned how to implement changes using Transaction SNOTE.

Finally, you learned about SAP Solution Manager and its role in helping a security administrator manage and implement security SAP Notes, produce SAP EarlyWatch Alert reports, and implement changes while following a change process throughout the entire landscape.

In the next chapter we will explore how to secure the TMS, which allows developers and business users to move changes between the systems in a landscape. It is important for a security administrator to properly safeguard this system to prevent malicious or untested changes from moving between systems, or into a productive system.

Chapter 10
Securing Transports

Before reading this chapter, you'll need to understand users and authorizations (covered in Chapter 7) and have a basic understanding of RFC connections (Transaction SM59).

Within an SAP landscape, changes to objects within the SAP system are managed using the TMS. The TMS is vital functionality for an SAP NetWeaver system. Software customizations, code changes, configuration changes, and table changes are all managed by TMS in transport requests. Transport requests are logical groupings of table entries that make up these changes.

Using the transport request mechanism, changes can be made in a development system and then copied to multiple downstream systems—and eventually to a production system. The arrangement of systems in a landscape is called the *TMS route*, which defines where transports go after they're created and imported.

Within an SAP NetWeaver ABAP system, code is moved from system to system using transports. A transport contains all the data and objects required for a change. There are several types of transports—but for now, just note that transports contain changes to the system.

One of the challenges of a security administrator is knowing which changes are authorized and which are not. This is purely an access control issue but nonetheless important. Periodic auditing of transport activities in all systems is a good way to identify any transport activities that cause risk to your system. A solid change control process also can be an indicator of risk. Any transport that doesn't go through such a process should be thoroughly vetted.

The subject of TMS is a broad one. Much documentation and many books have been written on the subject. For the security administrator's purposes, we'll only be coving the basics and the security aspects of TMS.

As for TMS and security, TMS is important to the security administrator because it's the mechanism by which changes can be introduced to an SAP landscape. Changes may not always be good or well-intentioned. A malicious party may attempt to introduce changes to the system that defeat or weaken security measures. Therefore, it's critical to have a secure TMS. In this chapter, we'll explore TMS and common threat vectors and how to address them.

Transport system management is not typically a day-to-day responsibility for a security administrator. The security administrator's involvement mainly centers on controlling access to the transport system and identifying to internal or external auditors who can use and has used the transport system.

10.1   Transport System Concepts

A *transport* is a numbered container that contains code to be moved between SAP systems. Transports can come from a development system, or even from SAP. (These are called *support packages*.)

Transports are all uniquely numbered and the system will log who creates, releases, and imports transports. This logging is often the target of audits, so it's important to maintain this data.

A *transport domain* is the grouping of systems that require development and customizing objects to be delivered by a transport. Traditionally, this is what's considered a landscape. However, in some scenarios, transport domains can be used to solve issues of a compliance nature. These situations are beyond the scope of this book. For the purposes of this text, we'll consider our transport domain to be made of a test SAP NetWeaver ABAP system. The figures in this chapter will show system SID JDM as a development system, QAS as a QA system, and PRD as a production system.

A *domain controller* is the system that manages the domain and all systems within it. In our example, system JDM is the domain controller. Production or development systems are commonly selected as domain controllers. All configuration is managed within the domain controller. This TMS configuration is then distributed to each system in the landscape. Each system knows other systems in the landscape, and transports can flow to and from systems in an order specified by the transport routes, which are also set up on the domain controller. Figure 10.1 shows an example of a transport route for a basic three-system landscape.

The *import queue* or *buffer* is the list of transports waiting for import into a particular system in the landscape. Maintaining this list is important because the order in which transports are imported is critical in ensuring that the versions of the objects they contain are the latest at the time of import.

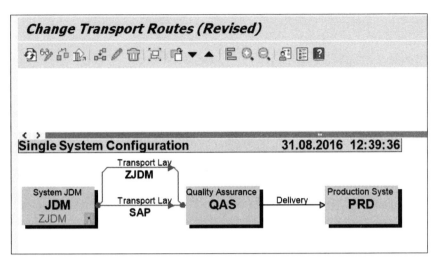

Figure 10.1 Sample TMS Routes

The transport system is managed with Transaction STMS. Within this transaction, an administrator can change the settings that govern the TMS's operation, as well as import transports.

10.1.1 Operating System-Level Components

The SAP NetWeaver AS ABAP application server plays a critical role in the TMS. Using the database and a shared OS-level directory, the SAP NetWeaver AS ABAP application server can move transports between systems. We'll cover OS-level security concerns in Section 10.3. For now, we'll walk through the process of moving transports between systems of a three-tier landscape.

The first component to understand is the shared transport directory. The shared transport directory (*/usr/sap/trans*) on the OS level is shown in Figure 10.2. Each system in the landscape will have access to this shared directory. The shared directory is the mechanism by which transports are moved between systems.

> **Hint: Mounted Directories**
>
> Some systems with special requirements won't have access to a shared directory across systems. These systems usually fall under government- or healthcare-related restrictions and may have a network gap between each system.

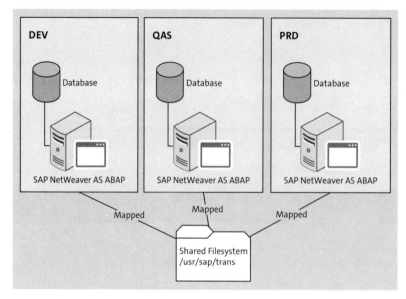

Figure 10.2 Physical TMS Landscape

When a transport is created in a development system, it's contained within the database of the SAP NetWeaver system it's been created on. Once a user, usually a developer or someone responsible for changing objects within the system, releases said transport, a copy of the objects that the transport contains is written to a file on the shared filesystem by the kernel utility tp. A header file is also written. These two files, the data file and cofile (header), are both written to the shared directory */usr/sap/ trans*. An entry into the buffer file is also made, indicating that the next system in the transport route can import the transport. The buffer file or import buffer is also located on the shared filesystem.

Once a transport operator is ready, the transport can be imported into the next system. In our three-tier example, this is QAS. When the import is triggered, the kernel utilities R3trans and tp work together to import the transport from the shared filesystem into the database of the next system down the line, as defined by the transport routes set up on the domain controller. The transport is imported and activated, then added to the next system in the transport route. This is usually PRD.

By using the database and file system, a controlled, trackable method of change movement and management can be established. This is a cornerstone of building a reliable and secure change management system. Next, we'll explore system settings that control which systems changes can be made in.

10.1.2   Controlling System Changes: Setting System/Client Change Options

The system and client change options define in which systems or clients changes to objects can be allowed. For example, development should be allowed in the development system or client. Development should *not* be allowed in the production or test systems or clients.

TMS Configuration

TMS configuration is client-independent, so it must be done in client 000.

There are two methods of controlling access to change objects in an SAP system: the system change option and the client change option. You can find more about changing the client-level change options in Chapter 4.

Setting the Global System Change Option

The global system change option can be set by following the steps:

1. Execute Transaction SE03 (Figure 10.3).

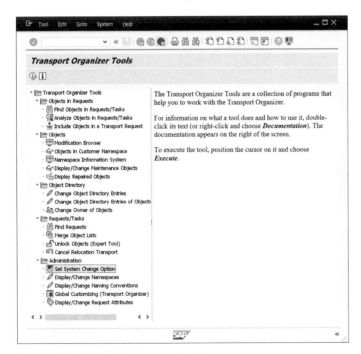

Figure 10.3 TMS Tools: Transaction SE03

2. Next, you'll see the **System Change Option** screen (Figure 10.4; note that the screenshot in this figure is a development system, so the **Global** system change setting is set to **Modifiable**).

3. To change settings within this screen, simply click the **Display/Change** button 🪛, make your changes, and click the **Save** button 💾.

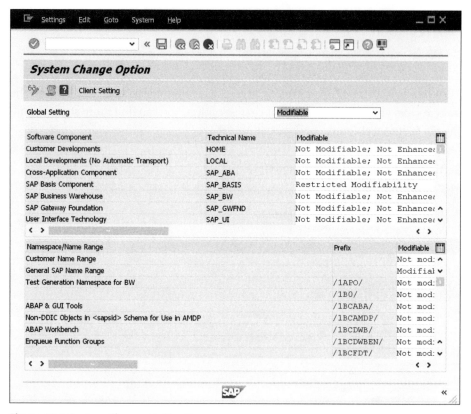

Figure 10.4 System Change Option Screen

4. Clicking the **Client Setting** button (Figure 10.5) will move you to a list of the clients on your system.

5. You can click a client to view its settings (Figure 10.6) or click the **Display/Change** button 🪛 to change its settings. We covered this in detail in Chapter 4.

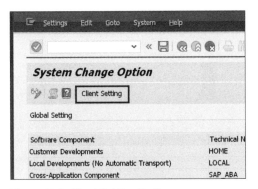

Figure 10.5 Client Setting Button

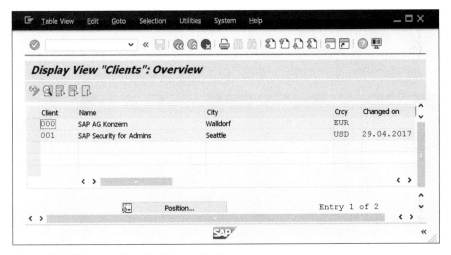

Figure 10.6 Clients Listing for Change Options

Viewing the Transport System Logs

Occasionally, especially during an audit, a security or system administrator may be asked to review the transport system logs. They can be found via the following steps:

1. Navigate to Transaction STMS. From the menu, select **Overview · Imports**. The **Import Overview** screen will appear (Figure 10.7).

2. From the menu, select **Goto · History · Import History**. You'll be prompted to select a system within your transport domain. Select a system and click the **Continue** button ✅.

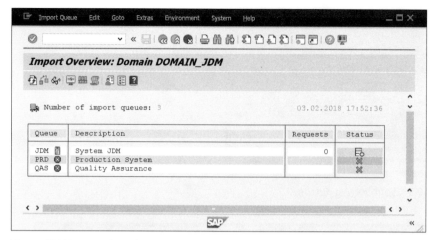

Figure 10.7 Import Overview Screen

3. The **Import History** screen will appear (Figure 10.8).

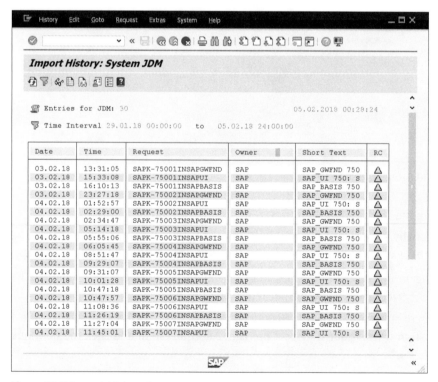

Figure 10.8 Import History Screen

The **Import History** screen can be used to trace which transports were imported by which person(s). It can be very useful during an audit or when a change has an unintended consequence and you need to find out who created the transport.

10.1.3   Transport Management System Users

For the TMS system to trigger import and release (export to filesystem) transports in systems remotely, two users are created for system use during the process (see Table 10.1).

Username	User Type	Description
DDIC	Dialog	This user is used for the execution of the application-level steps of the import. The most visible step for the system administrator is data dictionary activation.
TMSADM	System	This user is used for the RFC connection and triggering of the transport on the OS level.

Table 10.1 Users Required for TMS

The DDIC user's role in the SAP NetWeaver system is indicated by its name: DDIC denotes the data dictionary, and this user is used for activations in the data dictionary, among other things. SAP has two recommendations for securing your DDIC user:

- Secure DDIC against misuse by changing the default password in all clients.
- Lock DDIC and unlock it only when necessary.

The TMSADM user is used for connections between systems.

> **TMSADM Passwords**
>
> The old and new TMS default passwords are well-known. Change the password on every system in your landscape! It's critical to use a *strong* password for your TMSADM user. You can find more information about the TMSADM user and its password in SAP Note 1568362.

Because TMSADM's password needs to be identical on each system in your transport domain, we must set it using a special procedure. Let's walk through that now:

1. Login to client 000 of the domain controller of the domain you'd like to change the TMSADM password for.

2. Execute Transaction SE38. Enter the program name, "TMS_UPDATE_PWD_OF_ TMSADM" (Figure 10.9).

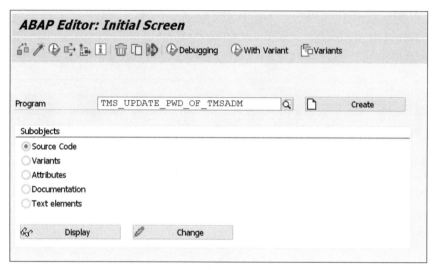

Figure 10.9 Execute Program TMS_UPDATE_PWD_OF_TMSADM

3. Click the **Execute** button 	.

4. Select the **User's Own Password Appropriate to System Setting** radio button (Figure 10.10). Next, enter your password in the **Password** and **Password Confirmation** boxes.

> **TMS Password**
>
> Again, we highly recommend using a unique, strong password.

It's a good idea to perform a connection test and fix any connection issues before continuing. Once you're ready, click the **Execute** button 	.

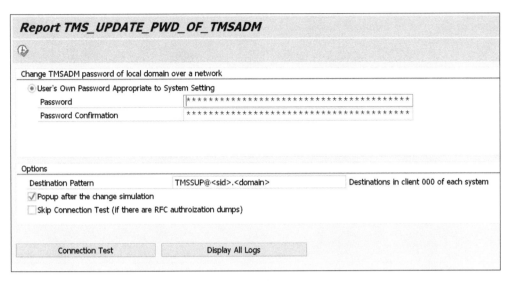

Figure 10.10 Program TMS_UPDATE_PWD_OF_TMSADM

5. The system will now ask for confirmation (Figure 10.11). Click the **Yes** button to continue. A second dialog box will ask if you'd like to use SNC-secured connections. Click the **Yes** button to continue.

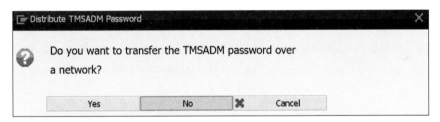

Figure 10.11 TMSADM Password Confirmation

6. The domain controller will now reach out to each system using the TMSUP@<sid>. <domain> RFCs and set the password in each system. If you encounter any issues, they'll be logged and can be retrieved using the **Display All Logs** button. Figure 10.12 shows a log from our example system.

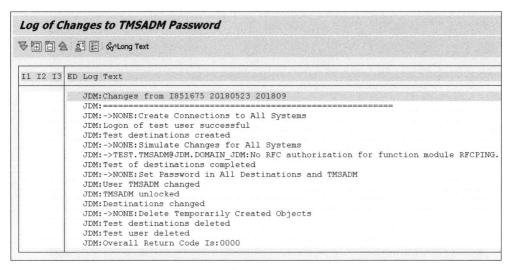

Figure 10.12 TMSADM Password Update Log

10.1.4   TMS RFC connections

TMS uses an RFC connection between systems, as well as between the SAP system and the underlying OS. A list of the system generated RFC destinations required for the transport system can be found in Table 10.2.

RFC Name	Description
TMSADM@TP<domain>.<system>	This RFC reads information back from the kernel utility tp.
TMSSUP@TP<domain>.<system>	This RFC can change information using the kernel utility tp.
CALLTP_<Operating System>	This RFC executes the tp command on the OS level.

Table 10.2 Standard RFC Destinations for TMS

The important takeaway here is that the destinations TMSADM and CALLTP both pose potential security risks. TMSADM is configured to use the password for the user TMSADM. As you know from earlier in this chapter, the TMS user has authorizations that allow for moving transports. We don't want this user account or RFC to be compromised. The CALLTP RFC calls down to the OS to execute the kernel utility tp to execute the move of a transport from a transport file to the database. We don't want malicious users to be able to have access to this functionality.

Secure RFCs and TMS

TMS gives you the option to use SNC-protected RFC connections. You can enable this by executing the steps below. SNC is covered in depth in Chapter 12. You must have SNC enabled on all systems in your domain to use this functionality.

Activating Secure Network Communications

Secure network communications can be enabled for the transport system to use between systems. You must have certificates installed for all systems involved. They can be self-signed, but CA-signed certificates are ideal. You can find more information about certificates and SNC in Chapter 12. The following steps assume you have certificates installed for each system in your transport domain.

1. Log in to client 000 of the domain controller of the domain you'd like to activate SNC for (Figure 10.13).

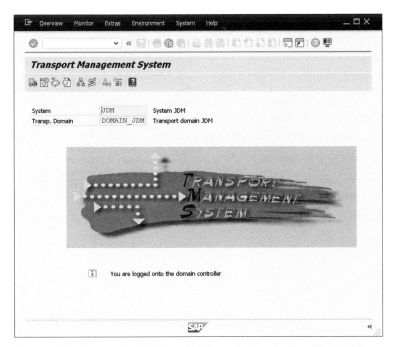

Figure 10.13 Transaction STMS on the Domain Ccontroller, Client 000

2. Navigate to Transaction STMS (Figure 10.13). You should see that you are logged into the domain controller. If not, log in to the domain controller, client 000.

3. From the menu, select **Overview • Systems.** The **System Overview** screen will appear (Figure 10.14).

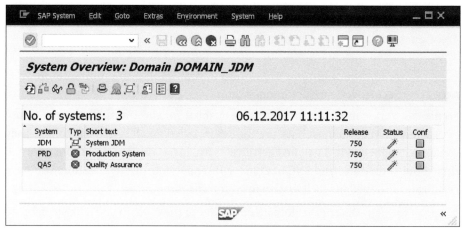

Figure 10.14 STMS System Overview Screen

4. From the **System Overview** screen, select **Goto • Transport Domains.** This will open the TMS configuration for your transport domain (Figure 10.15).

5. Click the **Display/Change** button 🖉. Change the **SNC Protection** radio button to **Active.**

6. The system will now check all TMS destinations within your domain for up to date configuration and prompt if there are any discrepancies.

7. Lastly, select the **Accept SNC Information** button 🖳 in the lower right-hand corner of the **Security Options** section. This will request SNC address information from all systems of your own and linked domains.

8. The system will now prompt you to distribute configuration. The process is now complete.

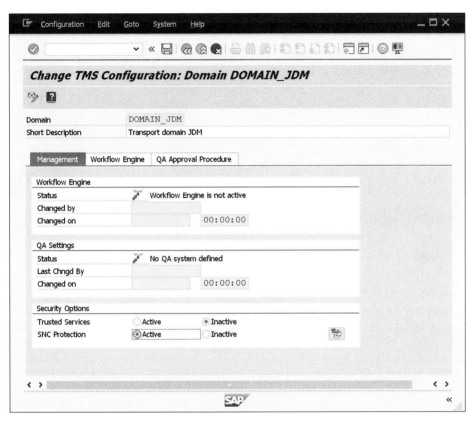

Figure 10.15 TMS Configuration for Domain

10.2   Transport Authorizations

It's important to control which users have access to the transport system. An inexperienced user and a malicious user may have an equally negative effect on an SAP system and its ability to serve business needs.

Within the SAP application, restricting access to Transaction STMS is a good first step. Recall that this is done with authorization object S_TCODE. Next, the authorization objects in Table 10.3 should be considered. Their values allow access to functionality required to perform imports. Be sure to carefully review each value you set for these objects.

Authorization Object Name	Description
S_CTS_ADMI	Controls Administrative functions of the CTS.
S_TRANSPRT	Controls access to the transport organizer
S_DEVELOP	Controls access to development functions
S_TABU_DIS	Controls access to edit/display tables
S_TCODE	Controls what transaction codes can be executed. Its value would be "STMS" if it allowed access to the transport organizer.

Table 10.3 Transport-Related Authorization Objects

SAP_ALL

Do *not* assign the profile SAP_ALL to the user TMSADM. This pairing often is found on customer systems and it's a *huge* security risk. Instead, use the SAP recommended S_A.TMSADM role.

TMS User Roles

Within the TMS system, there are several technical roles that users within functional roles will need to do their jobs.

Table 10.4 lists the SAP-delivered technical roles that are provided. When creating your own roles for your company, these can provide a good starting point.

SAP Delivered Role Name	Description
SAP_BC_CTS_DISPLAY	Display-only role for TMS
SAP_BC_TRANSPORT_OPERATOR	Allows execution of transports within TMS
SAP_BC_TRANSPORT_ADMINISTRATOR	Enables administration of TMS

Table 10.4 TMS Roles

Let's discuss the functional roles and the associated technical roles in more detail:

- **Transport viewer**
  This role should be assigned to a user that is responsible for diagnosing changes that are moving through TMS. It allows view-only functionality in the following transactions:

  - Transport Management System (Transaction STMS) and QA (Transaction STMS_QA)

  - Transport Organizer (Transactions SE01, SE09) and its tools (Transaction SE03)

  - Support Package Manager (Transaction SPAM) and Add-On Installation Tool (Transaction SAINT)

  - System settings (Transaction SE06) and client overview/settings (Transaction SCC4)

  Finally, this role is required for a user to be able to check and diagnose transport errors. A transport viewer would require the SAP_BC_CTS_DISPLAY role.

- **Transport operator**
  This functional role enables the management of transports, imports, releases, and import buffers. Be sure not to assign this to users that can create code as they would then have all the authorizations they need to create a change and move it to other environments. This also highlights that anyone given this role will be accountable for internal or external audit risks because they are able to move changes.

- **Transport administrator**
  A user with the transport administrator role is an administrator of the Change and Transport System. The tasks of this user include:

  - Configuring the system landscape with the TMS

  - Importing new SAP software, SPAM/SAINT, support packages, and add-ons

  - Routine transport tasks such as imports, approving changes, and so on

  The transport administrator role has all authorizations in the TMS. A transport administrator would require the role SAP_BC_TRANSPORT_OPERATOR. This role should be tightly controlled and only given to administrators that have a need to manage the transport domain. This role will also be tightly controlled in the case of an internal or external audit.

10.3   Operating System–Level Considerations

Although the primary method of moving transports is via Transaction STMS, it's also possible to move the at the OS level using the tp utility. Make sure you have restricted access on the OS layer and are regularly testing and reviewing who has access.

An SAP system being compromised at the OS level is one of the most dangerous threats that can be exploited. The reason for this is that with control of the underlying OS, signs of the compromise can be eliminated or obfuscated so that the intrusion may never be discovered.

Take special care to secure both the OS and its shared transport directory, */usr/sap/trans*. Take care to set strict permissions for your transport directory. Only administrators should have access, and it's probably best if only users that have SIDADM access can access your transport directory.

If you're using Linux/Unix, it's also best to use the "nosuid" option when mounting to a shared transport directory so that users that may have enhanced authorizations on remote systems can't change the permissions of the files in the shared transport directory.

Need More Info?

Full setup instructions for the transport directory can be found in SAP Note 28781 (Central Transport Directory NT/UNIX).

Remote Execution of TP Commands

Another attack vector on tp is remote execution through the gateway. Be sure to protect the gateway with an Access Control List (ACL).

Use the following ACL settings for securing tp:

```
P USER=* USER-HOST=local HOST=local TP=tp
D USER=* USER-HOST=* HOST=* TP=tp
```

Windows systems will require the exact name of the executable: tp.exe.

> **More Information**
>
> For more information about preventing the starting of tp via the gateway process, see SAP Note 1371799 (Correct Security Settings for Gateway Access Control Lists for Kernel Program tp).

10.4   Landscape Considerations

Take special care in development systems. Often, permissions in development systems are intentionally kept open to aid in the speed of development. Although this may help reduce barriers to getting things done, it's a big potential attack vector that should be addressed by security administrators. Figure 10.16 illustrates this point. If an unauthorized party can inject malicious code into development alongside legitimate development, it may slip through the change control process and be imported into QAS—and eventually PRD.

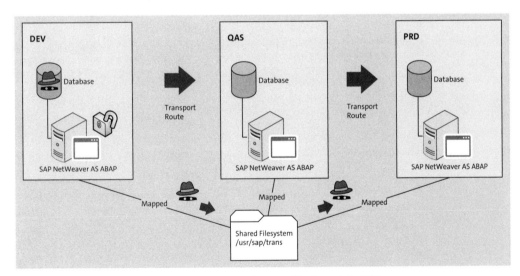

Figure 10.16 Exploitation of DEV Environment Can Lead to Breach in PRD

This raises the idea that a controlled and properly audited change process can be an asset in a security administrator's toolbelt. Software like SAP's ChaRM can be used to make sure that properly tested and vetted changes are being cycled through the environment. Using the tools we've discussed in this chapter on all systems in your environment will help in the constant battle against intrusion.

10.5   Summary

In this chapter, you learned about the basics of the TMS. You learned the process from creation to import for how a transport is moved between the database and application server layers. You also learned how to change the system modification settings and how to view the transport history.

You learned about the technical aspects of TMS to take care of, such as the */usr/sap/ trans* shared directory and the RFC connections, and users that enable its functionality. Finally, you learned about the user roles and considerations that should be taken into account on the OS level to keep systems safe.

In the next chapter you will learn about the logging and monitoring functions of SAP NetWeaver AS ABAP. These functions are used to provide a record of when changes, activity, or significant events happen in the system.

Chapter 11
Auditing and Logging

To keep a system secure, it's essential to have eyes on all parts of the system and the changes being made therein. Security audit logging records all security events for later analysis; table logging records changes made to tables, including when the changes were made and by whom. In this chapter, you'll learn to configure and enable security audit logging and table logging.

Certain activities in the SAP system are periodically checked and reviewed by an auditor. Therefore, you must ensure that those activities are recorded in the system. The security audit log provides a framework to record security-related events in the system—for example, Remote Function Calls (RFCs), logon attempts, changes to the audit configuration, and so on. The security audit log doesn't log changes to the data within the SAP system that are stored in the database. However, with the table-logging functionality, you can record changes to a table. It's not recommended to log all table changes—only the ones that are considered important and hence for which changes must be traceable. For example, important tables include table T000 (clients), table TCUR (exchange rates), and others.

To analyze the workload of the SAP system, you can use the Workload Monitor, which is also a neat tool to analyze a user's history. The Workload Monitor records historical usage data and allows you to drill down on a user level.

As data protection laws gain ground, protecting your data becomes more and more important. To protect the privacy of and personal information in your SAP system, along with sensitive and classified data, you can use Read Access Logging (RAL) to record read activity.

In this chapter, you'll learn how the different logging functionalities work, what makes them unique, and the impact on your system.

11.1 External Audits

Often, a security administrator will find herself being asked to help with an external audit. Before we tackle the task of assisting with an audit, first we'll cover what these audits do for a company.

External audits are typically financial; that is, they center on the financial records of the company. These audits typically focus on any customer running the SAP ERP or SAP S/4HANA finance functionality on SAP NetWeaver AS ABAP. Two common audits that organizations go through are to check compliance with the Sarbanes-Oxley Act (SOX) and the International Financial Reporting Standard (IFRS). Each of these audits is performed by an *external auditor*, an organization outside of your own that performs the audit. This organization will send one or several auditors who will be tasked with observing and recording proof that the practices of your organization comply with the controls required for your audit.

The Sarbanes-Oxley Act of 2002 set forth internal financial auditing controls in the United States that must be adhered to when preparing financial information for reporting purposes. US-based financial systems are routinely audited to SOX standards.

IFRS is an audit of accounting systems such that they can be compared between countries reliability. It's common to see IFRS audits performed for multinational companies.

Besides these two, there are many other audits that vary country by country. These auditing standards generally are prepared by a country's government-mandated accounting standards organizations and commonly follow Generally Accepted Auditing Standards (GAAS).

The external auditor will be working off a set of controls, in which the security administrator will most likely be the person that is running the queries in the SAP system to satisfy those queries. Most queries are run through the User Information System (UIS; Transaction SUIM). We'll cover the use of the AIS later in this chapter. Auditors may also ask for the output of some standard reports, among other things.

Often, auditors may also ask for access to your system to run reports on their own. Unless this is legally required, it's a good idea to deny this request. When given the choice, it's a more efficient practice for the SAP security administrator to run queries given to them by an auditor. This is done to keep the security administrator in control of the scope of the audit. If an audit is for financial compliance, the auditor should be looking at finance-related authorization objects. Too often, auditors are given free access to a system, which tends to change the scope of the audit to what-ever the auditor feels like digging into.

Often, external audits are focused into categories similar to the following:

- Internal controls
- Network activity
- Database activity
- Login activity (success and failures)
- Account or user activity
- Information access

For each such category, the auditor will require proof that the controls for that cate-gory are being applied. They may also ask for a random sample of users or transports, or even provide a time frame and ask to see logs or proof that controls were being adhered to for that time.

11.2   Internal Audits

Internal audits are performed by individuals within your own organization. Often, they focus on preparing for an external audit. However, this isn't always the case. Internal audits can be used to ensure that a specific control or policy is being followed by examining system activity, logs, or even user master records. This type of activity is usually mandated by either the security administrator or an internal audit depart-ment for the purposes of verification.

Quite often, when an internal audit is performed, the objective is to improve adher-ence to the controls that will be followed for an external audit. This will often leave the security administrator with a to-do list to satisfy the audit requirements. In addi-tion, the security administrator may be consulted to help create controls that will help keep compliance such that it's not a major effort when an external audit is per-formed.

One of the common tasks for an internally led audit is to manage the number of users that have powerful authorizations, like SAP_ALL, or access to perform business-criti-cal tasks, like pay vendors or create accounts. This is done by evaluating the roles and authorization objects that each user master record contains.

The internal audit is also a good time to determine the effectiveness of your general security operations and process. Defining a set of controls and evaluating your system and users based on those controls can help enforce a strong, consistent level of security.

11.3   Auditing Tools

SAP systems are equipped with a set of tools that can be used for auditing. Such tools include the security audit log, the system log, table logging, the Workload Monitor, as well as Read Access Logging and the User Information System. All these tools can be utilized to extract and analyze data about certain activities in the system, such as who logged on to a system, who changed a certain table, who accessed certain data, and more. We'll explore each of these tools in more detail in the next sections.

11.3.1   Security Audit Log

The security audit log (SAL) records security-related activities in the system, such as changes to user master records, logon attempts, RFCs, and so on. This tool is designed for auditors to log and review the activities in the system. With the SAL, an auditor can reestablish a series of events that happened in the system.

The SAL offers wide flexibility in its usage. You can activate and deactivate it, as well as change the filters as necessary. For example, you can activate the SAL before an audit takes place and deactivate it once the audit has been performed. Also, you can change the filters and, for example, monitor a user if you've detected suspicious activity in the system.

The audit log must be activated before it can be used. To activate the audit log, you have to specify which activities you want to record in the security audit log. The following activities are available:

- Successful and unsuccessful dialog logon attempts
- Successful and unsuccessful RFC logon attempts
- RFCs to function modules
- Changes to user master records
- Successful and unsuccessful transaction starts
- Successful and unsuccessful report starts
- Changes to the audit configuration

In addition to these events, the security audit log also logs certain activities that aren't categorizable, such as the following:

- Activation and deactivation of the HTTP security session management or instances in which HTTP security sections were hard-exited
- File downloads
- Access to the file system that coincides with the valid logical paths and file names specified in the system (particularly helpful in an analysis phase to determine where access to files takes place before activating the actual validation)
- ICF recorder entries or changes to the administration settings
- The use of digital signatures performed by the system
- Viruses found by the Virus Scan Interface
- Errors that occur in the Virus Scan Interface
- Unsuccessful password checks for a specific user in a specific client

Once activated, the system will record the activities into a log file on the application server.

Warning

Be cautious when activating the security audit log because it contains personal information that may be protected by data protection regulations—especially with the new GDPR regulation from the European Union but also other protection laws in other regions. Make sure that you adhere to the regulations in your area.

Versions

Your SAP_BASIS component affects your version of the security audit log. With SAP NetWeaver 7.5 SP 03 for SAP_BASIS, SAP has introduced new functionality in the security audit log.

In the old version, the main transactions for the security audit log were Transactions SM18, SM19, and SM20. In the new version, SAP introduced several new transactions:

- **Transaction RSAU_CONFIG**
  Maintenance of the kernel parameters and selection profiles relevant for the security audit log

- **Transaction RSAU_CONFIG_SHOW**
  Printable display version of Transaction RSAU_CONFIG

- **Transaction RSAU_READ_LOG**
  Audit log evaluation

- **Transaction RSAU_READ_ARC**
  Audit log evaluation in archive data

- **Transaction RSAU_ADMIN**
  Administration of integrity protection for files; reorganization of log data

- **Transaction RSAU_TRANSFER**
  File-based transfer of an audit profile

With the enhanced functionality and the new transaction codes, SAP delivers new features as well:

- Save the audit log into the database, either in full or in part.

- Filter by user groups with the user attribute **User Group for Authorization Check** from the **Logon Data** tab in Transaction SU01.

- Increase the number of filters from 10 to 90.

- Check the file integrity.

- Use an enhanced authorization concept with authorization object S_SAL.

- An API for evaluating log data is provided with the class CL_SAL_ALERT_API.

Tip

If you use the new security audit log, we recommend locking the old transactions with Transaction SM01_CUS in client 000. Parallel usage of the old and new functionality is possible but not recommended.

Usage Scenarios

Depending on your requirements, you can define usage scenarios differently. With the new security audit logging capability, you can define how and where you want to store the audit log, as well as how to access it. With the old security audit log, you could only save data on the file system of the application server; with the new functionality, you can either save on the file system of the application server or in its database. Also, shared scenarios are possible in which some parts will be stored in the database and the some in the file system.

Classical Approach

In the classical approach, similar to the old version, the audit log is only stored on the file system of the application server. You can read the data from the file system, as well as archive and delete old audit log files.

Database Logging

With the new functionality, it's possible to save the audit log into the database. However, system events are stored in the file system as well. Storing the audit log in the database might result in a quick growth of table RSAU_BUF_DATA, which holds the data. With the archiving object BC_SAL you can, however, archive the data in that table. With the database, you have an improved experience when accessing the data because it's quicker and the requirements for data privacy are met.

Mixed Scenarios

With the enhanced functionality, you can also activate mixed scenarios in which you generally save the logs on the file system but selective events in the database. When saving selective events in the database, you can access the data faster, which results in a significantly increased performance. That makes sense especially when using statistical data or if you run large evaluations against the log data.

In a second scenario, you can use APIs to transfer data from the security audit log to a central monitoring system (e.g., SAP Solution Manager). In that scenario, the SAL saves the data in the file system of the application server. Certain events that are relevant for the central monitoring systems, such as those to create alerts, are stored in the file system and in database table RSAU_BUF_DATA. The API that transfers the data will read the data from the table and then automatically delete it. Your logs are still available in the file system but will be removed from the database table and hence don't require archiving activities in the database.

Configuration

The new security audit log offers an enhanced configuration via Transaction RSAU_CONFIG. Let's explore configuration in detail now.

In general, the security audit log requires some parameters and the definition of filters that define which events will be logged.

To define the parameters, enter Transaction RSAU_CONFIG and open the **Parameter** folder (Figure 11.1).

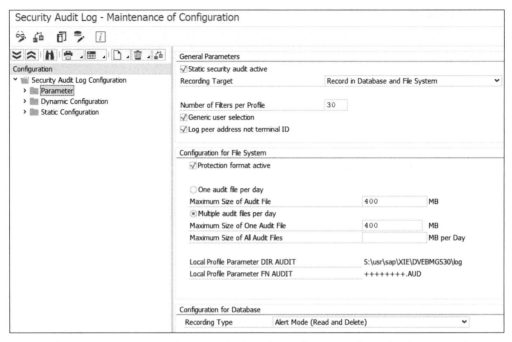

Figure 11.1 Parameter Maintenance in Security Audit Log Configuration in Transaction RSAU_CONFIG

The following can be configured:

- Activate or deactivate logging.
- Define the recording target, whether it's on the file system, in the database, or a combined recording in both the file system and database.
- Define the number of filters per profile, up to 90.
- Define if you'll allow generic user selection with an asterisk (*) character in the filters.
- Define if you log the IP address of the originator and not the terminal ID.
- Activate or deactivate integrity protection format for log files in the file system.
- Define the memory space usage when file system storage is used.
- Define the recording type in the database, whether it's temporary data or permanent data.

In the profiles, you define which events will be logged. To create a new profile or an additional profile, simply right-click the **Static Configuration** folder and choose

Create New Profile. Once the profile is created, you can go ahead and define the settings. Remember that each profile must have at least one filter. To add additional filters, you can simply right-click the **Profile** folder and choose **Create Filter**.

Regardless of the filter you create and specify, it's important to activate the filter once defined by clicking the **Activate** button (Figure 11.2). Only active filters will be selected at the next system start. You can define as many filters as you have defined in the parameter maintenance for each profile.

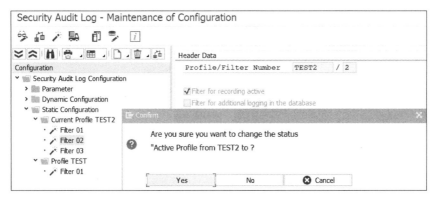

Figure 11.2 Activation of Filters in Transaction RSAU_CONFIG

Each filter that you add to a profile is linked via an OR connector. So, for example, if you have two filters, and the first filter logs everything for user group SUPER and the second filter everything for users starting with RFC*, then those two filters are *OR linked*. That means that all users that belong to user group SUPER and all users starting with RFC* will be logged. Note that user groups only allow for a specific value and that you can't use wildcards as you can for the user name.

In the **Standard Selection** screen, shown in Figure 11.3, where you define the client and whether you want to restrict the logging of a user name or user group, you can select the user group either positively or negatively. **Select by User Group (Positive)** means that you will log all users that are part of that user group. If you use the negative selection, the system logs the events for all users who aren't part of the user group. Possible scenarios for a negative selection can include wanting to log RFC function calls for all users who aren't technical and hence aren't part of a certain user group because those users shouldn't perform RFCs.

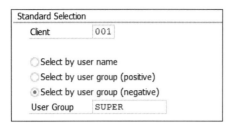

Figure 11.3 Standard Selection in Security Audit Log Configuration

In the **Event Selection** screen (Figure 11.4), you can define which events you want to log. In the **Classic event selection**, you get the same options as in the old security audit log.

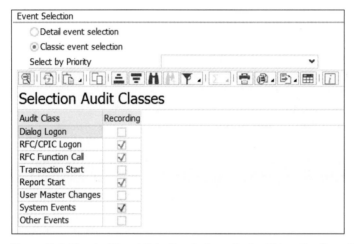

Figure 11.4 Classical Event Selection in Security Audit Log Configuration

In the **Detail event selection** (Figure 11.5), you can slice and dice on a more granular level and pick and choose events more specifically. For example, in the classical selection, you choose **Dialog Logon**, whereas in the detailed selection you can decide whether you want successful logons or failed logons.

If you defined the selection in the classic event selection, the underlying detailed events will be selected.

To start the logging of a filter, it's important that the switch **Filter for Recording Active** is selected. You can have active and inactive filters. Therefore, it's important to keep an eye on the **Active** checkbox, as well as if the filter has been activated.

Audit Class	Audit Class Recording	Message ID	System log message text (before setting variables)

Detailed Selection - Events

Audit Class	Audit Class Recording		Message ID	System log message text (before setting variables)
Other Events	Low	☐	AU0	Audit - Test. Text: &A
Dialog Logon	Medium	☐	AU1	Logon successful (type=&A, method=&C)
Dialog Logon	High	☐	AU2	Logon failed (reason=&B, type=&A, method=&C)
Transaction Start	Low	☐	AU3	Transaction &A started.
Transaction Start	High	☐	AU4	Start of transaction &A failed (Reason=&B)
RFC/CPIC Logon	Low	☐	AU5	RFC/CPIC logon successful (type=&A, method=&C)
RFC/CPIC Logon	High	☐	AU6	RFC/CPIC logon failed, reason=&B, type=&A, method=&C
User Master Changes	High	☐	AU7	User &A created.
User Master Changes	Medium	☐	AU8	User &A deleted.
User Master Changes	Medium	☐	AU9	User &A locked.
User Master Changes	Medium	☐	AUA	User &A unlocked.
User Master Changes	Medium	☐	AUB	Authorizations for user &A changed.
Dialog Logon	Low	☐	AUC	User Logoff
User Master Changes	Medium	☐	AUD	User master record &A changed.
System Events	High	✓	AUE	Audit configuration changed
System Events	High	✓	AUF	Audit: Slot &A: Class &B, Severity &C, User &D, Client &E, &F
System Events	High	✓	AUG	Application server started

Figure 11.5 Detailed Event Selection Options in Security Audit Log Configuration

Administration of Log Data

The administration of log data takes place in Transaction RSAU_ADMIN (Figure 11.6). In the administration cockpit, you can check the integrity of the file-based log data and reorganize obsolete files. For the database tables, you can use this cockpit to reorganize table RSAU_BUF_DATA by means of deletion or archiving.

Figure 11.6 Log Data Administration Initial Screen

Integrity Protection

With the integrity protection setting of the SAL, you can protect the security audit log from manipulation of its log files on the file system. However, it doesn't prevent the manipulation of the file but it will tell you if it was manipulated.

To protect the integrity of your files, you can create one hash-based message authentication code (HMAC) per system. To create the HMAC key, choose **Configure Integrity Protection Format** from the initial screen (Figure 11.7) and define your secret **Passphrase**.

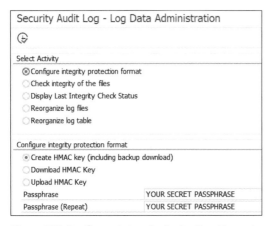

Figure 11.7 Configure Integrity Protection Format

If you wish to restore the key, a local backup file is generated that can be used in combination with the passphrase. Make sure to store the backup file and passphrase so that you can check the integrity of the system later.

If you decide not to create an individual system HMAC key, your integrity is at risk because the integrated key must be considered to be known, as it is set to a default value. That means that you can check the files only against unintentional corruption or change and not against malicious manipulation.

Once configured, all log files written forward will be checked by the integrity protection format. To check the integrity of the files, you can choose **Check Integrity of the Files** on the initial screen (Figure 11.8).

Shorter time frames can be analyzed in the foreground. However, larger periods will be run in the background. Once the check has been performed, you'll see an overview of all the files and their attributes (Figure 11.9). Also, you'll see the status, which indicates whether the file has integrity issues or not.

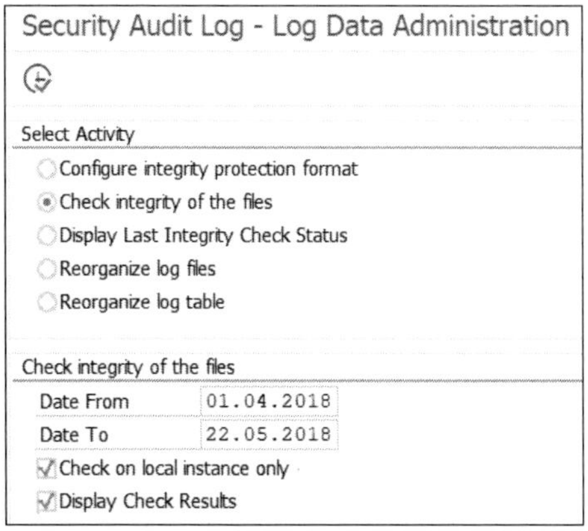

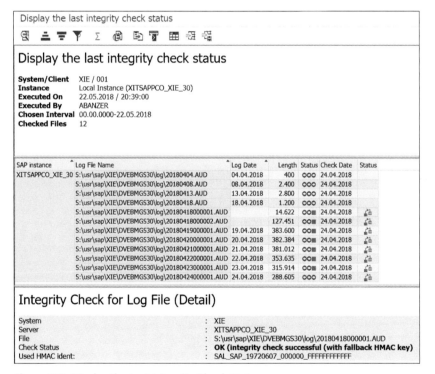

Figure 11.8 Check Integrity of Files

Figure 11.9 Display the Last Integrity Check Status

To quickly navigate back to the last integrity check, you can choose the **Display Last Integrity Check Status** option in the selection screen.

Reorganize Log Files

To reorganize log files by means of deleting the physical file from the file system, you can choose **Reorganize log files** from the initial screen (Figure 11.10). You can delete or display the data to be reorganized, as well as run a simulation mode first. The simulation mode lets you see what will happen if you deselect the checkbox.

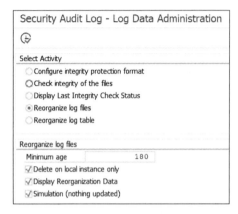

Figure 11.10 Reorganize Log Files

The minimum age decides which files will be deleted. Once executed, you'll see a results screen (Figure 11.11) indicating which old files will be deleted (if run without simulation).

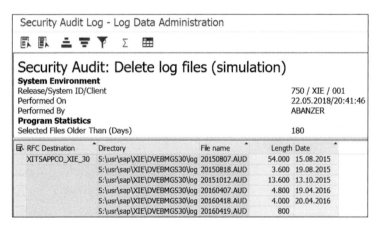

Figure 11.11 Delete Log Files

Remember, the deletion of log files should be carried out through this transaction because it performs an authorization check and follows the deletion process for files in the integrity protection format. Deleting files manually from the file system is considered a manipulation.

Reorganize Log Table

Reorganization of the database table is important when logging is activated to be stored exclusively in the database table. For all other scenarios, reorganization is not necessary; for example, APIs will delete the data after the transfer.

To delete data from the table, choose the **Reorganize log table** selection (Figure 11.12) and enter the date before which you want data to be deleted.

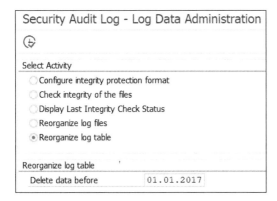

Figure 11.12 Reorganize Log Table in Database

Evaluation of Log Data

You can evaluate the log data in Transaction RSAU_READ_LOG (Figure 11.13). You can either evaluate the logs online in the foreground or send the report into the background. In the selection screen, you can set the time restrictions along with multiple other options.

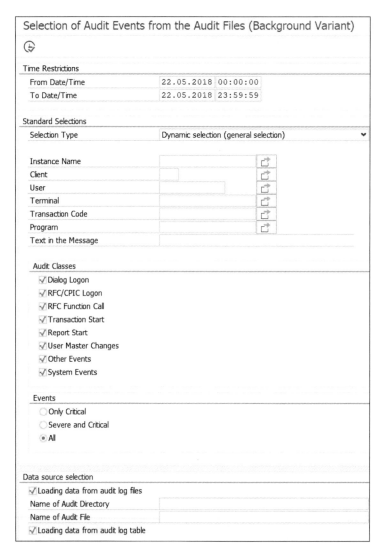

Figure 11.13 Evaluate Log Data Initial Screen

In the **Standard Selections** (Figure 11.14), you can set the selection type and, for example, search based on a specific user, client, terminal, or audit class or based on the criticality of the event. Also, you can reuse your filters and search for specific filters only.

The **Instance Name** field lets you input the instance that you want to evaluate. If you have multiple application servers and want to only include the current application instance, you can use the value <LOCAL>.

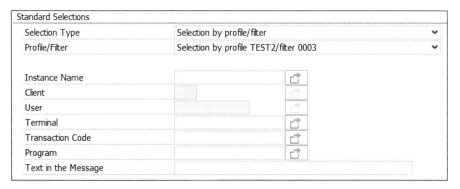

Figure 11.14 Standard Selection in Evaluation of Log Data

In the **Data source selection** (Figure 11.15), you can define if you want to read all your files, a specific file or directory, or your database tables.

11

Data source selection	
☑ Loading data from audit log files	
Name of Audit Directory	
Name of Audit File	
☑ Loading data from audit log table	

Figure 11.15 Data Source Selection in Evaluation of Log Data

The result screen shows the logged events in detail. For example, in Figure 11.16, you can see successful logons by user WF-BATCH.

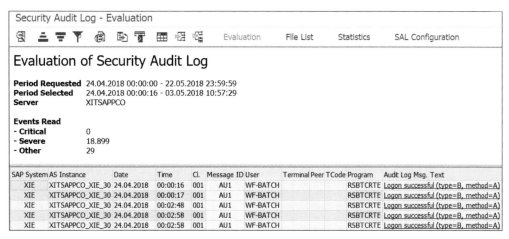

Figure 11.16 Evaluation of Log Data Result Screen

Evaluate Archived Log Data

To evaluate archived log data, you can use Transaction RSAU_READ_ARC (Figure 11.17). In the selection screen, you can set the period, as well as other selections like the client, user, terminal, and so on.

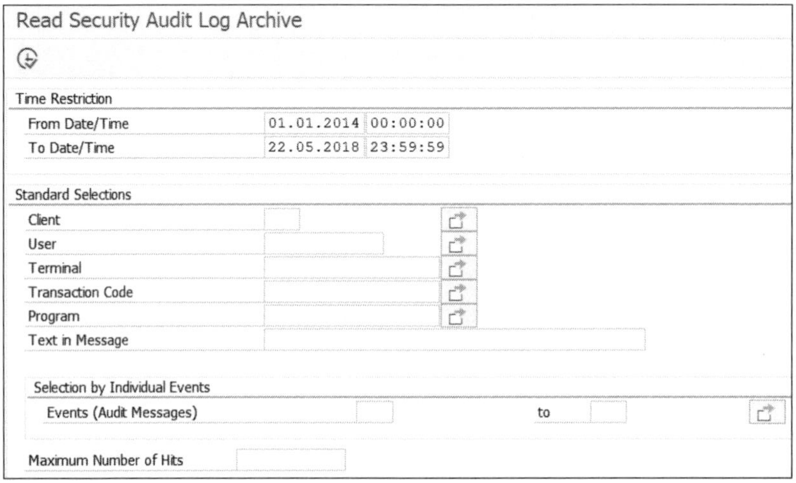

Figure 11.17 Read Security Audit Log Archive Data

11.3.2   System Log

Whereas the security audit log records security-related information about the system, the system log records information that may signal system problems. As an administrator, the system log is an important tool to maintain the healthiness of your system and keep the system up and running with good performance. The system log records warnings, error messages, database read errors, rollbacks, and so on.

The system log offers different types of logging depending on the host. On an UNIX host, you have local and central logging available. If you run on a Microsoft Windows NT host, you'll only have local logging. In the local scenario, the log is stored locally on the application server in a ring buffer. The ring buffer is overwritten once full. Therefore, the system log is only available for a certain time frame as the size is limited. In the central log, each individual application server sends its local log to a central server. Similar to the local log, the size of the central log is limited and hence it doesn't hold the information indefinitely.

In either scenario, we recommend analyzing the system log on a regular basis. Most administrators check the system log daily to avoid any disruption to the SAP system.

The local log is always up to date, whereas the central log might have a slight delay as the data must be written from the local application server to the central server.

The main transaction to analyze the system log is Transaction SM21 (Figure 11.18), in which you can read the system log and its messages. In the selection screen, you can define basic and extended attributes to get to the messages that are most important to you.

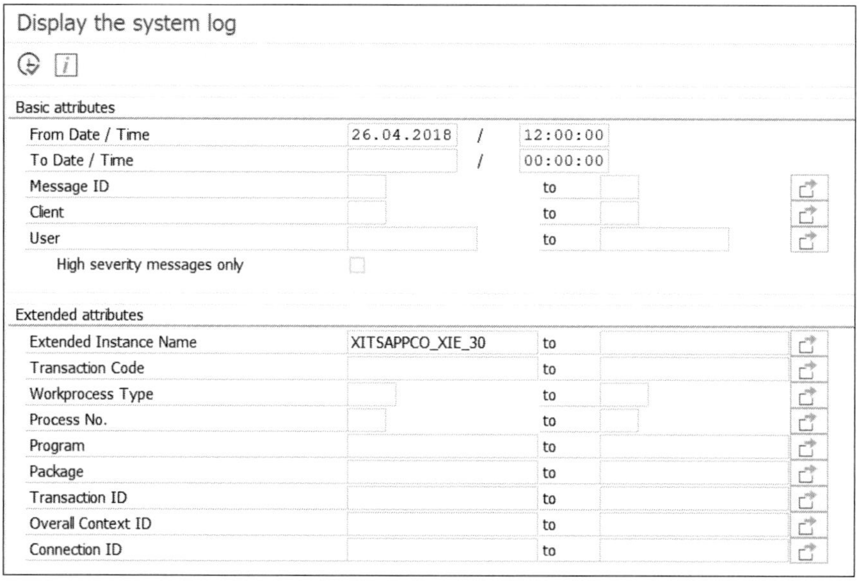

Figure 11.18 Initial Screen in Transaction SM21 to Display System Log

In the result screen (Figure 11.19), you get an overview of all messages that have been logged by the SAP system. For each entry, you see the time stamp, instance, client, user, and the priority of and information about the message. You can double-click any line item.

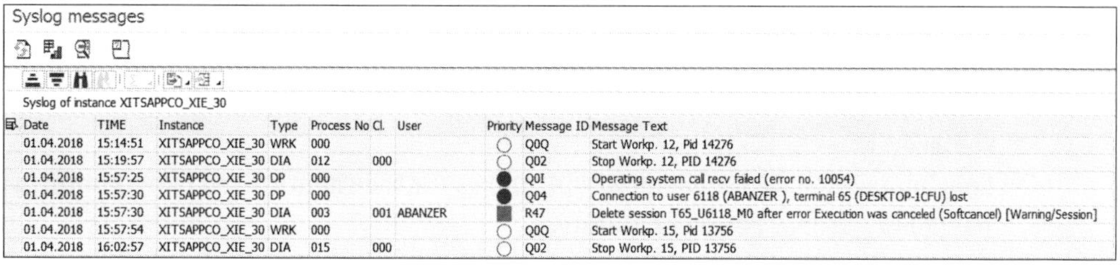

Figure 11.19 System Log Result Screen

After you double-click an item, you'll see to the details of the message (Figure 11.20) to dive further into the error. In addition to details about the message and the session, as well as technical and parameter details, you can also navigate to the trace from the menu bar.

Figure 11.20 System Log Detail View

In the trace, you can see all the steps that the system performed for the message that you selected. Analyzing traces requires a deep understanding of the SAP system and is definitely an expert-tool only.

11.3.3   Table Logging

To enable table logging in general, you have to activate the table logging in the profile parameter rec/client. Once activated, you can define tables to be logged in the table properties. The profile parameter rec/client knows four different values:

- **OFF**
  Logging is deactivated.

- **nnn**
  Logging takes place for client-specific tables only in the client listed (001, 100, etc.).

- **nnn,nnn,nnn**
  Logging takes place for client-specific tables for the clients listed (a maximum of 10 clients possible, comma-separated).

- **ALL**

  Logging always takes place; for client-specific tables, it takes place for all clients. *Caution*: This setting makes sense only in special cases. Note that in the case of ALL, changes are recorded in the log file for all test clients (including SAP client 000).

Once the table logging has been activated, you can define which tables will be logged. To activate logging for a particular table, you have to define the properties in the table itself. You can do that from Transaction SE13. SAP predelivers customizing tables with the table change logging activated.

For the example shown in Figure 11.21 for table RFCDES (RFC Destinations), the table change log is activated.

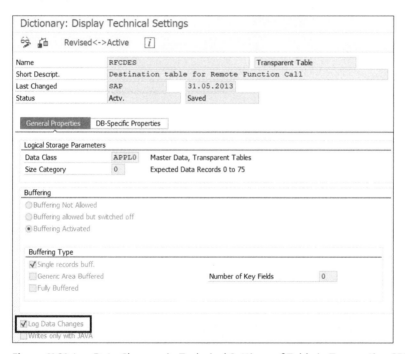

Figure 11.21 Log Data Changes in Technical Settings of Table in Transaction SE13

To check all tables that have the logging activated and to review the changes, you can use Transaction SCU3 (Figure 11.22). In Transaction SCU3, click **List of Logged Tables** to see an overview of all tables that have table change logging activated.

Analyze Changed Customizing Objects and Tables

List of Logged Tables

Analyze Logs

Figure 11.22 Initial Screen of Transaction SCU3

Warning

In an SAP NetWeaver 7.50 system with SAP ERP installed, SAP defined close to 30,000 tables with the table change log. Most of the tables are customizing tables and hence do not contain master data that changes regularly.

Analyze Logs

To analyze the changes that have been logged, you again can use Transaction SCU3. In Transaction SCU3, go to **Analyze Logs** and make your selections. In the selection screen (Figure 11.23), you must select one specific table or customizing object for analysis. This is enforced because the amount of data can be huge. For reporting purposes, we suggest using the ALV Grid Display, which lets you sort and filter the output.

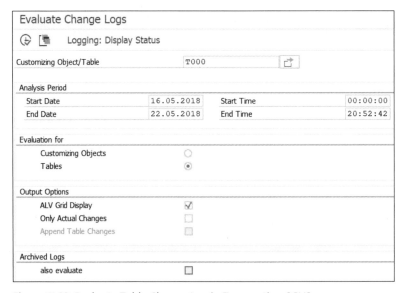

Figure 11.23 Evaluate Table Change Log in Transaction SCU3

In the output view, you can get the details of what's been changed in the table. In Figure 11.24, you can see changes to table T000 (clients). You can see the type of change, as well as which transaction and program were used to perform the change.

Display Change Logs

T000 Clients

Date	User Name	Time	TCode	Program	Type	Cl.	Name	City	Crcy	Role	CorrSys
01.02.2018	DKINDERMANN	09:13:54	SM30	SAPMSVMA	Created	200	SecArch Test	Schöfflisdorf		T	1
		10:34:21	SM30	SAPMSVMA	Created	300	Earlywatch	Walldorf		T	1
		11:06:14	SM30	SAPMSVMA	Created	066	e	Walldorf		S	1
		11:06:20	SM30	SAPMSVMA	Old	066	e	Walldorf		S	1
			SM30	SAPMSVMA	new	066	Earlywatch	Walldorf		S	1
		13:27:04		RSCLXCOP	Unchanged	200	SecArch Test	Schöfflisdorf		T	1
	SAP*	09:17:40		RSCLXCOP	Unchanged	200	SecArch Test	Schöfflisdorf		T	1
		09:34:27	SM30	SAPMSVMA	Old	066	EarlyWatch	Walldorf	EUR	S	1

Figure 11.24 Display Table Change Logs

The data being analyzed in Transaction SCU3 is stored in table DBTABLOG. Transaction SCU3 offers a fully functional cockpit to analyze the data efficiently.

> **SAP Note 1916**
>
> For more information about table logging, see SAP Note 1916 (Logging of Table Changes in R/3).

Performance Impact

Table change logging shouldn't have a performance impact if you only log customizing tables. Although SAP delivers many tables with table logging activated, those tables usually contain little data that rarely changes. Avoid logging for master data and transaction data tables because those tables are subject to mass changes and hence would have a negative impact on the system performance. For custom tables, you can define whether you want to activate table logging or not.

If you experience negative performance after activating table logging, you can find out which tables log the most amount of data. In Transaction SCU3, you can validate the table logging via the menu path **Administration • Number of Logs (Selection)**. In the selection screen (Figure 11.25), leave the **Table Name** field empty and analyze the last month (or extend the time if required).

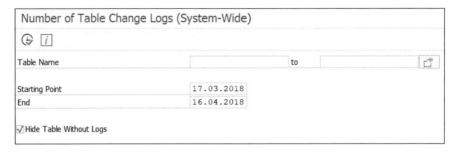

Figure 11.25 Number of Table Change Logs in Transaction SCU3

In the results screen, you can see the number of entries per table logged. For the example in Figure 11.25, table RFCDES logged 36 changes in the last 30 days, as shown in Figure 11.26. You can sort the number of logs in descending order to quickly get an indication of which tables might cause a performance issue.

Table Name	Short Description	No.of Logs
RFCDES	Destination table for Remote Function Call	36
RFCDOC	Description of Possible RFC Connections (->RFCDES)	24
RSADMIN	Data import administration settings	3
RSADMINC	Customizing Table General BW	4
RSAUPROF	Audit: Audit configuration parameters (audit profile)	87
RSAUPROFEX	SAL: Extended Audit Configuration Parameters (Audit Profile)	13
RSDATRNAVT	Navigation Attributes	136
SACF_ALERT	Collector for Failed Calls	31
SFOBUEV000	FoBuEv: Header Data of a Formula	335
SFOBUEV001	FoBuEv: Rows (Token) of a Formula	1.780
SSF_PSE_H	SSF: Personel Security Environment	2
SWD_EXPR	WF Definition: Expressions	411
SWD_HEADER	WF Definition/Runtime: Basic Data	15
T77ARRAYTP	Column Framework: Definition of Column Groups	2
T77ARRAYTT	Text Table for t77arraytp	2
TADIR	Directory of Repository Objects	1.284
TBDLS	Logical system	1
TBDLST	Text for logical system	2
TDDAT	Maintenance Areas for Tables	809

(Number of Table Change Logs (System-Wide))

Figure 11.26 Result Screen of Number of Table Change Logs

Table logging shouldn't have an impact on your overall system performance and hence is a helpful feature to ensure the traceability of changes to customizing and other important tables in your SAP system.

11.3.4 Workload Monitor

The Workload Monitor lets you analyze system statistics in the SAP system. You can report on different task types like background processing, dialog processing, update processing, ALE, RFC, and so on. You will also see detailed information on CPU time, number of changes to the database, number of users that use the system, and so on. You can start the Workload Monitor in Transaction ST03N.

Apart from all the analysis capabilities to check the workload of your system, the Transaction ST03N trace contains information that might be helpful for auditing purposes. In Transaction ST03N, you can analyze the activity of a user and reproduce the actions a user has executed in the system. In the user profile, you can see all the users in a certain time frame and details of the actions they performed. In Figure 11.27, you can see that user ABANZER executed several transactions (e.g., Transactions RSAU_ADMIN, RSAU_READ_LOG, and so on). You can also see how many dialog steps were executed along with the details of average response times.

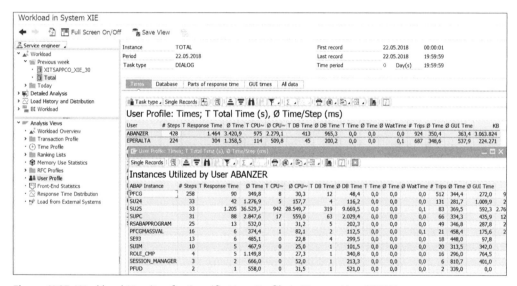

Figure 11.27 Workload Monitor for Specific User Profile in Transaction ST03N

The workload is deactivated by default as it increases the chances for performance implications. Therefore, we recommend activating it temporarily for specific analysis. Before activation, make sure that you adhere to the laws and regulations in your territory.

> **Warning**
>
> Analyzing user activities may not be permitted based on your area of operation. Also, personal data protection regulations like GDPR may prohibit the use of such information.

11.3.5   Read Access Logging

Read access logging (RAL) is a tool to monitor and record the read access to sensitive and classified data in your SAP system. The type of data that you want to monitor can be categorized as sensitive by law or by internal or external company policies. In the context of the GDPR, companies must comply with the regulations and adhere to standards about data privacy.

With the RAL framework, you can comply with the regulations because you always know who accessed which data from where and when. Also, in case of a security breach or a leak of information, you can report not only who had access to the data from an authorization standpoint but also who accessed the data through the logging.

The RAL framework works with different types of channels when a user is accessing the data. *Channels* are the way the data leaves or enters the system (e.g., through SAP GUI). On the UI side, the RAL framework works with Dynpro (logging of Dynpro UI elements and ALV grids) and Web Dynpro (logging of context-bound UI elements).

It also works with APIs such as the following:

- **Remote Function Calls (sRFC, aRFC, tRFC, qRFC, bgRFC)**
  Logging of server- and client-side RFC-based communication
- **Web services**
  Logging of consumer- and provider-side web service communications
- **OData channels**
  Logging of data consumed by SAP Fiori applications through OData services

> **Further Information**
>
> For more information about the OData channels for SAP Fiori applications, you can check SAP Note 2182094 (Read Access Logging in SAP Gateway).

The configuration and monitoring of the RAL is done in Transaction SRALMANAGER (Figure 11.28).

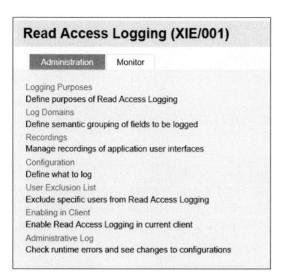

Figure 11.28 Read Access Logging Initial Screen

The configuration of RAL requires five steps, which are represented in the Web Dynpro application that starts with Transaction SRALMANAGER:

1. You have to identify and determine under what circumstances the RAL will log what type of data. For example, in view of GDPR, you have to protect personal information of your employees. Therefore, you have to monitor and protect transactions and tables that contain personal information, like Transaction SU01 (User Master Records), table USR02 (User Master Records), and so on.

2. In the second step, you have to define the purpose of the logging, which allows you to group certain requirements. You can freely define a name for the logging purpose. The logging purpose is used to organize the data in the context of a specific use case, such as for GDPR.

3. In the third step, you have to define the channels that you want to monitor. Common channels are Web Dynpro, RFCs, and so on.

4. Once you have the channels defined, you define the log domains. The log domains group semantically similar or related fields. For example, in the Basis area, an "account" is different than the "account" in the banking application. Therefore, you want to classify similar content into log domains.

5. Finally, you define the conditions that must be met for the application to log the data—for example, which fields are being recorded and whether the access is recorded only or the content of the data is recorded as well.

For simplified operation of the RAL, you can define an exclusion list of users that won't be logged. A common scenario is to exclude batch job users that perform multiple reads, which would lead to a significant number of logs.

Once the configuration has been activated successfully, you can start to monitor the log entries in the Web Dynpro application. To review the logs, you can go to **Read Access Log** in the **Monitor** tab. You can search channel-specific, date-specific, or user name-specific logs.

11.3.6   User Information System

The User Information System is one of the main tools required for both internal and external audits. This tool is a directory for several programs that facilitate the retrieval of information required for an audit. Most of the tools focus on users and authorizations. However, the AIS also contains a powerful change document feature. Each function is organized by its type in the menu tree and can be launched by double-clicking the **Execute** button to the left of the function name.

As an example, let's look up users with critical authorization combinations. This is a common report used by auditors to satisfy audit controls. Proceed as follows:

1. Navigate to Transaction SUIM.

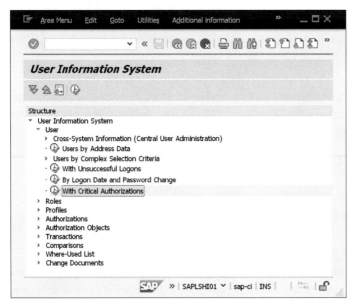

Figure 11.29 Transaction SUIM Main Screen

2. In the menu, click the **User** drop-down, then select **With Critical Authorizations** and click the **Execute** icon (Figure 11.29).

Direct Access

Alternatively, you can run report RSUSR008_009_NEW in Transaction SA38.

---

3. Next, choose the **For Critical Authorizations** radio button in the **Variant Name** box. For the variant name, choose the predelivered SAP_RSUSR009 variant (Figure 11.30).

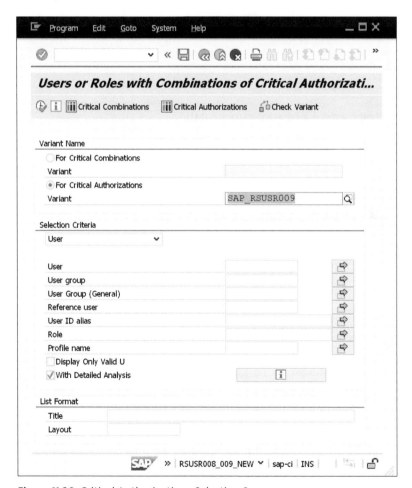

Figure 11.30 Critical Authorizations Selection Screen

Define Your Own Critical Authorizations

You can also define a list of critical authorizations. You may receive a list of critical authorizations or transaction codes from your internal auditor, external auditor, or functional business analysts. You may need to come up with this list on your own. A good starting point is to use the SAP delivered variant, SAP_RSUSR009, but be sure to adjust it for your auditing use.

4. Click the **Execute** button.

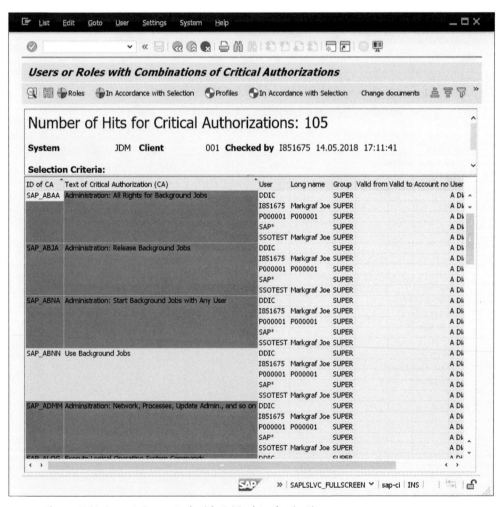

Figure 11.31 Report Generated with Critical Authorizations

The system will return a list of critical authorizations (Figure 11.31) that each user has in your system. If you have many super users, or administrators, this list could be in the thousands or tens of thousands. A review of this list and its users is done often, with the appropriateness of each user's access reviewed by either internal or external auditors.

11.4   Summary

In this chapter, you learned about internal and external audits and their purpose in an organization. You learned about auditing tools like security audit logging, the system log, table logging, the Workload Monitor, and Read Access Logging. Finally, you learned about the User Information System and how to use it to find users with critical authorizations.

In the next chapter, you'll learn about how to secure network communications to and from your SAP NetWeaver AS ABAP system. This is an important subject for a security administrator because most attacks against an SAP system use the network as an attack vector.

11

Chapter 12
Securing Network Communications

Before reading this chapter, you should know how to set parameters and how to restart the system. You should also have an understanding of the CommonCryptoLib.

This chapter will cover securing network communications both into and out of SAP NetWeaver AS ABAP. We'll be using encryption in this chapter, but a full explanation of the topic will be the focus of Chapter 13. The core concepts of encryption using SNC and HTTPS are identical.

The most secure way to operate an SAP NetWeaver AS system on a network is to block all traffic both into and out of the system. This is hardly a usable approach for obvious reasons. On the other hand, the most insecure approach to manage an SAP NetWeaver AS system is to open it up to the Internet. In a common business situation, a security administrator will be tasked with striking a balance between these two options. Ideally, you'd like the system as locked down as possible, while still allowing business end users to log on and perform work on the system.

Blocking can be accomplished with several tools. Good network design, firewalls, Access Control Lists (ACL), and encryption are the most commonly used tools used to secure network traffic both into and out of the SAP system.

In this chapter, we'll discuss the various methods for network security, how to implement them, and what to look for when executing your overall security strategy.

12.1 Choosing a Network Security Strategy

It's important to not make security overly cumbersome to the end user. If a security approach is too heavy-handed and prevents the business from accomplishing work, it will be eliminated—or, even worse, worked around. This creates a scenario that's easily exploited by malicious users. Convenience is the enemy of security. When implementing security enhancements, they usually come at the cost of the user's convenience. Often, this will be met with objection because the end user won't see the value of strengthened security. This is especially true when working with existing environments with limited security measures. End users have become accustomed to a low level of security and, to them, a low level of inconvenience. When designing your network security, keep this in mind. Restriction to the network must be balanced to add the required security but stay out of the way of the end user.

12.2   Securing Using Access Controls

The first method to be discussed is network access control. Network access control is the idea of limiting which network addresses or IP addresses can communicate with your SAP system. You can think of any network access control method as a gatekeeper that only allows authorized traffic to pass. There are three general methods of restricting access to your SAP system: firewalls, application-level gateways, and secure cells.

12.2.1   Firewalls

A *firewall* is a piece of hardware or software that helps keep malicious users or programs from accessing systems behind it by blocking ports or IP addresses. Firewalls are available from many different vendors. They can be deployed as physical appliances, virtual appliances, or software running on an OS. Most OSs have a built-in firewall that acts as the last line of defense against intrusion by malicious traffic. A simple diagram of a firewall on a network is shown in Figure 12.1.

As shown in Figure 12.1, the firewall acts as a gatekeeper to pass traffic that it deems acceptable and deny traffic that it deems unacceptable. A real-world example of this is allowing email or HTTPS traffic but disallowing all telnet or other service traffic. Firewalls deny or pass traffic using a variety of methods, the simplest of which is port numbers. For example, typical HTTP traffic occurs on port 80. If a server behind the firewall is hosting a website on port 80, the firewall would pass traffic through to port 80 of that system. However, port 22, or the SSH port, would be a good port to block because it's used to remotely manage servers. The firewall would be configured to deny traffic on port 22. It's important to note that an SAP system typically will operate on a known set of ports, so blocking or restricting access to ports that aren't typically used is a good practice.

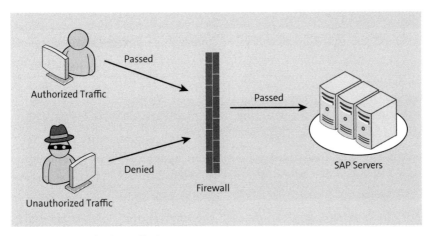

Figure 12.1 Simple Firewall Diagram

Firewalls can be set up to pass or deny traffic using a variety of rules based on ports, IP addresses, protocols, or even traffic type. Some firewalls can also intelligently determine which traffic to deny based on heuristics or traffic patterns. Setting up firewalls is beyond the scope of this book. We'll focus mostly on simply filtering traffic based on the port number. Often, a security administrator will be working with a networking or OS team that will have the responsibility of managing a firewall. The security or system administrator will be tasked with providing which ports to pass and block. The network or OS administrator will then implement the rules.

A firewall can be a security administrator's best friend—and a system administrator's worst enemy. It's very important to keep a careful eye on how the firewall performs because doing so can indicate the effectiveness of the rules it uses to block unwanted traffic. One of the worst situations that can occur is that too much traffic is passed because it's simply easier to pass traffic to alleviate an issue than it is to diagnose and fix the problem. This is a common practice that's easy to slip into. A security administrator should have a good understanding of his or her firewall rules and why each has been implemented.

Because SAP applications are often subject to *integrations*, or network communication with other SAP or even non-SAP systems, firewalls will play an important role in securing these landscapes. Due to their nature, firewalls are a source of difficulty for integration because they may block traffic that isn't a threat. It's very important to understand each integration and how it functions so that proper firewall rules can be developed.

12.2.2   Application-Level Gateways

Third-party products called *application-level gateways* or *application-level proxies* can be used in a similar manner to firewalls. Their responsibility is to control access to the SAP application, like a firewall, but operating on the application level itself. That is, the content of the network traffic is what determines if access is granted or denied. SAP generally recommends using these products. There are a few requirements that you can read about in SAP Note 833960.

SAProuter and SAP Web Dispatcher are considered application-level gateways and are great for filtering traffic. More information about SAP Web Dispatcher can be found in Chapter 13.

Using both firewalls and application-level gateways is the SAP-recommended method of securing your landscape. Using the demilitarized zone (DMZ), traffic passes from outside the network, through a firewall, and into the DMZ. In the DMZ, traffic is then passed through an SAP Web Dispatcher (HTTP/HTTPS traffic) or SAProuter (other application traffic). From there, it's passed through a second firewall and directed to the SAP landscape (Figure 12.2).

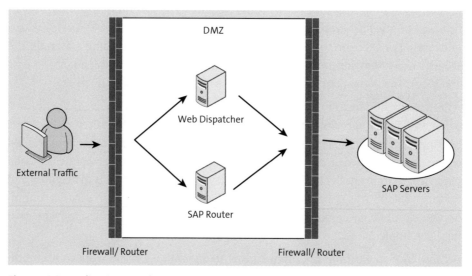

Figure 12.2 Application-Level Gateways and Firewalls for Network Security

For internal access, a DMZ isn't normally required. A single router sitting at the edge of the network that the SAP systems reside on is sufficient.

12.2.3   Business Secure Cell

When designing your network internally, special consideration must be taken. You must consider the corporate network to be more open for end users to perform normal business functions, such as share files, print to network printers, and have open access to the Internet—things that require a network to be less restricted. Your business systems however, should have a limited network. For this reason, we suggest maintaining a separate network, or *subnet*, for your business systems. Separating your business systems into their own "secure cell" will allow you to strengthen security by applying a more rigid network policy to these systems (see Figure 12.3).

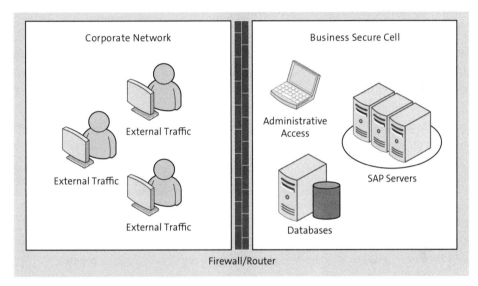

Figure 12.3 Business Secure Cell

SAP recommends that you install your systems as distributed systems. This means that you install separate application servers and a separate database server for each SAP system. Although central systems and multiple components, one database (MCOD) are technically possible, these setups add complexity to your systems that can lead to a lapse in security, as well as increased downtime.

Can I Use My Existing Network for SAP?

SAP strongly discourages placing SAP system servers into any existing subnet without first considering the appropriate security issues that exist in that subnet. This would mean that the subnet needs to be secured before adding SAP system, as existing vulnerabilities would directly affect SAP systems that were placed in the existing subnet. For the most secure SAP installation possible, place SAP systems in their own dedicated subnet.

It's also possible to segregate your application servers from your database in their own secure cell. Although this is more secure, it comes at the cost of increased complexity in your landscape. Most often, such a practice is not necessary. It would serve you better to spend more time securing your single business secure cell rather than create two different cells and secure both.

We recommend that both the database and application are kept within the same network for performance reasons. With that said, the connection needs of application servers and database servers are different. There should be no single template that can be applied to both. An application server will serve connections from end users. A database will only serve connections from application servers. No user should ever be connecting directly to a database server in a normal scenario. However, exceptions to this policy will be encountered and should be carefully considered.

It's also possible to separate each tier of your landscape (dev/QA/production) in its own network cell. It may be more secure, but it may add much more complexity that may not be worth the effort. In addition, it's a mistake to think that your development systems need a less secure network than your production systems. All your systems need the same level of security, both development and production. A bad actor will routinely look for neglected development or sandbox systems because they're easy targets.

Outside of the business secure cell, all traffic that is related to the systems within the cell should be encrypted. SNC encryption and SSL/TLS are further explored in Section 12.3.

12.2.4   Securing Common Ports

Securing ports happens on several levels: the first level is the firewall; the second is on the OS itself; third, an ACL is used. We recommend closing ports on all levels. For example, if you decide to block a port, it needs to be blocked at the external firewall, internal firewall, and OS levels, depending on the port and its use. Table 12.1 provides a list of commonly addressed ports as examples.

Port	Description	Notes
80	HTTP traffic	You should only allow encrypted traffic to your SAP systems.
36<NN> (3600)	Message server	The message server should only be reachable by appropriate parties.
32<NN>	Dispatcher/enqueue ABAP Central Services (ASCS)	The ASCS server should only be reachable by appropriate parties.
5<NN>16	Enqueue replication server	This should not be accessible by anything other than ASCS.
50013/14	SAP start service	The message server should only be reachable by appropriate parties.
23, 22, or 3389	Remote OS access	Telnet, SSH, or remote desktop.
Note: <NN> represents instance number		

Table 12.1 Commonly Attacked Ports:

Be sure to evaluate all open ports on your system for their appropriateness.

What Ports Does SAP NetWeaver AS Use?

SAP maintains a comprehensive catalog of ports that are used in SAP products at *https://help.sap.com/viewer/ports*.

Inevitably, someone will come to the technical/security teams and demand that they be granted an exception or pass for both the firewall and the ACL. *Be careful!* Granting such an exception isn't always the answer. Care must be taken to allow firewall exceptions in the proper firewalls. If a user asks for a pass on port 443 for internal corporate use, you must be sure that port 443 is still being blocked from external traffic.

12.2.5   Securing Services

Non-necessary services on any application or database server should be stopped and disabled. There is no reason to have things like printer sharing enabled on your database server. The goal of disabling unneeded services is one of attack vector

12

minimalization. We don't want to give adversaries any ways to attempt to compromise our systems.

In addition, it's important to remember that SAP systems will include services by default that you may not need. If you don't use the functionality behind a service, it's a good idea to disable it entirely to reduce the attackable footprint of your SAP systems. Just because SAP has it enabled by default doesn't mean that you need it. SAP has many customers with many requirements, so use caution: not all services are for you!

> **ICF Services**
>
> Often, in development or sandbox systems, all ICF services will be active. This is a significant security risk. Be sure to only activate services you need.

12.2.6   Access Control Lists

ACLs are present in many SAP products and are the basic building blocks of securing SAP NetWeaver ABAP. The ICM, SAP Web Dispatcher, SAProuter, and the gateway process all can use this method to permit or deny connections. Therefore, having a fundamental understanding of how they work is sensible.

ACLs work using text files on the OS. The path for these text files must be set with parameters. Table 12.2 shows some commonly used parameters for ACL files.

Use	Parameter to set	Notes
Enqueue server	enque/server/acl_file	
Start service	service/http/acl_file and service/https/acl_file	Use HTTPs for the start service if possible.
Internal message server	ms/acl_info	
Dispatcher	rdisp/acl_file	Be careful with syntax.
ICM	icm/server_port	ACL is specified with this parameter.
Gateway	gw/acl_file	

Table 12.2 Parameters for ACL Files

ACL Syntax

A line of the ACL follows this syntax:

```
<permit deny> <ip-address[/mask]> [tracelevel] [# comment]
```

Note the following:

- `<ip address>`
  The IP address must be an IPv4 address or IPv6 address of the following form:
  - IPv4: 4 byte, decimal, dot (.) separated—for example, 10.11.12.13
  - IPv6: 16 byte, hexadecimal, colon (:) or double-colon (::) separated
- `[mask]`
  If a mask is specified, then it must be a subnet prefix mask.
- `[tracelevel]`
  The trace level with which the denials or approvals of the ACL are written in the relevant trace file (default value 2). It's very important to keep an eye on the trace file for malicious activity.
- `[# comment]`
  Comment lines start with a hash sign (#).

It's important to remember that the rules are checked in sequence, starting from the top, and that you must always enter an explicit deny as the last rule.

Here's an example of what an ACL file might look like:

```
permit 10.10.20.0/24 # permit client network
permit fdf4:7e39:18e5:a127::/64  # permit server network, IPv6
permit 10.0.0.0/8 1 # screening rule (learning mode, trace-level 1-
 list all normal users/systems connecting to the system.)
deny 0.0.0.0/0 # deny the rest
```

> **ACL File Syntax**
>
> Be sure to carefully proofread and test your ACL files before attempting to implement them. Syntax errors could cause all ports to be blocked or your instance to fail at startup. For more ACL info, consult SAP Note 1495075.

12

Securing the Message Server

It's important to secure the message server from access from unknown or malicious application servers posing as legitimate application servers. The configuration of the ACL is slightly different than from other ICM based .

An ACL is set for the message server using the system parameter `parameter ms/acl_ info`.

The `ms/acl_info` parameter specifies a file (default file name/path: */usr/sap/<SID>/ SYS/global/ms_acl_info*) with access to the message server.

This file must contain all machine names, domains, IP addresses, and/or subnet masks for the application servers that are allowed to log on to the message server.

The entries in the ACL must have the following syntax:

```
HOST=[*| ip_adr | host_name | Subnet_mask | Domain ] [, ...]
```

Examples for valid ACL entries are as follows:

- `HOST = *` (all hosts are allowed, insecure)
- `HOST=host1,host2` (logons allowed from host 1 and host 2)
- `HOST=*.sap.com` (all hosts in the sap.com domain can log on)
- `HOST=10.10.10.135` (hosts with this IP address can log on)
- `HOST=10.10.10.*` (hosts with this subnet can log on)

On the OS level, set the access authorizations for the file to a value that prevents unwanted modifications.

Using Transaction SMMS (Message Server Monitor), you can dynamically adjust ACL entries for the message server. To do so, proceed as follows:

1. Navigate to Transaction SMMS (Figure 12.4).
2. From the menu, click **Goto · Security Settings**.
3. From this screen, you can view the loaded ACL for the message server by clicking **Display**. If you alter the ACL file on the file system and click **Reload**, you can view the results here.

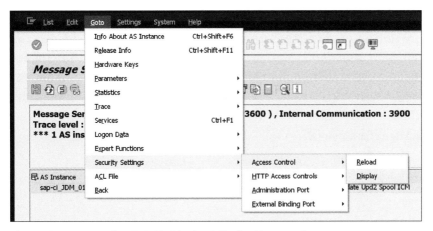

Figure 12.4 Transaction SMMS: Display ACLs for Message Server

4. The **ACL** menu option under **Goto** will show you other loaded ACL files (Figure 12.5).

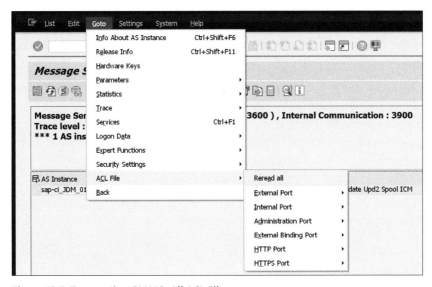

Figure 12.5 Transaction SMMS: All ACL Files

Message Server

For more information about secure configuration of the message server, refer to SAP Note 821875.

12.2.7   Tuning Network Access Control

In order to create access control lists for existing systems, it is helpful to observe normal traffic to set a baseline of typical network activity while the system runs. The easiest way to do this is to gather information from log files that are generated during a normal business period. This could be a day, week, month, or even a quarter. Observe the following logs for a specific time-period of your choosing:

- **Firewall deny/accept logs**
  - Network firewalls
  - OS firewalls
- **ALG logs**
  - SAP Web Dispatcher
  - SAProuter
- **ACL trace files**

While observing these logs, look at what's being allowed and denied. Be sure to look at the geographic source of your traffic. If you're in a US-based company that only has SAP users in North America, you might want to consider restricting any traffic that doesn't originate in your geographic region, for example.

Consider using a screening or learning rule (trace level 1 on an ACL). A screening rule will list all normal users/systems connecting to the system. Using a screening rule will give you an indication of where your traffic normally comes from. From the screening rule, you can reverse engineer where your traffic never comes from. Excluded IP ranges shouldn't ever have traffic flowing to your SAP system.

Finally, look at any network-based errors in the system logs. If you're too aggressive with your firewall and ACL work, you may cause issues with the application. Be sure not to impair your legitimate users' ability to perform work.

12.3   Securing the Transport Layer

When looking at communications across a network, a significant portion of traffic flows from computer to computer in an unencrypted manner. Anyone who's listening on the network may be able to eavesdrop and either capture traffic or capture, alter, and then resend traffic. This is a significant threat to SAP systems and must be protected against.

The method for safeguarding this is to encrypt traffic on the transport layer. By doing this, only the sender and receiver can decipher traffic, keeping it secure in transit. A listing of the common protocols and how they are secured can be found in Table 12.3.

Protocol	Method	Description
SAP-specific: SAP GUI, RFC	SNC	SNC is the SAP-specific interface for encryption.
Internet (HTTP, P4, LDAP)	SSL/TLS	SSL and TLS are the standard methods to secure Internet application protocols.

Table 12.3 Transport-Level Networking Protocols

There are two methods that are commonly used to secure the transport layer for SAP systems. First, we need to secure SAP GUI traffic. We use Secure Network Communications (SNC) to do this. Second, we need to secure Internet traffic. For that, we use SSL/TLS.

SNC is an interface with an external product that allows for the encryption of SAP traffic (see Figure 12.6). For the purposes of this book, the external product we'll use for SNC is SAP Single Sign-On 3.0. There are also other products on the market available to serve this purpose. Each one has different pros and cons and a different price point. SAP recommends SAP Single Sign-On for use with its products. We discussed how to setup SAP Single Sign-On and SNC in Chapter 8.

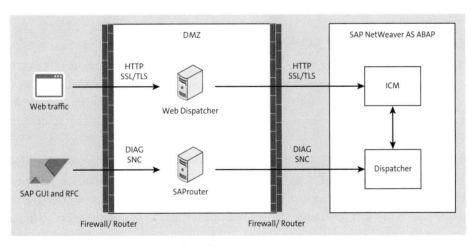

Figure 12.6 Securing with SNC and SSL/TLS

> **A note for clarification**
>
> SNC encryption only applies to connections that use SAP protocols (dialog, RFC, or CPIC). For Internet protocols, use SSL/TLS encryption for protection. SSL/TLS encryption will be covered in Chapter 13.

SSL/TLS is used to secure the HTTP protocol, along with several other protocols like LDAP or the P4 protocol. It's an industry standard that SAP NetWeaver supports.

The important takeaway from this section is that it should be the policy of any reasonable SAP shop to encrypt all transport layer network traffic. In this day and age, there really is no argument to be made against implementing strong encryption.

12.4   Connecting to the Internet and Other Networks

Careful consideration is required if your SAP NetWeaver AS ABAP systems require connectivity to the Internet or external networks. The external access scenario depicted in Figure 12.6 is the ideal way to accomplish this. For SAP GUI and RFC connections, we use SAProuter. For HTTP/HTTPS connections, we use SAP Web Dispatcher. Configuration of SAP Web Dispatcher for HTTP/HTTPS connections is covered in Chapter 13. In this chapter, we'll configure SAProuter for SNC and RFC connections.

External Configuration of SAProuter

The primary advantage of using SAProuter with your firewall system is that you'll only need to allow a single port through your external firewall. This port is 32<NN>, where <NN> is the instance number of your SAProuter. The default instance number for SAProuter is usually 99. An illustration of the port requirements is shown in Figure 12.7.

A secondary benefit to using SAProuter in your firewall system is that you can connect to other networks, like SAP, for support. SAProuter has the flexibility to allow connections from a wide array of services so that remote support can be delivered in a safe and secure manner. Using SNC, you can authorize SAP to open a secure channel and log on to your system over the Internet. This is useful in scenarios in which SAP global support may need to diagnose an issue on a running system.

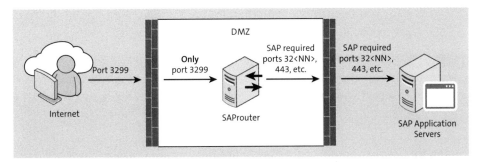

Figure 12.7 Port Configuration for SAProuter

Configuring SAProuter

Putting together what you've learned so far, we'll configure a basic installation of SAProuter. SAProuter has very low system requirements. We recommend that it run on its own system, behind a firewall.

SAProuter Documentation

You can find SAProuter documentation in SAP Note 30289.

---

1. Download the SAProuter executable package from SAP Support Portal, under **Support Packages and Patches · By Category · Additional Components · SAPROUTER**. Be sure to choose your correct OS and CPU architecture (32/64 bit).

2. Unzip the SAProuter executable package on the machine you intend to run SAProuter on. A good directory to use is */usr/sap/saprouter*.

3. Next, create a routtab file to tell SAProuter what to permit and what to deny. Open the text editor of your choice and enter the following:

D * * *

This simple file will deny all connections.

SAProuter Tip

Be sure to always enter a denial of all connections as the last line in an ACL file. This is done by D * * *. If a connection isn't matched by any of the existing rules, it's caught by this one and denied.

---

4. Save this file with the file name saprouttab. You should see the screen shown in Figure 12.8 in your */usr/sap/saprouter* directory.

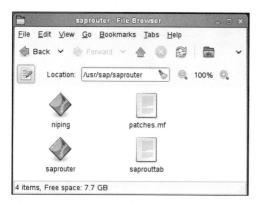

Figure 12.8 SAProuter Files

5. Now, it's time to start SAProuter. From the command line, navigate to the */usr/sap/saprouter* directory and start the SAProuter executable with the following command:

```
saprouter -r
```

6. At this point, SAProuter will begin running in your terminal (Figure 12.9). New connections will show as passed or denied. The log for SAProuter is dev_rout. It will aid in debugging when connections are being inadvertently blocked.

```
sap-router:/usr/sap/saprouter # ./saprouter -r

trcfile  dev_rout
no logging active

WARNING: wildcard character used in route target
```

Figure 12.9 SAProuter Process running

7. Next, you'll need to configure SAP GUI to use SAProuter to connect to your SAP system. In this example, we'll be using a test system. Your system numbers, hostnames, and ports will vary. Figure 12.10 shows the system entry properties screen of SAP GUI. Enter the hostname or IP address in this format in the **SAProuter String** field:

```
/H/<HOSTNAME>/H/
```

Where <HOSTNAME> is the hostname of your SAProuter.

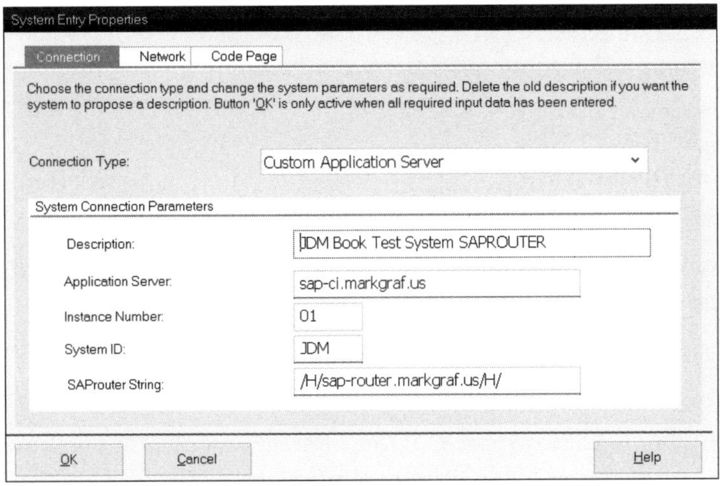

Figure 12.10 SAP GUI Configuration to Connect through SAProuter

8. Once you're finished, go ahead and launch your connection. You should see a failure message. If you go back to your SAProuter, in the */usr/sap/saprouter/* directory you should see a dev_route file. This file is the log for SAProuter. It should look similar to Figure 12.11.

```
sap-router:/usr/sap/saprouter # tail dev_rout
SAP Network Interface Router, Version 40.4

command line arg 0:     ./saprouter
command line arg 1:     -r
main: pid = 5599, ppid = 5546, port = 3299, parent port = 0 (0 = parent is not a
 saprouter)
reading routtab: './saprouttab'

Sun Jan 21 12:16:55 2018
checkRoute: route not permitted (1)
*** ERROR => NiRClientHandle: NiRExRouteCon for C9/-1 'SEAN00642323A.markgraf.us
' failed (rc=-94) [nirout.cpp   3488]
sap-router:/usr/sap/saprouter # 
```

Figure 12.11 dev_route with Refused Connection

The line reading Checkrout: route not permitted (1) indicates that the saprouttab file has blocked this attempt. By looking at blocked attempts, you can determine exactly where unauthorized attempts to access your SAP systems through SAProuter may be coming from. Often, a security or system administrator will check this file to determine why a session errored out or a connection was dropped.

Warning: Do Not Permit All Connections

Never, ever, permit all connections with P * * *. This defeats the purpose of SAProuter entirely and is insecure.

Securing SAProuter with a Password

Next, we'll secure SAProuter with a password.

First, you'll need to update your saprouttab file. Update the file located at */usr/sap/saprouter/saprouttab* to match the following:

```
P * * 3201 secure_password
D * * * *
```

This simple file will allow requests to port 3201 (the message server) if the password "secure_password" is used and will deny all other connections.

Now, set the following string in your SAP GUI configuration:

```
/H/<HOSTNAME>/W/secure_password/H/
```

Where <HOSTNAME> is the hostname of your SAProuter.

Again, this will only pass connections through SAProuter that are using the password "secure_password". This is more secure than just permitting everything, but overall it's still very insecure. Unless the dev_route log is being monitored, it would be a trivial task for a malicious user to brute-force attack SAProuter. To further secure SAProuter, it would be best to restrict the allowed hosts (columns 1 and 2 of the saprouttab file), as well as enable encryption.

There are three benefits to SNC encryption:

1. Secures user authentication so that passwords are never transmitted in cleartext
2. Establishes privacy protection and data integrity
3. Creates end-to-end security at the application level

Configuring SAProuter to Use SNC

One of the methods to connect your SAP landscape to SAP is to use an SNC-secured connection over the Internet. The following steps will enable that connection using an SAP-provided certificate:

1. Download the CommonCryptoLib from SAP Support Portal (see Chapter 5).

2. Extract the CommonCryptoLib files to your SAProuter directory.

3. Set the SNC_LIB and SECUDIR environment variables as follows:

   – SNC_LIB = <path to CommonCryptoLib>

   – SECUDIR = <saprouter directory>/sec

4. *Optional*: Register your SAProuter with SAP to get your specific common name (CN).

Get a Signed SNC Certificate from SAP

SAP will sign a certificate for your SAProuter free of charge. To request a certificate, head to *https://launchpad.support.sap.com/#/saproutercertificate*.

Otherwise, you can use a signature signed from the Certificate Authority (CA) of your choosing.

---

5. Generate your PSE files. For this, use the sapgenpse command as follows:

```
sapgenpse get_pse -v -a sha256WithRsaEncryption -s 2048 -r <certreq>
-p local.pse -x <password> "CN=<YOUR SPECIFIC CN>"
```

Where <certreq> is the filename you'd like for your certificate signing request (CSR), <password> is a password you set to import the certificate, and <YOUR SPECIFIC CN> is the CN you wish to use. The latter will be provided by SAP if you are using an SAP-signed certificate. Run the command in the directory where you placed your SAProuter files (see Figure 12.12).

6. Submit the CSR. The file generated by the sapgenpse command (certreq in our example) will need to be sent to your CA. For this example, it's provided to SAP using the following URL:

https://launchpad.support.sap.com/#/saproutercertificate

Once you have receive your certificate, copy it's contents to a fileon your SAProuter system. For this example, we've named our certificate "srcert". To import your certificate, issue the following command:

```
sapgenpse import_own_cert -c <srcert> -r <root CA certificate> -p local.pse
```

Where <srcert> is the response from the CA and <root CA certificate> is the root certificate from the CA that has signed the systems you're connecting to. (This is needed for verification in network-to-network scenarios.)

```
sap-router:/usr/sap/saprouter # ./sapgenpse get_pse -v -a sha256WithRsaEncryption -s 2048 -
r certreq -p local.pse "CN=sap-router.markg, OU=0000033018, OU=SAProuter, O=SAP, C=DE"
Got absolute PSE path "/usr/sap/saprouter/local.pse".
Please enter PSE PIN/Passphrase: ***********
Please reenter PSE PIN/Passphrase: ***********
 Supplied distinguished name: "CN=sap-router.markg, OU=0000033018, OU=SAProuter, C=D
E"
 Creating PSE with format v2 (default)
 succeeded.
 certificate creation... ok
 PSE update... ok
 PKRoot... ok
Generating certificate request... ok.
Certificate Request:
 Signed Part:
  Subject:                          CN=sap-router.markg, OU=0000033018, OU=SAProuter, O=
SAP, C=DE
  Key:                              rsaEncryption (2048 bits)
  Attributes:                       None
 Signature:
  Signature algorithm:              sha256WithRsaEncryption (1.2.840.113549.1.1.11)
  Signature:                        <Not displayed>

sap-router:/usr/sap/saprouter # █
```

Figure 12.12 Generation of PSE

7. Next, you'll need to generate your credentials file. This file enables encryption on the SAProuter side using the certificate you provided in the previous step. Issue the following command using the PSE password you created the CSR with:

```
sapgenpse seclogin -p local.pse <pse password>
```

8. Once you've generated your credentials file, you can test to see if you've installed everything properly (Figure 12.13). To test, run the following sapgenpse command:

```
sapgenpse get_my_name -v -n Issuer
```

If you've installed your certificate correctly, you should see the Issuer string displayed when running the command above.

9. Next, you'll need to set your saprouttab file to allow an SNC connection. Let's set our SAProuter to accept SNC from sapsrv2 at SAP. This server can serve SNC connections over the Internet. Create a saprouttab entry with the following:

```
# SNC connection to and from SAP
KT "p:CN=sapserv2, OU=SAProuter, O=SAP, C=DE" 194.39.131.34 *
```

This saprouttab entry specifies that SNC is being used for the connection and that it will allow the SNC name.

```
sap-router:/usr/sap/saprouter # sapgenpse get_my_name -v -n Issuer
 Opening PSE "/usr/sap/saprouter/local.pse"...
 PSE (v2) open ok.
 Retrieving my certificate... ok.
 Getting requested information... ok.
SSO for USER "root"
  with PSE file "/usr/sap/saprouter/local.pse"

Issuer              :   CN=SAProuter CA, OU=SAProuter, O=SAP Trust Community II, C=DE

sap-router:/usr/sap/saprouter #
```

Figure 12.13 Testing SAProuter Config

10. Next, start your SAProuter. Be sure to start it using its SNC name—for example:

    saprouter -r -K "p:CN=example, OU=0000123456, OU=SAProuter, O=SAP, C=DE"

> **Troubleshooting**
>
> Troubleshooting information can be found at *https://support.sap.com/en/tools/con-nectivity-tools/saprouter.html.*

12.5   Summary

In this chapter, you learned about the balance of network security and usability and how to choose a network strategy to better secure your network. You learned about how firewalls and application-level gateways control the flow of traffic to your SAP systems. You also learned about the business secure cell strategy and how to implement a firewall system using firewalls, application-level gateways, and network segmentation. Next, we looked at ports, as well as services, and how to limit their exposure. Using Access Control Lists (ACL), a major tool in your network security toolbox, was discussed next. Finally, you learned about SAProuter and its architecture and configuration.

In the next chapter, you will learn about encryption and it's use with SAP's solutions. Encryption is a key concept that every security administrator will need to use to keep data private over the network. In today's business environment, much of the data that is manipulated in an SAP NetWeaver system is transmitted over the network, so it is critical to have a solid understanding of how encryption is configured and maintained.

Chapter 13
Configuring Encryption

*Before reading this chapter, you need to have an understanding of
setting system parameters, restarting the system, and navigation on
the OS level for SAP NetWeaver AS ABAP.*

One of the key responsibilities of a security administrator is understanding how
encryption is configured in SAP NetWeaver AS ABAP. Despite being a key attack vector that affects all systems on a network, encryption knowledge seems to be in short
supply. Because of this, many vulnerabilities executed against an SAP system are
directed toward unencrypted points of entry. Do not let your organization become
an unencrypted target. Following the principals and practices in this chapter will
allow you to enable strong encryption for your system and keep your system and its
data in transit much more secure.

This chapter will first focus on the basics of cryptography, how it's used, and what
techniques are needed for to function effectively. Next, we'll discuss the technical
steps required to implement and manage encryption in SAP NetWeaver AS ABAP.
Finally, the ICM and its related applications like Web Dispatcher will be covered from
both an encryption and access control point of view.

13.1 Introduction to Cryptography

Cryptography is the practice of securing communications in the presence of
untrusted third parties. In our daily lives we use cryptography every day: HTTPS,
VPNs, and cellphones can and do use cryptography to keep our data private and safe.

Cryptography is a tool that security administrators use to keep our systems and data
safe. Our goal, within an SAP NetWeaver system, is to be able to establish trusted end-
to-end communication in any environment, including over the Internet.

There are three approaches to achieving this goal. The first approach is to verify that
we're talking to whomever we are talking to. This approach is called *authentication*.

The second approach is to keep secret the communications between our end and the other end. This approach is called *encryption*. The third approach is *integrity*. We need to be certain that what we receive is what was sent by the other party. It mustn't be tampered with while in transit.

The specific tool we use to accomplish our cryptographic goals is called the *Common-CryptoLib*. We'll dive deep into the CommonCryptoLib later in Section 13.2. For now, think of it as the part of the SAP NetWeaver kernel that makes advanced cryptography possible.

SAP systems can possibly face many threats on networks—for example, man-in-the-middle attacks or network traffic routed from an SAP system to a trusted individual but intercepted on the way by untrusted people. A real-world example of this approach is the POODLE attack or the Heartbleed attack. Utilizing these attacks, adversaries can compromise an otherwise secure connection and sniff out things like passwords or sensitive data, all of which could be copied without any trace of evidence. So, our challenge becomes protecting our systems from communicating with any third party that isn't someone we trust.

A third party can be anyone: Internal unauthorized users, external bad actors, foreign governmental agencies—they could have access to the networks you are using to communicate or could be listening in on the open Internet. Our goal is to eliminate the risk of these parties being able to compromise our communications in any manner.

A difficult aspect of modern cryptography is simply understanding the significant amount of terminology used whenever the subject is written about. A fundamental understanding can help with that, along with knowing the history of the adoption of cryptography into the field of computer networking.

As time goes on, more and more processing power and clever exploits increase the need for strong encryption. Our goal as security administrators is to apply the fundamentals of cryptography to make certain that when our systems communicate, only a trusted party can read said communications.

13.1.1   Encryption in Depth

The practice of encryption has existed for as long as people have had the need to keep secrets. In its most basic form, encryption is the practice of taking a message, scrambling it, and then giving that scrambled message to the receiver, who should have the ability to unscramble it.

A basic example of encryption is as follows:

1. A sender scrambles a message intended for the receiver (Figure 13.1).

Figure 13.1 Encryption Using Simple Cipher Method

2. The message is transferred, at which point, the receiver unscrambles or *decrypts* the message (Figure 13.2).

Figure 13.2 Decryption Using Simple Cipher Method

An important aspect of this communication is that the message shouldn't be understandable if intercepted by a third party. But once it's received by the authorized second party, it can be decoded and read.

It is assumed that both the sender and receiver have agreed on a method of scrambling beforehand. The technical term for a method of scrambling is a *cipher*. Formally, a cipher is a secret method used to encode or decode a message. The cipher in this example is simple, even if it appears not to be. Each letter was shifted one letter forward in the alphabet: an H becomes an I, an E becomes an F, and so on. This is known as a *shift cipher*. The text that's transmitted is called the *ciphertext*—"Ifmmp" in our example. Unless you know the cipher method, it's difficult to understand this message at first glance.

Of our assumptions, pre-agreement of the cipher is troublesome because it requires both the sender and receiver to meet and exchange this information in a secure manner. In our world of computer networks, this type of exchange is time-consuming and difficult. Imagine having to physically exchange ciphers with each and every connection that may need to take place over encryption. Such a task isn't feasible in real-world applications.

13

The second assumption made is that when the message is transferred it's in no way intercepted, overheard, or read by an untrusted third party. This is also difficult be certain of. Again, in the world of computer networks our data may travel over may networks to get to its destination. It may not be safeguarded on that route; it may be recorded or, worse, intercepted and retransmitted. If our cipher is compromised, the third party can decode our message.

Cipher Suites

Today, many complex ciphers are available for use. A cipher usually has a number of other functionalities and algorithms included to add to its usefulness. A *cipher suite* is the set of algorithms used to generate or decode ciphertext, the actual data that is transmitted over an unsecured network. As a general rule, the more complex a cipher, the more processing power is used to encrypt or decrypt data, which translates into a slower connection. This also means that the more complex a cipher is, the more difficult it is to defeat. SAP NetWeaver supports many ciphers, from simple to very strong. You'll need to select which ciphers are available in the system. We'll talk about this more in Section 13.2.1. For now, know that different ciphers will be used for different types of encryption of differing strengths. Also know that you'll need the same cipher on both sides of the connection, the client and server sides. Depending on the clients, this may be a challenge for your organization.

Once key feature of a cipher suite is its ability to detect tampering. This key capability is what gives us the integrity portion of our three requirements for encryption. This feature enables us to check messages that are incoming and warn that they weren't signed by the proper key or that they lack a proper signature.

Private Encryption Keys

Modern ciphers incorporate private encryption keys as a foundation for encryption. Encryption keys are mathematical number sequences used in the transformation of plaintext into ciphertext and vice versa. Each encryption key is able to both encode and decode the same ciphertext. As you learned previously, a cipher is a method of encryption, or an algorithm. When given a key and text, an cipher outputs encrypted text, or ciphertext (Figure 13.3).

Keys can also be used to sign certificates and authenticate messages, two features that help establish the identity of another party.

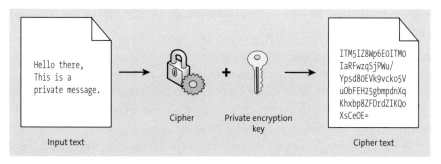

Figure 13.3 Example of Cipher and Private Key Encrypting Text

Private encryption keys are to be kept secret. Anyone with a copy of a private encryption key is able to encrypt and decrypt anything else that is encoded with that private encryption key. Therefore, it's of utmost importance to keep private encryption keys just that: *private*.

Symmetric Encryption

Now, we've got the two things we need to encrypt and decrypt messages securely: a cipher and a private key. Using these two tools, we can perform symmetric encryption. *Symmetric encryption* relies on a cipher and private key that's preshared between two parties (Figure 13.4).

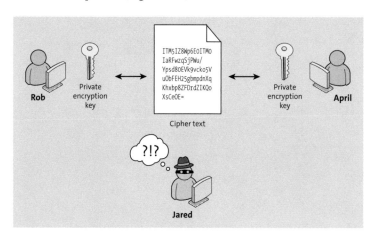

Figure 13.4 Example of Symmetric Encryption

The specific combination of the cipher and key can both encrypt and decrypt text. Therefore, to communicate securely, each party will be using the identical cipher and private key combination. What's encrypted by one party thus can be decrypted by the other.

Let's look at a practical example with two parties; we'll call them Rob and April. Both parties want to communicate in the clear, but they don't want to be heard by a malicious third party, named Jared. Rob and April can securely meet in person and agree on a cipher and private key to use. Then, using the agreed-upon cipher and private key, Rob can encrypt a message and send it to April. April can receive that message and use the identical cipher and private key to decrypt the message and read it. April can then reply with another encrypted message that Rob will be able to decrypt and read. Jared is left in the dark because without the private key he can't decrypt the ciphertext.

However, if Jared is able to gain access to the private key and can intercept messages, he can read them, change them, and relay them to the other party without either party knowing that this has happened. This is called a *man-in-the-middle attack* (Figure 13.5) and is something we want to safeguard against.

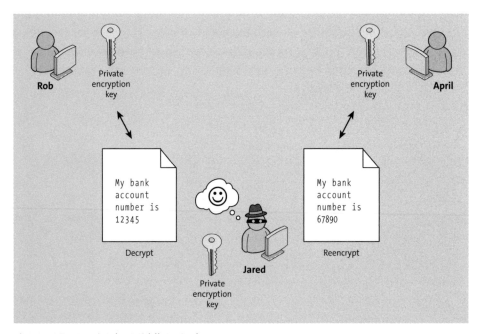

Figure 13.5 Man-in-the-Middle Attack

Unfortunately, because symmetric encryption relies on a shared key, it's difficult to defend against a man-in-the-middle attack. We'll need to use other tools to help keep the malicious party, Jared, at bay. The upside of symmetric encryption is that if you can keep the keys private, it's secure. It's also very efficient when it comes to performance.

Asymmetric Encryption

Simple encryption and symmetric encryption both highlight two key challenges with simple and private key encryption. These challenges, cipher selection and transit security, can both be addressed with a method called *asymmetric encryption*.

Before we dive into asymmetric encryption, you first need to learn about the concept of encryption key pairs. *Encryption key pairs* are used as part of a cipher process to both encode and decode messages, as well as establish identity (Figure 13.6).

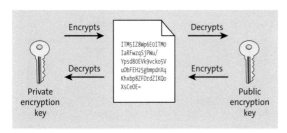

Figure 13.6 Public and Private Keys

Each party, the sender and receiver, creates a set of keys. Each set of keys contains two keys; let's call them key A and key B. These two keys are mathematical functions that are used in a special way to encode and decode messages. These sets of keys work in what's called an *inverse relationship*. If a message is encoded with either key, the opposite key can decode it. So, if we encode something with key A, key B can decode it. If we encode something with key B, key A can decode that. Only those two keys can encode or decode messages from each other. You also can't use key A to guess key B, or key B to guess key A. This makes them secure.

One of our two keys, let's say key A, we will keep private so that only we have that key. No one else is allowed access. The other key, key B, will be made public. We'll provide this key to anyone that needs it in cleartext, out in the open. Even third parties that are attempting to read our messages may have key B, or our public key. In summation, a private key is kept secret, only to be used by the owner of the key. A public key, on the other hand, is known to everyone and can be used by anyone. *Only* the public key can decode anything encoded by the private key, and the *only* the private key can decode anything encoded by the public key.

So, if Rob wants to send a message to April, he can give April his public key over cleartext because his public key isn't a secret. The message he is sending is encoded with his private key. By doing this, he can assure April that the message she is receiving is truly coming from Rob because that message can *only* be decoded with his public key (Figure 13.7).

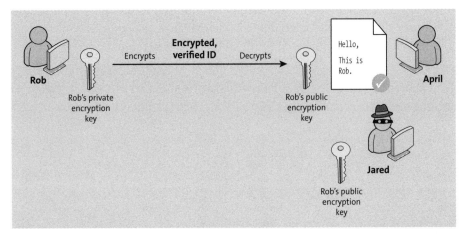

Figure 13.7 Verifying Identity with Key Pairs

Jared wouldn't be able to send a message to April pretending to be Rob because Jared doesn't have Rob's private key. In technical terms, this protects us from a man-in-the-middle attack. If April were to receive a message encrypted by Jared, as in Figure 13.8, and April attempted to decrypt it using Rob's public key, the cipher would indicate that the message is not trusted. This is a key feature of modern ciphers that we rely on to keep malicious parties such as Jared from performing man-in-the-middle attacks. One thing to note is that Jared *would* be able to decipher Rob's initial message to April. This is a limitation of using a single private/public keypair and is why we don't recognize this as true and "full" encryption.

Now, anyone who has a copy of this message can decode it with the correct public key. Strictly speaking, we don't have encryption. What we do have, however, is authentication. The second party knows that the message must have come from us because the appropriate public key is able to decode it.

Key sets are just a part of our cipher method. We perform additional steps within our cipher method to overcome the issue of a third party having both public keys because public keys are known to everyone. We'll talk more about that in the next section.

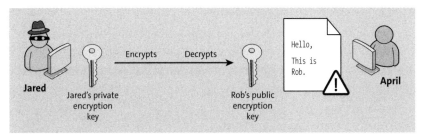

Figure 13.8 Attempting to Spoof Identity in Key Pair Scenario

At this point, we've been able to establish Rob's identity. Next, we need to establish the identity of April. To do this, we use the same method. As before, April sends her public key to Rob. With this, Rob can decode messages from April that are encrypted with her private key (Figure 13.9). Therefore, if Rob receives a message from April and April's public key can decode that message, he knows that he must be communicating with April.

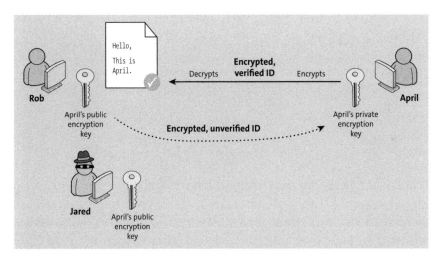

Figure 13.9 Reversing Process of Private-Public Key Pairs

As before, whenever a message is encoded with a public key and sent, it can only be decoded with the private key. This means that anything that is sent using this public key is encrypted. However, because public keys are public by nature, they can be used by anyone to send an encrypted message to the private key holder. We're still subject to the same issue of Jared being able to decrypt what April sends to Rob using her private key.

Asymmetric Encryption: Putting It All Together

Now, using each piece of this puzzle, we can send messages that are authenticated and secure. Here's how: First, Rob encodes a message with his private key. Next, he encodes the already encoded output from his private key again with April's public key. He now sends this doubly encoded message to April. April can decode it by first using her private key and then Rob's public key. Jared is left in the dark because he doesn't have April's private key (Figure 13.10).

This message is fully encrypted and cannot be decoded by a third party, and, we are assured of the identity of both parties because it was encoded with the sender's private key and the receiver's public key. We also know that the message hasn't been modified in any way because to do so, you would need both the public and private keys.

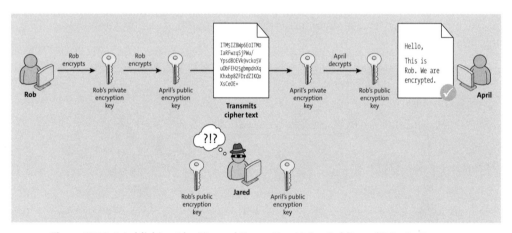

Figure 13.10 Establishing Identity and Encrypting Using Public and Private Keys

Now that we've covered both symmetric and asymmetric encryption, we can explore how and when they're used. Symmetric encryption is fast. Comparability, it's much faster than asymmetric encryption. However, it relies on a key that must be previously shared. Asymmetric communication is much slower but can be established without a commonly shared key. Ultimately, we want to get to the point at which we're using symmetric encryption due to its increased speed.

Now for the final trick: if we establish asymmetric communication using a public key, we can use that encrypted communication channel to share a one-time-use shared private key and switch over to fast symmetric communication without exposing the key (Figure 13.11). Problem solved!

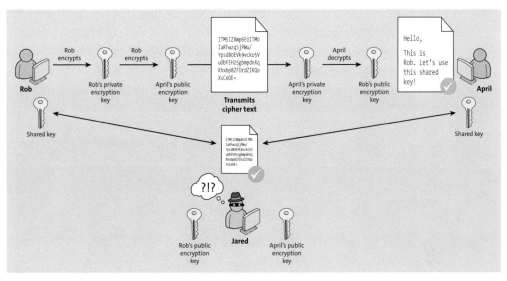

Figure 13.11 Switching from Asymmetric to Symmetric Encryption

Using this asymmetric to symmetric method to exchange a private key in a secure environment allows us to have both the security of asymmetric encryption and the performance of symmetric encryption.

Digital Certificates

The next challenge we must face is how to identify and exchange public keys in a safe and trusted manner over an untrusted medium such as the Internet. The tool that we use for this challenge is a digital certificate.

A *digital certificate* is an encoded data file that contains several pieces of information that are used to identify another computer, device, website, or even an actual person. A digital certificate almost always contains the following three main items: information about what the certificate represents, a public key, and a signature. It's much like a passport or identification card that you may carry with you. It will positively identify a party and allow encrypted communications to occur. Let's walk through each of the main items that a certificate will contain.

Ownership Info

Every digital certificate contains information about who owns it. Each certificate will have an owner and a validity date for which the certificate is valid. The owner or purpose of the certificate is indicated by a common name (CN). For example, the CN of the certificate in Figure 13.12 is *www.sap.com*. This indicates that the certificate is for SAP's webpage. Other information about the certificate is also classified in this manner. The common naming conventions for a digital certificate can be found in Table 13.1.

Key	Meaning	Use
CN	Common name	The exact website, computer, or person that the certificate represents—in our example, www.sap.com.
OU	Organizational unit	The division or department the certificate represents, such as SAP Global IT.
O	Organization	A company name, such as SAP SE.
S	State or province	The state or province, such as Baden-Wuerttemberg.
L	Locality or city	The city or town name, such as Waldorf.
C	Country name	Typically, a two-letter code for a country, such as DE for Germany.

Table 13.1 Certificate Naming Conventions for SSL Certificates

The distinguished name (DN) is the complete chain of information. In this example, the DN would appear as follows:

```
CN=www.sap.com, OU=SAP Global IT, O=SAP SE, S=Baden-Wuerttemberg, L=Waldorf,
C=DE
```

You can see this reflected in the actual certificate in Figure 13.12.

Public Key

A public key is included because it provides anyone that is sent a certificate with a public encryption mechanism that corresponds with the certificate owner's private key. Because of this, anyone can establish secure encryption with the private key holder. We covered public keys earlier in Section 13.1.1. They are a critical part of establishing security and are included with a certificate.

Signature

The signature in a digital certificate establishes trust. It tells us with certainty that the computer presenting it really is the one we expect. A digital certificate can be signed by an organization called a *Certificate Authority* (CA), such as Verisign, Thawte, or

DigiCert—or your company may run its own CA. In addition, digital certificates may be self-signed. Self-signed certificates are technically valid, but because their authenticity can't be checked against a trusted third party, they're considered insecure.

A certificate can be signed in such a matter that it's singed by multiple CAs. The primary CA is called the *root CA*. Additional CAs are called *intermediary CAs*. These CAs must have their certificates signed by the root CA and the intermediary CAs below it. This is called a *trust chain*. For a certificate to be valid, the signature of each of the intermediate and root CAs must be verifiable.

In addition to the three major parts, certificates contain additional information for establishing secure communication and preventing unauthorized parties from impersonating or spoofing who they are.

Our example in Figure 13.12 was an SSL certificate, but other types of certificates exist. Most often, these certificates conform to or are like the X.509 standard that governs SLL and personal digital certificates. The details may be slightly different, but the overall concepts are similar in almost all certificate-based encryption approaches.

Figure 13.12 Certificate for sap.com

In the real world, certificates are being used in smart cards, passports, and driver's licenses to positively identify the holders in both a physical and digital manner.

X.509 Certificate Standard

X.509 is a standard for digital certificates that defines the public key infrastructure we use to create, exchange, and verify certificates. The standard is published by the International Telecommunications Union's Standardization sector (ITU-T) and is widely used in computing. When someone is referring to a certificate, it's most likely that certificate is a X.509 certificate. Within SAP's applications, X.509 is the supported certificate type for user authentication and SSL/TLS.

SSL and TLS

Now that we've discussed how encrypted communications work, let's go over the guidelines for how to set up and maintain these encrypted communications. These guidelines are called *protocols*, and for HTTP communications the TLS and, historically, SSL protocols are used commonly. Other popular encryption protocols include SAP's SNC for system-to-system communication, SFTP for secure file transfers, and SSH for secure shell access, to name a few. Our focus in this section will be HTTPS, so we'll start with TLS/SSL.

Transport Layer Security (TLS) is a cryptographic protocol used by many computers to secure communications over networks. The TLS protocol specifies the exact process of a connection, just as we laid out in this chapter. If two computers use TLS, then you can be assured they will be "speaking the same language" to each other when it comes to establishing encryption. TLS is a newer version of Socket Secure Layer (SSL), which has been used extensively since the early days of the Internet. SSL has gone through through multiple versions, the latest being SSL 3.0. Due to significant vulnerabilities discovered in SSL 3.0 in 1999, the protocol was completely rewritten and became TLS 1.0. Currently, as of the writing of this text, TLS 1.3 is in a draft status, with TLS 1.2 being the current standard of use. The older protocol SSL 3.0 is still widely used because of its standardization but is slowly being phased out due to attacks such as Heartbleed and POODLE. As time goes on, more discovered vulnerabilities will make SSL 3.0 a security risk and applications will be forced to move to TLS.

TLS versus SSL

In SAP NetWeaver, TLS is fully supported and should be the default choice of the security administrator. Only use SSL if absolutely required by a legacy application, and take all available precautions to prevent outside access to these communications because they're a weak link in an otherwise strong chain of encryption.

Technical Encryption Steps for TLS/SSL

Now that you have the concepts down, we'll dig into how this process technically works between the client and server. Figure 13.13 provides an overview of the process handshake for TLS/SSL:

1. The client says hello and tells the server what protocols and ciphers it supports. If the client has a certificate, it provides it to the server. This initiates the handshake.

2. The server says hello to the client, tells the client which protocols and ciphers it supports, and specifies the protocol/cipher it's going to use. The server also sends its certificate, which contains its public key. Once this is done, it sends a *hello done* message.

3. The client validates the server's certificate. Next, the client generates a premaster code and encrypts it with the server's private key. It then sends this encrypted key to the server. Once it's done sending, it creates the symmetric key using the premaster code and sends a *change cipher spec message* to the server to tell the server it's ready to converse using this key. Once it's done all of this, it sends a *client finished* message to the server.

4. The server uses its private key to decrypt the message from the client. Using the premaster code from the client, the server generates a symmetric key that will be used for the encryption. It then sends a *change cipher spec* message and then a *server finished* message. This completes the handshake.

5. Encrypted communication begins, using the private key on each end. This is symmetric key encryption.

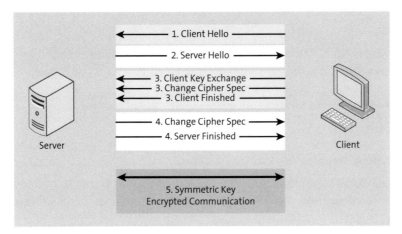

Figure 13.13 TLS General Diagram

This general process is used in almost all secure connections: server to client, server to server, and from SAP systems to non-SAP systems.

13.1.2   Secure Communication in SAP NetWeaver

Now that you know how the process of cryptography works, we'll next explore the application of this process in SAP NetWeaver AS ABAP.

Encryption and authentication takes place using the ICM, SAP's web-facing component of SAP NetWeaver AS ABAP. SAP NetWeaver AS ABAP manages the certificate handshake and SSL/TLS process as follows:

1. **Certificate exchange**
   The certificates that are exchanged are maintained in the Trust Manager.

2. **Cipher selection**
   The cipher selection is determined with the profile parameter. The cipher is provided by the Common Cryptographic Library.

3. **Handshake**
   The handshake is performed by the ICM, using the CommonCryptoLib for certificate verification and encryption.

Common Cryptographic Library

Why is specifying your cipher important? The mechanism that determines which SSL cipher is chosen when negotiating between a server and client is vulnerable for attack, so we need to make sure that we set an appropriate baseline for cipher strength. We don't want our servers to support strong encryption only to handshake and agree with the client to use weak encryption. It would be better to deny the connection outright rather than support weak encryption.

CommonCryptoLib is a collection of ciphers and related cryptographic code that an SAP NetWeaver AS system uses to handle encryption and decryption. This package is highly configurable and easy to manage. It can be upgraded independently of the kernel because it's an entirely separate subsystem. We covered upgrading CommonCryptoLib in Chapter 5. In this section, we'll focus on configuring it.

Cipher selection is done with profile parameters. The profile parameter we're configuring is ssl/ciphersuites. The following are sample values for strong TLS encryption:

```
ssl/ciphersuites = 135:PFS:HIGH::EC_P256:EC_HIGH
ssl/client_ciphersuites = 150:PFS:HIGH::EC_P256:EC_HIGH
```

Warning: Cipher Values

These values are the values as of the writing of this book. They are certain to change. Please consult SAP Note 510007 for the most up-to-date values.

Please be aware that the ICM requires both a server cipher value and a client cipher value. This is because when an SAP NetWeaver AS ABAP system is communicating in a role in which it is the client (talking to another server), it must also have the cipher specified.

Transaction STRUST (Trust Manager)

The Trust Manager, Transaction STRUST, allows the administrator to perform certificate maintenance functions such as generating key pairs, creating certificate requests to be signed by a CA, and maintaining the list of trusted CAs that the server accepts. Transaction STRUST also stores certificates that the system trusts such that these systems will be available for secure encrypted communication. A screenshot of Transaction STRUST is shown in Figure 13.14.

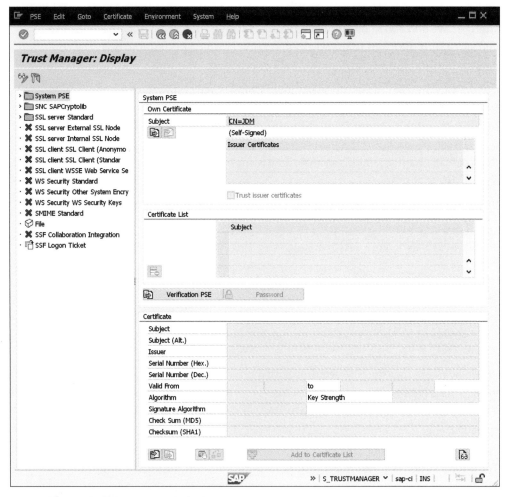

Figure 13.14 Transaction STRUST

Personal Security Environment

A Personal Security Environment (PSE) is a container that holds the certificates and credentials necessary to perform authentication and encryption. PSEs are created and maintained for specific purposes, such as the SSL server (the SAPSSLS.pse file) or the SNC PSE (SAPSNCS.pse).

The PSE files are created on the OS of each app server and are required for cryptography. They are called when the server is running to verify the identity of other systems. The directory for these files is the SECUDIR directory. This can be found by viewing the environment variable for SECUDIR in the OS.

Some PSEs are system-wide because they apply to every system in the landscape—for example, if the system is using a specific alias for access to any application server. A copy of these system-wide PSEs is required on each application server. Other PSEs are created for specific application servers. These PSEs only reside on the application server they're used for. For example, if you are creating an SSL/TLS server and its URL is the host name of a particular application server (not a DNS alias), that application server must have its own instance-specific PSE.

13.2   Enabling SSL/TLS

Enabling SSL/TLS is often thought of as a very difficult task. Although it may be a bit complicated, it's not difficult at all once you familiarize yourself with the different parts of the SAP NetWeaver AS ABAP system.

> **Don't Use Unencrypted HTTP!**
>
> Don't be tempted to use unencrypted HTTP connections with your SAP system. With a network connection and a sniffer program, adversaries can discover passwords and critical business data being transmitted over unsecured HTTP connections. HTTPS is fully supported, industry-standard, and secure. It may be a little more work to set up but it's truly worth the investment of time and effort to secure your system against security threats.

Properly planning and documenting your SSL/TLS implementation is important. Deciding on what the parameter values and settings should be beforehand is a great way to think through the complexity before you begin. As you walk though this section, make a note of what your values should be from start to finish.

13.2.1   Setting System Parameters

First, we'll need to tell the system that we need an ICM node to listen using SSL. You'll need the profile parameters listed in Table 13.2 to be set.

Profile Parameter	Value	Example
icm/ssl_config_ <xx>	CRED=<credential> [, CACHESIZE=<cache size>, LIFETIME=<max. lifetime>, VCLIENT=<SSL client verifi- cation>, CIPHERS=<Cipher Suites>]	CRED=SAPSSLS.pse, VCLIENT= 1, CIPHERS= 135:PFS:HIGH::EC_P256:EC_ HIGH?
icm/server_port_ <xx>	PROT=HTTPS, PORT= <port>,TIMEOUT=<timeout_ in_ seconds>	PROT=HTTPS, PORT=8443, TIM- EOUT=900
icm/HTTPS/verify_ client	0: Do not use certificates 1: Allow certificates (default) 2: Require certif- icates	1

Table 13.2 Required Parameters for SSL/TLS Configuration

To set these parameters, we'll have to do some preparation work to decide what we want to use for both ports and ciphers.

Choosing a Port

Choosing a port could be as simple as using the standard SSL port, port 443. Often, ports in a higher range are used because on Unix/Linux systems only root can bind a port under port 1000. Often, port 8443 is used for SSL, but you can use any open port.

Choosing a Cipher

The cipher choice is important. The most prudent choice would be as strong a cipher as is available. However, we must keep in mind the clients that are connecting to our system. Clients can be anything from end user web browsers to other servers. If you have legacy servers as clients, you may be required to fall back to less secure ciphers because the legacy servers may not support the latest and most secure ciphers. If this is the case, be cautious. Often, attacks on weak or old ciphers can compromise systems that for the most part are secure. If you're forced to use an old cipher, consider setting up an isolated server identity for that system and segregate its traffic to a different port than your end users or Internet users. We'll cover this approach more in Chapter 15.

It's important to read the cipher section of SAP Note 510007 (Setting up SSL on Application Server ABAP).

Cipher Recommendation

As of the writing of this book, the current recommended strong cipher value is `135:PFS:HIGH::EC_P256:EC_HIGH`.

Be sure to check the latest information in SAP Note 510007. Vulnerabilities are often discovered and this SAP Note will list the most recent recommendations directly from the security experts at SAP.

If the parameter value is `icm/HTTPS/verify_client= 1`, then any users who use Microsoft Internet Explorer as their web browser and who do not possess a client certificate will receive an empty certificate selection dialog box when they access SAP NetWeaver AS for ABAP. If your users aren't going to use client certificates for authentication, then set this parameter to the value 0.

Entering the Parameters and Testing

Using Transaction RZ10, enter the parameters provided ahead after adjusting them to your needs. In this example, we're using port 8443 and a very secure cipher. Note that these parameters are case-sensitive.

1. Enter the following parameters:

```
#SSL Configuration
icm/server_port_1 = PROT=HTTPS, PORT=8443, SSLCONFIG=ssl_config_1
icm/ssl_config_1 = CRED=SAPSSLS.pse, VCLIENT=1, CIPHERS=135:PFS:HIGH
icm/HTTPS/verify_client = 1
```

Tip: Which Profile to Set SSL Settings?

Use the instance profile if you'd like to maintain different settings for each application server. Use the default profile if you'd like all servers to match. Remember that if you set something in the instance profile, it will override what's in the default profile.

---

2. Stop then restart your SAP NetWeaver AS ABAP server.
3. To test, you first need to verify that your configuration is active on the SAP NetWeaver AS ABAP side. Navigate to Transaction **SMICM** and click **Goto · Services** (Figure 13.15).

You should see your service running on the port you specified in the profile. It's important to note that your service is not yet active. You will need to create the PSE, which is our next step. Also notice any other running services on your system. Any service with a 0 for the port is not listening for outside connections and can safely be ignored.

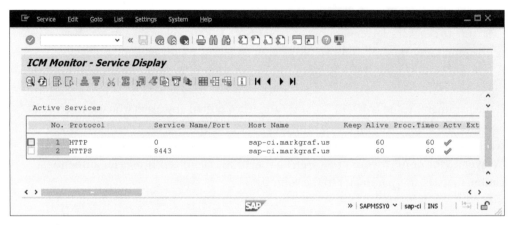

Figure 13.15 ICM Services Screen

Troubleshooting Tips

Be sure your profile parameters are correct and are being evaluated during system startup. Checking the ICM log in Transaction SMICM via **Goto • Trace File • Display All** will help you identify what the ICM does as it evaluates the parameters passed to it. Also, checking **Goto • Parameters • Display** will tell you what the ICM is reading from the system profile. If your parameters are missing here, it means they're inactive or have an error.

13.2.2   Creating the TLS/SSL PSE

The next step to enabling TLS/SSL is to create a PSE for the TLS/SSL server.

Before You Begin

You must know the DN of the server(s) you intend to setup. The syntax of the DN depends on the CA you use. DN syntax is explained in the Ownership Info section of this chapter.

To create a PSE for the TLS/SSL server, perform the following steps:

1. In client 000, execute Transaction STRUST.

2. Click the **Display <-> Change** 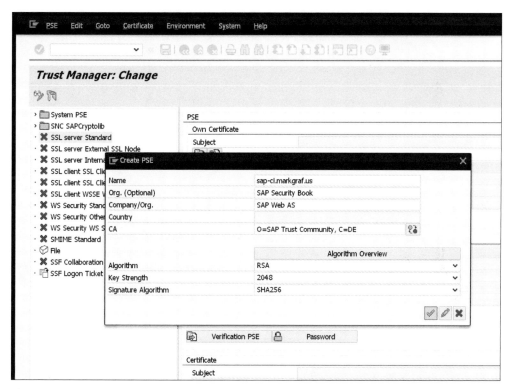 button to enter change mode.

3. Right-click the **SSL Server Standard** entry and select **Create**.

4. At this point, you'll see a **Create PSE** screen. Enter the **Name** of your system, your organization (**Org.**) name, and the correct **CA** values (O and C, which are organizational unit and country, respectively). For the purposes of this example, we've used our testing environment values. Yours will be different (Figure 13.16).

Figure 13.16 Create PSE Screen

5. Click the **Revise DN** button .

6. Revise the DN as required. This is important to specify correctly because it will be used in the certificate request process. See Section 13.1.1 of this chapter for more info.

> **Choosing a CA**
>
> If you use SAP's CA service, the naming convention is CN=<host_name>, OU=I<installation_number>-<company_name>, OU=SAP Web AS, O=SAP Trust Community, C=DE.

7. Click the green checkmark ✅ to create the PSE (Figure 13.17).

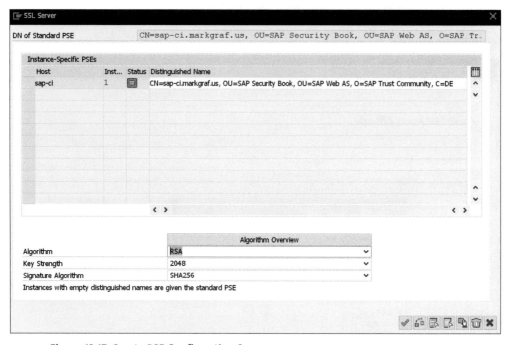

Figure 13.17 Create PSE Confirmation Screen

> **Server Identities**
>
> If you have multiple instances, in the screen shown in Figure 13.17 you can decide which DNs they will receive. If you're creating SSL certificates for these specific systems, they will most likely need their hostnames in the **CN** field. See the next subsection for more discussion of this topic.

8. The **Instance-Specific PSE** screen will now appear. If you have a single instance, you can simply click the green checkmark ✅ to finish creating the PSE.

The newly created PSE will now exist on the filesystem in the directory */usr/sap/ <SID>/<INSTANCE>/sec*.

Server Identities

Transaction STRUST can become complicated because an SAP NetWeaver system can support multiple SSL identities. For example, an SAP CRM system might act both as an internal SAP CRM portal at the address *internal.mycompany.com* and an external portal at the address *external.mycompany.com*. In a situation like this, no one certificate will satisfy both situations. You need one for each. Therefore, you'll have to set up a PSE and SSL configuration for each scenario.

In the example in Figure 13.18, we have two server identities: an internal identity and an external identity. Each identity needs a separate certificate and TLS/SSL configuration while being hosted on a single SAP NetWeaver AS ABAP server.

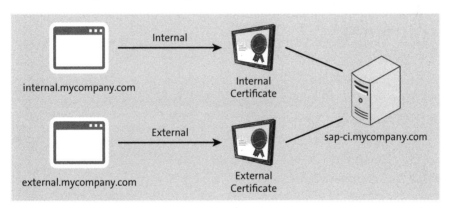

Figure 13.18 Server Identities

Wildcard Certificates

Wildcard certificates, or certificates issued for *.mycompany.com, are widely discouraged because of severe issues related to their security and management. Some CAs for these reasons refuse to sign wildcard certificates, so a security administrator shouldn't use them.

If you have two or more server identities, the following procedure will allow you to correctly set up SSL for each. In this example, we'll be using an internal host and an external host on our test system.

For each identity, create an ICM service. The required parameters are as follows:

```
#Internal Server Identity
icm/server_port_2 = PROT=HTTPS,PORT=8444,SSLCONFIG=ssl_config_2
icm/ssl_config_2 = CRED=SAPSSLS_INT.pse,VCLIENT=0
#External Server Identity
icm/server_port_3 = PROT=HTTPS,PORT=8445,SSLCONFIG=ssl_config_3
icm/ssl_config_3 = CRED=SAPSSLS_EXT.pse,VCLIENT=0
```

To set up your PSEs, proceed as follows:

1. From the Trust Manager screen in Transaction STRUST, choose **Environment • SSL Server Identities** (Figure 13.19).

Figure 13.19 SSL Server Identities Menu Entry

2. Click the **Change** button on the toolbar.

3. The **SSL Server Identities Maintenance** screen appears. The table contains entries for the standard PSEs for this PSE type.

4. Choose **New Entries**.

5. The **New Entries: Overview of Added Entries** maintenance screen appears. Enter the PSE's information (**Identity** and **Description**) in the appropriate columns. Click the **Save** button on the toolbar (Figure 13.20).

6. For each server identity you've created, there will be a new PSE entry created in Transaction STRUST. To create the PSEs on the file system, click **Edit** on the toolbar, then right-click each new PSE and select **Create**. From here, perform the normal certificate request and response for each (Figure 13.21).

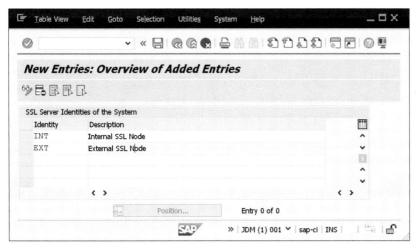

Figure 13.20 Adding Multiple SSL Identities

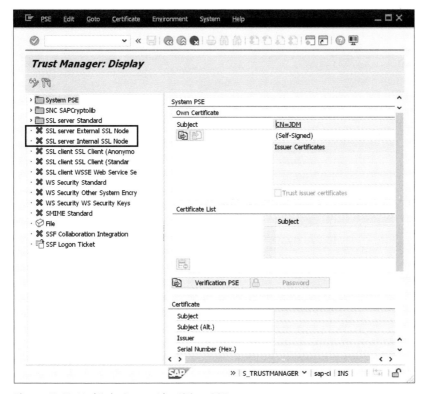

Figure 13.21 Multiple Server Identities: PSE

13.2.3 Testing TLS/SSL

1. After enabling the parameters and creating the SSL server PSE, we're ready to test TLS/SSL:

2. Stop then restart your SAP NetWeaver AS ABAP server.

3. Navigate to Transaction SMICM and click **Goto • Services**.

4. A green checkmark ✔ should now appear under the **Active** column for your service. This indicates it is active and the server is listening on the specified port for connections (Figure 13.22).

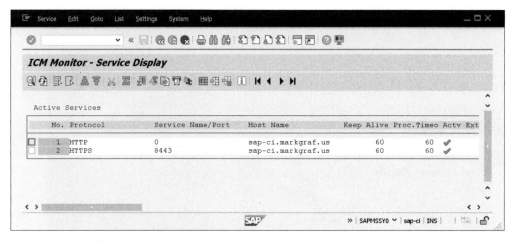

Figure 13.22 ICM Services Screen

5. Next, navigate to Transaction SICF.

6. In the **Service Path** field, enter "/sap/public/info/" (Figure 13.23).

7. Click the **Execute** button 🔁.

8. Right click **Info** and select **Activate Service** (Figure 13.24).

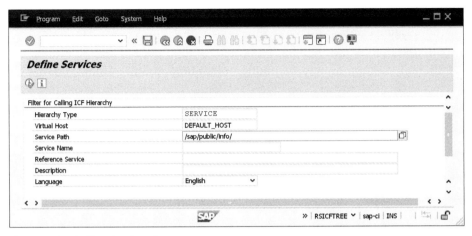

Figure 13.23 Define Services Screen

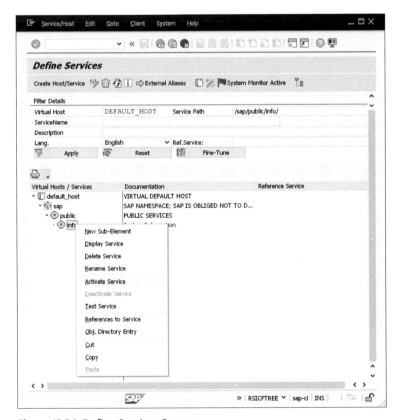

Figure 13.24 Define Services Screen

9. Click the leftmost **Yes** button in the **Activation of ICF Services** confirmation window (Figure 13.25).

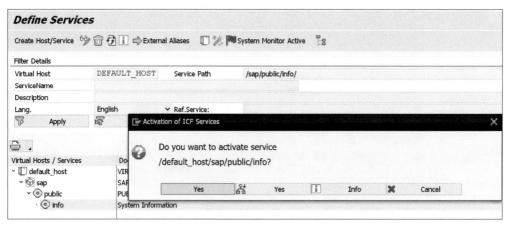

Figure 13.25 Activation of ICF Services Confirmation Window

10. Open up a web browser and navigate to *https://<hostname>:8443/sap/public/info*.

You'll most likely get a certificate warning; that's OK. We haven't given the system a certificate to present yet. Click **Continue** in your web browser.

If you can see XML output with information about your system (Figure 13.26), your test is a success! What this test represents is that our web browser was able to successfully negotiate a TLS connection with our SAP NetWeaver AS ABAP server. If you don't see this output, you'll need to go back and check your parameters and that the PSE exists.

In addition, using an SSL testing and auditing tool, a security administrator can independently inspect what the SAP NetWeaver AS ABAP server is offering during its handshake and cipher negotiation phase. Figure 13.27 shows the output of a very useful tool called SSL Audit, created by security researcher Thierry Zoller.

Figure 13.26 Web Browser Output of Test Service

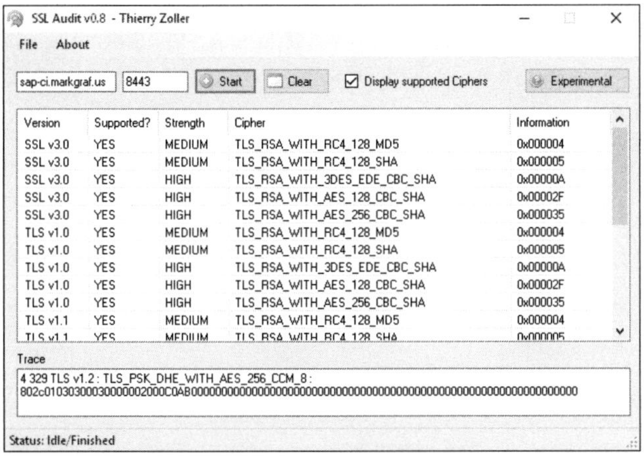

Figure 13.27 Output of TLS/SSL Auditing Tool

These tools are very useful in detecting situations in which SSL implementations are broken or support ciphers that are weak or compromised. We'll cover the strategy of testing our systems for these types of situations in Chapter 15, using network scanning tools.

This concludes the configuration of TLS/SSL. Next, we'll obtain a certificate for our server and remedy the trust/certificate errors.

13.2.4   Requesting and Installing Certificates

There are five main steps in configuring SSL/TLS authentication with a certificate:

1. Request a certificate from a CA.
2. The CA creates a certificate and signs it with its key.
3. The certificate is installed in the SAP NetWeaver server.
4. The browser is issued root certificates.
5. The browser trusts correctly signed certificates.

You must generate an individual certificate request for each application server that uses a server-specific PSE. If you use a system-wide SSL server PSE, then you only need to generate a single certificate request that will serve the entire system. System-wide PSEs are required for the use of DNS aliases, in which one DNS name will be directed to multiple application servers in your SAP NetWeaver AS ABAP system.

Determine the DN of Each Application Server

To determine each unique SSL server PSE, expand the **SSL Server PSE** node in the Trust Manager and select each application server by double-clicking. The server's DN appears in the **Owner** field. For each application server with a unique DN, you must generate a certificate request.

Procedure to Generate Certificate Signing Request

In order to request a signed certificate from a certificate authority, a CSR must be created. To create a CSR, follow these steps:

1. Navigate to Transaction STRUST.

Transaction STRUST

Changes to Transaction STRUST should generally be done in client 000 because they're system-wide changes.

2. From the Trust Manager screen, for each unique SSL server PSE (each server-specific PSE or a single system-wide PSE), select the application server. The application server's certificate appears in the **PSE Maintenance** section in the **Owner** field. In our example, this is sap-ci_JDM_01 under folder **SSL Server Standard**.

3. In the menu, choose **Edit**, then **Create Certificate Request**. A dialog appears showing the certificate request that was generated (Figure 13.28).

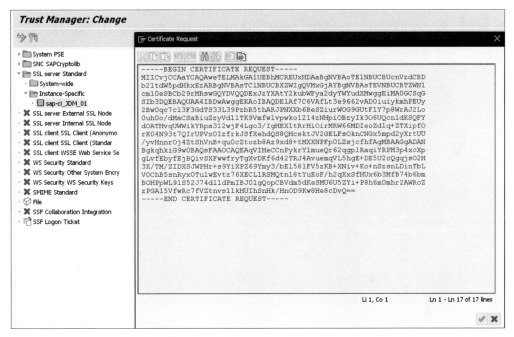

Figure 13.28 Generation of Certificate Signing Request

4. Save the certificate request to a file using the **Save as Local File** button.

This certificate request will then be sent to the CA for signing. Once your certificate is signed, the CA will send it back to you in the form of a certificate response.

Procedure to Install a Signed Certificate Response

Next, you'll need to install the certificate response on your system(s).

1. Navigate to Transaction STRUST.

2. Click the **Display <-> Change** button to enter change mode.

3. From the Trust Manager screen, for each unique SSL server PSE (each server-specific PSE or a single system-wide PSE), select the application server. The application server's certificate appears in the **PSE Maintenance** section in the **Owner** field. In our example, this is sap-ci_JDM_01 under folder **SSL Server Standard**.

4. Click the **Import Certificate Response** button 🔁.

5. Use the **Paste** 📋 or **Import** 📥 button to import your response file.

6. You certificate will now appear in the **Own Certificate** section, in the **Subject** field. If you click it, the certificate details will appear in the **Certificate** box below (Figure 13.29).

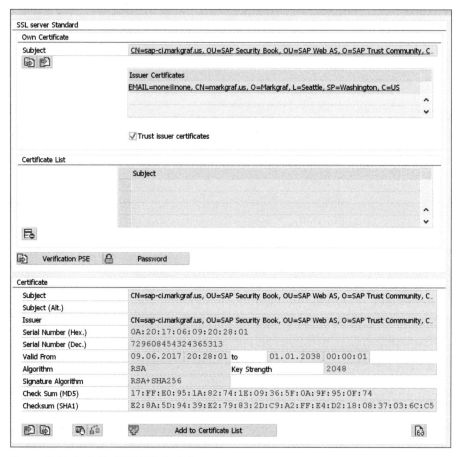

Figure 13.29 Installed TLS/SSL Certificate

7. Stop then restart your SAP NetWeaver AS ABAP server.

Testing TLS/SSL Certificate Configuration

To test your SSL certificate installation, open a web browser and navigate to *https:// <hostname>:8443/sap/public/info*. If your certificate is installed correctly, you shouldn't see any warnings. You should see a lock icon, as well as that the site is trusted (Figure 13.30).

Figure 13.30 Successful SSL Test in Internet Explorer

If you don't see correct certificate validation, first check to see if your SAP NetWeaver AS ABAP server is actually sending the certificate you imported. Next, you need to make sure that the root certificate from the CA is installed on your computer. Most major CAs root certificates come preinstalled on Windows or Mac. However, if you are using a CA that is internal to your company, you must install the CA's root and intermediate certificates on your computer. Consult your CA for instructions on how to install their root certificates.

> **Reminder: Deactivate Unused Services**
>
> Once you finish testing, go back to Transaction SICF and deactivate the info service. Leaving this service active gives any potential attacker information about your system.

13.3   The Internet Connection Manager

One of the key features of an SAP NetWeaver AS ABAP system is that it's designed to interface with the Internet in a robust and business-process-focused way. One of the downsides of being Internet-connected is that without the proper safeguards an SAP system can be subject to attack from many hostile or malicious users.

When configuring the ICM, take great care to create a system that is as secure as possible. SAP provides many tools to create a very secure system, but if they aren't configured and used properly your system may be at significant risk.

13.3.1   ICM Concepts

The ICM is how an SAP NetWeaver system interfaces with the Internet over a network. The ICM isn't limited to HTTP, however. The ICM can use other protocols, like SMTP (email). This allows developers to send emails for, say, approval requests or notifications. A developer can even use this functionality to read email sent to the SAP system from end users. Although an interesting use case, it's a security risk we should be aware of.

The ICM is configured using system parameters. The ICM itself is a collection of running server processes that can be adjusted and restarted on the fly. The ICM is monitored using Transaction SMICM, using OS-level tools, or from a web administration interface. Be sure to secure each of these methods because you wouldn't want an unauthorized user to be able to change the settings of your ICM.

Because the ICM is network-facing, it's a component of the SAP system that a security administrator must know inside and out. Much effort on the part of unauthorized users is spent trying to determine weaknesses of the ICM and its operation. It's up to the security administrator to be sure that the ICM is sufficiently safeguarded against both internal and external threats.

If your ICM is intended to be Internet-facing or connected to the Internet, you must be extra vigilant because this opens your SAP NetWeaver AS ABAP system to many exploits coming from anywhere and everywhere. We'll speak about this more in Chapter 15.

13.3.2   Important ICM Security Parameters

The first step in controlling the ICM is making sure the administrative interfaces are as secure as possible. The biggest risk is with the web administration interface. Be sure to address this first. Beyond initial configuration, the ICM can tuned in a variety of ways depending on your situation.

Web Administration Interface

The ICM Web Administration Interface is a great tool for administration of the ICM without using SAP GUI or OS tools. However, it's a security risk because it can be more easily accessed by nefarious parties in an Internet or corporate intranet networked scenario. Therefore, unless you have an explicit need for the ICM Web Administration Interface running on the same port as your HTTPS traffic, we suggest running it on a nonstandard port that isn't open to end users.

If you use the Web Administration Interface, the following safeguards are suggested:

- Run on a secure port that doesn't allow end user traffic.
- Use X.509 certificate authentication.
- Only allow access from your internal administrative network.
- Use an auth (authorization) file to restrict access.

13.3.3   Controlling Access Using Access Control List

One key security feature to take advantage of when it comes to the ICM is its built-in access control functionalities. An ACL is a whitelist or blacklist that either permits or denies a connection based on its IP address. For example, if all your end users are in the 10.10.10.0/24 address range, then it'd be simple to only allow connections from that range and deny everything else.

From a security perspective, establishing a whitelist and blocking all other URLs is preferred. The tool we use to control access to the ICM is an ACL file.

Syntax of the ACL File

Lines in the ACL must have the following syntax:

```
<permit or deny> <ip-address[/mask]> [tracelevel] [# comment]
```

A breakdown of each parameter can be found in Table 13.3.

Parameter	Description
Permit	Allows a connection
Deny	Denies a connection
IP address	An IPv4 or IPv6 address
Mask	Optional: a subnet mask to deny a network (CIDR notation)
Tracelevel	The trace level in which the logging system writes a permit or deny to the trace file (default value is 2)
#	Anything after # is ignored

Table 13.3 Syntax of ACL File

For example, if you want to exclude the 10.10.20.0 network from being able to access your system, you'd enter the following line in your ACL file:

```
deny 10.10.20.0/24 #Deny a specific network.
```

If you want to deny a specific IPv4 address and log it to the trace file, use this syntax:

```
deny 10.10.20.20 1 #Deny a specific ip address.
```

Some notable aspects of ACL files include the following:

- The file can contain blank lines.
- Entering comments is a good practice to identify why certain rules were implemented.
- The ACL rules are checked sequentially from the top down.
- The first relevant rule determines the action taken.
- If no rule applies, the connection is rejected.
- An explicit deny (deny 0.0.0.0/0) should always be entered as the last rule.

A good ACL file can take quite a long time to create. However, this time is well-spent as the ACL functionality can enhance system security greatly if implemented correctly.

Trace Level

The trace file for the ICM can be used to diagnose issues or show the security administrator when the ACL is being triggered to permit or deny connections. The trace file can also be used for audit. When tracing is used, it can create a record of system access that a security administrator can report on. A second and very useful use of the trace file is as a screening rule.

To change the trace level of the ICM, in Transaction SMICM, select **Goto • Trace Level • Set**.

> **Tracing**
>
> Be sure to keep your tracing level as low as possible. Higher trace levels may have a negative impact on system performance. Always evaluate the security needs of your trace and audit requirements.

Using a Screening Rule

A *screening rule*, or *learning rule*, is a rule put in place to permit connections and write their information to a log file. Doing so gives the security administrator a good idea of the normal pattern of traffic that will commonly be accessing the server. Using a screening rule, a security administrator can identify the entries required for a whitelist by looking at what IPs commonly are trigging the ACL. The security administrator can also verify which IPs do not normally trigger the ACL and proceed to block them using deny ranges. Using screening rules can be a time-saving tool to develop accurate white- and blacklists without the headache of opening or closing the ACL for individual requests.

These ACL activations will be written to the dev_icm log on each permit or deny that is at or above the current trace level of the ICM. Denied connections will also be written to the dev_icm_sec trace file.

Activating the ACL

The ACL is activated by adding an option to the `icm/server_port_<xx>` parameter.

> **Caution**
>
> The ICM must have a valid ACL File when the `ACLFILE` option is used. If it doesn't have a valid or syntactically correct file, the ICM will stop in an error state. In many cases, the SAP system will fail to start due to an ACL file error.

In our example system, the `icm/server_port_<xx>` parameter is modified as follows:

```
icm/server_port_1 = PROT=HTTPS, PORT=8443, SSLCONFIG=ssl_config_1,
ACLFILE=/usr/sap/$(SAPSYSTEMNAME)/$(INSTANCE_NAME)/data/ICM_ACL
```

Our ACL file is created in the directory */usr/sap/<SID>/<INSTANCE>/data/*.

The ACL file used is as follows:

```
permit   10.10.10.0/24    1        #Screening Rule
deny     0.0.0.0/0        2        #Deny all others
```

To enable an ACL file, follow these steps:

1. Using Transaction RZ10, add the required `ACLFILE` option to the `icm/server_port` parameter.
2. In the text editor of your choice, create the ACL file. For this example, we're going to allow our end users and deny all other connections.
3. Stop then restart your SAP NetWeaver AS ABAP server.
4. Navigate to Transaction SMICM and click **Goto · Services**.
5. A green checkmark ✔ should appear under the **Active** column for your service. This indicates it is active and the server is listening on the specified port for connections. The column **ACLFILE** should list the path to your ACL file (Figure 13.31).

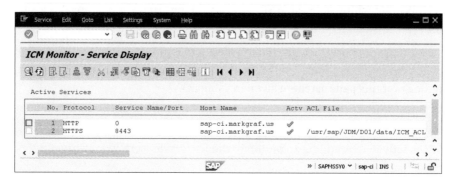

Figure 13.31 ACL Status: Enabled

Often, organizations don't bother with ACLs because they feel that if an intruder is able to bypass all other network security, an ACL won't stop them. This is a bad practice and should be avoided. If an unauthorized user is within your organization, an ACL could be your critical last line of defense, preventing them from accessing your SAP NetWeaver system.

13.3.4   Security Log

The ICM security log is a powerful tool that can alert a security administrator to potential issues.

The following events are logged in the security log:

- Data sent to the ICM with invalid syntax
- Attempts to access objects that don't exist
- Access to objects that is not permitted due to filter rules
- ACL-based denials
- Logon errors to the Web Administration Interface

Here are some examples of log entries:

```
Error: Permission denied (-13), authorization failed for user >sap< [http_
auth_mt.c 745]
Error: Protocol error (-21), illegal request version: 1009
Error: Protocol error (-21), NULL bytes in HTTP request [http_plg_mt.c 4037]
```

As you can see, this information would be valuable to a security administrator. Potential actions from this information would be to review a user that triggers a large number of authorization failures or deny an IP address in the ACL that triggers a large number of protocol errors because they may be looking for SSL/TLS exploits.

The default value for the icm/security_log parameter is as follows:

```
icm/security_log = LOGFILE=dev_icm_sec,MAXSIZEKB=10000
```

The options for this parameter are given in Table 13.4.

Option	Values	Description
LOGFILE	security_log-%d-%m-%y_%h:%t:%s	Name of the output file in the file system.

Table 13.4 Options for icm/security_log Parameter

Option	Values	Description
LEVEL	1–3	This value indicates the level of detail recorded in the trace in accordance with the trace level.
MAXSIZEKB	File size in KB, up to 2TB	Maximum size of the security file in kilobytes. If this size is exceeded, the current file is closed and a new one (with a new name) is opened.
SWITCHTF	Hour, day, month	A new security log can be created not only if the file reaches a certain size, but also when the time changes.
FILEWRAP	On, off	If FILEWRAP=on is active, every time a new file is opened (due to time or size limits being exceeded), the existing security file is reset and overwritten.

Table 13.4 Options for icm/security_log Parameter (Cont.)

Additional options for inserting the date in the log filename are as follows:

- %d: Day of the month (1–31)
- %m: Month (1–12)
- %y: Year, in four-digit format YYYY
- %h: Hour (0–23)
- %t: Minute (0–59)
- %s: Seconds (0–59)

Additional options for setting the logging level are as follows:

- 1: Only the reason for the entry is recorded
- 2: Additional information about the status of the connection and the start of the data that gave rise to the entry is recorded (default value)
- 3: All the data that gave rise to the entry is logged

If your security policy requires one month of detailed records to be kept, then the configuration of this parameter would be as follows:

```
icm/security_log = LOGFILE=security_log-%d-%m-%y_%h:%t:%s, LEVEL=3, MAXSIZEKB=
50000, SWITCHTF=day, FILEWRAP=off]
```

> **Security Log File Size**
>
> One thing to keep in mind is that if filewrap is turned off or the log/trace level is set higher than the default value, a situation in which the application server's file system may fill up due to large logfiles is much more likely to occur. A full filesystem can halt a running SAP NetWeaver AS ABAP system, so it's prudent to keep logfiles on a separate filesystem that has a backup/archiving strategy defined.

13.3.5   Controlling Access Using a Permission File

The ICM can be configured to evaluate incoming requests and treat them differently based on criteria that the administrator defines. The following restrictions are possible using this mechanism:

- URL
- Client IP address
- Server IP address
- User name/user group and password
- String search in the URL

The following parameter applies to the ICM and SAP Web Dispatcher:

```
icm/HTTP/auth_<xx>
```

The <xx> index is a number without a leading 0. By using the index, you can specify which ICM node you'd like to filter. This is assuming you have more than a single ICM node.

This parameter is powerful tool that allows the security administrator to control access by IP address and by user if needed. Traditionally, ICM controls by user were more difficult to implement in SAP NetWeaver AS ABAP. Using this parameter, this task can be accomplished with ease and flexibility.

The following parameter syntax is used:

```
icm/HTTP/auth_<xx> = PREFIX=<URL-Prefix>
[,PERMFILE=<permission file>, AUTHFILE=<authentication file>,
FILTER=<name>]
```

Descriptions for the values in the `icm/http/auth_<xx>` can be found in Table 13.5.

Value	Description
auth_<xx>	
PREFIX	URL prefix for which the HTTP subhandler is to be called.
AUTHFILE	Name of the user file or system for authentication of an OS user.
PERMFILE	Name/path of the permission file in the file system.
FILTER	Name of the profile for the search template. The default value is SAP. The filter will be deactivated if you omit this parameter. The filter can be dynamically activated/deactivated by setting the parameter `csi/enable`.

Table 13.5 icm/HTTP/auth_<xx> Parameter Values

This parameter is not dynamically changeable, meaning that the ICM must be restarted before this parameter will take effect.

Permissions File Syntax

A permissions file requires a specific syntax so that it can be properly read by the ICM. Failure to follow this syntax will cause the ICM to start without the permission file in place.

The full syntax for a permissions file (permfile) used by the ICM is as follows:

```
P/D/S <URI pattern> <USER><GROUP><CLIENT IP><SERVER IP>
```

- P (permit) allows the request to be passed.
- D (deny) denies the request and sends a message to the client.
- S (secure) only allows secure connections (HTTPS) for the URL prefix.

- `<URI pattern>` is the URL that is being allowed or denied. This doesn't include the hostname, just the path that would come afterward. Because of this, a Perm file can be used for multiple hosts with no changes.

You can use the wildcard character * for the URI pattern, but only at the start or the end of the path. For example, you can enter */sap/admin or /sap/admin*. There are two IP ranges that can be used. They are as follows:

- Client IP address/address range: The range or address from which the end users' request may originate.

- Server IP address/address range: The range or address in which the server being called is allowed.

For the client and server IP address you can use an exact address, the wildcard character *, or a net mask syntax.

Restricting Authfile Use by Users or Groups

An authfile can be restricted using users or groups. The following list defines the function of this feature:

- User: This is the named user permitted to access or denied from accessing this URL.

- Group: This is the named user group that is permitted to access or denied from accessing this URL.

User and group restrictions are implemented using an authfile. This is generated on the OS level maintained using programs wdispmon and icmon (option -a). It has the following structure:

`<User>: <Password hash>: <User group>: <DN Client certificate>`

An example of authorization file creation is as follows:

1. On an application server or SAP Web Dispatcher, run the icmon or wdispmon tool. In this example, we'll be using the wdispmon tool on an SAP Web Dispatcher box. Include the -a flag to generate an authfile (Figure 13.32).

```
wdsadm> wdispmon -a
```

Figure 13.32 wdispmon Tool

2. Choose the name of the file you'd like to edit. If you're a creating a new file, specify the name of the file you'd like to create here. For this example, we've chosen *icm-auth.txt* (Figure 13.33).

```
Maintain authentication file
============================

Filename (icmauth.txt): icmauth.txt█
```

Figure 13.33 SAP Web Dispatcher: Name Authfile

3. If the file doesn't exist, the tool will prompt you to create the file (Figure 13.34).

```
Maintain authentication file
============================

Filename (icmauth.txt): icmauth
Error reading file icmauth

do you want to create new file ? y█
```

Figure 13.34 SAP Web Dispatcher: Create Auth File

4. The tool will now display its main menu. It's important to understand that you could edit the file on the filesystem with a text editor, but the necessary password hashes wouldn't exist. To create a sample user, we'll choose the a option (Figure 13.35).

```
Maintain authentication file: icmauth
=====================================

    a - add user to set
    c - change passwd of existing user in set
    g - change group of existing user in set
    x - change client cert data of existing user in set
    d - delete user from set
    l - list users of set
    s - save changes of set to file
    q - quit (without saving)

--> █
```

Figure 13.35 SAP Web Dispatcher: Main Menu

5. Enter your user's details. You'll have to enter the user's password and the subject value of a client certificate, if required. We strongly recommend using certificates

in securing the ICM/SAP Web Dispatcher. Once you've finished, press the [Enter] key to create your new auth file (Figure 13.36).

```
Maintain authentication file: icmauth.txt
=========================================

    a - add user to set
    c - change passwd of existing user in set
    g - change group of existing user in set
    x - change client cert data of existing user in set
    d - delete user from set
    l - list users of set
    s - save changes of set to file
    q - quit (without saving)

--> a
User name: i851675
Enter new password:
Re-enter password:
Group name: admin
Subject value of client cert: i851675
new entry locally created

Press <RETURN> to continue
```

Figure 13.36 SAP Web Dispatcher: Add User Functionality

6. Next, be sure to save the file using the s menu option. This will write the file out to the file system. After you've written the file, you can use the q functionality to quit the utility and go back to your shell (Figure 13.37).

```
Maintain authentication file: icmauth
=========================================

    a - add user to set
    c - change passwd of existing user in set
    g - change group of existing user in set
    x - change client cert data of existing user in set
    d - delete user from set
    l - list users of set
    s - save changes of set to file
    q - quit (without saving)

--> s
changes saved to file icmauth

Press <RETURN> to continue
```

Figure 13.37 SAP Web Dispatcher: Save File Dialog

7. If you view the file that's created, you can see that the tool took the password (which was *password*) and created a hash (Figure 13.38).

```
wdsadm> more icmauth
# Authentication file for ICM and SAP Web Dispatcher
 authentication
i851675:{SHA384}qLZLq9CsqRpZvbt3YbQh1PK7OCgNOnW6DyHy
vrxFWD1EbFmGYMlM5oDEfRnDB4On:admistrators

wdsadm> ▐
```

Figure 13.38 icmauth File

This is important because we don't want to actually store the password on the filesystem. We want to transmit and compare the hashes so that the password is never transmitted. On the client side, when the password is entered, it's hashed and then sent to the ICM or SAP Web Dispatcher. ICM or SAP Web Dispatcher then compares the hash it received with the hash stored in this file. If they match, access is granted. If not, access is rejected.

General Authfile Guidelines

Any line that begins with a hash (#) is a comment line. It's ignored by the ICM but useful to communicate the intent of entries in your permissions file.

There are several things to keep in mind when using a permissions file:

1. The permission file conditions are evaluated from top to bottom.
2. If one of the conditions for deny or permit is true, the check ends, and the request is permitted or denied by the ICM.
3. If none of the conditions in the permission file are met, the request is denied.
4. The default value of empty entries is *, which permits everything. Because of this, it's important to deny all and permit as needed.

Example Scenario

Now, let's put it all together.

Our authfile, saved at */usr/sap/wd/permfile.txt*, is shown in Table 13.6.

	ICM Path	User	Group	Source	Destination
S	/sap/bc/gui/sap/ its/webgui	*	administrators	10.10.10.0/24	10.10.10.100
S	/sap/bc/gui/sap/ its/	*	administrators	10.10.10.0/24	10.10.10.100
D	/sap/*	*	*	*	*

Table 13.6 Sample Authfile

Our permfile is as created in Figure 13.38. It's also saved at */usr/sap/wd/icmauth.txt*.

Therefore, our ICM/SAP Web Dispatcher parameter would look like this:

```
icm/HTTP/auth_00 = PREFIX=/, PERMFILE=/usr/sap/wd/permfile.txt, AUTHFILE=/usr/
sap/wd/icmauth.txt
```

The goal of this example is to deny access to SAP GUI. Only secure (SSL/TLS) access is granted to the ICM path /sap/bc/gui/sap/its/webgui, and only for the administrators group, which must be in the 10.10.10.0/24 subnet, and only on the server at IP 10.10.10.100.

13.4   SAP Web Dispatcher

SAP Web Dispatcher is an intelligent software load balancer. In its most simple form, SAP Web Dispatcher takes HTTP or HTTPS requests from users and load-balances them to ABAP application servers. You might notice that the ICM and the SAP Web Dispatcher seem very similar. That's because they share a common code base. The primary difference between the two is that the ICM passes its request off to local work processes to execute code and return an HTTP response back through the ICM. SAP Web Dispatcher, on the other hand, will take a request and distribute it to an ABAP application server. From there, the ICM on that application server will handle the request and assign it a work process. See Figure 13.39 for the overall architecture. As discussed in the previous section, parameters for the ICM often also will apply to SAP Web Dispatcher.

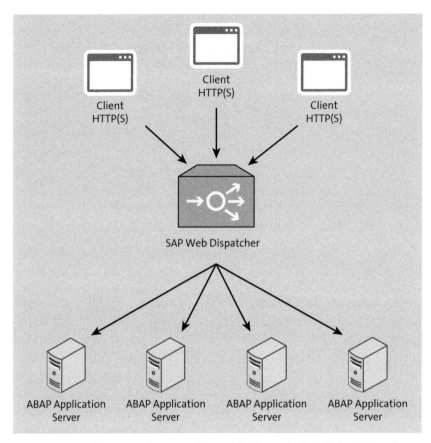

Figure 13.39 Architecture Diagram of SAP Web Dispatcher's Role in SAP Landscape

SAP Web Dispatcher is recommended when your SAP system has multiple applica-tion servers that you'd like to load-balance HTTP/HTTPS connection among. SAP Web Dispatcher works for ABAP systems, Java systems, and dual ABAP/Java stack sys-tems. SAP Web Dispatcher is also a good choice for Internet communication because it limits the attack area that potential adversaries can exploit. SAP Web Dispatcher is simple, which makes it easier to protect.

SAP Web Dispatcher is commonly used for the following functions:

- Selection of appropriate application server—which includes persistence with stateful applications and load balancing.

- SSL forwarding, termination, and decrypt/(re)encrypt.

- URL filtering, to define URLs in a file that you want to be rejected, and by doing so restrict access to your system.

- Configuration for load balancing to multiple systems: SAP Web Dispatcher can be placed in front of multiple SAP systems, and configured to route requests to different systems. SAP Web Dispatcher can also perform load-balancing across system boundaries.

- Web caching to improve response times.

- URL rewriting, including manipulation of HTTP header fields: SAP Web Dispatcher can manipulate inbound HTTP requests in general using predefined rules.

There are two main advantages to using SAP Web Dispatcher in your landscape: first, it can connect to the ABAP message server and determine the system load. Not many load balancers have this ability. Second, it can be deployed with no license cost.

The downside to SAP Web Dispatcher is that it's software-only. In situations in which excessive load may occur, several large, dedicated, hardware load balancers may be appropriate.

Hardware Load Balancers

Many types of hardware-based load balancers exist. They will all work with an SAP ABAP system. Hardware load balancers are often placed in front of web dispatchers to add hardware load balancing and accomplish redundancy between two web dispatchers. In this configuration, you've got the best of both worlds: message server load awareness and integration due to the web dispatchers and hardware load-balancing performance.

13.4.1   Initial Configuration of SAP Web Dispatcher

SAP Web Dispatcher configuration is simple. There are only three configuration parameters that must be set. One of the greatest features of SAP Web Dispatcher is that once it's connected to the ABAP message server, it can read the SAP system configuration and set itself up automatically.

The three parameters in Table 13.7 are the minimum required to get SAP Web Dispatcher running, but it's important to properly set up authentication and security also. Consult the installation and configuration guides on SAP Support Portal for more information about the day-to-day operation of SAP Web Dispatcher.

Parameter	Description
`icm/server_port_ <xx>`	Port on which HTTP/HTTPS requests are to be received
`rdisp/mshost`	Hostname of SAP message server
`ms/http_port` or `wdisp/system_ <xx>`	HTTP port of SAP message server

Table 13.7 Required Parameters for SAP Web Dispatcher Operation

Parameters

Parameters in SAP Web Dispatcher are set in the default parameters directory, which can be reached by the alias cdpro. This is identical to how parameter files are managed in SAP NetWeaver AS ABAP (Figure 13.40).

```
wdsadm> cdpro

wdsadm> pwd && ls -alt
/usr/sap/WDS/SYS/profile
total 20
drwxr-xr-x 2 wdsadm sapsys 4096 Jun 11  2017 .
-rw-r--r-- 1 wdsadm sapsys  471 Jun 11  2017 dev_rfc.trc
-rw-r--r-- 1 wdsadm sapsys 1863 Jun 11  2017 WDS_W00_sap-wd
-rw-r--r-- 1 wdsadm sapsys   74 Jun 11  2017 DEFAULT.PFL
drwxr-xr-x 5 wdsadm sapsys 4096 Jun 11  2017 ..

wdsadm> ▌
```

Figure 13.40 Parameter Directory for SAP Web Dispatcher

SAP Web Dispatcher's day-to-day management occurs in the SAP Web Dispatcher Administration console (see Figure 13.41).

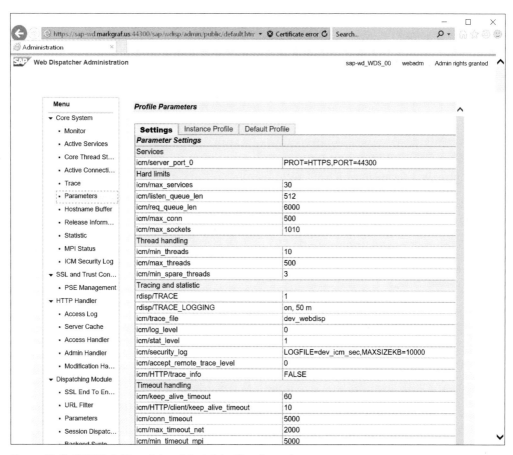

Figure 13.41 SAP Web Dispatcher Administration Console

Securing the Administration Console

It's imperative that the system administrator secures the Administration console of SAP Web Dispatcher. There are a variety of methods to do so. The best is configuring certificate logon using an authfile (Section 13.3.5).

Encryption of the Administrative Console

We recommend using HTTPS for administration. If you use HTTP, the administrator passwords are transferred unencrypted and can therefore be listened to. It's best to work with client certificates.

13.4.2 SSL with SAP Web Dispatcher

There are two SSL scenarios that SAP Web Dispatcher supports, along with SSL for its own administrative interface.

SSL Termination

In an SSL termination scenario, the SSL-secured connection is decrypted at SAP Web Dispatcher. A second call (which may be either unencrypted or encrypted) is made from SAP Web Dispatcher to the ABAP application server. The following steps illustrate the process in which SSL termination is setup.

1. Install CommonCryptoLib on SAP Web Dispatcher (see Chapter 5).

2. Create the SAP Web Dispatcher PSE and your cert request.

   The command to generate a CSR is as follows:

   ```
   sapgenpse get_pse <additional_options> -p <PSE_Name> -r <cert_req_file_
   name> -x <PIN> <Distinguished_Name>
   ```

   For example:

   ```
   sapgenpse get_pse -p SAPSSLS.pse -x yourpin -r certreq.req "CN=
   host123.mycompany.com, OU= MyCompany, OU=SAP Web AS, O=mycompany, C=US"
   ```

   You'll notice that this procedure is nearly identical as that for SAP NetWeaver AS ABAP. Again, the reason is that the ICM is nearly identical for SAP Web Dispatcher.

3. Once you've received your signed certificate from the CA, you can import it with the following command:

   ```
   sapgenpse import_own_cert <Additional_options> -p <PSE_file> -c <Cert_file>
   [-r <RootCA_cert_file>] -x <PIN>
   ```

   For example:

   ```
   sapgenpse import_own_cert -c mycert.cer -p SAPSSLS.pse -r rootCert.cer -x
   yourpin
   ```

   Notice you need to import the public root cert as well. The reason for this is that the chain of trust must be intact for the cert to be valid. Once you've imported the certificates, you should be able to test SSL by going to the SSL port of SAP Web Dispatcher: *https://<hostname>:<ssl port>/sap/wdisp/admin/public/default.html*.

End-to-End SSL

In an end-to-end encryption scenario, SAP Web Dispatcher will forward the HTTPS request directly to the ABAP application server without decrypting it.

Why would you use one scenario over the other? Encryption in environments with heavy user load can cause significant hardware workload. It may be prudent to separate this workload from the ABAP server to a web dispatcher. In other situations, regulations may require that the SSL connection is encrypted all the way to the application server. This choice will be dependent on the desired outcome of load balancing.

Implementing end-to-end SSL is simple. Set the following parameter in the SAP Web Dispatcher profile:

```
icm/server_port_<xx> = PROT=ROUTER, PORT=<port>, TIMEOUT=<timeout_in_seconds>
```

No PSE or trust setup is required because SAP Web Dispatcher will forward SSL requests to the target system.

13.5 Summary

In this chapter, you learned the basics of encryption. From there, you learned about encryption keys, ciphers, and how they're used verify and encrypt data between two parties. We talked about symmetric encryption and its primary use to keep data private between two parties. You also learned about asymmetric encryption and its use to verify identity and establish an encrypted channel. From there, you learned that asymmetric encryption is used to establish trust and to exchange keys, then symmetric encryption is used.

We discussed SAP NetWeaver AS ABAP's adaptation of SSL/TLS and how it uses the CommonCryptoLib to establish encrypted sessions between clients and servers. You learned about Transaction STRUST and the PSEs, the building blocks of SSL/TLS configuration. Certificates and the trust chain came next, and you learned how they're validated using data within the PSE. Finally, you learned about the parameters required and how to set them to configure the ICM for SSL/TLS. Finally, we talked about SAP Web Dispatcher and how to set it up for both SSL/TLS and end-to-end SSL.

In the next chapter we'll learn about securing the database, both on the access level and on the physical level. Database security is important to a security administrator because the compromise of the database can expose all application data to an attacker.

Chapter 14

Database Security

Before reading this chapter, you need to know the basics of network security (Chapter 12), encryption (Chapter 13), and patching (Chapter 9).

The database of an SAP system contains a wealth of sensitive information. Although the primary point of access for SAP applications is through the UI using an application server, it's possible with enough knowledge to extract sensitive data directly from an unprotected database.

Databases are commonly overlooked for security hardening: few administrators consider the risks of database compromise because it's a very technical attack vector. You must be intimately familiar with SAP to know it's database structure and vulnerabilities. You also must have access to the network or access to the OS level of the database server in order to perform an attack. These attack surfaces are usually secured as a first step. However, if for some reason they are not secured, they're an ideal way for an attacker to get into your database.

Due to exploit framework tools like Metasploit, performing complex attacks on proprietary databases has become a simple click-through process. These tools give a wealth of ability and complex knowledge to relatively inexperienced users. For this reason, we must do everything we can to lock down the database as securely as possible because of the ease of these tools' use.

There are a few reasons that databases are common targets for malicious users:

- **Corporate espionage**
  The database of an SAP system holds all the company's data, from production schedules to parts lists, technical diagrams, customer and vendor data, and financial information. It's very important to protect this information from bad actors. At the database level, this data exists and can be accessed with the right knowledge and an administrative level of access.

- **Fraud**
  Malicious users could introduce data into the system at the database level that creates or modifies sales orders or purchase orders, changes bank account numbers, or alters finical statements to hide illicit activity.

- **Disruption**
  A malicious user with database access could destroy or corrupt data, preventing the organization from doing businesses entirely.

For these reasons, it's important to take database hardening into account when designing a security strategy for your organization. The database is often forgotten when it comes to security, and as you can see, it's a critical part of the system.

14.1   Platform-Independent Database Considerations

SAP NetWeaver AS ABAP runs on several databases produced by different database vendors, including SAP itself. Each of these databases have slightly different procedures for operation and security, but the general concepts are all the same. In this chapter, we'll cover some of the most popular databases, but keep in mind that procedures may vary from release to release and from vendor to vendor for both the database itself and the OS the database and application servers run on.

The following sections contains recommendations that apply to all databases that run SAP NetWeaver AS ABAP, regardless of the OS or vendor.

14.1.1   Database Patching

This is very simple: stay patched. It's easy to forget that the database and database client need regular patching. The database client is the software layer in which SAP NetWeaver AS ABAP interacts with the database itself. It's important to stay on a current supported version. The database software itself will require regular patching to stay up to date. Always be sure to consult the proper SAP Note for your database release and the PAM when considering upgrades. Always follow the latest security SAP Notes and implement all relevant ones. See Chapter 9 for more information about security SAP Notes.

In addition, it's important to keep your database client up to date on each of your application servers. The database client runs on each application server and contains the executables needed to allow the application server to initiate and use a connection to the database. Each database vendor will maintain a client for its database and it's important to keep it up to date.

> **Database Client**
>
> Be certain to stop the application server before upgrading the database client. Failure to do so could cause data integrity issues within your database!

14.1.2   Networking

When considering networking, keep in mind that database and application servers generally should be kept in the same network within your landscape. We refer to this as the *secure cell* concept. Within this cell, don't allow connections to your database from anything other than known application servers. Why? If an attacker can initiate a denial-of-service attack from a malicious appserver, preventing the attacker's access could help prevent this. Also, close any unneeded ports between the corporate network and your database systems, as well as unneeded ports between application servers and the database.

Typically, there's no need to have a connection from the end user directly to the database. If you've determined that this is the case, don't allow connections from your corporate network to the database. Think about it this way: if a malicious user gains physical access to your network by breaking into the lobby of your building and plugging into your network via a network jack, she shouldn't be able to have access to your database.

Don't forget about interdatabase communications. Some databases utilize a multiple-node architecture and use internal ports to communicate. Again, attackers can attempt to create their own malicious nodes that can utilize this communications channel to compromise the database. Only allow communications on the port and network level that you know and trust.

Creating a closed architecture that only allows for communications between known hosts is a significant asset to your security measures. It may be more difficult to add new hosts to your landscape, but it'll help fight anyone who attempts to add malicious hosts.

14

14.1.3   User Accounts

It's important to recognize that all database systems have a user account concept that needs to be managed by a system administrator. It's as simple as securing database user accounts that aren't being used and managing the credentials of the user accounts that are required for normal operation.

Don't allow anyone access to the database directly that doesn't need it. Only Basis or database administrators should be allowed access to the database. Pay close attention to the authorizations that users are granted to the database schemas and tables. You should have a good understanding of every user and why they have access levels set to whatever their values are. It's also a good idea to look for users created during upgrades. These users are usually a target of malicious parties.

> **Direct Database Manipulation**
>
> Don't allow anyone except SAP support to manipulate data in the database on the database level. Doing so can void your support contract and may lead to corrupted data that in some cases is unrecoverable.
>
> Whenever possible, only use SAP-provided tools to access the data in the database.

Database Password Changes

Actively manage any database credentials and change passwords regularly in a safe manner. A common pitfall for the administrator is changing a database password that results in downtime. After the downtime, an organization will alter or eliminate the need to change passwords for a database, which is a terrible idea. The security administrator needs to walk the line between keeping the system highly available and regularly introducing password changes. Create a solid, technically well-thought-out and well-tested plan to make sure that important passwords are changed with limited disruption to the business applications' availability.

> **SAP Recommendation: DB Password**
>
> SAP strongly recommends that you change the default password for database users. Your database users may be SAPR3, SAP<SID>, or SAPABAP1. Check which database user the application server is using by executing R3trans -d and reviewing the trans.log file. Be sure to disable any unneeded accounts.

Sensitive Tables

SAP recommends that you do not grant any access for other database users to the following tables:

- Table USR*

- Table T000 (no write access)

- General tables (such as table SAPUSER or RFCDES) or application-specific tables (such as tables PA* or HCL*)

In general, you should avoid storing data that other database users need to access within your SAP database. A separate database or container would be a better approach.

14.1.4   Database Backups

In many cases, a database backup is a literal copy of your entire database. If obtained by a malicious party, it will contain all the confidential data that you're protecting within your database. Don't underestimate the risk of physical theft of a disk or backup media. For this reason, it's crucial to protect your backups from being compromised both physically and over a network. Often, many organizations overlook the threat related to backups. The following topics should be considered when designing your backup strategy.

- **Encrypt**
  Always encrypt your backups. You should be able to obtain access to the file physically and still not be able to access the data without a proper encryption key. Many database vendors, storage vendors, and OS vendors offer mechanisms to encrypt data. We highly recommend encrypting both in transit and at rest.

- **Store**
  Be sure to store redundant copies of your encrypted database backup. Preventing disruption by sabotage is a good security practice. Be sure to enforce a strong data storage security policy for each copy of your backups. If you store two copies of your backups using military-grade encryption in a secure bunker, but your third copy sits on a USB drive at your desk in a lightly monitored office building, you're still at risk of having your data compromised.

- **Test**
  Testing your database backups by a restoration activity is always a good practice. It will help prove your disaster-recovery procedures, as well as prove that you can

recover from a malicious activity that threatens the integrity of your data. It's also a prudent practice to do negative testing. Test that given a physical copy of the database, it's not possible to decrypt it and gain access to its unencrypted data.

14.1.5   Additional DB Functionality

Each database certified for SAP NetWeaver AS ABAP features extended functionality that isn't required to run the system. This functionality can be useful but is also an additional attack vector for potential attackers. We recommend tightening security on these features or, better yet, disabling them completely if they're not being used.

SAP HANA XS Application Server

SAP HANA XS application server is a very powerful tool for utilizing the SAP HANA database without a full SAP NetWeaver system. It's important to secure it if it isn't being used.

We recommend configuring SSL for all communications. We also recommend forcing the use of SSL.

> **SSL Encryption for SAP HANA XS**
>
> To enable SSL encryption for SAP HANA XS, consult SAP Note 2300943.

Be sure to review SAP HANA XS features, like SAP HANA user self-service. This service is turned off by default. If turned on, the request account functionality and the forgot password functionality can both be used to potentially break into the system. At the very least, only allow trusted hosts or networks to access this service. These types of services can be very useful but pose a threat if they are left wide open to an entire network or the Internet. When evaluating services, it's best to use the same approach used with the ABAP ICM: only activate services you're going to use.

Management Consoles

Don't forget management consoles, like SAP HANA Cockpit, Oracle Enterprise Manager, or SQL Server Management Studio. Leaving these open or with default credentials may lead an attacker to have full control over the database. Just because a system administrator doesn't use these tools doesn't mean that they aren't exploitable. Be sure to secure them against unauthorized use as per the database vendor's recommendations.

14.2 Securing the Database Connection

The database connection is a critical part of the client/server architecture. Each SAP NetWeaver application server must be connected to the database. In connecting, credentials must be passed from the application server to the database to authenticate the system user that the application server uses to do its work. Each ABAP work process connects to the database and manipulates data. Because of this architecture, a security administrator must take steps to secure this connection.

14.2.1 Understanding the Database Connect Sequence

When connecting to the database, the application server will use stored credentials to submit to the database. This sequence can be observed by running the R3trans tool.

The following command will print connection details to the trans.log file (Figure 14.1):

```
R3trans -v
```

```
4 ETW000 R3trans version 6.25 (release 745 - 04.09.15 - 20:15:09).
4 ETW000 unicode enabled version
4 ETW000 ===========================================================
4 ETW000
4 ETW000 date&time    : 14.04.2018 - 09:13:50
4 ETW000 control file: <no ctrlfile>
4 ETW000 R3trans was called as follows: R3trans -d
4 ETW000  trace at level 1 opened for a given file pointer
4 ETW000 [     dev trc,00000]  Sat Apr 14 09:13:50 2018
4 ETW000 [     dev trc,00000]  Loading DB library '/usr/sap/JDM/SYS/exe/run/dbhdbslib.so' ...
4 ETW000 [     dev trc,00000]  Library '/usr/sap/JDM/SYS/exe/run/dbhdbslib.so' loaded
4 ETW000 [     dev trc,00000]  Version of '/usr/sap/JDM/SYS/exe/run/dbhdbslib.so' is "745.04", patchlevel (0.13)
4 ETW000 [     dev trc,00000]  switch DBSL TRACE LEVEL from 3 to 1
4 ETW000 [     dev trc,00000]  DBHDBSLIB : version 745.04, patch 0.013 (Make PL 0.15)
4 ETW000 [     dev trc,00000]  HDB shared library (dbhdbslib) patchlevels (last 10)
4 ETW000 [     dev trc,00000]    (0.013) Use connection variables instead of table M_CONNECTIONS (note 2207349)
4 ETW000 [     dev trc,00000]    (0.008) Session variables processing via dbsl (note 2182777)
4 ETW000 [     dev trc,00000]    (0.005) Substitute literals in select list (note 2182777)
4 ETW000 [     dev trc,00000]    (0.004) Cancel FDA SQL statement (note 2177669)
4 ETW000 [     dev trc,00000]
4 ETW000 [     dev trc,00000]  Loading SQLDBC client runtime ...
4 ETW000 [     dev trc,00000]  SQLDBC Module  : /usr/sap/JDM/hdbclient/libSQLDBCHDB.so
4 ETW000 [     dev trc,00000]  SQLDBC Runtime : libSQLDBCHDB 1.00.097.00 Build 1434028111-1530
4 ETW000 [     dev trc,00000]  SQLDBC client runtime is 1.00.097.00.1434028111
4 ETW000 [     dev trc,00000]  Try to connect via secure store (DEFAULT) on connection 0 ...
4 ETW000 [     dev trc,00000]  Sat Apr 14 09:13:51 2018
4 ETW000 [     dev trc,00000]  Attach to HDB : 1.00.102.02.1446663129 (fa/newdb100_maint_rel)
4 ETW000 [     dev trc,00000]  fa/newdb100_maint_rel : build_weekstone=0000.00.0
4 ETW000 [     dev trc,00000]  fa/newdb100_maint_rel : build_time=2015-11-04 20:04:49
4 ETW000 [     dev trc,00000]  Database release is HDB 1.00.102.02.1446663129
4 ETW000 [     dev trc,00000]  INFO : Database 'HDB/00' instance is running on 'sap-db'
4 ETW000 [     dev trc,00000]  INFO : Connect to DB as 'SAPABAP1', connection_id=200038
4 ETW000 [     dev trc,00000]  INFO : set parameter for SQLSCRIPT, Enable_Select_Into_Scalar_UDF
4 ETW000 [     dev trc,00000]  INFO : DATA AGING feature is supported by HANA
4 ETW000 [     dev trc,00000]  INFO : FDA feature is supported by HANA
4 ETW000 [     dev trc,00000]  INFO : FAE with FDA feature is supported by HANA
4 ETW000 [     dev trc,00000]  INFO : DEFERRED LOB WRITING is activated
4 ETW000 [     dev trc,00000]  DB max. input host variables  : 32767
4 ETW000 [     dev trc,00000]  DB max. statement length      : 1000000000
4 ETW000 [     dev trc,00000]  DB max. array size            : 100000
4 ETW000 [     dev trc,00000]  use decimal precision as length
4 ETW000 [     dev trc,00000]  ABAPVARCHARMODE is used
4 ETW000 [     dev trc,00000]  use DBSL marker map
4 ETW000 [     dev trc,00000]  use DBSL session variable handling
4 ETW000 [     dev trc,00000]  INFO : DBSL buffer size = 1048576
4 ETW000 [     dev trc,00000]  Command info enabled
4 ETW000 [     dev trc,00000]  Now I'm connected to HDB
4 ETW000 [     dev trc,00000]  00: sap-db-HDB/00, since=20180414091350, ABAP= <unknown> (0)
4 ETW000 [     dev trc,00000]  Connection 0 opened (DBSL handle 0)
4 ETW000 [     dev trc,00000]  INFO : SAP RELEASE (DB) = 750
4 ETW000 [     dev trc,00000]  NTAB: Structure of NTAB on DB is VERS_B, unicodelg of executable is 2, unicodelg c
4 ETW000 Connected to DBMS = HDB ---  SERVER = '' PORT = '' --- SYSTEM = 'JDM'.
```

Figure 14.1 R3trans Log File

> **R3trans Output May Vary**
>
> The output of R3trans may be slightly different depending on the database you're using. The output in these figures is on an SAP HANA system. Because each database will use its own client, it may connect differently.

Note the following line:

```
Try to connect via secure store (DEFAULT) on connection 0 ...
```

This is where the database client is attempting to connect to the database using the secure store credentials.

And this line:

```
Now I'm connected to HDB
```

This line indicates a successful connection to the SAP HANA database.

In the event of an issue with credentials, the failure will be several lines below the Try to connect line. You shouldn't see the Now I'm connected to HDB.

The connection process is also observable in the work process logs (Figure 14.2) when the system is starting up. Remember that each work process will initiate its own connection to the database.

From this log, you can observe some of the same information that R3trans tells you. First, the system is using credentials from the secure store to connect. Second, you've successfully connected when you see the same Now I'm connected to HDB entry.

R3trans is a critical tool for a system administrator to utilize during database issues. For a security administrator, it gives you the ability to test a password change and the authentication mechanism before attempting to start the system.

Finally, it's very important to test any changes to database authentication on each application server in your system. Changes to the database password need to be made on every application server and tested before attempting to start your system.

```
M Thu Mar 29 22:39:15 2018
M  kernel runs with dp version 253000(ext=117000) (@(#) DPLIB-INT-VERSION-0+253000-UC)
M  length of sys_adm_ext is 500 bytes
M  ThStart: taskhandler started
M  ThInit: initializing DIA work process W1
X  MMX: use precise segment size globally
M  ThStopHeapLockChecker: stop heap lock checker
M  ***LOG Q01=> ThInit, WPStart (Workp. 1 1 10310) [thxxhead.c   1077]
M
M Thu Mar 29 22:39:18 2018
M  ThInit: running on host sap-ci
I  MtxInit: 1 0 0
M  calling db_connect ...
B  Loading DB library '/usr/sap/JDM/D01/exe/dbhdbslib.so' ...
B  Library '/usr/sap/JDM/D01/exe/dbhdbslib.so' loaded
B  Version of '/usr/sap/JDM/D01/exe/dbhdbslib.so' is "745.04", patchlevel (0.13)
C  Callback functions for dynamic profile parameter registered
C
C  DBHDBSLIB : version 745.04, patch 0.013 (Make PL 0.15)
C  HDB shared library (dbhdbslib) patchlevels (last 10)
C    (0.013) Use connection variables instead of table M_CONNECTIONS (note 2207349)
C    (0.008) Session variables processing via dbsl (note 2182777)
C    (0.005) Substitute literals in select list (note 2182777)
C    (0.004) Cancel FDA SQL statement (note 2177669)
C
C
C  Loading SQLDBC client runtime ...
C  SQLDBC Module  : /usr/sap/JDM/hdbclient/libSQLDBCHDB.so
C  SQLDBC Runtime : libSQLDBCHDB 1.00.097.00 Build 1434028111-1530
C  SQLDBC client runtime is 1.00.097.00.1434028111
C
C  Try to connect via secure store (DEFAULT) on connection 0 ...
C
C Thu Mar 29 22:39:19 2018
C  Attach to HDB : 1.00.102.02.1446663129 (fa/newdb100_maint_rel)
C  fa/newdb100_maint_rel : build_weekstone=0000.00.0
C  fa/newdb100_maint_rel : build_time=2015-11-04 20:04:49
C  Database release is HDB 1.00.102.02.1446663129
C  INFO : Database 'HDB/00' instance is running on 'sap-db'
C  INFO : Connect to DB as 'SAPABAP1', connection_id=200067
C  INFO : DATA AGING feature is supported by HANA
C  INFO : FDA feature is supported by HANA
C  INFO : FAE with FDA feature is supported by HANA
C  INFO : DEFERRED LOB WRITING is activated
C  DB max. input host variables  : 32767
C  DB max. statement length      : 104857600
C  DB max. array size            : 100000
C  use decimal precision as length
C  ABAPVARCHARMODE is used
C  use DBSL marker map
C  use DBSL session variable handling
C  INFO : DBSL buffer size = 1048576
C  Command info enabled
C  Now I'm connected to HDB
C  00: sap-db-HDB/00, since=20180329223918, ABAP= <unknown> (0)
B  Connection 0 opened (DBSL handle 0)
```

Figure 14.2 Work Process Log when Connecting to Database

14.2.2 SAP HANA Database: HDB User Store

The SAP HANA database uses a mechanism called the HDB User Store to authenticate to the database. Credentials are saved in an encrypted data file that's saved on the OS level of each application server. These credentials are evaluated by the SAP HANA database when the user attempts a login.

Changing the Database Password: SAP HANA Database

Changing the database password is a simple procedure on the database side.

1. Stop your SAP instance.
2. Open SAP HANA Studio.
3. Connect to the database you'd like to change the password for.
4. Open the SQL Console for the system you'd like to change the password for.
5. Issue the following command:

   Alter user SAPABAP1 password <password>;

   Where <password> is the new password (Figure 14.3).

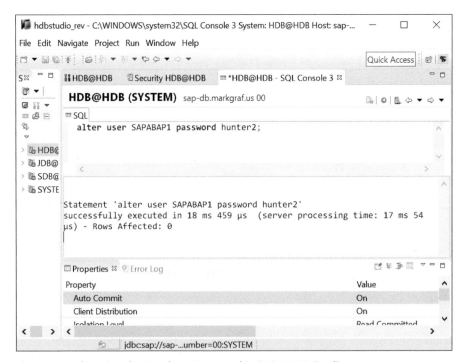

Figure 14.3 Changing the Database Password in SAP HANA Studio

This can also be accomplished using the hdbsql command line utility. Consult the SAP HANA documentation for instructions on how to use this tool.

If you run R3trans on an application server at this point, you'll see the failure shown in Figure 14.4 in the trans.log file.

```
switch DBSL TRACE LEVEL from 3 to 1
DBHDBSLIB : version 745.04, patch 0.013 (Make PL 0.15)
HDB shared library (dbhdbslib) patchlevels (last 10)
   (0.013) Use connection variables instead of table M_CONNECTIONS (note 22073

   (0.008) Session variables processing via dbsl (note 2182777)
   (0.005) Substitute literals in select list (note 2182777)
   (0.004) Cancel FDA SQL statement (note 2177669)

Loading SQLDBC client runtime ...
Sat Apr 14 13:28:22 2018
SQLDBC Module  : /usr/sap/JDM/hdbclient/libSQLDBCHDB.so
SQLDBC Runtime : libSQLDBCHDB 1.00.097.00 Build 1434028111-1530
SQLDBC client runtime is 1.00.097.00.1434028111
Try to connect via secure store (DEFAULT) on connection 0 ...
*** ERROR => Connect to database failed, rc=1, rcSQL=10
SQLCODE    : 10
SQLERRTEXT : authentication failed
***LOG BY2=>sql error 10      performing CON
***LOG BY0=>authentication failed
DBMS = HDB                              --- SERVER = '' PORT = '''"
```

Figure 14.4 R3trans Failure

The next step in the password change process is to change the password on your application servers.

DB Credentials on the Application Server: HDB

The tool in which database credentials are managed is called HDB User Store. The HDB User Store will store connection information securely on the OS level in an encrypted format. It's important that the security administrator protect the OS access to your data and key files. These files hold the credentials that are used to connect to the SAP HANA database.

A list of the credentials on your application server can be returned with the following command (see Figure 14.5):

```
hdbuserstore LIST
```

In the example in Figure 14.5, you can see that the user on your SAP NetWeaver AS ABAP system is named SAPABAP1. The file located at */home/<sidadm>/.hdb/<hostname>/SSFS_HDB.DAT* contains the encrypted password for the database. Even though the file is encrypted, it's important to keep it secure. Make sure the permissions for the file are properly set and that it isn't accessible by users other than <SIDADM>. Also make a note of the environment (env) value; it's the fully qualified domain name (FQDN) and port for your SAP HANA database.

```
sap-ci:jdmadm 57> hdbuserstore LIST
DATA FILE        : /home/jdmadm/.hdb/sap-ci/SSFS_HDB.DAT

KEY DEFAULT
  ENV : sap-db.markgraf.us:30015
  USER: SAPABAP1
```

Figure 14.5 HDB User Store

To change the password, issue the following command (Figure 14.6):

```
hdbuserstore -i SET DEFAULT <hostname>:3<instance Number>15 <user>
```

Changing Database Password

When changing the database password, you must be sure to update it on each application server. Failure to do so will cause that application server not to start and may lock the database user, preventing all other application servers from functioning.

```
sap-ci:jdmadm 61> hdbuserstore -i set DEFAULT sap-db.markgraf.us:30015 SAPABAP1
Password:
sap-ci:jdmadm 62> R3trans -d
This is R3trans version 6.25 (release 745 - 04.09.15 - 20:15:09).
unicode enabled version
R3trans finished (0000).
sap-ci:jdmadm 63>
```

Figure 14.6 Changing HDB Password on Appserver

14.2.3   Oracle Database: Secure Storage in File System

Secure Storage in File System (SSFS) is the method by which an SAP NetWeaver AS ABAP-based system connects to its Oracle database. In the past, SAP has used an OPS$ remote connection procedure that allowed the ABAP work processes to connect to the database to retrieve an encrypted database password, which allowed them to login to the database for productive work. Because it relies on the host OS's authorization mechanism, this method has been discontinued.

The new database connection method is called *Secure Store Connect*. It's supported on all SAP NetWeaver AS ABAP 7.x systems. The SSFS mechanism can be used for several databases, including Oracle, SAP HANA, SAP MaxDB, and Sybase ASE.

Oracle Database Connections

SAP recommends that you use the newer method for security reasons. If you need to transition from the old method to the new SSFS method, follow the steps in SAP Note 1622837.

Changing the Database Password: Oracle

BR*Tools is the SAP-provided toolset to manage Oracle databases. We advise that the administrator use BR*Tools to manage the database. The following procedure will change the Oracle database password:

1. Execute the following BR*Connect command to change the database password for the SAPSR3 user (see Figure 14.7):

   ```
   brconnect -u / -f chpass -o sapsr3 -p <password>
   ```

```
ora-db:oraadm 23> brconnect -u / -f chpass -o sapsr3 -p hunter2000
BR0801I BRCONNECT 7.40 (33)
BR0280I BRCONNECT time stamp: 2018-04-15 13:16:55
BR0828I Changing password for database user SAPSR3 ...
BR0256I Enter 'c[ont]' to continue, 's[top]' to cancel BRCONNECT:
c
BR0280I BRCONNECT time stamp: 2018-04-15 13:17:02
BR0257I Your reply: 'c'
BR0259I Program execution will be continued...

BR0280I BRCONNECT time stamp: 2018-04-15 13:17:02
BR0829I Password changed successfully in database for user SAPSR3
BR0831I Table SAPUSER not found for user SAPSR3

BR0280I BRCONNECT time stamp: 2018-04-15 13:17:02
BR1525I Setting password for database user SAPSR3 in secure storage /usr/sap/ORA
/SYS/global/security/rsecssfs/data/SSFS_ORA.DAT ...
BR0256I Enter 'c[ont]' to continue, 's[top]' to cancel BRCONNECT:
c
BR0280I BRCONNECT time stamp: 2018-04-15 13:17:11
BR0257I Your reply: 'c'
BR0259I Program execution will be continued...

BR0280I BRCONNECT time stamp: 2018-04-15 13:17:17
BR1526I Password set successfully for database user SAPSR3 in secure storage /usr/sap/ORA/SYS/globa
l/security/rsecssfs/data/SSFS_ORA.DAT

BR0280I BRCONNECT time stamp: 2018-04-15 13:17:17
BR0802I BRCONNECT completed successfully
ora-db:oraadm 24> █
```

Figure 14.7 Changing Database Password Using BR*Tools

2. Be sure to run this command using the `<SIDADM>` user, on the database. Also, be sure that the application is not running.

   As shown in Figure 14.7, BR*Connect executes more than just the password change on the database. It also sets SSFS on the database OS. If this isn't done, scripts and BR*Tools can be broken by a password change.

What about Other Oracle Accounts?

For more info on how to reset other Oracle user passwords, consult SAP Note 562863.

---

3. Next, test on your application server to make sure that the password has been properly changed both on the database and the application server. The procedure to test on the application server is the same as previously covered in Section 14.2.1

   `R3trans -d`

   0000 is a successful return code. Issues can be diagnosed in the trans.log file.

DB Credentials on the Application Server

On the application server, the existence of database credentials can be checked using the following command (see Figure 14.8):

`rsecssfx list`

```
ora-ci:oraadm 40> rsecssfx list
|-----------------------------------------------------------------------------
| Record Key                      | Status               | Time Stamp of Last Update
|-----------------------------------------------------------------------------
| DB_CONNECT/DEFAULT_DB_PASSWORD  | Encrypted            | 2018-04-15  17:56:40  UTC
|-----------------------------------------------------------------------------
| DB_CONNECT/DEFAULT_DB_USER      | Plaintext            | 2018-04-15  17:56:37  UTC
|-----------------------------------------------------------------------------
| SYSTEM_PKI/PIN                  | Encrypted            | 2018-04-15  01:56:34  UTC
|-----------------------------------------------------------------------------
| SYSTEM_PKI/PSE                  | Encrypted (binary)   | 2018-04-15  01:56:40  UTC
|-----------------------------------------------------------------------------

Summary
-------
Active  Records : 4 (Encrypted: 3, Plain: 1, Wrong Key: 0, Error: 0)
Defunct Records : 4 (180+ days: 0; Show: "list -withHistory", Remove: "compact")

ora-ci:oraadm 41> █
```

Figure 14.8 rsecssfx: Display Existing Credentials

We can see both `DEFAULT_DB_PASSWORD` and `DB_USER`. These are the two pieces of information the SAP NetWeaver system uses when attempting to connect to the database using SSFS.

To test if the existing credentials work, simply execute `R3trans -d` and observe both the return code and contents of the logfile, trans.log.

To update the DB password, issue the following command:

```
rsecssfx put DB_CONNECT/DEFAULT_DB_PASSWORD <pwd>
```

If you run the list command, you should see that the timestamp of your key has been updated.

> **More Info about SSFS**
>
> For more information about the SSFS mechanism, consult SAP Note 1639578.

Database Users: Oracle

The Oracle RDBMS software will be preinstalled with standard SAP users, along with several different users that are unique to Oracle. Table 14.1 lists the standard Oracle user accounts.

Login Name	Type
<SAPSID>ADM	OS user
ORA<DBSID>	OS user
SYS (internal)	Database user
SYSTEM	Database user
SAP<SAPSID>	Database users (SAP system)

Table 14.1 Oracle Standard Logons

The <sapsid>adm password is changed at the OS level. For Linux/Unix-based systems, the utility password is used. On Windows, passwords can be changed in the Windows Local Users and Groups Administrative Management Console (MMC). Be sure to adjust the passwords in the running services and restart them.

The ORA<DBSID> user is used for Oracle-specific maintenance. Its password, like the <SAPSID>ADM user's, is changed on the OS level. With both accounts, be sure that passwords are regularly reset and that OS users able to use this account are carefully monitored.

The SYS and SYSTEM users are used by the oracle software during normal database operations. Because of the special nature of this account and its settings, SAP recommends that you only use the BR*Connect tool to reset its password. Although it's technically possible to reset its password in SQLPLUS, there are dependencies that need to be set which are automatically handled in BR*Connect.

The SAP<SAPSID> database user is used for Oracle logon for the system to perform work. This user was formerly responsible for the OPS$ logon mentioned earlier. We recommend changing this user's password through the SAP-supplied BR*Connect application.

> **BR*Tools**
>
> The BR*Connect application is part of the BR*Tools package delivered by SAP. More information can be found about BR*Tools in SAP Note 12741.

14.2.4   Microsoft SQL Server: Authentication

There are two choices in Microsoft SQL Server (MSSQL) for authentication methods:

- **Windows-only authentication**
  This authentication type requires that a user connecting to the database have a Windows account and be validated by the OS. This is the recommended type of connection for an SAP NetWeaver AS ABAP system. This is only valid for Windows application servers.

- **SQL Server and Windows authentication**
  This authentication type allows either Windows OS authentication or a password set in SQL Server. This type of authentication is used when your DB runs on Windows and your application servers are of another OS or if you're running an SAP NetWeaver AS JAVA or dual-stack system. Because of this configuration, anyone who knows the password of the SQL Server login SAP<SAPSID>DB or <sapsid> or sa account can connect interactively to SQL Server. If you don't need this, turn it off.

> **SQL Server and Windows Authentication Mode**
>
> If you require the use of SQL Server and Windows authentication mode, be sure to set a strong Windows password for the sa account.

Changing the Database Password: MSSQL

MSSQL account passwords can be changed by following these steps (see Figure 14.9):

1. In the SQL Server Management Studio, open Object Explorer.
2. Expand the server and **Security**.
3. Expand **Logins**.
4. On the left you'll see a branch of logins defined for the server.

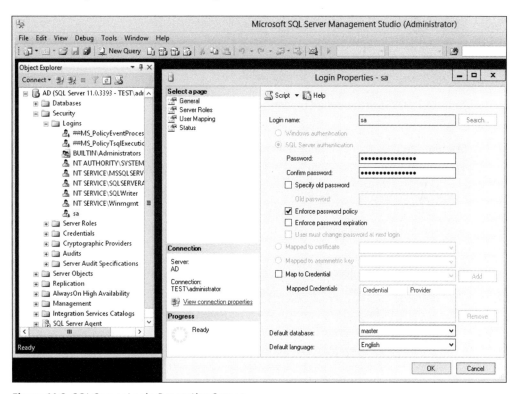

Figure 14.9 SQL Server Login Properties Screen

5. Right-click the login for which you want to change the password and choose **Properties**.

6. The **Login Properties** dialog box opens.

7. On the **General** page, enter a new password for the login you've selected, and confirm the password with **OK**.

It's important to understand that if you're using OS accounts for authentication, they'll authenticate automatically. You don't need to update an application server like you would for an SAP HANA- or Oracle-database-based systems.

Table 14.2 shows the default MSSQL users created at install.

Login Name	Type
SA	SQL Server system administrator
<SAPSID>	SQL Server login for ABAP database user
<SAPSID>ADM	Login for OS account
SAPService<SAPSID>	Login for OS account

Table 14.2 SQL Server Standard Logons

Standard MSSQL Management Users

The following paragraphs will detail the methods used to secure these accounts.

The *SA* user has system administrative privileges for the entire MSSQL server. It isn't needed for SAP NetWeaver AS ABAP standard operations and should not be used. We recommend setting a strong password for this user after installation and then disabling it.

The <SAPSID>ADM account is the main account used by SAP administrators. It should be protected with a strong password.

The <SAPSID>ADM and SAPService<SAPSID> logins have system administrator rights. This means that all systems on the same database are accessible by these accounts. Keep this in mind in an MCOD environment.

The <SAPSID>ADM and SAPService<SAPSID> logins connect to the SQL Server using the Windows authentication mode. Therefore, these accounts should be protected with strong passwords.

Be aware that after changing the password for <SAPSID>ADM and SAPService<SAP-SID>, you also need to specify the new password in the services used for the SAP system and restart these services. These services can be found in the Microsoft Management Console (MMC) services snap-in.

14.3   Logging and Encrypting Your Database

When considering the physical storage of data, you must consider: if an attacker can gain access to data, or the systems that contain it, what can you do to protect it? Database encryption protects the files stored on the database from being read without a proper key file. In some applications, database encryption will also protect database backups from being read or restored without the proper key.

As with any encryption, there are performance implications for the increased workload associated with encryption and decryption. These depend on the RDBMS software and the strength of encryption used. The remedy could be faster or more hardware, or limitation of performance based on the encryption being used. The security administrator must weigh the security advantages against the potential performance hit that database encryption may require. It's also important to understand that the performance effects may vary wildly based on the activity in your system. It's a good idea to benchmark before making any final decisions. One factor to keep in mind is that with SAP HANA data volume encryption, there is no performance loss because the database resides in memory. SAP HANA data volume encryption encrypts only the persistence layer on disk, which isn't read by the application as a part of normal reading/writing.

In addition, logging and auditing features may be required or requested by the business. These requests usually don't consider performance implications. They can be significant, so be sure to weigh this against the potential benefits. It's also a good idea to create a policy to review and delete these logs because they can grow to be many times larger than the database's total size in a matter of weeks or months depending on your system's activity.

Finally, it's a terrible idea to rely on database encryption instead of proper OS and network security techniques. Be certain to secure all other areas of your installation

14

before deciding to attempt a database encryption project. An easily accessible unsecured database that is encrypted is an easy target for any malicious attacker. If they can find a way to access or brute-force the encryption key, they have access to all the data. Good security involves multiple areas of hardening, which makes the task much more difficult for the attacker.

14.3.1   SAP HANA Data Volume Encryption

SAP HANA database encryption will encrypt the pages that the database saves to disk as a part of its persistent storage. Pages that exist in memory as part of normal operation of the database are not encrypted. To activate SAP HANA data volume encryption, follow these steps:

1. Back up your SAP HANA system using the SAP HANA database backup tools.

2. *Optional:* You may wish to format your hard disks and reinstall the SAP HANA database software. This step is not required but may be performed to achieve the maximum level of security possible.

3. Next, you must change your root encryption key. To do so, open the SQL console in SAP HANA Studio and issue the following command (Figure 14.10):

```
ALTER SYSTEM PERSISTENCE ENCRYTPION CREATE NEW ROOT KEY
```

This will create a new root encryption key that is used to encrypt the data written to persistent storage.

Figure 14.10 Creating New Root Encryption Key

4. You will now enable data volume encryption to encrypt your SAP HANA data volume on disk. In SAP HANA Studio, right-click the database you wish to encrypt and select **Security · Open Security Console** (Figure 14.11).

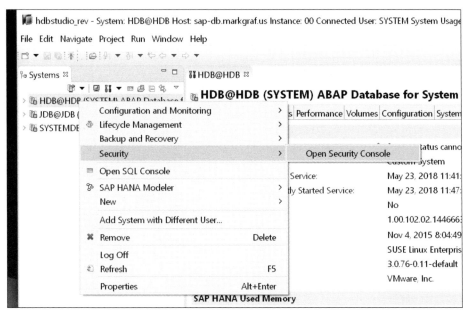

Figure 14.11 Opening Security Console in SAP HANA Studio

5. Check the **Encrypt data volumes** checkbox as shown in Figure 14.12. Next, click the **Save** button on the taskbar.

6. The SAP HANA database will now begin encrypting data. The **Status** column in the security console will show the current status of encryption (Figure 14.13).

7. *Optional*: If you had re-created your database, you will now need to recover your backup. Use the backup and recovery functionality in SAP HANA Studio. As your data is written back to persistent storage, it will be encrypted using the root encryption key.

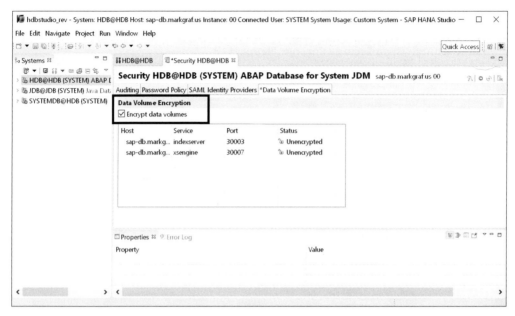

Figure 14.12 Security Console

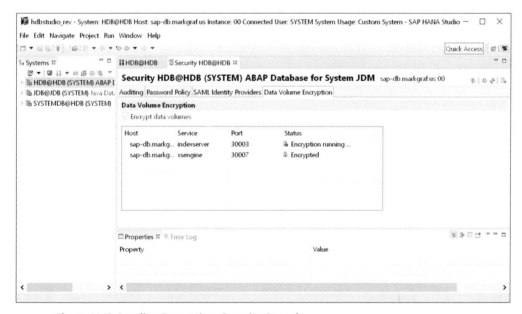

Figure 14.13 Pending Encryption: Security Console

14.3.2 Oracle Transparent Data Encryption

Oracle Transparent Data Encryption (TDE) is an encryption method offered by Oracle to encrypt data files in the database. It is transparent to the application, meaning that the SAP application doesn't need to be aware of the encryption to function. However, tools like BR*Tools and the application and database startup mechanisms need to be adjusted. This process is fairly complex and is best described by the SAP Note 974876.

Oracle TDE stores its encryption keys in an OS-level storage mechanism called the *Oracle Wallet*, which integrates with backup applications and SAP's BR*Tools suite. It's important to back up your Oracle Wallet separate from your database backups. It's also advisable to test your separate backups of the Oracle Wallet because they will be required to restore the database from backup.

In addition, Oracle TDE requires a separate Oracle Advanced Security Option license that can be obtained through SAP.

> **More Info: Oracle Transparent Data Encryption**
>
> For more information about Oracle TDE and SAP NetWeaver, consult SAP Note 974876.

14.3.3 MSSQL Server

Microsoft's offering, SQL TDE, is also available for MSSQL databases. It offers the same type of transparent encryption that's available from both Oracle and SAP.

MSSQL's TDE uses a certificate system to store its keys. It's very important to keep backups of your certificates, but not alongside your database backups.

> **More Info: SQL Server Transparent Data Encryption**
>
> For more information about SQL Server TDE and SAP NetWeaver, consult SAP Note 1380493.

14.4 Summary

In this chapter, you learned about the importance of database security. Most importantly, you learned how attackers may adversely manipulate the database to cause harm or distress to the business. Next, we covered database patching, networking hardening, and unused or inappropriately authorized user accounts. Then, we discussed sensitive tables, backups, and additional database functionality that may need to be hardened.

The second section of the chapter covered securing the database connection. This primarily centered on changing the password of the main database users both on the database side and the application server side. You learned that you must change passwords on all application servers that connect to the database. You also learned about transparent data encryption and its role in keeping our at-rest data safe, both on the OS and in our backups.

In the next chapter, you will learn about infrastructure security. This is important to understand because it's often within the security administrator's responsibility to make sure that each critical portion of the SAP system is protected against attack in order to limit exposure and risk.

Chapter 15
Infrastructure Security

Before reading this chapter, you need to be familiar with common IT infrastructure, such as networking, hypervisors, and OSs.

In reading this book, a security administrator may think: There's a lot of information here. Where do I begin? The best place to start is with a thorough evaluation of your business systems. First, we must define what a business system is. A *business system* can be defined as all parts or components required to operate the business functionality being used. For example, if the SAP product being used by the business is SAP S/4HANA, then the SAP S/4HANA software, roles, user accounts, architecture, SAP NetWeaver layer, OS, database, policies, network, hypervisors, physical servers, and so on make up the entire business system.

Critical business systems require a higher level of security and it's important to separate them from normal corporate devices, systems, and users. Always keep in mind that a business system is more than just the SAP installation itself. Attackers will be focused on getting into business systems by any means necessary, and the weakest part of your business system will be the easiest place for an attack to occur.

Because the corporate network is a significant attack vector, we tend to think in terms of networking when evaluating our business systems from a security perspective. This makes logical sense because it's the easiest way to group our business systems. However, don't let this move your focus away from parts of your business system that are not part of the network.

As you read this chapter, you will find that its focus touches all parts of a typical business system. When performing planning around security, make sure you are focusing broadly. When you conceptualize your design, review it from all angles to make sure you haven't left anything out. As vulnerabilities are discovered in the wild, evaluate your design against those vulnerabilities. If an attacker had gained access to your system, or a part of your system, would your business be at risk due to that vulnerability?

Finally, many security administrators will inherit a business system that was previously set up and may have been operating for many years. It may or may not be secure by today's standards. Going forward, it's important to map out the entirety of the business system as it exists. Then, review that system and look for gaps. Prioritizing and classifying the risk of the discovered gaps comes next. This could take a day, or a year, depending on the situation. Don't underestimate the task. Planning and implementation is the final step in taking in an existing business system. Operate slowly and carefully, step by step, until you've mitigated all that you've classified as a risk to the business. Again, this could take a significant amount of time.

Once you have established a secure business system, the daily tasks of a security administrator move to more of a maintenance mode. This means keeping up with discovered vulnerabilities, patches, and ever-evolving threats. Remember that attackers are working against security at all times, and the evolution of computer hardware and vulnerability techniques improves every day. Therefore, security also is ever-evolving and should become an ongoing practice, not a single task.

15.1   Business Secure Cell Concept

In Chapter 12, we covered the creation of a business secure cell in which network access is tightly controlled. The secure cell concept is best applied to all aspects of your business system, however. Topics such as access, connectivity, and patching should all be controlled by policy that governs your business secure cell.

Figure 15.1 shows a corporate network with a business secure cell residing within it. The business secure cell is *hardened*, meaning that it's designed to be more secure than other systems within the organization. This is because of its criticality and the value of the business data and process that it holds and enables.

The question must be asked: Why don't we just harden the entire network? It should be as secure as possible, right? There's a saying within the security community: "Security is the enemy of convivence." This means that often, if something is convenient, seldom is it secure. Inversely, something secure is seldom convenient. This saying reflects why a business secure cell is necessary within an organization. Some services don't require the utmost security because they aren't critical. So, a task accomplished by the implementation of a business secure cell is the segregation of what requires the increased security (and decreased convivence) and what does not.

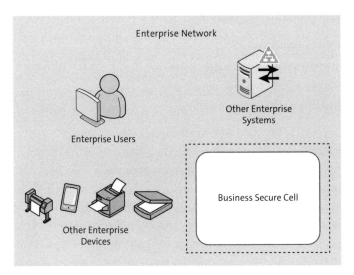

Figure 15.1 Simple Diagram for Business Secure Cell

As we'll further discuss in Section 15.3, high security can be cumbersome. If you're in a government military base, this is probably acceptable. However, if you're in a private business that manufactures bubble gum, an absurd level of security is going to upset your users because it's a waste of their time and the company's money. It may even lead to a catastrophic failure of security entirely (more on that later).

15.2   Secure Landscape

A common deficiency in many SAP landscapes is the treatment of nonproductive systems. This situation is often worsened with time and the development nature of these systems. Consider the standard landscape in Figure 15.2.

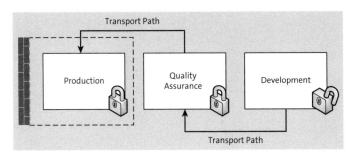

Figure 15.2 Standard Landscape

There are several important things to observe:

- Enhanced security around production
- Lesser security in nonproductive systems; many users with super user authorizations
- Transport paths that link the entire environment

This three-tier landscape is typical for most SAP installations. Often, a focus is put on production due to its productive nature. End users log into this system and perform work. However, attackers will commonly target quality assurance, development, sandbox, or demo systems because they typically are left unsecured or with lower security standards. Often, these nonproductive systems are copies of production. If the attacker's objective is to gather sensitive information, then they've got that sensitive information if they compromise these nonproductive systems.

The second and most important attack vector to guard against is the propagation of malicious code through the transport path. An attacker gains access to a nonproduction system and creates or inserts malicious code into that system (Figure 15.3). The attacker then packages this code in a transport and includes it in the import queue of the next downstream system. It's then imported and available in systems that the attacker didn't previously have access to. Eventually, this code could make it to a productive system, giving that attacker access in the productive system.

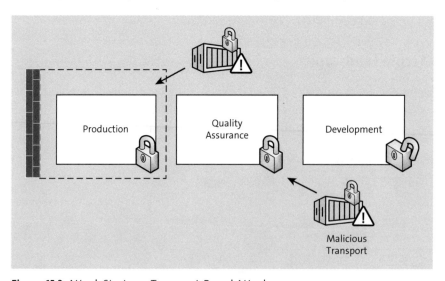

Figure 15.3 Attack Strategy: Transport-Based Attacks

How do we guard against attacks of this nature? The solution is simple: The security administrator *must* apply security measures consistently across the *entire landscape*. The following subsections highlight mitigation strategies for these landscape-based attacks. This activity is especially relevant to security administrators that are retrofitting existing business systems. In landscapes that have been operating for many years, the cumulative effect of security neglect can be quite significant.

What about Disaster Recovery?

Don't forget your disaster recovery site and its associated infrastructure. It should be considered an extension of your business secure cell.

Establishing a Plan for Secure Landscape Design

Redesigning or adjusting your SAP landscape can be a complex and technically challenging project. It's important to address the following steps when planning to secure your landscape:

1. Identify the most critical systems. It's important to safeguard your most critical data first. Identifying which systems contain your organization's most sensitive business information is an important step to deciding which systems to address first.

2. Within these critical systems, determine how many people have access to them. Define your overall access strategy and start with these critical business systems.

3. Once systems have been selected, look at each tier in the system. Are their settings, profile parameters, users and roles, and functions similar? Evaluate the appropriateness of each deviation from production.

4. Map each system and its integration with other systems. Look at the security level for each integration and how it could be improved. Do production systems talk to nonproduction systems? Is this a risk?

5. Finally, establish and apply a security policy to all systems within your secure cell.

6. Secure landscape design and security policy are two separate subjects. When focusing on secure landscape design, be sure to focus on the landscape and its specific vulnerabilities. A strong design can help prevent some attacks from even being viable.

Secure Design in the Real World

Consider a long-running SAP NetWeaver application server running integration with legacy manufacturing mainframes on an assembly line. For years, this integration has been leveraged using an old, unpatched FTP server, which took output from the main frame and provided it to SAP NetWeaver as a flat file. An attacker has quite an opportunity for exploits with an old, unpatched FTP server. Instead, consider designing integration using a web service that leverages encryption and strong SAML authentication. This design is much more difficult to compromise.

As you establish your plan for your landscape, be sure to explicitly address the following areas:

- **Manage users and roles**
  Although users require more authorizations in a development system, this doesn't mean that they require all authorizations. Spend time crafting appropriate roles that fit the user's requirements.

Super User Authorizations

Do not allow users to have super user profiles in nonproductive systems. SAP_ALL or SAP_NEW may temporarily solve authorization issues, but if that user is compromised, they have access to all functions of the system.

- **Obfuscate or protect production data**
  Often, nonproduction systems are copied or refreshed from productive systems. Along with configuration, production data is copied. This can be a requirement for testing because some situations will require production or production-like data.

  Products such as SAP's Test Data Migration Server (TDMS) can be used to obfuscate, transform, and reduce the test data required for testing. TDMS can reduce the frequency or entirely replace refreshes as a method of updating testing data. In addition, TDMS can be used to mask sensitive user data that may be required to meet privacy or data security standards like Payment Card Industry (PCI) or the General Data Protection Regulation (GDPR).

  It's also important to protect sensitive data using proper authorizations. See Chapter 7 for more information about authorizations and their use.

- **Implement ticketing**
  Ticketing systems are a critical part of a modern IT landscape. Your organization may already be using one. It's a good idea to mandate the use of a ticketing system for system maintenance procedures and incidents within your organization. It's much easier to defend and audit when you've got a clear source of documentation for what and why something was done. SAP Solution Manager is a good candidate for this role because it has a robust SAP-centric ticketing system available for use.

- **Practice change management**
  Catching malicious transports before they're imported into downstream systems can be accomplished using a robust change management process. SAP's ChARM functionality that's built in to SAP Solution Manager is a robust system that can help a security administrator manage changes to SAP systems.

15.3   Policy

One of the most useful tools for securing your business secure cell is a well-thought-out policy. A *policy* is a set of guidelines for operation of your business systems, processes, and procedures.

The security policy and practices you may develop should apply equally to all tiers of your landscape, from sandboxes to production. However, security policy for your business secure cell may be too strict for the general enterprise. Keep in mind the scope of your policy and set its intensity based on that scope.

When planning your policy, ask your organization the following questions:

- What's the required minimum level of security protection?
- What level of security protection would be too much?
- What would happen monetarily if the organization were to experience a security breach?

Asking these questions will help narrow the scope and level of security you will need to enforce. Often, a company will elect to adopt the highest security level possible. Although secure, this choice is nearly impossible to maintain. When use of the SAP systems become highly onerous, users will take shortcuts to avoid the inconvenience of strict high security. This completely defeats the intent of increased security. This is exceptionally true when a user doesn't understand why he must suffer the increased workload of strict, high-security systems.

A practical example of this is requiring users to reauthenticate after two minutes of inactivity via 2FA—and you could compound this with requiring users to change passwords every 30 days and locking them out if they type their password incorrectly three times. Although more secure, the inconvenience of this policy could result in the following effects:

- **End users**
  - Use the same password with different variations each time
  - Use simple passwords so they can be remembered
  - Write passwords down near their computers
  - Lose productivity because they're performing 2FA multiple times daily
  - Lose productivity because they're locking themselves out often
- **Administrators**
  - Spend time unlocking users
  - Have a greatly increased load for authentication and 2FA backend hardware

It's easy to see that creating an overzealous security policy can have real effects on the business. The question that must be evaluated by a security administrator is this: Will these requirements significantly decrease our risk of being compromised? Or will we be forcing users to increase that risk by taking shortcuts?

Therefore, security policy must be approached in a thoughtful manner: enough protection to mitigate the risks identified, but not so much that the business is paralyzed by too much security.

Once you decide on the level appropriate for your security policy, write it down. Having a written policy or set of written policies governing the operations of your business secure cell will help justify any actions taken to uphold it. Users will not take kindly to a policy that appears to be arbitrary.

Written security policies have the following benefits:

- Provide consistent measurable criteria in which the effectiveness of an organization's security measures can be evaluated
- Implements controls that may be required for audits
- Coordinates the efforts of administrators and internal and external auditors
- Demonstrates management support for actions taken by security administrators

Your organization might already have an IT or physical security policy. The policy you create will go hand in hand with what's already in place. Policy developed for a business secure cell will strengthen existing policy such that it is sufficient to mitigate risks to your SAP systems. All components, networks, hypervisors, and OSs that reside in the business secure cell should be required to comply with its security policies, as well as the overall company policies.

Within the organization, you may have several established policies already, such as IT or security policies (Figure 15.4). Consider your secure cell policy an extension of this policy that enhances the guidelines already set up by other policies. The difference between the policy you will create and other corporate policies is that your policy should be *SAP-centric* or *businesses system-centric*, meaning that its focus is on keeping your business systems or SAP systems safe.

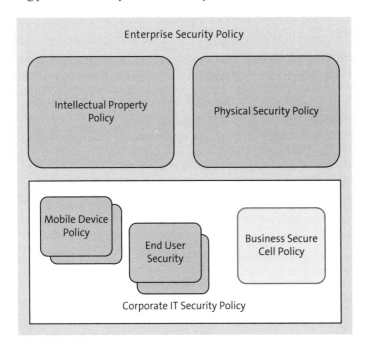

Figure 15.4 Business Secure Cell Policy

15.3.1   Establishing Security Policy

When establishing your security policy, it should fully define and address the following question: What are the challenges to the organization, both security-wise and business-wise, as it relates to SAP systems?

The answer to this question can be several sentences to several pages. The more verbose your reply, the better your starting policy position will be. As you develop this policy, it'll grow into a more defined set of guidelines, rather than the loose ideas that are the answer to the question noted earlier.

The goals of your policies should be centered on the following:

- Protecting the business
- Passing audits and regulatory compliance checks
- Promoting the improvement of security overall

Each item in the policy should be able to positively benefit each of these points. It's a good practice to define how each item in your policy will reach each each goal, but not a requirement.

In addition, policy can be shaped around audit regulations like GDPR, PCI, or SOX. Alternatively, policy can also be based generally around what your organization feels is prudent. This approach is more in line with the strategy of beginning with a few simple questions and working towards refinement, but either method works. The end goal is to get to a listing of what needs to be done to best meet the security objectives.

Once you have an initial draft of your policy, meet with each group of stakeholders that will be affected. This will normally include the following:

- Leadership or management
- The business—specifically, power or key users that use the modules that your SAP systems have installed, such as finance, procurement, human resources, and planning
- System and security administrators involved in the support and operation of your business secure cell
- Developers and business analysts
- Internal auditors
- External auditors
- End users

Meetings should consist of brainstorming, planning, and eventually approval of the designed policies. Signoff from each of the groups noted in the preceding list is critical to the acceptance and success of any policy created.

Once established, review each policy you create from both a security/system administration point of view and a business point of view. Outdated or irrelevant policy will do very little to further security and in some cases may become a hinderance to progress. Make sure that what you're proposing and enforcing is relevant to the situation.

15.3.2   Starting Points for Your Policy

The following are several subject areas that it would be a good idea to make sure that you address in your policy. This is not an exhaustive list and should be taken only as a starting point. Again, start with your security objectives and work toward granularity.

The subject areas are as follows:

- **Authentication**
  Address the minimum criteria for authentication of users. This includes password policy, password complexity, expiration, and SSO. Be sure that your password policy is enforced using the parameters set in your SAP NetWeaver AS ABAP system.

- **Access control**
  Be sure to specify that access must be controlled for every part of your business system, including network devices, OS accounts, hypervisor management accounts. Include criteria that set out a time table to perform access reviews, and make sure that terminations have a process and are enforced.

- **Communications security**
  It's important to set a standard by which communications are secured entering, within, and while leaving the business secure cell. It's a good idea to mandate SSL\TLS encryption for all devices and services.

  Also, be sure to specify in what circumstances remote access is available or authorized. Use tools like 2FA to better secure remote access.

- **Data security**
  Standards for data security topics such as encryption at rest and data storage security should be addressed. Be sure to cover all parts of your business landscape, not just your SAP NetWeaver systems.

  Backups are also critical from both a data theft and data integrity standpoint. Specify a data retention policy, as well as a restore and backup handling policy.

15

- **Change management**

  Change management serves the purpose of preventing both malicious and potentially destructive untested changes from moving between systems in your environment. A change approval and vetting process is a good item to include. Be sure to differentiate between vendor-delivered and custom-developed changes; you're likely to have both moving through your environment.

  A separate section of your policy should be directed to non-SAP systems that are part of your landscape. The use of patching tools can be beneficial. See Section 15.4for more information.

- **Patch and upgrade management**

  SAP Notes, support and enhancement packages, and upgrades are activities that require extensive planning. It's important to prevent security becoming an afterthought during these critical activities. As an organization, have an SAP upgrade planning meeting. Most of the effort of this activity falls on the business to define its needs and upgrade pace. However, it's important for the security administrator to be a part of the process. This is because business users may not see risks that the security administrator may notice right away. An example of this is the continued use of an old, unpatched, unsupported system. To a business user, this system may be reliable and known. However, to a security administrator or attacker, this system represents a large target with many attack surfaces that need to be secured or patched. This activity falls within change control, but it's different from normal day-to-day corrections. Its significance justifies a separate section or even a separate policy.

Keep SAP Requirements in Mind

When using non-SAP patching management tools, remember that you must still stay within the supported versions for SAP software. Consult the PAM to verify versions for non-SAP products.

- **Auditing**

  Most of your auditing policy should be centered on *internal audits*, self-imposed audits performed by your own staff. Internal audits are a very powerful tool to see if you're in compliance before undergoing an external audit. *External audits* are audits in which the auditors are external to your company. These can be security audits, financial audits, or regulatory compliance audits.

To assist in internal auditing, a small staff could use network vulnerability scanning, discussed in Section 15.7.1, to quickly audit hundreds of systems over the network. Another beneficial practice is reviewing and acting on SAP EarlyWatch Alert reports from SAP Solution Manager.

Other internal auditing objectives that are useful include the following:

- Log auditing: reviewing access logs
- ACL review: determining what attempts are made to access restricted portions of your network
- Client opening and closing: reviewing when and why clients are opened for changes
- Role audits: auditing which users hold critical roles in your business systems

- **Educating**
  Make users and the organization aware of the policy or any policy changes in a reasonable timeframe. Policies that users are educated about are much more likely to be successful in the areas of acceptance and compliance. A policy that isn't enforced or that users don't know about isn't really a policy at all. Be sure your users know and understand the policies that they are being expected to comply with.

15.3.3   Further Policies

This chapter contains recommendations for securing various parts of your business secure cell. It's up to the administrator to decide what parts of the infrastructure stack should require their own policy. Some organizations opt to develop a "host policy" in which each host must conform to a specific set of guidelines, like backups, antivirus, and configuration. Others are more granular, differentiating between things like database hosts and application server hosts, specifying exactly what criteria must be met by that host to satisfy the policy. Add whichever policies you find best fit your organization and achieve your goal of strengthening security.

15.3.4   Adopting Policy

In smaller organizations, it's the SAP system or security administrator that will be responsible for all aspects of security policy. In larger organizations, multiple positions may be responsible for areas of infrastructure that make up the SAP system design. It's important for the security administrator to act in an advisory role such that each position fulfils its duty to comply with the chosen policy. For example, an operating system administrator may be in charge of patching all of the OS for the entire corporation. This includes OSs that reside under the security policy developed for your business secure cell. The focus of the SAP security administrator in this situation is guiding the OS administrator to understand the intricacies of the SAP systems, their technical requirements, and the security requirements defined by the business secure cell policy. It's a good idea to develop your policy together with other administrators so that they understand its purpose and can lend their expertise in its creation.

> **Focusing on Business Systems**
>
> Remember that your policy is specific to your business secure cell. This means that not end users but the business systems themselves are the direct focus of this policy. It's the business systems themselves.

As you complete your policy and move toward adoption, keep in mind that business and management buy-in for your security policy are critical. Policies that don't have support of users and management don't stand a chance to be effective. Gain the buy-in of each critical part, both when planning and before adoption.

15.3.5   Auditing and Reviewing Policy

After adoption of your policy or group of policies, hold an audit and policy review meeting monthly or quarterly. In this meeting, review the effectiveness of, inconvenience of, and overall sentiment about the policy. It may be difficult to take criticism about a policy that was well-thought-out and implemented, but keep in mind that users are the ones who have to suffer the inconvenience of stricter security. If they're unhappy, they most likely will look for ways to make the policy easier to live with, which can defeat the usefulness of the policy. Be sure to adjust based on the feedback of your end users.

In addition, be sure to discuss and remedy policy violations. Try to identify any trends and adjust your policy accordingly. Do a postmortem on both downtime and discovered security vulnerabilities and how they could be avoided by a prudent change or adjustment in your policy.

15.4 Operating System Considerations

One of the first steps to strengthen your overall security level is to harden your OS. OS hardening, or security hardening in any capacity, is taking the steps necessary to improve the overall security of your system. This can mean closing ports, updating software, eliminating unneeded services, and so on. These small steps when added together strengthen security overall.

When choosing or evaluating the choice of the OS you're running SAP NetWeaver on, it's important to keep in mind that any OS can be secured. Don't be tempted to stray from your core OS competency, because a poorly secured OS is worse than a less secure OS that has been secured. If you're historically a Windows shop, focus on securing Windows and not moving to Linux unless you're willing to put in the time and effort to learn the OS inside and out. Properly securing whatever you're running is the takeaway here.

Because security threats are ever evolving, you must keep your OS up to date with the latest patches. We recommend using a patch management system such as Microsoft WSUS, or SSCM, SUSE Manager, Red Hat Satellite, VMware Go, or IBM Tivoli Endpoint Manager. It's important to understand that patching is required both on your servers and the end user's systems. A compromised end user's system could easily lead to a greatly increased attack surface for an intruder to exploit. This isn't as dangerous as a unpatched server, but dangerous nonetheless.

Supported Software Levels

In general, SAP supports the latest patches for supported OSs. However, be sure to check the PAM before patching to make sure you're on a supported version of your OS.

The following are general recommendations for all OSs:

- Disable any unneeded services.
- Manage default accounts and passwords.
- Use password policies.
- Change administrative passwords often.
- Use a repeatable process, create a checklist of hardening items, and audit your systems frequently.

15.4.1   General Linux Recommendations

The following recommendations apply to all Linux-type OSs:

- The hardening process for most Linux OSs is similar. Consult your OS vendor for specific security guides and scripts to harden your system.

- Avoid use of SUID/SGID programs with known vulnerabilities. The best way to prevent exploits of this type is to keep your system up to date.

- If you don't require them, do not run X window systems. Other than ease of use, there's no requirement for an SAP NetWever server to run the X windows subsystem.

- Do not use FTP and Telnet for file transfer. Instead, use secured versions, SSH, SCP, or SFTP.

- Prohibit root logons remotely over SSH.

- Configure the default file mask such that new files are created with appropriate permissions.

- Carefully protect your passwords file (passwd). Consider making it only readable by the root user. Take care in using an access-management system because your password file could be read over the network.

- Follow your OS vendor's recommendations when securing NFS. NFS uses a host-based authentication system, so do not configure your SAP NFS shares like SAP mounts on systems that don't require it.

- Check keys/signatures on downloaded patches to verify their authenticity.

- Check the integrity of the OS and its installed packages often.

- What about security mechanisms such as SELinux or Apparmor? Although SELinux and Apparmor are both very good security tools, at the time of writing there are no SELinux polices available for SAP HANA or SAP NetWeaver, so enabling SELinux or Apparmor isn't recommended.

SUSE Linux

SUSE Linux is a popular choice for SAP NetWeaver because it's widely supported by SAP, especially with SAP HANA. SUSE produces two security hardening guides, one for SAP software in general and a second for SAP HANA. We advise consulting these guides as a starting point for securing SLES.

Notable recommendations are as follows:

- Install the SUSE security checker. This utility can notify an administrator of security changes via email. Seccheck can be installed with the following command:

  `Zipper in seccheck`

- SUSE recommends that you forward your system logs to a system-logging server. You can read more about system-logging servers in Section 15.5.1.

Linux Filesystem Recommendations

SAP's recommendations for filesystem permissions on Linux are provided in Table 15.1.

Path or File(s)	Permissions (Octal)
/<sapmnt>/<SAPSID>/exe	775
/<sapmnt>/<SAPSID>/global	700
/<sapmnt>/<SAPSID>/profile	755
/usr/sap/<SAPSID>	751
/usr/sap/<SAPSID>/<Instance ID>	755
/usr/sap/<SAPSID>/<Instance ID>/sec	700
/usr/sap/<SAPSID>/SYS	755
/usr/sap/<SAPSID>/SYS/*	755
/usr/sap/trans	775
/usr/sap/trans/*	770
/usr/sap/trans/.sapconf	775
The home directory of <sid>adm	700
The home directory of <sid>adm/*	700

Table 15.1 SAP's Recommendation for Linux File Permissions

Important: Linux File Ownership

The user and group for all files in Table 15.1 is <SID>ADM:sapsys.

It's a good idea to write a shell script to routinely check the permissions and ownership of these files and alert a security administrator in the event of a discrepancy. In additiony, be sure that any NFS shared file systems are properly protected and only authorized on hosts that require access.

15.4.2   Microsoft Windows

The single most important guidance on Windows systems is to stay up to date with your patching. Because Windows is a widely used desktop OS, much attention is given to it by attackers. This doesn't mean that Windows is an unacceptable or insecure choice for your systems. It's important to review Microsoft's patching schedule and act accordingly.

The following specific tasks are good starting points when hardening your Windows systems:

- Use domain accounts where possible. Local administration accounts are popular targets for attackers.
- Secure remote desktop.
- Disable unneeded services and accounts.
- Remove unneeded windows components, features, and roles.
- Use NTP. Out-of-sync time can break things like Kerberos.

Windows Domain Controllers

Do not install your SAP NetWeaver AS ABAP systems on your Windows domain controller because this will make your local SAP administrative accounts known to all domain controllers of the domain.

SAP's recommendations for filesystem permissions on a local Windows installation are given in Table 15.2.

Path	Permissions
\<usr>\<sap>	Full Control
\<usr>\<sap>\<trans>	Full Control

Table 15.2 SAP's Recommendations for Local Windows File Permissions

Path	Permissions
\<usr>\<sap>\<SID>\<sys>\<global>\ <security>	Full Control + deny all for Administrators group

Table 15.2 SAP's Recommendations for Local Windows File Permissions (Cont.)

Important: Windows File Ownership

The user groups for all files in Table 15.2 are SAP_<sid>_LocalAdmin for local user groups and SAP_<sid>_GlobalAdmin for domain user groups.

15.4.3   Operating System Users

When securing your OS, be sure to monitor the following:

1. Who has access to the root users?
2. Who has access to the super users?
3. Who are the domain users?

Once you've set up monitoring, track the changes and make review of this process a regular practice. It's a good target for internal audits.

For each system, restrict access to the root, SAPSID, and DBSID users on each of your systems. Be sure to lock the <DBSID> user on your application servers, which have no need for this user.

On Windows, use groups to manage your privileges. Domain groups have the advantage of being managed through the domain and not restricted to a local user.

15.4.4   Viruses and Malware

Viruses and malware are a threat to be taken into account when your SAP NetWeaver AS ABAP system accepts uploads. Common scenarios for this type of activity include collecting user-submitted resumes from a recruitment system or documents uploaded by vendors, customers, or other business partners.

Before opening or storing these files, it's important to check them for malicious code using a virus-scanning solution.

Tip: Stop Viruses before They're Uploaded

Be sure to mandate enterprise virus and malware scanning on end users' desktops. This practice can prevent malicious files from being uploaded in the first place. However, in some scenarios, like e-recruiting, the administrator has no control of the end user's system. It's therefore important to perform a scan on any file that's uploaded to the SAP NetWeaver AS ABAP system.

In an SAP NetWeaver system, virus scanning is accomplished using an interface that calls a virus-scanning solution. The mechanism for this is the SAP NetWeaver Virus Scan Interface, referred to as the Virus Scan Interface or NW-VSI (Figure 15.5).

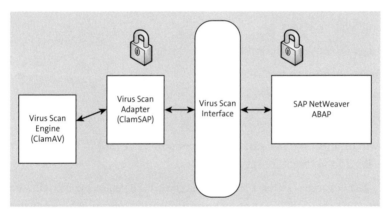

Figure 15.5 SAP NetWeaver Virus Scan Interface

There are many ways and multiple methods to configure virus scanning. In this simple example, we'll configure a method that uses the ClamAV scanner and a shared library developed by a third party. See Figure 15.5 for the architecture of the VSI. In this figure, we've labeled the parts (ClamAV and ClamSAP) that we'll be using in the example ahead. Keep in mind that any supported virus-scanning solution can be used with the VSI. Before choosing a specific method or product, be sure to consult both the SAP NetWeaver documentation and the SAP Notes for the NW-VSI and your specific product.

Approved Virus Scan Applications

A list of approved antivirus providers can be found in SAP Note 1494278 (NW-VSI: Summary of Virus Scan Adapters for SAP integration).

Before you begin configuring virus scanning, you must fulfill the following prerequisites:

- ClamAV must be installed on your OS.

- Install the ClamSAP library package available at *https://sourceforge.net/projects/clamsap/*.

   You'll require the clamsap.so library for your platform and CPU architecture. For SLES 64x, this is libclamsap.so, contained in the clamsap_linux_x64_glibc23.tar.gz file. If you wish, these files can be compiled by source.

Let's start by installing and configuring ClamAV on your application server—in our case, SLES:

1. Install ClamAV and ClamSAP on your OS. In SLES Linux, this can be done by launching the YaST2 package manager (Figure 15.6) and selecting the ClamAV package and the clamsap package.

   You can also install both packages using the following terminal command:

   ```
   sudo zypper install clamav clamsap
   ```

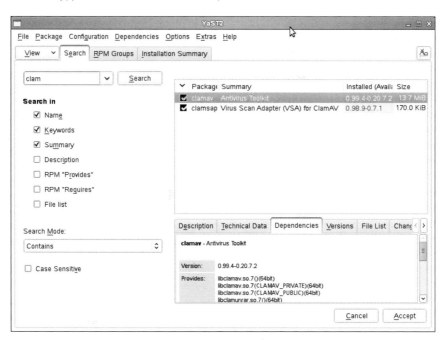

Figure 15.6 Installing ClamAV on SLES Using YaST2 Package Manager

2. From the terminal of an application server, execute the cdexe alias to move to the exe directory.

3. Execute the following command to see the status of the kernel program vcand_rfc (Figure 15.7):

```
vscan_rfc -i
```

This will show the status and version of the kernel program which is used to call the virus scanner.

```
*   [-c SAP codepage] [-V VSA_LIB path] [-p VSA profile name]      *
*   [-T max. threads] [-m min. threads] [-L SNC_LIB path]          *
*   [-S SNC name of this instance] [-P SNC name of SAP instance]   *
*   [-Q SNC protection quality] [-I timeout in sec. for instances] *
*   [-n max. memory trace lines] [-h hold time for memory trace]   *
*   [-apptrc append lines to trace]                                *
*   [-daemon start the server as daemon]                           *
*                                                                  *
********************************************************************
==================================================================
SAP Virus Scan Server for Virus Scan Interface, (c) 2002-2018 SAP AG
==================================================================
Server info
      VSI Version   : 2.00
      Versiontext   : Final Release of SAP Virus Scan Server
      Startup time  : Mon Apr 30 13:22:20 2018
      Build release : Release 745, Level 0, Patch 15
      Build date    : Oct 12 2015
      Build platform: AMD/Intel x86_64 with Linux
                      (mt,opt,unicode,SAP_CHAR/size_t/void*=16/64/64)
Server configuration
      Command line  : vscan_rfc
      RFC commands  :
      Config file   : <not set>
      Codepage      : <not set> (default)
      Tracefile     : dev_VSCAN.trc (default)
      Tracelevel    : 0 (default)
      GW program ID : <not set> (default)
      GW host       : <not set> (default)
      GW service    : <not set> (default)
      Min. threads  : 5 (default)
      Max. threads  : 20 (default)
      VSA_LIB       : <not set> (default)
      SNC_LIB       : <not set> (default)
      SncMyName     : <not set> (default)
      SncPartnerName: <not set> (default)
      SNC protection: <not set> (default)
      Inst. Timeout : 60 (default)
      MMTrc maxlines: 10000 (default)
      MMTrc maxhold : 86400 (default)
sap-ci:jdmadm 56> █
```

Figure 15.7 vscan_rfc Kernel Executable

4. Run the following command to update the ClamAV signature files:

`freshclam`

Note: You may need to run this command as a super user.

5. Next, perform a test scan to make sure the scanner is working:

`clamscan`

This should scan the current directory and report the results to the terminal.

Now, let's create the virus scanning group:

1. Navigate to Transaction VSCANGROUP.

2. Click the **Display -> Change** button to enter change mode.

3. The system will warn that this activity accesses a table that is cross-client. Click the green checkmark to continue.

4. The **Scanner Groups: Overview** screen will appear. Click the **New Entries** button to create a new scanner group. Name the scanner and click the **Save** button. Do not click the **Business Add-In** box. You may be prompted to create a transport depending on your system settings (Figure 15.8).

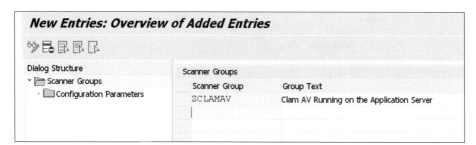

Figure 15.8 Creating Scanner Group

Next, let's create the virus scan provider:

1. Navigate to Transaction VSCAN.

2. Click the **Display -> Change** button to enter change mode.

3. The system will warn that this activity access a table that is cross-client. Click the green checkmark to continue.

4. The **Virus Scan Provider Definition: Overview** screen will appear. Click the **New Entries** button to create a new provider definition group.

5. The **Change View: Virus Scan Provider Definition: Details** screen will appear (Figure 15.9).

   Configure the following:

   – **Provider Name**: Adapter (Virus Scan Adapter)

   – **Provider Name**: VSA_<hostname>

   – **Scanner Group**: The scanner group that you previously set up.

   – **Server**: This should be prepopulated to your application server.

   – **Adapter Path**: libclamsap.so

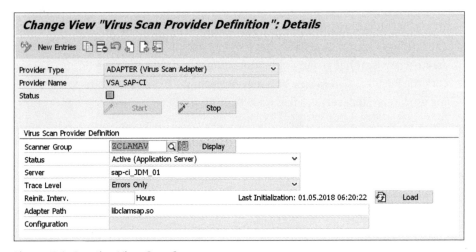

Figure 15.9 Creating Virus Scan Server

6. Once complete, click the **Start** button to start your adapter.

7. Once your adapter starts, you should see a summary appear in the bottom pane of the screen. You should see a ClamSAP VSA version and drivers loaded for ClamAV (Figure 15.10).

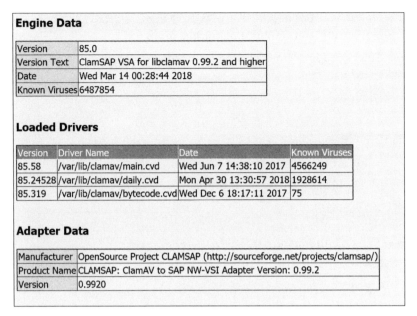

Figure 15.10 Output Showing ClamSAP and ClamAV Active.

15

Update Your Definitions

Don't forget to schedule a background job to update your virus scan definitions. You can either schedule this on the host OS or using the SAP job scheduler to run and OS command. The command to update ClamAV is freshclam.

Finally, let's test the virus scanning configuration:

1. Read SAP Note 666568. This note explains testing the virus scan interface using a test file provided by a third party.

2. Navigate to Transaction VSCANTEST (Figure 15.11).

3. In the **Object to be Checked** box, select **EICAR Anti-Virus Test File**.

4. In **Scanner Selection**, click the radio button for Virus Scan Provider. Then, click the provider that you created. In this example, we created the group **VSA_SAP-CI**.

5. Click the **Execute** button.

Figure 15.11 Testing Screen for Virus-Scanning Interface

6. The system will prompt you to make sure you have read and understood SAP Note 666568. If you haven't already, read the SAP Note, then click **Yes** to continue (Figure 15.12).

Figure 15.12 SAP Note 666568 Warning

7. The system will now display scanning results for the test file. You should see results that match Figure 15.13.

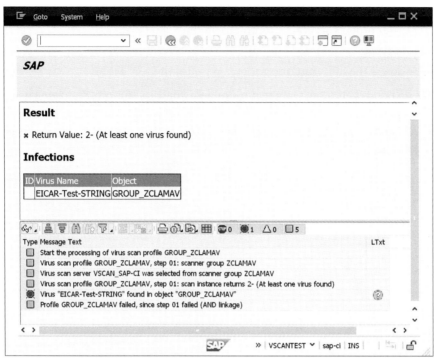

Figure 15.13 Successful Test Scan of Test File

More Info: Virus Scan Interface

Consult SAP Note 797108 for more information about the Virus Scan Interface.

15.4.5 Application Server File System

For most files, the normal user and group is <SID>ADM and SAPSYS. Refer back to Table 15.1 and Table 15.2 for a list of OS authorization values for your OS. Because of the <SID>ADM and SAPSYS group authorization model, it's important to tightly control access to this super user and group. In addition, administrative or root access should also be tightly controlled. Perform periodic reviews to determine which personnel have access to these accounts and the reasoning behind the access.

Using OS tools to monitor your system profiles is a good idea to prevent systems from having incorrect or out-of-sync values. In general, your profiles should be relatively in sync across your environment. Development and test systems often have relaxed profiles, allowing things like nonsecure HTTP access. This is a security risk. Be sure that your profiles accurately represent production.

Guard your transport path from the OS level. Make sure that only the <SID>ADM user is able to access the transport directories and transport tools like TP.

Finally, do not export directories that contain SAP data to arbitrary recipients using NFS. Export to trustworthy systems only—that is, only the systems that are part of your SAP landscape. There is no need for transport files (data and co-files) to be accessed by any other systems.

15.5   Monitoring

Many tools exist to monitor logs via algorithms from many different sources. They range in complexity from simple to highly configurable log parsers. At a minimum, a security administrator should focus on determining what suspicious log entries look like (login attempts or potential brute force attacks) and monitor logs for those activities.

> **Warning: Log Management**
>
> Be sure to copy or archive logs to another filesystem before performing any monitoring operations. You don't want to fill up a filesystem with logs. This may cease productive operation of your systems, both SAP and non-SAP.

15.5.1   OS Logs

In your OS logs, you're looking for repeated access attempts, as well as attempts to compromise the OS functionality in any way. This could include denied attempts to login via SSH, Telnet, FTP, or any other service that the host is running.

It's a good idea to configure a logging server in which your OS logs are forwarded for review and analysis. Don't forget your nonproduction systems!

15.5.2   Application Logs

Refer to Chapter 11 for more information about audit logs and how they can be used to monitor the security of your system. Application logs can be compared between systems and may indicate when a breach or security vulnerability is being executed.

15.5.3 Certificate Revocation Lists

In Chapter 13, we covered digital certificates and their use in SSL/TLS configuration. It's important to know that the certificate authorities that sign digital certificates commonly maintain a list of certificates that are no longer trusted. This list is called a *certificate revocation list* and it indicates when the certificate signer wants to revoke trust on a certificate.

It's a good idea to monitor certificate revocation lists for certificate authorities that you may commonly trust across your enterprise. This can be done with enterprise PKI tools and by configuring revocation lists in SAP NetWeaver AS ABAP. The following steps will guide you through setting up monitoring of a certificate revocation list.

First, let's enable the SSF certification revocation PSE:

1. Navigate to Transaction SSFA.
2. Click the **Display -> Change** button on the toolbar.
3. This will launch the **Change View: "Application-Specific SSF Parameters": Overview** (Figure 15.14).

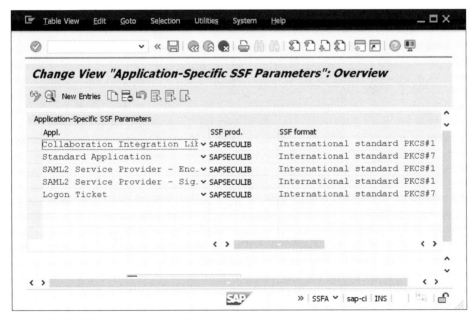

Figure 15.14 SSF Parameters Overview

4. Click the **New Entries** button on the toolbar.

5. Select **Manage Certificate Blocking** (Figure 15.15).

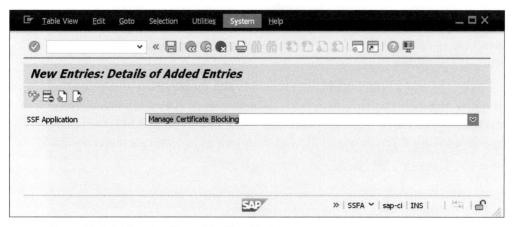

Figure 15.15 Adding Certificate Blocking SSF Entry

6. If prompted, create a transport and click the green checkbox.

7. Click the **Save** button.

Now it's time to obtain your CRL. CRLs are usually specific to a root CA. However, most CAs use a chain of trust to sign their certificates. Because of this, the CRL can usually be found in the properties of an *intermediate certificate*, which is the certificate that signs the SSL/TLS certificate. For our example, we're looking for the CRL for the CA that signs the SSL/TLS certificate for the *sap.com* website. This will provide us with the CRL for the CA that signs SAP's certificates. We suggest that you configure CRLs for any CA that signs certificates that your systems will communicate with. These could be internal or external CAs.

8. To determine the CRL, simply look for the **CRL Distribution Point** field of your certificate (Figure 15.16). This will give you the URL from which the CRL can be downloaded.

Figure 15.16 Determining CRL Distribution Point to Download CRL

Next, we'll need to add the certificates that represent the CA we're going to be checking against. Download the root certificate and all intermediary certificates so that you can add them in Transaction STRUST. The following steps describe how to add them in Transaction STRUST.

1. Navigate to Transaction STRUST.

2. Click the **Display <-> Change** button to enter change mode.

3. Right-click the **SSF Manage Certificate Blocking** PSE and select **Create** (Figure 15.17).

4. Adjust the PSE creation parameters to your needs. For our needs, the defaults are sufficient. Click the green checkmark to create the PSE (Figure 15.18).

5. Double-click- the PSE and import the root certificate of the CA you'd like to configure a CRL for. To do so, click the **Import** button in the certificate section, then the **Add to Certificate List** button. Do this for both your root certificate and each intermediate certificate (Figure 15.19).

6. Click **Save** to save the PSE.

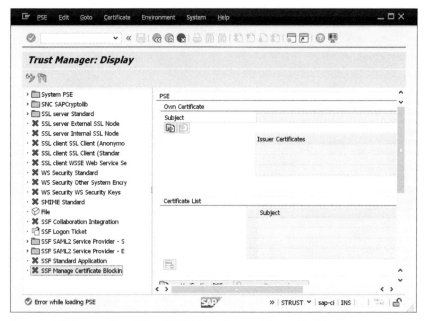

Figure 15.17 Transaction STRUST PSE Entry for Certificate Blocking

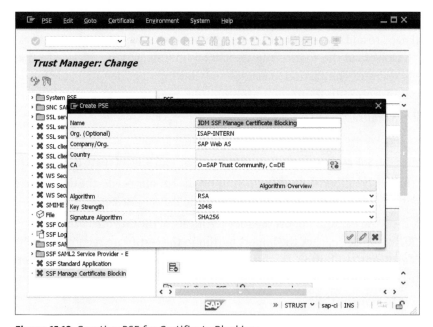

Figure 15.18 Creating PSE for Certificate Blocking

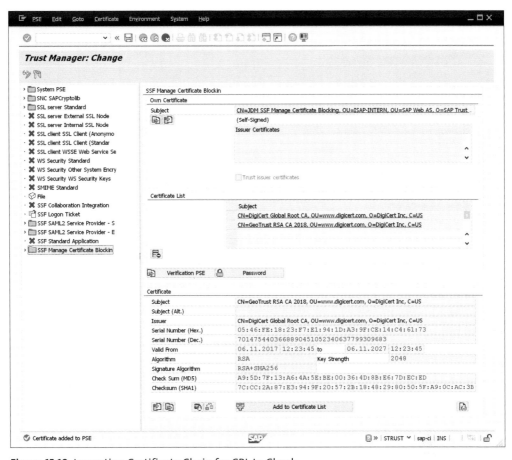

Figure 15.19 Importing Certificate Chain for CRL to Check

Now, let's create the CRL profile:

1. Navigate to Transaction CRCONFIG (Figure 15.20).

2. Click the **Display/Change** button on the toolbar to enter change mode.

3. In the **SSL_SERVER** row, check the **Active** box (Figure 15.21). This will enable CRL checking for SSL/TLS connections. If you intend to use other CRL lists, you can check the **Active** box for those profiles here.

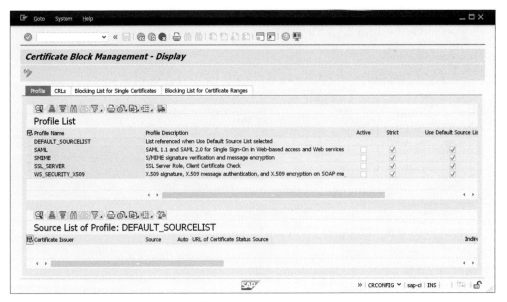

Figure 15.20 Transaction CRCONFIG

Profile Name	Profile Description	Active	Strict	Use Default Source Lis
DEFAULT_SOURCELIST	List referenced when Use Default Source List selected			
SAML	SAML 1.1 and SAML 2.0 for Single Sign-On in Web-based access and Web services	☐	✓	✓
SMIME	S/MIME signature verification and message encryption	☐	✓	✓
SSL_SERVER	SSL Server Role, Client Certificate Check	✓	✓	✓
WS_SECURITY_X509	X.509 signature, X.509 message authentication, and X.509 encryption on SOAP me	☐	✓	✓

Figure 15.21 Profile Box

4. Double-click **DEFAULT_SOURCELIST** to select it.

5. In the bottom pane, select the **Create Source** button.

6. In the **Issuer** box, enter the issuer of your CRL list. This will be the same issuer as for the root or intermediary certificate. Click the green checkbox to continue (Figure 15.22).

7. Under the **Source** column, select **CRL**.

8. Enter the URL of the CRL in the **URL of Certificate Status Source** column.

9. You can test your CRL by clicking the **Check CRL Availability** button. The status of the test will be shown in the lower left-hand corner of the window (Figure 15.23).

10. Click the **Save** button. Create a transport if required.

Figure 15.22 Creating CRL Source

Figure 15.23 Configured Source and Successful CRL Test

The next step is to update the CRL:

1. Navigate to Transaction SA38.
2. Enter the following report name: "S_TRUST_DOWNLOAD_CRL" (Figure 15.24).

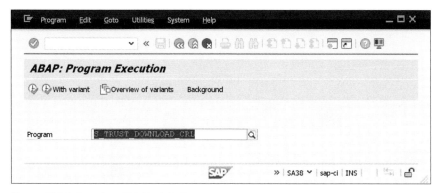

Figure 15.24 Running CRL Update Program

3. Click the green **Execute** button on the toolbar.

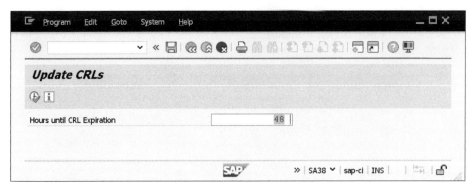

Figure 15.25 Update CRLs: Expiration Value for Downloaded CRLs

4. Click the green **Execute** button to accept the default CRL expiration of 48 hours (Figure 15.26).

CRL Expirations

By default, the system downloads CRLs that are due to expire within 48 hours. Enter "-1" to download all CRLs immediately.

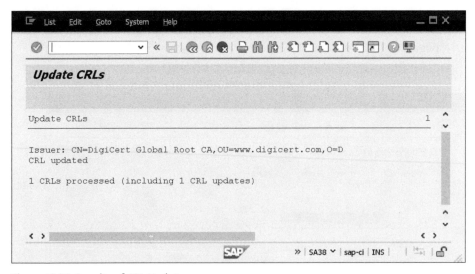

Figure 15.26 Results of CRL Update

5. You should now see that your CRL is updated. (Figure 15.26) To verify this, navigate to Transaction CRCONFIG. If you encounter errors during the update, they can be addressed in Transaction CRCONFIG.

Scheduling the CRL Update

It's a good idea to schedule a CRL update to occur as a background job every 48–72 hours. Background jobs can be created using a variant in Transaction SM36.

---

6. Click the **CRLs** tab. You should see your CRL and up-to-date timestamps (Figure 15.27).

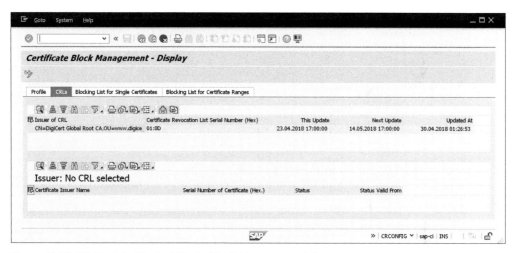

Figure 15.27 CRL Updated in Certificate Block Management Screen

Now, you can manually check the revocation status of a certificate:

1. Navigate to Transaction STRUST.
2. Click the **Display <-> Edit** button to enter change mode. You won't be making any changes.
3. Select a certificate by double-clicking it so that it appears in the **Certificate** area of the screen.
4. From the menu, click the **Check Block Status** button 🔒 (Figure 15.28).
5. Select the **SSL_SERVER** profile and click the **Check** button. The system will check the certificate against the CRL and display the results (Figure 15.29).

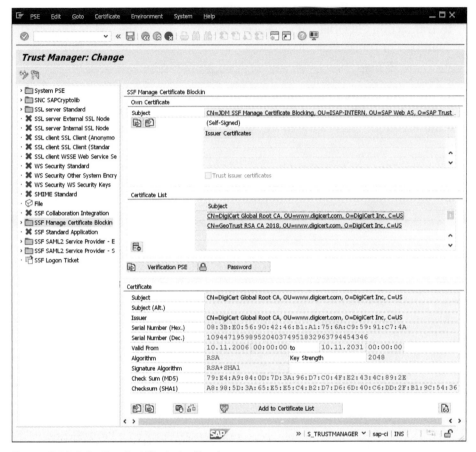

Figure 15.28 Selecting Certificate to Check

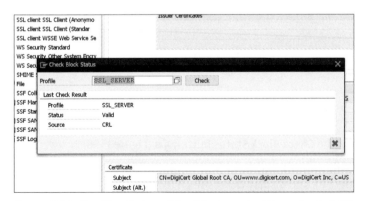

Figure 15.29 Checking Status of Certificate against Downloaded CRL

The results listed in Table 15.3 are possible.

Status	Description
Valid	When a certificate does not appear in any CRL, this is the result.
Revoked	The certificate appears either in the manual revocation list or in the CRL of the CA.
Unknown	The revocation check has a source for the CRL but cannot reach it due to network error or file not found. The validity of the certificate depends on whether the **Strict** flag for the profile is set.
Hold	CAs list certificates in CRLs with this value to indicate that the CA doesn't want to permanently revoke the certificate. The CA may remove the certificate from the revocation list in the future.
Unchecked	The profile used to check the certificate isn't active. The system doesn't perform a certificate revocation check.

Table 15.3 CRL Check Status Codes

In addition, you can manually block certificates:

1. Select the certificate in the same manner as in the previous example.
2. Click the **Block Certificate** button. This will add it to the internal block certificate list (Figure 15.30).

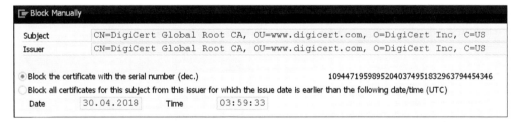

Figure 15.30 Manually Blocking Certificate

If this certificate is checked, it will come back as **Revoked** (Figure 15.31).

Figure 15.31 Revoked Certificate

If the system were to attempt to initiate SSL/TLS communication and checked the revoke list, the connection would be terminated. This would appear in the ICM and security logs, if activated.

Custom CRL Checking

CRL checks can be implemented in custom-written ABAP programs as well. This can be done using a custom profile and the STRUSTCRT_CHECK_CERTIFICATE function module.

The block list can be viewed by performing the following procedure:

1. Navigate to Transaction CRCONFIG.
2. Click the **Blocking List for Single Certificates** tab (Figure 15.32).

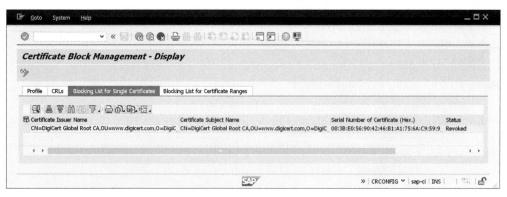

Figure 15.32 Viewing Certificate Block List

Certificates can be removed from the block list by performing the following procedure:

1. Navigate to Transaction CRCONFIG.
2. Click the **Blocking List for Single Certificates** tab.
3. Click the **Display <-> Edit** button on the toolbar to enter change mode.
4. Select the certificate by clicking on it.
5. Click the **Delete Certificate** button on the toolbar.
6. Save by using the **Save** button on the menu bar.

15.6   Virtualization Security Considerations

Virtualization, or abstracting hardware from software using virtual machines, is a core technology that has quickly made its way into the enterprise. With virtualization comes a rich feature set that allows administrators the ability to decouple software from hardware, both saving money and adding flexibility. The hypervisor is a key piece of software that enables this. A *hypervisor* is a system in which virtual machines are created, run, and managed. Popular hypervisors at the time of writing include VMware ESX, Microsoft HyperV, and the open source Xen hypervisor. The specific hypervisors all differ in configuration, but the general concept is identical for each. Figure 15.33 illustrates the role of a hypervisor in the application stack.

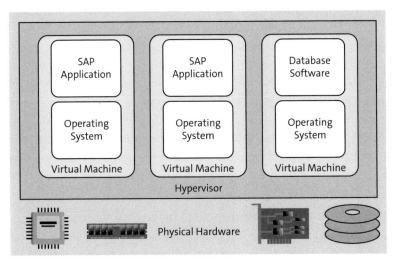

Figure 15.33 Illustration of Hypervisor

Hypervisors are often chosen for the SAP NetWeaver AS ABAP central instances and application servers. This is a favorable strategy because it allows flexibility in the management of each system. Clustering and high availability may be done in a manner that can resist several hardware failures with little application configuration. The same can be done with databases; however, due to the high memory requirements of databases like SAP HANA, more often these systems will be physical. With the continuing enhancements of memory technology, we'll most likely see large in-memory database systems fully virtualized in the near future.

> **Virtualizing SAP NetWeaver AS ABAP**
>
> When running SAP NetWeaver AS ABAP on a virtualized host, be sure to follow all SAP Notes on configuration of the guest environment. Failure to do so could cause performance or stability issues.

Securing a hypervisor is very similar to securing a physical server. However, keep in mind that a vulnerability can lead to a number of systems being affected rather than just the single physical system.

It's important to observe that virtual machines (sometimes called *guests*) are managed by the hypervisor but generally do not have access to the hypervisor or its management functionalities. A common attack vector is to attempt to break out of the virtual machine and gain access to either the hypervisor or the underlying physical hardware. This is referred to as *virtual machine escape* and is a highly sought-after exploit.

In addition, many attacks exist to compromise the hypervisor. A successful attack would give the attacker access to the virtual hardware and possibly the software of each virtual machine running on the hypervisor. This is problematic because with access to the virtual hardware and physical hardware of the hypervisor host, many attacks can become possible. From the network side, hypervisor hosts are often plugged into many different networks. Having access to networking hardware or virtual hardware may give the attacker access to each of these network segments that are assumed to be separated. Thus, a hypervisor is a critical piece of infrastructure to keep secure.

Thankfully, most hypervisors are fairly secure out of the box. They take steps to isolate VMs and have been hardened to a level that is much more secure than the typical OS. However, as always, it's very important to keep your hypervisor up to date. Given the portability of virtual machines (i.e., you can move them from one hypervisor to another while running), there really is no excuse for lapsing on patching.

How do we combat the attacks on hypervisors? In the following ways:

1. Patch your hypervisor. Be sure that you have enough spare capacity to move all running virtual machines to another host to be patched so that they can be patched on the fly without causing downtime.

2. Be sure to patch each guest OS.

3. Make sure the guest's integration tools or agents are kept up to date. These tools enable communication between the VM guest and its hypervisor host. This communication is for management and functionality enablement but can be used as an attack vector.

4. Separate management, storage, and VM network traffic.

5. Patch the BIOS and remote management interfaces such as IPMI and make sure they're secured on each hypervisor physical host.

6. It's important to stay informed. Look for vulnerabilities that threaten stability as well as security.

7. Observe the network exposure of the hypervisor hosts that your systems run on. You don't want to run your systems on a hypervisor that has a network interface that's connected to the Internet.

Additionally, be careful when allocating rights and permissions to the hypervisor system and any management systems that may be associated with your hypervisor.

- Allow only the access explicitly needed to support the business environment.

- Turn off things like remote access if not needed (e.g., SSH or RDP ports).

15.7   Network Security Considerations

Attackers can use a number of unimaginable methods to attempt to compromise a corporate network. Some of the more interesting attacks involve things like unpatched printers or even, in one recent case, an Internet of Things (IoT) fish tank thermometer that leaked network credentials to a very creative attacker. In a business secure cell, it's a good practice to fully catalog all networked devices and eliminate anything that isn't necessary. For example, it may be easier to connect something like a check printer directly to the same network that your SAP NetWeaver system resides on. However, this creates a larger attack surface for an attacker to try to compromise. So, to minimize the attack surface, be sure to remove any nonessential devices from your business secure cell's network.

After removing nonessential network devices, it's a good idea to map your network to understand what needs to be protected. Although it's possible to map your network by hand, it's much more efficient and repeatable if you use a tool such as a network vulnerability scanner. For a full explanation for security in your secure cell, refer to Chapter 12.

Regardless of the extensive effort we put into securing our SAP systems, the corporate network should be secured with the same type of effort. However, this isn't usually a direct responsibility of the security or system administrator.

Administrative interfaces are required for management of network equipment but are often left set to default credentials. Make sure these interfaces are protected by a virtual LAN (vlan) and have strong, frequently changed passwords.

We recommend that MAC address authorization/authentication is implemented on your network. Although MAC address authorization and authentication isn't a strong security countermeasure, it still has value overall in increasing the security of your network. This is recommended in your business secure cell, as well as on your corporate network.

Finally, the use of geographic IP bans can be very useful in determining which traffic to be block. Evaluate the sources of your normal traffic by looking at access and firewall logs. If your traffic is all domestic, then it's fairly safe to block traffic from other countries or regions. This type of traffic categorization can be useful in preventing intrusion from places that don't need access to your systems.

15.7.1   Auditing Using Vulnerability Scanners

One of the most challenging aspects of the role of an SAP administrator is that there are many non-SAP products and technologies associated with an SAP installation. This makes the required knowledge set for the position very broad. One of the most useful tools to help a security administrator manage this broad responsibility is the network vulnerability scanner.

> **Network Vulnerability Scanners**
>
> Although useful, a network vulnerability scanner is no replacement for knowledge about the entire software stack of your SAP installation. Be sure to stay up to date on the vulnerabilities for your OS, database, and networking equipment.

These tools perform scans over the network, looking for open ports, vulnerabilities, and attack surfaces. They are also able to log into systems with credentials and report patch levels and vulnerability status. Configuration templates exist for popular OSs and databases, which allows the security administrator to perform many checks in an easy-to-perform scan. This is a highly useful tool that can save many hours of work and missed vulnerabilities. However, keep in mind that often this functionality requires a username and password on the target OS, so be certain to use a service account and a tightly controlled, secure password.

Remember to run your scanners during nonpeak times, preferably when user load on the system is lowest. Also be sure to test your scanning settings on nonproduction systems before moving to production. You don't want to inadvertently perform a denial-of-service attack on your own systems.

A scanner worth mentioning is Nessus scanner by Tenable Network Security (Figure 15.34). It's a good, multipurpose scanner that works well with SAP landscapes. Its main advantages are as follows:

- Nessus can scan SAP NetWeaver systems, looking for published vulnerabilities.
- It integrates well with SUSE SLES and Windows OSs.
- It integrates with patch management systems.

Scanners can easily be set up on virtual machines inside (and outside of) your business secure cell. Setting up the Nessus scanner is simple but is beyond the scope of this book. You can find more information about Nessus by visiting Tenable's website at *http://www.tenable.com/*.

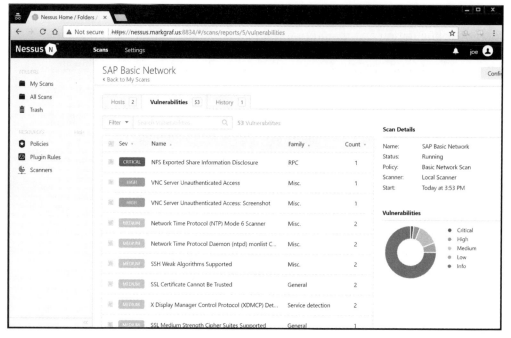

Figure 15.34 Sample Nessus Vulnerability Scan on Test Systems

15.7.2   Network Intrusion Detection

Network intrusion detection (NID) or network intrusion prevention (NIP) systems sit on your network and investigate network traffic for abuse, intrusion, and vulnerability exploitation, such as cross-site scripting, buffer overflows, or application unreality exploitation attempts. It's the application vulnerability exploitation scanning that an SAP Security administrator should be most interested in. These systems can either alert you of or stop suspicious behavior over the network. They work in conjunction with firewalls and network equipment like load balancers and routers. These devices work using a variety of rules that match specific behavior, signatures, heuristics, or deviations from standard traffic patterns.

IDS/IPS

At the very least, an IDS/IPS should be run on the corporate network. We advise that an installation is run in your business secure cell.

15.7.3   Firewall

Firewall configuration and monitoring is typically a responsibility of an organization's networking team, but the security administrator should be on the lookout for attempted attacks to specific SAP-related ports like the dispatcher or message server. Activities like reviewing the month's firewall logs and determining trends and threats would be good practices for the security administrator to engage in. For more information about firewall architecture and configuration, see Chapter 12.

15.7.4   Load Balancing

Load balancers should be used anytime an SAP system is connected to the internet to mitigate the threat of denial-of-service attacks. This doesn't replace a firewall or IDS/IDP system but works to add flexibility to the number and size of systems responding to HTTP(s) requests.

Figure 15.35 illustrates a configuration in which a hardware load balancer is added in front of two SAP Web Dispatchers.

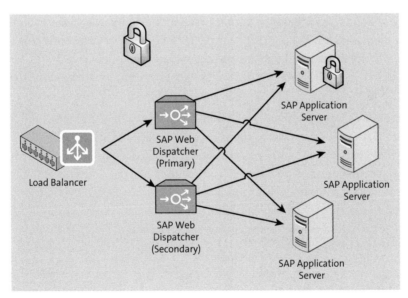

Figure 15.35 Example Load Balancer/Web Dispatcher Configuration

This allows traffic to flow from the load balancer to one of the two SAP Web Dispatchers, then on to SAP application servers. This configuration allows the maximum level of flexibility and redundancy, allowing for patching/maintenance on each of the application servers and the SAP Web Dispatchers. We also recommend segregating network traffic that has potential to create a high load on the system to a specific set of application servers that are designated only to serve this traffic.

The goal of this strategy is to protect the system in the event of high load. If these systems become overloaded, the system should still be reachable using the nonweb traffic designated application servers.

The hardware load balancer and the SAP Web Dispatchers can be configured to drop traffic that meets certain criteria defined by the administrator. Consult the documentation provided by your load balancer provider for information on configuration. For SAP Web Dispatcher, an ACL or ICM rule can be implemented. Consult Chapter 12 for more information.

15.8   Physical Security

When evaluating your critical business systems, it's important to not lose sight of the fact that your systems physically run on hardware that exists somewhere, even if your environment is virtualized. When running in a building or datacenter, it's a good idea to conduct an analysis of all threats that your system might face. Malicious parties that could potentially gain physical access to your systems might be at the top of your list.

It's a good idea to explore what happens to your backups. Are they on tapes, optical media, or hard disks? What happens to them once they reach the end of their useful life? Are they destroyed? The same questions should be asked about hardware. What happens when you decommission a server? Is it securely deleted or destroyed? The risk is that a malicious party may be able to obtain your hardware after you destroy it. If it's backup media, they may be able to restore your backup to their own hardware and exploit it. If it's hardware, they may gain enough information to expose a vulnerability, which they'll try to exploit.

> **Tip: Be Vigilant!**
> Be sure to securely destroy any decommissioned backup media, disks, or anything that may have contained proprietary information at some point.

Along with access to your hardware, physical access to your network must be secured. Make sure that any access point to the network (drop) is in a location that's secured. Often, attackers will scout the lobbies of corporate buildings looking for network jacks via which access can be obtained. Often, companies will secure their premises using things like keycards or ID badge systems, but these presecurity access points exist nonetheless. Mitigating this risk is as simple as not activating network drops in unused areas, conference rooms, waiting rooms—even the bathroom!

In the datacenter, it's important to adhere to security practices that comply with today's security standards. The primary standard being used is SSAE 16 (Statements on Standards for Attestation Engagements no. 16). This datacenter auditing standard will produce several reports (SOC 1, 2, or 3) and should be closely reviewed to maintain the most secure environment possible.

As general guidance for a security administrator running small installations that may not be in a dedicated datacenter, use the maximum amount of security control you can manage. Use high-security door locks, rack locks, and physical locks. Use locking rack bezels. Every little bit helps. When protecting your systems physically, every obstacle you can put in the way to raise the difficulty of obtaining a system raises your overall security level.

It may not be the security administrator's primary function to implement or oversee these physical security measures, but keeping these factors in mind while developing a security policy for business-critical systems is a good practice. Details like physical security are often scrutinized by attackers so a vigilant security administrator can make all the difference in making sure each vulnerable area is addressed.

15.9 Summary

In this chapter, we explored the secure system design concept, creating a secure landscape within a business secure cell. We went on to explore creating the policy your business secure cell is governed by. Next, you learned about what can be done in infrastructure to secure your business systems. This included OS considerations and monitoring. Within these two subjects, we explored specific steps to secure your OS, as well as what can be done to prevent viruses and malware from compromising your SAP NetWeaver AS ABAP system. We went on to cover what can be done with monitoring to keep an eye on your environment. Next, checking SSL/TLS certificates against certificate revocation lists was demonstrated.

Continuing on the infrastructure stack, we covered things to look for when securing your hypervisor and network. Auditing using vulnerability scanning and intrusion detection/prevention rounded out this section, which can potentially save the security administrator a great deal of time and effort protecting systems and preventing regression to a vulnerable state.

If you take away one thing from this chapter, be *sure* to keep things up to date!

The Authors

Joe Markgraf is a senior cloud architect and advisor for SAP HANA Enterprise Cloud at SAP. Before joining SAP he worked as Basis and security administrator, contributing to both small and large-scale SAP system implementations. He holds a business degree with a focus on information system management from Oregon State University. He enjoys playing vintage video games and shooting sports with his family in Washington State.

Alessandro Banzer is the Chief Executive Officer of Xiting, LLC. He has worked in information technology since 2004, specializing in SAP in 2009. Since then, Alessandro has been involved with global SAP projects in various roles. Alessandro is an active contributor and moderator in the Governance, Risk, and Compliance space on SAP Community, as well as a speaker at SAPPHIRE, ASUG, SAPInsider, and other SAP-related events. He holds a degree in Business Information Technology, as well as an Executive Master of Business Administration from Hult International Business School in London, UK.

Index

- The comprehensive guide to SAP HANA security, from authentication to auditing

- Learn to develop a complete security model using practical examples and case studies

- Identify the critical settings necessary to pass an SAP HANA security audit

Jonathan Haun

SAP HANA Security Guide

How do you protect and defend your SAP HANA database and application development platform? This comprehensive guide details your options, including privileges, encryption, and more. Learn how to secure database objects, provision and maintain user accounts, and develop and assign roles. Then take an in-depth look at authentication and certificate management before seeing how to enable auditing and security tracing. Up to date for SAP HANA 2.0!

541 pages, pub. 05/2017
E-Book: $69.99 | **Print:** $79.95 | **Bundle:** $89.99

www.sap-press.com/4227

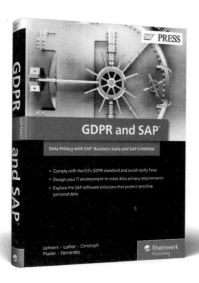

- Comply with the EU's GDPR regulation and avoid costly fines
- Design your IT environment to meet data privacy requirements
- Explore the SAP software solutions that protect sensitive personal data

Lehnert, Luther, Christoph, Pluder, Fernandes

GDPR and SAP

Data Privacy with SAP Business Suite and SAP S/4HANA

Can your data privacy protocols prevent data breaches? With this guide, you'll develop and implement a privacy policy that protects your data and complies with GDPR. Learn to block and delete data, implement purpose-based processing, and determine who can access what information in your SAP system. Use the Information Retrieval Framework, SAP MDG, Read Accessing Logging, and other tools to support your data privacy efforts. Get compliant before it's too late!

430 pages, pub. 07/2018
E-Book: $99.99 | **Print:** $109.95 | **Bundle:** $119.99

www.sap-press.com/4652

www.sap-press.com